The

CRIMEAN TATARS

Alan Fisher

HOOVER INSTITUTION PRESS
Stanford University, Stanford, California

The Hoover Institution on War, Revolution and Peace, founded at
Stanford University in 1919 by the late President Herbert Hoover,
is an interdisciplinary research center for advanced study on
domestic and international affairs in the twentieth century.
The views expressed in its publications are entirely those of
the authors and do not necessarily reflect the views of the staff,
officers, or Board of Overseers of the Hoover Institution.

Hoover Institution Publication 166

for Carol, Elizabeth, Christy, and Garrett

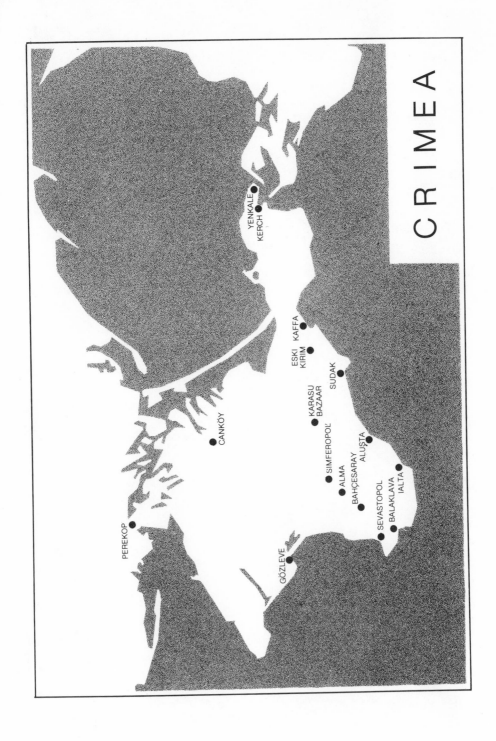

CRIMEA

PEREKOP

CANKÖY

GÖZLEVE

PEREKOP

ALMA

SIMFEROPOL

BAHÇESARAY

SEVASTOPOL

BALAKLAVA

ALUŞTA

IALTA

KARASU BAZAAR

SUDAK

ESKI KIRIM

KAFFA

YENKALE

KERCH

Contents

Foreword

In most surveys of the history of Russia and the Soviet Union, the more than one hundred non-Russian peoples receive far less attention than their histories and cultures merit. Moreover, such general works tend to give only superficial attention to such important topics as the Russian conquest of foreign nationalities and lands, the development and administration of ethnic minorities under Tsarist and Soviet rule, Russia's role in transmitting both Russian and West-European ideas and institutions to their own Asian and non-Slavic groups, and Russia's character as a melting pot of different ethnic peoples and cultures.

The Crimean Tatars is the first in a series of volumes that discuss the history and development of the non-Russian nationalities in the Soviet Union. The subject of this book is especially appropriate for the opening volume of the series, because a study of this particular people vividly illustrates a number of the problems encountered by Soviet leaders in their attempt to create a multinational society. Except for the Volga Germans, the Crimean Tatars are the only one of the component nationalities of the USSR who, having once been granted an autonomous territory, appear to have had this privilege permanently revoked.

The problems discussed here have parallels which are examined in the remaining volumes of the series. Since the beginning of the rapid industrialization of the Soviet Union, the requirements of economic development and political control have transformed the ethnographic map of the Soviet Union and created in many national autonomous territories situations nearly as acute as that in the Crimea. Many of the nationality groups have found themselves outnumbered and politically displaced by immigrating Great Russians, Ukrainians, and others. This movement of peoples and its results has called into question the functioning of the Soviet federal solution and has created discontented local nationalisms to plague the rulers in the Kremlin.

A new pattern, however, is now emerging. The difference in birth rates between the dominant Slavs and the non-Russian nationalities is changing the ethnographic balance more and more in favor of the latter. It appears possible or even likely that in the relatively near future the Great Russians will be outnumbered by the other nationalities.

As a result of these dynamics of development the study of the past and present of the non-Russian nationalities is extremely important. It is also significant in what it portends for the future. Thus, studies such as the one presented here, and those that follow, should provide the Western reader with a fuller understanding of the complexities of Soviet reality. Comparable volumes on several other major nationalities, a total of seventeen, are currently in preparation. Included are separate studies of the principal nations of Soviet Central Asia, the Caucausus, the Baltic region and the Ukraine, as well as special groups such as the Jews and the Crimean Tatars. Each volume examines the history of a particular national group in both the Tsarist and Soviet eras with an emphasis on determining its place in the Soviet federation as well as its impact on the evolution of Soviet society.

Hoover Institution   WAYNE S. VUCINICH, editor

Preface

The Crimean Tatars are today a nationality living in a diaspora. Denied the right to return to their homeland in the Crimean peninsula, their communities are scattered throughout the USSR, the Turkish republic, and the West. Like other nationalities that have experienced the same disasters (the Jews come to mind), the Tatars' claim to national identity and a national home are based on historical, cultural, and linguistic foundations.

Appearing first in the Crimea in the thirteenth and fourteenth centuries, the Crimean Tatars soon displaced the existing political and cultural entities with their own; they established their first state there in the middle of the fifteenth century. From that time until the Russian annexation of the peninsula in 1783, the Crimean Tatars organized and lived in a state, called the Crimean Khanate, that was ruled by their own Giray dynasty. From 1783 until 1918, the Tatars lived within the Russian Empire as subjects of the tsars.

During the latter period, the Tatars were displaced gradually by immigrating Slavic settlers, officials, and landowners. Despite concerted efforts by their Russian rulers to eliminate Tatar culture and identity and to assimilate them into the fabric of Russian society, the Tatars were able to preserve their national awareness. With the fall of the tsarist system, the Tatars were temporarily successful in reestablishing their own state and independent society. But the advent of Bolshevik power soon put an end to their success, if not to their efforts.

Since 1920, the Crimean Tatars have experienced one calamity after another: collectivization and its related famines, the elimination of their political and cultural elites between 1928 and 1939, the ravages of war and occupation from 1941 to 1944, and finally, their wholesale deportation to remote areas of the USSR where they now reside. Yet there have been developments in the Tatar community that show accomplishment in the face of adversity—developments that show that the Tatars possess almost unequalled courage to struggle for what they consider to be a just solution to their problems. Applying pressure upon the Soviet authorities who were responsible for the denial of their national existence, they have succeeded in the years since 1944 in gaining partial restitution of what was taken from them by Stalin. In 1967, in a decree issued by the Soviet government, the charges made against the Tatars in 1944 were removed; they were "rehabilitated" as a nationality. Yet their rehabilitation was virtually meaningless, for the punishments under which they suffered were not removed. They cannot return to their homeland. Their national and cultural rights remain denied to them, and their struggle for these rights continues today.

I have two primary purposes in this volume, and the book's organization reflects both. First, there is no account in any language of the history of the Crimean Tatars from their first appearance in the Crimea until today. In this book, I have offered a short summary of the Crimean Tatars' history, including their political, economic, social, and cultural life. It is based on both primary and secondary sources in the important East European languages as well as in Tatar and Turkish.

Second, the main problem the Crimean Tatars face today is based on the facts that Soviet and most Western observers deny the existence of a separate Crimean Tatar entity in the Turkic world; Soviet historians ignore the khanate and its history; Soviet and Western writers accept the charges made against the Tatars in 1944 and are ignorant of or conveniently gloss over the removal of those same charges in 1967. In this volume I have tried to place in historical perspective the fallacies in these positions.

In the preparation of this book I have incurred a variety of personal and academic debts that I wish to acknowledge. Research for this project was made possible through a grant from the Hoover Institution at Stanford University. The historical methodology I have used owes whatever skill it manifests to my mentors at Columbia University a decade ago, Professors Marc Raeff and Tibor Halasi-Kun. I wish to thank my colleagues Robert Slusser and William O. McCagg, Jr. for the benefit of their knowledge of the workings of the Soviet political system and its police apparatus, and for reading portions of the manuscript and offering advice for revision. Bey Turgut Işiksal, staff member of the Başbakanlik Arşivi in Istanbul, has educated me for years on the Turkish archival matters so important to my studies on the Tatars. I want to thank Bey Mustecip Ülküsal of the Crimean Tatar National Center in Istanbul for much information and many difficult-to-acquire Tatar publications. Melissa Devereaux acted as courier for the manuscript across various national frontiers at a critical stage in its preparation. My thanks also go to Jessie Garrett for reading proofs. Finally, my wife Carol, who helped enormously in the preparation of the manuscript, and my children, Elizabeth, Christy, and Garrett, who had to put up with my schedule over the past year, deserved more thanks than I can offer.

East Lansing, Michigan   ALAN W. FISHER

Acknowledgments

Grateful acknowledgment is made for permission to reprint the following previously published material:

Excerpts from Pyotr Grigorenko's speech at the funeral of Aleksei Kosterin, from *Samizdat: Voices of the Soviet Opposition*, edited by George Saunders. Published by Monad Press. Copyright 1974 by the Anchor Foundation. Reprinted by permission.

An excerpt from page 95 of *Sakharov Speaks* by A. D. Sakharov, copyright 1974. Reprinted by permission of Alfred A. Knopf, Inc.

Numerous excerpts from the English edition of *A Chronicle of Current Events*, nos. 11–28. Reprinted by permission of Amnesty International.

An excerpt from Osman Turkay's translation from Cengiz Dagci's novel, appearing in *Index on Censorship 1–1974*, published by Writers and Scholars International Ltd., London. Reprinted by permission.

Excerpts from pages 249, 253, 254–55, and 258–59 of *Uncensored Russia* by Peter Reddaway, copyright 1972. Reprinted by permission of McGraw-Hill Book Company.

Excerpts from pages 208–13 of *In Quest of Justice: Protest and Dissent in the Soviet Union Today* by Abraham Brumberg, copyright 1970. Reprinted by permission of Praeger Publishers, Inc.; and, in the British Commonwealth, Phaidon Press Ltd.

PART ONE

THE CRIMEAN TATAR KHANATE

1. The Origins of the Crimean Tatar Khanate

Notwithstanding a certain self-assuredness that pervades most accounts of Crimean history, the origins of the Crimean Tatars are as obscure as the origins of most peoples. The task of finding these origins would be considerably easier, in fact, if there were general agreement among historians as to the definition of *Crimean Tatar*. The question of their origins predates the first Crimean Khanate, which appeared in the early 1440s under the leadership of Khan Haci Giray. This khanate's existence is attested to by historical sources from both Asia and Europe. Who were the peoples who made up the population of the new khanate? Where had they come from, and when? The paucity and unreliability of contemporary sources makes the answers to these questions difficult.

The Crimean peninsula is divided into two parts that are separated by the mountainous ridge north of the Black Sea's coastline. Along the coast, in Haci Giray's time, there were several large towns—Kaffa (Kefe), Evpatoria (Gözleve), and Tana (Azov, Azak)—that by eastern European standards were really cities. They were inhabited for the most part by Greek, Armenian, and Jewish populations, yet there was a sizeable Italian and Frankish minority in political and economic command. From contemporary accounts of visiting merchants and travelers, these cities were teeming urban areas, each with a full complement of public buildings, market places, harbor complexes, and crowded living quarters. Although the architectural style of the cities, which emphasized the utilitarian rather than the beautiful, was by no means comparable to that of the Italian and Frankish homelands, visitors from both east and west could not mistake the fact that these cities were European in influence.

To the north of the mountains, the land was inhabited by various nomadic tribes who were for the most part Islamic and who spoke various Turkic dialects. For centuries, these tribes had intermittently passed through the northern Black Sea area on their excursions into eastern Europe, and during this period, their main impact upon the area seems to have been a disruptive one. It consisted of breaking up or seriously damaging existing local political and economic organization.

In the mid-thirteenth century, during the invasions by the armies of Batu Khan, founder of the Golden Horde, these Turkic nomads gained political ascendancy over the previously settled Slavic and Italian populations.[1] Slavic sources show that, just before Batu's invasion in the 1220s, the towns of Sudak and Korsun in the southern Crimea paid the Polovtsy a tribute in order to protect themselves against nomadic raids. Sudak itself was leveled by the Tatars just after the battle of the Kalka in 1223 and again soon after by an army sent by Ala ed Din, the Seljuk sultan of Rum (Konya). It was in the years following this last attack that Seljuk and Oğuz Turkish groups, most of which came from Anatolia, began their settlement of the northern Crimean plains.[2]

Turkish sources clearly indicate that during the second half of the thirteenth century, under the encouragement of Berke Khan, ruler of the Golden Horde, many Seljuk Turks settled in the Crimea. According to the Ottoman chronicler, Münicimbaşi, one of the four daughters of the Seljuk sultan married Berke Khan. According to Seid Lukman's Ottoman chronicle, Izz ed Din, a son of this Seljuk wife, received from Berke the lands and towns of Solhat and Sudak in the Crimea and brought Anatolian Turks to settle there. By the end of the thirteenth century, Arab travelers through the region reported that the population of Sudak was largely Turkish.[3]

At first this settlement of the Crimean interior and of Sudak on the coast proceeded without interfering with the Frankish and Slavic populations on the southern shore of the Crimean peninsula. But at the end of the thirteenth century, Emir Nogai, governor of the Crimean and steppe province of the Golden Horde, demanded payment of taxes and tribute from the Genoese city of Kaffa on the southeastern coast of the Crimea. On the latter's refusal, he attacked and pillaged the city. Clearly the relationship between the Turkic population in the north and the Christian population of the south was entering a new stage.[4]

One of the immediate results of this attack was the recognition by the Genoese of the Tatars' right to exact payment of taxes, and with this came partial acceptance of Tatar political authority over the whole region. Turkish settlement on the shore of the Black Sea itself followed. It is after this point that many Tatar names appear among the inhabitants of Kefe and Sudak.

Throughout the fourteenth and early fifteenth centuries, the Tatar khans at

Saray on the Volga considered themselves the rulers of the Crimea. They made good this claim by appointing governors of the Crimean and steppe province, whose seat of power was Solhat, later to be called Eski Kirim ("Old Crimea"). This city remained the main Tatar center on the peninsula until the formation of the Giray dynasty in the mid-fifteenth century. It was a religious center with mosques, dervish monasteries, and schools (*medresses*) all with their *mulla*s, *sheikh*s, and *kadi*s (legal scholars and judges). Solhat served as a source of Muslim missionary activity in the north and in the Caucasus. In addition, Arab travelers reported a large number of *caravan-sarais* and a strong fortress of stone. Iakobson provides a picture of a school and mosque in Solhat, built by Khan Uzbek in 1314 and still extant.[5]

Solhat was never the official residence for the khans of the Golden Horde, but it became a place of refuge for unsuccessful aspirants to the throne. It also served as the locale for diplomatic relations between the Golden Horde and the Turkic Mamluk dynasty of Egypt. Sultan Baybars built a large mosque in Solhat and modestly named it for himself.[6]

It was not until the end of the fourteenth century that any of the Tatar governors in the Crimea began to attempt to establish an independent political power based on their control of the Crimea. The first appears to have been Taş Timur who had his name inscribed on coinage minted and intended for exclusive use in the peninsula. He called the Crimea his *yurt* ("patrimony"), and with the policy continued by his sons, granted the position there as a hereditary position: thus, Taş Timur rightly may be considered as the creator of the base for a future independent polity in the Crimea.

Haci Giray Khan

Historians of all persuasions are agreed that one of Taş Timur's successors, Haci Giray, was the first khan of an independent Crimean Khanate.[7] There is some controversy, however, about Haci Giray—his character, the origin of his name, his exact relationship to the khans of the Golden Horde, and his relationship to Taş Timur. The reasons behind this controversy (which centers primarily around Haci's genealogy) relate to the Crimeans' desire to show their legitimacy as heirs of some of the horde's political and territorial traditions. In the sixteenth century, the Muscovite grand princes (and later the tsars) made similar claims to the legitimate inheritance of these horde traditions. It was felt that the ruler who could make the best case for his own horde traditions had the best chance of becoming the ruler of the Golden Horde's territories—the steppe between southern Poland and central Asia.

The most reasonable account of Haci Giray's appearance seems to be that provided by V. D. Smirnov, who bases his views on Lithuanian and Polish chronicles. Stryikovski's Polish chronicle explains it thus: "That year (1443)

the Tatars of Perekop, Barin, and Şirin, whose khan died without heir, sent to
Casimir, grand prince of Lithuania, with the request that he give them Haci
Giray as khan, who having fled from the Great Horde, was there in refuge."[8]
According to this view, Haci Giray had been born in Lithuania, made an
attempt for supremacy in the Golden Horde in 1428, and after his failure had
returned to Lithuania. When he was invited by the Tatars in the Crimea to
come and rule over them, he accepted and began to base his political
authority solely on the fact that he was khan in the Crimea. At that time
Crimean coins began to bear his name, and in place of the former Tatar
kipçak seal, a new seal for the Crimean khans was initiated. It bore the image
of an owl.[9]

There is little ground for debate, however, about the policy that Haci Giray
pursued once he was khan in the Crimea. After his attempts to gain the throne
of the Golden Horde for himself, Haci set about to establish an independent
state in the Crimea. To accomplish this, he needed (1) to gain as many allies as
possible from among his and the horde's neighbors, and (2) to attract as many
Tatar clans and nobles to his side as he could. There was no question that the
khans of the horde would oppose his policy. If he failed to build a strong base
in the Crimea, it was likely that his attempts at independence would fail.

Haci Giray's first step was to seek as many allies as he could. He was not
particular with regard to the religion or nationality of the neighboring rulers
and states whose support he sought. Before 1453, when Sultan Mehmed II
captured Constantinople and began to incorporate all of the shores of the
Black Sea into his empire, Haci vacillated between friendship and alliance
with Poland-Lithuania and the Muscovite Russia (Muscovy). So long as his
major threat came from the Golden Horde, Muscovy was his natural
ally—Muscovy's grand princes had been struggling against Tatar overlord-
ship for some time. But there were occasions when close relations with the
Kingdom of Poland seemed to offer more advantages to the Crimean ruler. In
1445 at a time when the khan of the Golden Horde was threatening both
Crimean and Polish territory in the south, Haci Giray made his first
Polish/Lithuanian alliance with Casimir IV. In 1452 Haci attacked the
invading khan, Seyyid Ahmed, and together with Polish/Lithuanian forces
was able to defeat him.[10]

Relations with the Ottoman Empire

The year 1453 brought a dramatic change to the geopolitical situation in
the Black Sea region. The Ottoman sultan, Mehmed II, achieved the
centuries-old Muslim and Turkic dream of seizing Constantinople, the capital
of the East Roman Empire. This event showed that the relatively new
Ottoman Empire was without doubt the greatest power in southeastern

Europe. It created a completely new situation for the Italian colonies along the Crimean shore whose trade had to pass through the straits now controlled by the Turks.

As a self-proclaimed heir of the political and some of the territorial traditions of the Golden Horde, Haci Giray had from the beginning considered the Italian colonies to be within his sovereign domains. According to Ankarali Hekim Yahya, a mid-fifteeth-century Ottoman chronicler, Haci Giray was sovereign of Kirkyer, Eski Kirim, Taman, Kerch, the Kuban, Kipçak, and—most important—Kefe.[11] With the Ottomans on the Bosphorus, Haci Giray and Mehmed II had complementary interests in the activities of the Genoese in the Crimea. In 1454, the Crimean khan made an agreement with Mehmed II to attack and capture Kefe from the Genoese. While an Ottoman fleet approached Kefe, the khan laid siege to the city by land with a force of 7000 Tatar cavalry. But on this occasion, the town was able to withstand the joint attack. Finally, after the Genoese agreed to pay to the Tatars an annual tribute of 1200 gold pieces, Haci Giray and the Ottomans withdrew. After this date, coinage from the khanate bears both Tatar and Genoese markings.[12]

Although this joint attack was the first sign of the future Crimean-Ottoman political and military relationship, the final connection was not to be made until the reign of Haci Giray's successor, Devlet Giray, twenty years later. Until then, in defense of his own independence and sovereignty, the khan's main attention was still directed toward the steppe and horde politics. Constant struggles against the Golden Horde khans marked the last ten years of Haci Giray's life.

Tatar Migrations

Haci Giray's second major step in setting the basis for Crimean independence from the Golden Horde was the attraction of many Tatar clans and aristocrats. The fact that the horde khans proved unable to end his claims to a separate sovereignty led many of the most important Tatar clans to move to lands under Haci Giray's authority. Between 1453 and 1466 at least three such clans (the Şirins, the Barins, and the Konghurats) made the westward move. The rulers of the Golden Horde had relied on support of these clans in the past. Ironically, this immigration created both the basis for khanate strength vis à vis the Golden Horde and the basis for internal khanate weakness. The fact that so many of the horde's leading clans and leaders transferred their loyalty to the fledgling Crimean Khanate greatly strengthened the position of the Crimean khans in their struggles against the horde. Their migration added numerically to the Tatar population on the peninsula and gave to the khan both a larger military force and increased economic power. It also brought to

Battle between Ottoman Turks and Crimean Tatars before the
Fortress of Kefe between 1453 and 1475.
(From the *Şuca'at-name* of Aşafi Paşa, made in 1586. In the library of
Istanbul University, Yildiz 2385/105, fol. 207.)

the khanate the causes of internal weakness that had plagued the horde in past decades—competing claims for power and sovereignty on the part of the clan leaders against their khan.

It was not only large numbers of Tatars who moved west, but also clans that had a long tradition of political power, clans that for centuries had played important roles in the politics of the horde. The leaders of these clans were not willing to abandon their own power completely, whether the khan be a khan of the Golden Horde or a khan of the Crimean Khanate. Internecine struggle was to be the major characteristic of Crimean political life until its last days. According to Inalcik, in 1456 the Genoese in Kefe were able to persuade leaders of some of the new clans to turn against Haci Giray and depose him in favor of his son Haydar Khan. Although this interlude lasted only a few months and Haci regained his throne by the end of the year, this was an omen for the future.[13]

The last recorded event in Haci Giray's life was his preparation in 1460 for a major struggle with Khan Küçük Mehmed of the Golden Horde. Haci was involved in these plans when he suddenly died, probably of poison administered by some of the clan leaders who resented his growing claims to internal power. Haci's death opened a period of intense internal fighting that was only resolved with the conquest of the shores of the Crimean peninsula by the Ottomans in 1475 and with the political supremacy over the khans achieved by the Ottomans a couple of years later.[14]

2. Ottoman Hegemony in the Crimea

One of the major historiographical issues in Crimean history concerns the way in which and the extent to which the Crimea became dependent upon the Ottoman Empire. The most important questions about which historians disagree are: (1) When the Ottoman Turks captured Kefe and the southern shore of the Crimean peninsula in 1475, did they also conquer the fledgling Crimean Khanate, or did the Crimea merely enter under the protection of the Ottoman sultan? (2) Was the Crimean khan, after 1475, a sovereign and heir to the political traditions of the steppe, or was he a vassal of the Ottoman sultan? If the khan was a vassal of the sultan, how does one explain the facts that the khans often did not act in concert with the Ottomans, that they continued to maintain their own separate diplomatic relations with both Poland and Muscovy, and that they acted within the Crimea as officials with historic prerogatives of independence and sovereignty?

In order to make some sense of the issue of Crimean-Ottoman relations, events of the years 1466–1478 (the year of Haci Giray's death—the year in which Mengli Giray offered himself as an obedient servant of his sovereign, the *padishah* of the Ottoman Empire) must first be examined. Then the development of political and economic relations between the Ottomans and the Crimean Tatars must be analyzed.

The death of Haci Giray in 1466 produced a struggle for succession that raises serious questions about the existence of a dynasty at all. The political traditions of the Golden Horde made it clear that Haci's eldest son, Nurdevlet, should have inherited the throne, yet the succession was not so easily solved. The clan leaders who had migrated to the Crimea during Haci Giray's reign refused to accept a khan over whom they had no authority. For the next twelve years there ensued a struggle between proponents of three theories of politics that were embodied in three power centers: the horde itself; the clan leaders, led by the *bey* of the Şirin clan; and the Ottoman sultan. There were only two contenders for the throne: Nurdevlet and his brother Mengli Giray. The Genoese intervened first on behalf of one, then of the other. The problem was only solved in 1478 with the installation of Mengli Giray as khan and as a vassal of the Ottoman sultan. One may conclude that the khanate as a stable political entity dates from this period rather than from the "founding of the khanate" by Haci Giray thirty years earlier. Mengli Giray ruled in the Crimea from 1478 until his death in 1514.

The sources from the period 1466–1478 (Ottoman and Tatar chronicles; diplomatic correspondence between the Crimeans, Ottomans, Poles, Muscovites, and the horde; and Genoese documentation) are contradictory and incomplete. The construction of a clear account of the struggle for succession is almost impossible. Yet Professor Inalcik has been able to surmount these difficulties in his famous article in which he offers the best possible account of the events available.[1] In summary, his findings are that, according to historical tradition, the eldest son, Nurdevlet, should have inherited the throne easily. Throughout the struggle between himself and Mengli Giray, Nurdevlet consistently received support from the khans of the Golden Horde. However, the clan leaders, particularly the Şirins, usually chose to oppose the horde's leadership and support Mengli Giray. In the face of the political traditions, Mengli Giray could win the struggle only with the support of the clans. Thus, the clan leaders believed, he would be dependent upon their support to keep his power. The balance between these factions within the Crimea seems to have been fairly even, so that no solution could have been found without outside intervention. This intervention was sought both from the Genoese in Kefe and from the Ottomans. The Genoese, since the Ottoman conquest of Constantinople, were themselves in a position of confrontation with the Ottomans; therefore, these two powers usually supported rival claimants within the Crimea.

Nurdevlet in Power

First Nurdevlet succeeded in achieving the throne. He received a *yarlik* ("charter of authority") from the Golden Horde recognizing his authority in the Crimea. Mengli Giray was forced to take refuge in Kefe where he remained until 1468. It is possible that Mengli did not receive official support from the Genoese since Kefe had many Tatar inhabitants at the time. In the early 1470s, the Genoese may have only seemed to be switching from one side to the other with increasing rapidity; it may have been the Tatars in the city who, without official sanction, often provided refuge for the Crimean rivals. This would help explain the fact that both Nurdevlet and Mengli Giray received help of one sort or another from Kefe.

In 1468, Mengli Giray gained control of part of the peninsula and established himself on the throne in Kirkyer with the help of the Şirin *bey*, Mamak, and the Genoese. Mengli's main opposition, the Golden Horde, helped thrust him into a policy of friendship with Muscovy and hostility toward Poland—a fact that, according to Russian historiography, has made Mengli Giray one of the most outstanding of Crimean khans. In 1469, Mengli Giray also sent a letter to Sultan Mehmed II addressing him as a friend.

But Nurdevlet and his horde allies (in the Crimea these were primarily nomadic Nogay Tatars) had not come under the political or economic control of the Tatar aristocracy. He was able to remain in power in the steppe regions between the Ozu river and the mouth of the Don. In late 1469, Nurdevlet, with an army of Nogay Tatars and a contingent from the Golden Horde, succeeded in driving Mengli Giray from Kirkyer to Kefe, thus temporarily ending the period of dual rule in the Crimea. However, in 1471, Mamak and almost all of the Crimean clan aristocracy retook the central region of the peninsula and paved the way for Mengli Giray's return. Nothing is known of Mengli Giray's activities until 1474, when a rebellion against his rule was led by the new Şirin *bey,* Eminek Mirza. This rebellion, supported by most of the aristocracy and the Genoese leadership in Kefe, forced Mengli Giray from power and brought back Nurdevlet.

On the basis of what is known of Mengli Giray's activities after 1478, it seems probable that the cause of this rebellion was his attempt to strengthen his position at the expense of the clan leaders; the Genoese could have been expected to support the weakest part in the Crimea. Russian sources show that in 1472 Mengli Giray entertained Nikita Beklemishev, an envoy from Muscovy, and an agreement was made by which Ivan III was to act in concert with the Crimeans against the horde while Mengli Giray would aid Muscovy against Poland.

Invitations to the Ottomans

In early 1475 the Şirin *bey* again found reason to quarrel with the khan. This time it was Nurdevlet, who had been acting in close agreement with the Genoese. The Şirin *bey* formally requested that Sultan Mehmed II attack Kefe and bring it under his sovereignty. It is clear from the letter published by Professor Kurat, that this was not the first communication from a clan leader to the sultan and that there had been contact between the Crimean aristocracy and the Ottomans for some time. This request coincided with the policy that Mehmed II had been pursuing since his conquest of Constantinople: completion of Ottoman expansion around the shores of the Black Sea. There was to be no room in such a scheme for an area controlled by Christian Europeans. Although Nurdevlet supported the Genoese against the attack of Grand Vezir Gedik Ahmed Paşa and a large Ottoman fleet, the Turks captured Kefe, and in a few months they completed their conquest of all Genoese-held areas along the shore.

Mengli Giray, who was in Kefe at that moment, immediately arranged with the Ottoman commander that he, as khan, would accept the suzerainty of the Ottomans in the Crimea. Six months later he confirmed this agreement with a letter to the sultan in which he promised to be "the enemy of your enemy, the friend of your friend." It quickly became clear that the foundations of

Crimean vassalage to the Ottomans had been laid. This acknowledgment persuaded the khan of the Golden Horde, Seyyid Ahmed, to make one last major attempt to regain the area he had never ceased to claim. In 1476, he made a full-scale invasion of the Crimea, successfully driving Mengli Giray from the throne and replacing him once more with Nurdevlet. However, this time Seyyid Ahmed left behind another representative, Janibek, as *vali* ("governor") to oversee Nurdevlet's activities. Thus for a short time Nurdevlet and the horde were able to sever the new ties between the Crimea and the Ottomans. For the moment it appeared that the Ottomans were willing to accept this division of power in the Crimea. They of course retained the southern shore and the cities along it, including Kefe. Mengli Giray fled to Istanbul where he was detained by the Ottomans in their new prison of the Seven Towers. Mehmed II seemed satisfied to deal with Nurdevlet as khan, partly because Nurdevlet sent a letter to Istanbul in which he promised to be the sultan's servant.

The last episode in this complicated series of events took place in late 1477. The Şirin *bey*, Eminek Mirza, representing all of the Crimean *bey*s and clan leaders, sent a secret request to Mehmed II in which he asked that the sultan return Mengli Giray as khan to the Crimea. In early 1478, accompanied by an Ottoman army, Mengli Giray invaded the Crimea, driving Nurdevlet and Janibek from their respective seats of power. It is clear that Mengli Giray returned as the protégé of the sultan. He depended upon Ottoman support in gaining his throne, and his former pledges of obedience were repeated, this time with greater force. In this his third khanate, which lasted until his death in 1514, Mengli Giray was able to establish the Crimean Khanate on a sound basis.[2] The presence of Ottoman authority in the Crimea became unquestioned, and attempts of the Golden Horde khans to regain their sovereignty in the Black Sea region ended.

Ottoman-Crimean "Treaty"

For some time, Russian and Western historians have believed that in 1478 Mengli Giray and Mehmed II signed a treaty that laid out in some detail the forms of Ottoman authority in the Crimea. These historians took at face value an account of such a treaty in the multivolume travelogue of a seventeenth-century Ottoman traveler, Evliya Çelebi. According to this tradition—which has been accepted by such historians as Khartakhai and Howorth, and believed by the eighteenth-century French observer, Peysonnel—the treaty included the following five points: (1) Internal authority within the khanate would remain within the hands of the khan, and appointment of political and military officials would be solely his concern; (2) the Crimean aristocracy would select their choice for khan from among eligible members of the Giray family; (3) the Ottoman sultan, as sovereign in the Crimea, could require that the khan support him in military campaigns, and external relations of the khanate would be in the hands of officials appointed by the sultan; (4) since the sultan was caliph, he would have authority to appoint all religious and judicial officials in the Crimea; and (5) the khan was to be allowed to have his name mentioned in the Friday noon prayers and engraved on coinage issued in the khanate.[3]

Professor Inalcik has proven that such a treaty could not have existed in the fifteenth century and that it probably never existed at all.[4] By the late seventeenth century, when Evliya Çelebi was writing his epic descriptions of Ottoman territories and institutions, the points believed to have been included in the treaty may have represented the realities of the relationships between the khans and sultans, and in the eighteenth century, they may have been believed by all parties involved, but there is no possibility that such a treaty would have been drawn up by Mengli Giray and Mehmed II. Mehmed made no claims to be caliph. Sultan Selim I in the next century only claimed to be the "Servant of the Two Holy Cities [Mecca and Medina]" after his conquest of Egypt. Also, according to an important Tatar chronicle, the name in the Friday noon prayer was inserted only during the reign of Khan Islam Giray I in 1584.[5]

The New Ottoman Role in the Crimea

There can be no doubt, however, that in 1478 some agreement was made that set the pattern for future relations. Although the Ottomans played a role in the choice of khan, they usually accepted the selection made by the Crimean aristocracy in their traditional *kurultay* fashion. According to the contemporary documents, such choices were made *ittifak-i cumu'i tatar ile* ("by the Tatar notables assembled together").[6] This procedure would become an occasional source of dispute since the clan leaders viewed Ottoman participation as limited to confirmation (*tasdik*) of their selection, while the Ottomans maintained their claim to the right of appointment (*tayin*). Kefe and the whole of the Crimean shore did pass into the hands of the Ottomans and came to form a special Ottoman province, the *eyalet* of Kefe, which in time included not only the Crimean shore but also the forts and trading centers of Taman and Azov. The Crimean khans, from Mengli Giray until the end of the khanate in the late eighteenth century, had political prerogatives over the rest of the peninsula and over most of the territories that had been claimed by Haci Giray in 1454.

The relationships between the Crimean Tatars and the Ottoman sultans were built on two main foundations: (1) political ideology based on historical and legendary traditions, and (2) geopolitical necessity. By the time of Sultan

Suleiman I in the sixteenth century, the Ottoman rulers based their claims to power on three historical traditions: (1) Islamic—they controlled the holy places in Arabia and Palestine, and their empire had been formed in the process of *gazi* ("religious") warfare against the Christian world; (2) Byzantine-Roman—they possessed the capital of Byzantium with its imperial prerogatives, and they had conquered almost all of the lands that had been within the Byzantine Empire; and (3) Turkic—they included in their imperial title the terms *khan*, and *Padişah-i Deşt-i Kipçak* ("Sovereign of the Kipçak Steppe").[7] It was this last element in Ottoman political ideology that was important for their relations with the Crimean Tatars, for political connections with Jengiz Khan was the one way to prove legitimate political authority over the Turkic-Tatar steppe that reached into central Asia.

While the Ottoman chroniclers tried to show that the Ottoman sultans inherited the political prerogatives of the Jingizids (descendants of Jengiz Khan), the Giray dynasty in the Crimea claimed to be able to prove physical as well as political descent from the first khan of the Golden Horde. The Ottomans in their correspondence with the Girays used the term *cingiziye* for the Crimean khans, thus admitting this distinction. Even Suleiman I, in a letter to Khan Mehmet Giray I, called him "descendant of Crimean sultans and of Jingizid *hakhan*s."[8] Of all of the subjects of the Ottoman sultans, the Crimean khans held a special position because of the importance of their genealogy.

In the realm of geopolitics, the relationship between the khans and the sultans was also important. In the sixteenth and seventeenth centuries the steppe was an area contested increasingly by Muscovy and Poland-Lithuania. Muscovy claimed that it had inherited the Golden Horde traditions; therefore it challenged Crimean and Ottoman monopoly over the steppe. The presence on this frontier of an effective military force under Crimean leadership permitted the Ottomans to concentrate their attention on their major western and eastern rivals—the Habsburgs and the Iranian Safavids.

Ottoman-Crimean Finances

As a result of both their Jingizid heritage and their military service to the Ottomans, the khans received large financial and social rewards.[9] They received annual pensions, grants when they ascended the Crimean throne, landholdings in both Rumelia and Anatolia, a subsidized personal elite guard called *sekban*s, and large grants for participation in each Ottoman campaign. The Ottomans also allowed the Girays to collect an annual tribute from Muscovy and Poland. Although the origins of this tribute had been the customary payments to the khans of the Golden Horde and the Girays had merely inherited this right, the collection of tribute from foreign states without Ottoman supervision implied the Ottomans' recognition of special Crimean rights in the steppe. In addition, the Tatars were permitted to collect a similar tribute from subjects of the sultan in the Danubian Principalities.

From the financial evidence, it seems that the khans were neither independent of nor subject to the Ottoman sultans. Those areas that made up the *eyalet* of Kefe were under direct Ottoman rule and were completely separate from this relationship. There, the Ottomans collected taxes, assigned revenues, and appointed officials in the same way they did in the other areas of their empire.

The Ottomans made good use of the leverage of their financial grants. The *sekban* troops and the economic influence over the ruling elite allowed the Ottomans to interfere in many matters of internal Crimean interest. Although never codified, this practice became increasingly frequent in the seventeenth century until there developed within the Crimean élite a movement that demanded separation from the Ottoman Empire and a return to independent political existence.[10]

Crimean Prerogatives

The khans at no time abandoned their prerogatives in the steppe; these prerogatives they had received from their Jingizid heritage, not their Ottoman overlords. On their correspondence with both their northern neighbors and the Ottomans, they used one of the most important symbols of steppe sovereignty, the Jingizid seal (*tamga*). The khans reserved the right to maintain diplomatic relations with Muscovy and Poland (again proving the falsity of the supposed treaty of 1478 which had prohibited this). Crimean envoys appeared in Moscow with a greater frequency than did Ottoman; they resided there in a special building named the Krymskii Dvor. This building served not only as the collection point for the Muscovite tribute but also as a place where normal diplomatic functions were performed.[11]

Since the conduct of diplomacy is one of the prerogatives of a sovereign state, one must conclude that here again is evidence of an incomplete Crimean dependence upon the Ottomans. A further sign of partial independence is the fact that, until the last half of the eighteenth century, the khans continued to mint their own coins—coins that bore the seal of the Girays, not of the Ottoman sultans.[12]

The claims made by many Soviet historians that the Crimean Tatars were marionettes in Ottoman hands are incorrect. They have been made in an attempt to show that the Tatars were not an independent entity in the steppe region during the khanate period and thus never did have political legitimacy there. The logical conclusion of such arguments is that the Tatars were interlopers whose annexation and eventual removal from the area by the Russians was fully justified.[13]

The Reign of Mengli Giray

Mengli Giray proved to be an able ruler, one whose ambitions were equalled by his skill in dealing with the internal problems that the clan leaders frequently caused and his skill in using his new relationship with the sultan to the best advantage of the khanate. Mengli Giray realized that the attention of the clan leaders could easily be directed toward foreign adventures, relieving him at home from the sort of pressure he had faced during the period after his father's death. In 1484, he received an invitation from Sultan Bayezid II to take part in his campaign in Moldavia to capture the stronghold of Akkerman. As a reward for Tatar participation in the campaign, Mengli Giray extended his own holdings to include the Bessarabian towns of Kavshan, Tombasar, and Balta; at the same time, the booty the Tatars earned proved so irresistible that they willingly became tied to Ottoman foreign expansion in the west.

The booty included scores of human captives who were brought to Kefe and sold to slave merchants for a great profit. This set the stage for the slave trade that became one of the most important economic resources of the khanate. Mengli Giray's military support for the Ottomans served both to strengthen the internal position of the khan's administration and to provide the Ottomans with a welcome addition to their own awesome military power against Poland and the Habsburgs.[14] On the other hand, this policy made the khans more and more dependent upon Ottoman successes, and when the eventual decline of the Ottoman Empire set in, the khanate declined with it.

In his own Crimean external affairs, Mengli Giray turned his attention northward in 1502 and made strong attempts to increase his influence on the Turkic steppe as far as the Volga. He personally led an army against the Golden Horde and entered and partially destroyed its capital of Saray. His son, Sahib Giray, was to carry this struggle further by achieving the throne in Kazan and winning temporary familial unity between the khanates of Kazan and the Crimea. Clearly, such activities were inimical to the interests of the rising Muscovite state, and to help his northern flank, Mengli Giray made an alliance with the Polish Jagellonian monarchy against Moscow in 1511. As part of this agreement, the khan abandoned his claim of historical rights (based upon those of Jengiz Khan) to any lands in White Russia or the Ukraine within the Polish kingdom. Although this alliance proved to be a fragile one, the khan's relations with Poland were maintained on a friendly basis so long as he perceived a danger to the north.

In a way that Haci Giray had not, Mengli Giray realized that a strong khanate required internal development that would include the establishment of a capital worthy of the state, a religious and cultural life that would give the state some purpose within, and an economic structure that could sustain the first two. That he did not succeed in completing any of these tasks was due to a lack of time rather than a lack of effort.

In 1503, in Solhat, which was later to bear the historic name of Eski Kirim ("Old Crimea"), Mengli Giray constructed a palace, called Aşlama Saray, that became famous for the beauty of its portal and towers. The door was built by a follower of the Venetian school of architecture of the fifteenth century—probably the architect Aleviz, whom Ivan III employed to build some additions to his Moscow Kremlin. Aleviz is known from Russian sources to have been detained in the Crimea in 1502 and 1503 on his way to Moscow, and the inscription on Mengli Giray's portal bears the date 1503.[15]

In his capital and palace in Solhat, Mengli Giray laid the foundations of the Crimean administrative structure. He created the Khan's *divan* ("council"), which was attended by representatives of the clans, the khan's heir apparent who bore the title of *kalgay,* and the chief administrative offical of his government, the *vezir.* In later years, the composition of the *divan* changed, but its preeminent position in government was established by Mengli Giray.[16]

Mengli Giray constructed several higher schools of learning, or *medresse*s. A particularly large and important *medresse* was the Zinjirli Medresse in Salajik, whose ruins can still be seen today. Likewise, a large mosque, presumably modeled after the cathedral of Hagia Sophia in Istanbul, was built in Solhat. Unfortunately, the mosque was destroyed in the mid-nineteenth century.[17]

In economic matters, Mengli Giray paved the way for the Tatar policy of depending almost entirely upon tribute payments from Muscovy, Poland, and the Danubian Principalities; upon frequent payments from Istanbul; and upon booty gained from campaigns against the infidel, booty that included with ever greater frequency human captives to be sold as slaves. In the late seventeenth century, when the balance of power changed in favor of Muscovy and the Habsburgs and against the Ottoman Empire, the economic resources of the Crimean state proved inadequate. Their lack was the greatest cause for the Crimea's own decline and eventual elimination.

When Mengli Giray died in 1514, he left behind a mixed legacy: a close dependency upon the Ottomans, a fragile internal unity that had to be maintained by foreign adventures, the beginnings of a sound internal administrative structure, and a ruling Giray dynasty. In regard to the latter, it is important to note that Mengli Giray's early rival, Nurdevlet, did not use the dynastic name of Giray even when he was acting as khan; nor did any other of Mengli Giray's brothers use the name of Giray. Yet all of Mengli's own sons and their sons appended the Giray dynastic name to their Muslim one. Thus Mengli, rather than Haci Giray, may be considered the real founder of the Giray dynasty in the Crimea.

3. The Political System of the Crimean Khanate

The Crimean Tatar Khanate was one of the most important states in eastern Europe from the early sixteenth century until the end of the seventeenth century. This is true despite the fact that most historians have considered the Tatars to be, at best, vassals of the Ottoman sultan and a northern extension of his aggressive imperialistic policies against the Christian world, or, at worst, semicivilized brigands whose only function was to raid and devastate the steppe, living upon their more civilized neighbors.

In fact, however, the Crimean Khanate met all of the prerequisites for early modern statehood. It possessed a viable government with a central administration that provided leadership in military, political, and economic affairs. Its administration was based on both historical tradition and a well developed legal system. The legal system was modeled primarily on the Ottoman Islamic example although it contained some remnants of the Tatars' central Asian traditions. The khanate had a clearly defined social system, with at least as high a proportion of urban population as its northern and eastern neighbors. Its economy depended greatly upon trade, including trade in slaves, agriculture, and livestock. Its educational system was as complex and thriving as that of the Ottomans and more advanced than that in Muscovy. Finally, the Crimean khans were patrons of the arts. They built both sacred and secular monuments. Historiographical literature written by Tatar authors extolled the development of the khanate and was a sophisticated contribution to Islamic literature. In view of all of this, it is strange that today in the historiography of eastern Europe the Crimean Tatars can be considered to have been without state or civilization.

Giray Dynasty

At the pinnacle of Crimean society stood the Giray dynasty that provided all of the khans and the highest court officials. The Girays traced their genealogical origins through the Golden Horde to the Great Horde and Jengiz Khan. This tradition gave the dynasty a sense of historical legitimacy and a political pretension that was embodied in the khan's titles. Mengli Giray was called:

> the Crimean Khan, born of the pure race, descended from the Great Khan, through the dynasty of Khans, whose rank provided him with sovereign power,

the possessor of the state, the possessor of the highest praise of God, which has brought to him great dignity, and has earned for him great happiness, who raising the flag of the dynasty shows great obstinacy in battle against the enemy.[1]

A century later, the Crimean khan was called "of the Great Horde, and Great Yurt, of the Kipçak Steppe, Crimean State, of the innumerable Tatars and Nogays, Great Sovereign."[2] While these titles were meant for internal consumption, the khans used similar ones in diplomatic correspondence with foreign states. A note to the Muscovite tsar in the 1680s described the khan: "By God's grace of the Great Horde, of the Great Crimean Yurt, of the Kipçak Steppe, of the many Tatars of the right and left lands, also of the Circassians, blessed Khan, We the great Murat Giray Khan."[3]

According to a Tatar chronicler of the sixteenth century, a khan should be a noble (Giray) in origin, have a handsome appearance, be intelligent, have an authoritative air, be a wolf against injustice and a sheep toward the just, protect the land against all enemies, and hold to all agreements.[4] It is important to notice that there is no mention of the form of political power that the khan should or does possess. The concept of autocracy is conspicuously absent. This is where the political ideology of the khanate diverges from the Ottoman model. The Ottoman sultan not only governed; in many respects he actually was the state. Instead, the Tatars followed the ideology and practice of the hordes: The khan and his dynasty were the symbols of the khanate, but they governed with the active participation of the leaders of the most important clans. In theory, the lands of the khanate were the patrimony of the Girays. It was expected that the eldest member of the dynasty would occupy the throne in the same way that the eldest member of each clan would act as *bey*. But the actual member of the Giray family who became khan was selected by a complicated procedure that often varied from the traditional. This involved the wishes of the clan leaders expressed in their *kurultay*. In theory, the Ottoman role in the selection of the Crimean khan was supposed to appear as an act of confirmation of the *kurultay*'s decision. The Ottomans granted the nominee some Ottoman symbols of political authority—robes of honor and a large monetary sum delivered to the khan-elect by a special representative.

During the sixteenth and seventeenth centuries, however, patterns of selection emerge that often differ from the theoretical model. Beyond the fact that only members of the Giray family serve as khan, there is no established form of succession to power. In one form, the eldest brother of the reigning khan succeeds; in another, the eldest son of the khan succeeds; in still another, it is another brother or son who succeeds.

According to tradition and practice, the Giray dynasty possessed two other official positions, those of *kalgay* and *nurredin* sultans. According to Crimean political theory, these two officers were considered heirs to the throne. In practice, this was seldom the case. While the *kurultay* chose the khan, and its choice was confirmed or rejected by the Ottoman sultan, the khan himself made the selection of these two positions.

Thus the khan's power derived from three streams: Tatar tradition, his personal selection by the *kurultay*, and his acceptance and subsequent financial support from the Ottoman sultan. Once he assumed the throne, the khan's position depended upon his ability to satisfy the demands and needs of the other members of his Giray family and of the leaders of the important Crimean clans. Such satisfaction demanded both effective leadership within the state and lucrative foreign adventures. It is no accident that those khans with the longest reigns were the khans who brought to the Crimea both booty from military campaigns and a strong internal rule.

Giray Finances

The economic resources of the khan were only sufficient to support his court activities and the upkeep of his palaces. Much of the peninsula was outside of his financial control. Most of the economically productive land was in the hands of the clans, the Muslim institutions, and the Ottomans. In addition to the taxes that the Girays could expect from their own lands, they also owned the monopoly of salt production. Until the end of the seventeenth century, the Girays also received tributes in varying amounts from Muscovy, Poland, and the Danubian Principalities.[5]

Monies were needed for several courts. As visible evidence of his sovereignty, the khan maintained both a large palace in Bahçesaray and country estates at Ulakli and Alma. (By the end of the sixteenth century, the khan's first palace at Solhat had fallen into disuse and disrepair.) The *kalgay* and *nurredin* sultans also kept palaces of their own in Akmeçet. Foreigners who visited these palaces during the early seventeenth century indicate that there seemed to be no official business conducted there. They remarked that the palaces seemed to be mostly pleasure centers for the Giray heirs to the throne.[6]

The last element of the ruling dynasty was made up of the large number of Giray sultans that included all of the living Giray males who had never held one of the three top positions. From Ottoman records it appears that these sultans numbered as many as fifty at a time.[7] Both the ruling khans and the Ottomans had difficulty keeping these sultans active while keeping them from striving to gain one of the top positions. Some of these sultans were assigned as the khan's representatives among the Nogay hordes; some were sent to Circassia to administer the khan's interests there; a few were kept on estates assigned to the Girays by the Ottoman sultans. These latter originally bore the title *rehin* ("hostage"). The *rehin*s were sent to Istanbul to ensure the tractability of the khan in relation to Ottoman policy. Ironically, the efforts of the khans to keep the khanate sultans away from the court contributed to internal unrest within the khanate during the eighteenth century, when some of the sultans representing the khan among the Nogay hordes precipitated rebellion and initiated independent relations with Russia for their personal advancement.[8]

Administration and Law

As the khanate developed during the sixteenth century, the khan's palace administration grew into a large bureaucratic establishment. The number of officials under his authority grew until the khan's resources became inadequate to maintain them. The bureaucracy included a number of offices staffed by servitors (*kapikulu*), members of the scholarly profession (*ulema*), and lower-ranking nobles from the other great clans.[9] Knowledge of the actual operation of this system prior to the mid-eighteenth century is almost nonexistent. The archives of the khanate's bureaucracy have not been studied, and since the end of the nineteenth century they have disappeared from view.[10]

It is known that the legal system of the khanate was based on several traditions: Islamic law, interpreted and administered by officials of the Muslim institutions; traditional Tatar law, based on that believed to be inherited from the Great Yasa ("law code") of Jengiz Khan; and to a lesser extent, Ottoman law in the areas of the peninsula that were under the control of the Ottoman sultan, or in relations between the khans and Istanbul.

One of the major problems between the Ottomans and the Crimeans arose from the difference between Tatar customary law and the Ottoman *kanun* law on the question of succession to the throne. The Ottoman practice was that of a vertical line of succession, to the eldest son of the ruling sultan; historically, Tatar practice, which was based on the Great Yasa, was horizontal. The eldest living male member of the dynastic family succeeded the ruling khan. According to tradition he would occupy the position of *kalgay* sultan until he became khan. Although the Crimean Tatars did not always adhere to this tradition, it is clear from various disputes with the Ottomans that they did not want to permanently abandon their traditional system.[11]

Tatar law was followed in questions of royal succession, and it determined the relationships between the khans and the other Tatar clans. The clans, according to Tatar custom, manifested their own authority through a periodic assembly (the *kurultay*) that had no Ottoman parallel. Likewise, in the area of social relationships, the Tatars preferred the practice of the Golden Horde to that in use in the Ottoman Empire. On the other hand, Ottoman administrative practice was the model for the khan's *divan* ("council") and many of his court officials.

Finally, Islamic law, which was administered by Muslim officials outside of the khan's civil administration, determined the day-to-day legal behavior of the Muslims in the khanate. The leader of the Muslim establishment was the *mufti,* who was selected by and from among the local Muslim clergy. His major duty was neither judicial nor theological; it was financial. The *mufti*'s administration controlled all of the *vakif* lands (land owned by the Muslim institutions) and their enormous revenues, both of which belonged to the Muslim institutions. Another Muslim offical, appointed not by the clergy but by the Ottoman sultan, was the *kadiasker.* He oversaw the khanate's judicial institutions. The peninsula was divided into small judicial districts, each under the jurisdiction of a *kadi.* In theory, the *kadi*s were under the authority of the *kadiasker;* in reality, they answered to the demands and needs of the civil bureaucracy of the khan or the clan leaders in their areas. Their appointments by the khan or clan leaders were given *pro forma* approval by the *kadiasker.*[12] It is interesting to consider the sultan's use of the *kadiasker* in assuring Ottoman lines of information and authority, but unless Ottoman sources on these relations emerge, one can only speculate.

Thus, when examining the characteristics of the khan's administrative institutions and his symbols of authority, one finds the skeleton of a sovereign state with a well developed centralized governmental structure. Looking more closely at the social organization of the Tatars, however, and then at the khanate's economic resources and the distribution of control, the outline of the khanate's political authority becomes more complex. Unlike its neighbors, the khanate was not a feudal monarchy, an absolute monarchy, a patrimonial state, or an oriental despotism. It was something quite different, perhaps without European or eastern European parallel.

Tatar Clans

The Girays possessed the symbols of sovereign power, and because of their relationship to Jengiz Khan, their preeminent position in the Tatar hierarchy was not challenged. Yet their actual authority in the khanate was limited by the overwhelming power of the great Tatar clans. These clans had virtually hereditary possession of the vast majority of productive lands on the peninsula, economic and political authority over most of the population, and a much larger military force than the khan. The combination of these factors made it impossible for the khan to act without the cooperation and approval of the *bey*s of these clans.

The traditional Tatar hierarchical system governed the relations between the various clans and between the clan leaders and the khan. Over the centuries, this sytem was under constant change, as various clans gained in importance at the expense of others, but throughout the khanate's existence, the Şirin clan always occupied the first position.[13]

As was the case with the Girays, the Şirins owed their position to the role their ancestors had played in the Golden Horde. The Şirin clan held almost all of the eastern part of the peninsula that was not in the Ottoman district, the land north and east of Kefe, and the land along the shores of the Sea of Azov. The Şirin *bey* directed the clan's vast holdings from his palace of Katirşa Saray near the *beylik*'s capital, Karasu Bazaar. From the khanate's beginning, when the Şirin *bey*, Eminek Mirza, supported Mengli Giray at the Ottoman court, the Şirins' desires were always taken into special account by the Ottoman sultan. The Şirins' position as first among the nonroyal families is shown by the fact that they were the only Tatars other than the Girays who could legally marry a Giray prince or sultan.[14]

Along with the Şirin *bey*, the *bey*s of three other Tatar clans made up the exclusive circle of the Crimean aristocracy called the Karaçi *bey*s. As a group, the four Karaçi *bey*s exerted great influence over the khan, determined the success or failure of Tatar military campaigns by granting or withholding support for the khan's ventures, and usually represented before the sultan the wishes of the Tatar *kurultay* on the matter of the selection or removal of a khan. They sat on the *divan*, and by their presence could effectively determine the main contours of Crimean policy. Together, their power was considerably greater than the khan's, and he refused to take heed of their wishes at his own peril.[15]

At first, the four Karaçi *bey*s were the leaders of the Şirin, Argin, Barin, and Kipçak clans. Other clans that rose to this important rank in the seventeenth and eighteenth centuries were the Mansur Oglans and the Sicuvuts.[16] The functions of the *bey*s were divided into three main categories: (1) advising the khan as part of the *divan*, (2) representing the wishes of the *kurultay* before the Ottoman sultan, and (3) governing their own lands or *beylik*s. Unfortunately, the evidence for the first function is scanty since the khanate's archives have not been available to scholars. However, source material explaining the other two is plentiful, first because the Ottoman archives are being examined for information on the Tatar question, and second, because the evidence on the *beylik*s was studied carefully by F. Lashkov during the nineteenth century.

In recognition of their role in the selection of a new khan, the *bey*s directed the ceremonies in which the nominee was presented with the formal trappings of Crimean sovereignty by the representatives of the Ottoman sultan. When Sahib Giray, on the request of the Karaçi *bey*s, was confirmed as khan by Sultan Suleiman I, this confirmation took place at the mouth of the Bug (Ozu) River. It began with the khan emerging from a tent, wearing the robes of his new position and accompanied by the Ottoman *çavuş* ("messenger"). He was met by the four Karaçi *beys* who had also been given robes of honor as gifts from the sultan.[17]

On their own lands, the Karaçi *beys* were considered by their clans as defenders of their interest against those of other clans and of the khan. When on military campaign, each *bey* assumed command of whatever military force his clan provided for the Tatar army. Each force fought under its clan's banner. The Karaçi *beys* had both their own palaces with their own court officials and subservient officers, named *kalgay* and *nurredin,* after those of the Girays. The selection of a *bey* was a jealously held prerogative of the clan, and although it often went to the eldest male almost automatically, the khan had no right to interfere in the selection at all. In addition, the *bey* controlled the activities and selection of the *kadis* in their own *beyliks.*[18]

Beneath the *beys* of the Karaçi clans, other families of the aristocracy were led by *mirzas* (Tatar nobles).[19] Their lands were theoretically parceled out by the *bey,* but evidence seems to indicate that *mirza* families held their lands in a substantially hereditary fashion. It is not possible to determine if these *mirza* families were genealogically tied to the clan, although it is likely that many merely joined one clan or another and could transfer their loyalty from one *bey* to another at will. Unfortunately, evidence of the type that Lashkov found about the origins and conditions of the clans has not turned up to answer similar questions about the *mirza* families.

As the khanate fell more under Ottoman influence during the late sixteenth century, some purely Ottoman institutions replaced their Tatar counterparts in the realm of social organization. The Ottoman *timar* or *kapikulu* system— through which the sultan kept absolute control over large portions of the empire's lands, granting only temporary use of them to his personal servants—began to appear in the Crimea after 1550. This had a destructive effect on the position of the great Tatar clans who held their land independent of the khan's authority. It must be suspected that conflicts between the two systems arose. Tatar nobility occupying these *timar* lands were surer allies of the khan than were the Karaçi *beys,* and they were often used by the khan to offset the latter's power. Exactly how land on the peninsula was procured for *timar* purposes is a mystery; in any case much of it was taken from the Caucasus and parts of Bessarabia which in time were added to the khan's domains.[20]

Lower Classes

Most of the Tatars living on the peninsula were not members of the Crimean elite. Rather, they were either herdsmen or peasants. Their relationship with the lords of the land was not feudal in character. Most of the peasants were Muslims and Islamic law exempted them from the possibility of losing their rights. Apportioned by village, the land was worked in common and the tax was assigned by the lord to the village as a whole. The *bey, mirza,* khan, or *kapikulu* was permitted to collect three types of tax from his Muslim peasants. He was owed one-tenth of the value of the grain harvest, one-twentieth of the livestock production, and a variable corvée (unpaid labor). Since the peasants were free to leave if they wished, those who collected and assigned taxes were careful not to abuse their rights for fear of losing the producers on their land.[21]

Nogay Tatars

After the Girays, the Tatar nobility, and the peasants, there were two other important elements in Tatar society: the Nogay Tatars, and to a lesser extent, the Circassians under the khan's authority. The Nogay Tatars had been an integral part of the Golden Horde as one of its tribal confederations. Completely nomadic, they had lived in the steppe north of the Caucasus between Azov and Astrakhan until the middle of the sixteenth century. When the Tatar khanate of Astrakhan was conquered by Muscovy in 1556, many of the Nogays from that region migrated to the steppe north of the Crimea and submitted in an informal way to the suzerainty of the Crimean khan. It was not long, however, before these Nogays split into a number of confederations that would play an important role in the khanate's history until the end of the eighteenth century. The Kuban Nogays roamed the steppe north of the Sea of Azov; at times they showed themselves loyal to the khans, at others to the tsars. The Yediçkul Nogays lived in the steppe north of the Crimean peninsula and roamed as far into the Ukraine and southeastern Poland as the Cossack groups would permit. Other Nogays who played an important role in both Crimean and Ottoman relations with eastern Europe were the Bucak Nogays (from the Danube to the Dnestr rivers), the Yedisan Nogays (from the Dnestr to the Bug rivers), and the Jamboyluk Nogays (from the Bug River to the beginning of the Crimean peninsula).

After the Nogays accepted Crimean suzerainty, they were required to recognize the authority of the khan's representatives sent from Bahçe-saray to govern them. These representatives, called *seraskers*, were not able to establish a firm allegiance from the Nogays for the Crimea, nor were they very successful in introducing any sort of Crimean administration among the Nogays. As steppe nomads, the Nogays had for centuries considered their way of life superior to that of the settled populations represented by the khanate. They participated in numerous rebellions against Tatar supremacy, carrying their disputes to the point of killing khans and their representatives when the demands made by them were deemed excessive.

In 1523, the Nogays killed Mehmed Giray I, and during the reign of Sahib Giray I, they invaded the peninsula. On several occasions during the seventeenth century some of the Nogay chieftains broke their ties with the Crimea and offered to recognize the Muscovite tsar. In the late eighteenth century, when Catherine II was attempting to end the relationship between the khanate and the Ottoman Empire, it was among the Nogays that she found her most attentive audience. Yet the Nogays served a useful purpose for the khanate: They prevented the establishment of solid Slavic settlements in the steppe and provided the Crimean slave markets with a never-ending supply of captives.[22]

As for the Circassians, the khans merely inherited claims of authority left after the demise of the Golden Horde. The Girays had a special arrangement with certain Circassians under which some Crimean sultans were educated in military affairs under Circassian direction. Also the Circassians were a great source of slaves, especially those for use as wives and concubines of the khans and of Tatar nobility. In Circassia in the late sixteenth century, the khans built a number of fortifications in which they settled Nogays who were to defend the area against the depredations of Cossack raiders and Kalmyks (the true Mongolian remnants of the Mongol/Tatar empire). The Ottoman government recognized the khan's right to exercise political authority in much of Circassia, in return for which the khans provided the Ottoman sultan with an annual tribute of Circassian slaves.[23]

In summary, until the beginning of the eighteenth century, the political system of the Crimean khanate appeared to be a combination of several systems. The ruler belonged to a hereditary dynasty and occupied the position of symbolic sovereign. His administration was well developed and included every variety of court and palace official that one is accustomed to find in an early modern state. Yet his authority within the khanate was restricted by the power exercised by the clans, their leaders, and the primary allegiance of the great majority of *mirzas* to the *beys*.

The khans on occasion found support against rebellious Tatar nobles among the Nogays and Circassians, yet this support was extremely fragile and subject to transferral either to Muscovy or to the Ottoman sultan. The khan's authority was at best equal to that of the other elements of society. It was in the realms of economic and cultural life that the real basis for the importance of the Girays as rulers of the khanate was found.

4. Economic and Cultural Life in the Khanate

In their campaign to justify the elimination of the Crimean Tatars in 1944, Soviet historians have dismissed them as raiders and brigands who lived by the collection of booty and tribute from their neighbors and did not create an urban network and peasant economy in the Crimea. These historians argue that for these reasons the Tatars cannot be considered as having either territorial or national claims for existence today. Good examples of this view may be found in the work of Novosel'skii, who combines the Tatars with Turks in his title, and in Iakobson's book on the Crimea in the middle ages, in which only the short last chapter deals with the period of "Turco-Tatar occupation" in the period around the mid-fourteenth century.[1] Should Soviet historians admit the fact that the Crimean Tatars once possessed an economically and culturally developed state that paralleled their own, they would find it difficult to justify the fate of these Tatars since 1944.

Slave Trade

One has only to state the fact that the slave trade was the most important element in the Crimean Tatar economy from the mid-fifteenth century to the eighteenth century, and the reader regretfully accepts the Soviet judgment. How could a slave trade provide the basis for the economy of an early modern state? The Western reader has little sympathy for or understanding of the enslavement of Christians by Muslims or by any other non-Christian people. This alone seems to be enough to cause a negative reaction to the Tatar economy and society. Yet participation in slavery and the slave trade seems to have had little deleterious effect on the culture of Venice, Genoa, or the Netherlands during the same centuries. This chapter will examine the nature and extent of the Crimean slave trade and the towns it spawned. The flowering of Crimean Tatar culture that emerged from these urban centers will also be discussed.

In the Crimean area, a slave trade had existed as early as recorded history for the region exists. In the period just prior to the Ottoman conquest of Constantinople and the appearance of the Tatar khanate, the shores of the Black Sea were an important source of slaves for foreign buyers.[2] After 1475, when the Ottomans and the Crimean Tatars defeated the Italians, the Muslims merely replaced the Italians as the major slave merchants in the

Crimea. With the introduction of war into this area and the resulting captives, the Muslims legitimized their slave trade (according to both Christian and Muslim legal theory, capture during war was the only acceptable means of enslavement).[3]

The Crimean Tatars were well suited to continue and expand this form of trade. Many of them had retained nomadic skills and predilections despite the fact that, by the sixteenth century, most had settled down to an agricultural or urban way of life. The Tatar aristocrats were both hostile toward the Christian populations that lived beyond the frontiers of Islam, and disdainful of the peasant populations that they found there. From 1468, the time of the first recorded Tatar raid in the northern steppe, until the end of the seventeenth century, Tatar raiders made almost annual forays into Slavic agricultural communities in the north searching for captives to sell as slaves. It is understandable that Slavic historians describe these events with dismay; yet viewed from a less emotional or nationalistic perspective, these slave raids can be seen as a very successful economic activity that produced the means by which the Tatars developed a lively urban and cultural society.[4]

The Ukrainians and Poles possessed a literature of tales about the resulting slavery under the Turks and Tatars. The "Dumy o nevol'nikakh" told of being sold first in Kefe, then in Istanbul, and eventually in Arabia. Another tale read:

> A poor slave in Turkey sends greetings
> From the land of Mohammed to the Christian cities,
> To his father and mother;
> He cannot greet them,
> But he greets the gray pigeons,
> "O thou gray pigeon
> That fliest high and wanderest far!
> Fly thou to the Christian cities, to my father and mother,
> Remind them of my Kozak fate."[5]

Added to the profits gained from the capture and sale of slaves, ransom (the sale of the captives back to representatives of their native lands) became a lucrative offshoot of the slave trade. The ransom system was closely related to the maintenance of Tatar political prerogatives in the steppe vis à vis Poland and Muscovy. When one remembers that Muscovite political ideology in the sixteenth century made extravagant claims to power not only in eastern Europe but in the whole of eastern Christendom, it is strange, indeed, to find that Muscovy permitted the Crimean Tatars to make such slave raids in its territory and then took part in ransoming the unfortunate captives.

Collection of funds for ransom became a serious financial burden for the Muscovite government. In 1535, Tsar Ivan IV issued an order to his governor in Novgorod saying, "last year the Tatars came to the Ukraine, and according to our representatives, captured men, women, and children. In order to buy them back, we are asking for silver from the monasteries."[6]

In 1551, the Zemskii Sobor regularized the ransom of Russian slaves held in the Crimea. Ivan IV went so far as to encourage merchants in the Crimea possessing these slaves to bring them to Moscow for sale.[7] Finally, in 1649, the Ulozhenie ("law code") of Tsar Aleksis created a special fund, collected as an annual tax, to take care of the increasing sum needed for slave ransoms. That the Muscovite government was willing to do this indicates that it was not yet strong enough either to prevent Tatar slave raids or to free the slaves by force. Added to the Muscovite tribute, the khans thus received a substantial and growing yearly sum from their Russian neighbors.

Poland likewise was in a position of submission to the Tatar government through payment of an annual tribute. Polish historians have characterized this tribute as appeasement to prevent raids. The tribute was financed by a special poll tax on Jews within the kingdom. Over a five-year period in the mid-seventeenth century, this Polish appeasement amounted to more than 700,000 *zlotys*.[8]

Although the khans did not possess sufficient land to permit them economic control of the khanate, they did have large financial resources. These derived from a combination of the tribute monies from Muscovy and Poland, from their percentage of all captives brought to the Crimea, and from the large donations of various sorts they received from the Ottomans. After the end of the seventeenth century, when the khans lost all of these resources save the last, their authority within the khanate rapidly deteriorated.

Urban Society

The Crimean economy depended primarily upon trade, the greatest part of which was the slave trade. This is easily seen in the location of the Crimean towns, in the proportion of the Crimean population that the towns represented, and in the sorts of urban population they contained. In the sixteenth and seventeenth centuries, foreign travelers remarked on the size and beauty of the cities. In their accounts, they expressed considerable surprise at the liveliness of the culture, occasionally comparing them to towns in Muscovy at the expense of the latter.

The khan's own port city was Gözleve (Evpatoria), which, like Kefe, had been an important trading center under Italian rule before the khanate was founded. After the Tatar capital of Bahçesaray, Gözleve was the largest city belonging to the Girays. Beauplan, visiting the Crimea in the sixteenth century, described the city as having more than 2000 homes. In 1850, even after the depredations such towns underwent during the eighteenth and nineteenth centuries, Gözleve still retained several large mosques, the old Tatar customs house, and two *medresses*.[9]

Other cities developed as important centers too. Karasu Bazaar, the capital of the Şirin *beylik*, had as its central feature an enormous *caravan sarai* and bazaar (the Taş Han) that particularly struck the eye of Pallas when he passed through it at the end of the eighteenth century. It had twenty-three mosques and twenty *han*s (combination market places and inns) at the beginning of the eighteenth century. It was the headquarters of the Şirin *bey* and the site of the Karaçi *bey*s' periodic meetings. Heavy fighting around the city in the years before the Russian annexation seems to have destroyed all traces of the nearby Şirin palace, but it is probable that it was a building worthy of its occupants.[10]

During much of the khanate's history, Akmeçet (Simferopol'), which was under control of the *kalgay* sultan, was the largest town not under Ottoman control. In the early eighteenth century, its population exceeded 8000 male inhabitants. However, Pallas wrote that by the time of his travels the *kalgay*'s palace had been entirely demolished and the site was "now occupied by breweries."[11]

The khanate's primary city was Bahçesaray, the capital of the khans. That it was a city with a large, varied population was reflected in the many mosques and churches it contained. By the end of the eighteenth century, Pallas reported thirty-one mosques, a Greek church, an Armenian church, and two synagogues. The city was the major trading center for the Crimean peninsula and thus contained numerous *han*s and merchant quarters; it also had a major leather-working industry and was a milling center for the grain production of the state.[12]

Bahçesaray Palace

The city's central feature was the palace of the Girays. A sprawling complex of relatively low buildings, its layout differed considerably in style from either European or Russian palaces. Although it was not comparable in decoration and elegance with Topkapi Palace in Istanbul, its size and structure had great similarities with the latter. The palace was divided into the customary Islamic three-courtyard system with the innermost court reserved for the royal family and its personal servants.

Most Tatar and Western accounts give the date of its construction as 1503, the date found on the Golden Door at the entrance to the third court. Yet Professor Ernst, through a careful examination of diplomatic sources from Muscovy and Poland, has decided that the palace was most probably built between 1533 and 1551, during the reign of Sahib Giray I. Ernst has discovered that northern diplomats, at least until 1533, delivered their notes and received responses from "the khan and/or his representatives" in what they called the Crimean capital at Solhat. After this date, the name of

Bahçesaray appears in the sources as the Crimean capital. Thus it is likely that Khan Sahib Giray I brought the famous door from his earlier palace to emphasize the continuity in political authority.[13] Further evidence for this proposition is the fact that in the late sixteenth century Bahçesaray was not a large city; it only began to grow in the early seventeenth. Bronevskii had described mid-sixteenth-century Bahçesaray as "a small town with a stone house in which the khan lives."[14]

Unfortunately, the khans' first palace in Bahçesaray was destroyed by the invading Russian army in 1735, and beginning in 1738, was rebuilt according to a somewhat different style. The many surviving detailed descriptions of the palace are only of the later version.[15]

A legend that was used by the Crimean Tatars to explain the authority of the Giray khans, and that served as the title of an important Tatar history of the Crimea, is the *Rose Garden of the Khans*. This legend was inscribed on the portal of the main royal mosque, just outside of the palace. It read:

> Who is Haci Selim? This was the most famous of all of the khans, the heroes inspired by God. That God grant him all thanks for the construction of this mosque. The person of Selim Giray is comparable to a rose garden; the son who is born to him is a rose. Each in his turn has many honors in the palace. The rose garden is ornamented by a new flower; its unique and fresh rose has become the lion of the padishah of the Crimea, Selamet Giray Khan.[16]

Non-Muslim Minorities

Almost all of the non-Muslims lived in the cities of Gözleve, Karasu Bazaar, Akmeçet, and Bahçesaray. It is interesting to note that many of these non-Muslims (for the most part Armenians, Georgians, Greeks, and Karaim Jews) had taken on the way of life of the Crimean Muslims—with the exception of religion. The Karaim Jews spoke a Turkic language, lived according to Turkic traditions, and even sang purely Turkic songs. The Greeks and Armenians who were moved from the Crimea to the Russian Empire in 1779 were found to speak a Turkic language.[17]

The non-Muslims lived in distinct quarters in these cities, or in special suburbs just outside. As was normal in most Islamic states, they controlled business, trading, shipping, and private financial affairs. According to the *millet* (religious community) traditions in effect in the Ottoman Empire, the non-Muslims in the Crimea enjoyed the use of their own religious courts which had jurisdiction in domestic matters in their communities. Taxes on non-Muslims were relatively high. In addition to the taxes in effect on all Crimeans, non-Muslims also were required to pay a *cizye* ("capitation tax"). In theory this took the place of their having to perform military service. There is no evidence, however, that they were subject to any of the discrimination or persecution that infidel subjects experienced in the Christian states in the north.[18]

General view of Bahçesaray in 1800.

Bahçesaray Palace in 1800.

Courtyard, Bahçesaray Palace (restored 1737).

Inscription above the great
portal, Bahçesaray Palace
(restored 1737).

Interior, Bahçesaray
Palace (restored 1737).

The great portal, Bahçesaray Palace, in 1800.

The Karaim Jewish community lived in different circumstances from other non-Muslims. Concentrated in one town, Çufut Kale, near Bahçesaray, they had a number of special rights and privileges that Christian subjects were denied. They were exempted from a number of Crimean taxes and had rights to "ownership" of their town and to total noninterference in their local political life. The evidence on the origin of these privileges is not clear. Çufut Kale had been an important Tatar fortress before the founding of the capital city and was the site of the tombs of several early Tatar khans and aristocrats. Its former name had been Kirkyer (*Çufut Kale* meant "Jewish fortress"), and according to some Tatar sources, it had been the first site of Tatar political authority in the Crimea in the early years of the Golden Horde. Its largest tomb was that of Nenekecan Hanim, a daughter of Toktamiş Khan (Khan of the Golden Horde), who according to legend fell in love with a Genoese nobleman and fled with her lover to the impregnable walls of Kirkyer.

The Karaim community explained their privileged circumstances with the story that in the "ancient past" their ancestors had been able to cure a *uluhane* (a first wife of a Tatar khan) of a terminal disease. In return for this favor, they were granted the use of the fortress and a number of important financial and legal privileges. The one verifiable element of this story is the fact that in the late sixteenth century, the capitation tax on these Jews was attached to the office of *uluhane* in Bahçesaray.[19]

Ottoman Lands in the Crimea

The Ottoman province of Kefe should be mentioned briefly at this point. At the time of the Ottoman conquest of the Crimean shores in 1475, the areas taken from the Genoese were placed under the jurisdiction of an Ottoman *pasha* in Kefe, and the region was assigned the provincial rank of *sancak*. But eighty years later, when a large-scale Ottoman campaign was prepared against the Muscovites in the Volga area, this region was made an *eyalet* and given an Ottoman commander. According to a late-sixteenth-century list of *eyalets*, the province of Kefe included the towns of Kefe, Akkerman, Bender, Azov, Kilburun, and Kerç; thus this *eyalet* extended all along the northern shores of the Black Sea, rather than being simply on the peninsula.[20]

By 1640, this large province had been divided into two *eyalets*. The new *eyalet* with its capital at Ochakov included the western and southwestern portions of the former. This change reflected the Ottomans' changing perceptions of their dangerous neighbors in the early part of the seventeenth century. Cossacks from Poland and Habsburgs in the west were now far more dangerous than potential threats from Muscovy or the steppe nomads in the east.[21]

The town of Kefe, which was larger than Akmeçet or Bahçesaray, was a port that handled more trade than Gözleve, and had more architectural monuments than the rest of the Crimean towns combined. Ottomans who visited Kefe often saw it as a Küçük Istanbul ("small Istanbul"). It perhaps paralleled Kiev, which had tried in the early centuries to reproduce some of the attributes of Constantinople. Dortelli, in the first half of the seventeenth century, pictured Kefe as being five miles in circumference and having a population of at least 80,000. It contained more than seventy mosques, and its port handled on an average of ten ships per day. If these figures are correct, Kefe at this time was a larger city than any in Muscovy. Among the most impressive buildings in Kefe was the Great Mosque, built in 1623, of which only ruins remain.[22]

Tatar Chronicles

Besides the mosques and palaces that the khans built, the most important survivals of the flourishing Crimean Tatar culture are the historical chronicles describing Tatar history and life in these centuries. If one can assign one major characteristic to all of these chronicles, it is that they all present both historical and ideological justifications for considering the Crimean Khanate as a separate state—a state under Ottoman suzerainty, yet with its own institutions that bore traces of the khans' central Asian heritage that had been received directly from Jengiz Khan.

Sixteenth-century Crimean historians were interested in the problems of Tatar separateness and Tatar identity, and in those khanate traditions that were purely Tatar in origin. The first such chronicle, the *Tarih-i Sahib Giray Khan*, written soon after the death of Sahib Giray, emphasizes throughout that the genealogical traditions of the Giray dynasty were second to none (either Muscovite or Ottoman) in legitimacy and longevity. It is noteworthy that Sahib Giray was a contemporary both of Sultan Suleiman I and of Tsar Ivan IV. In this chronicle, much information is given about the cultural life at the court of Sahib Giray, among whose scholars the leader was Keffevi Alşayh Abu Bakr Efendi, who had been to Jerusalem and Baghdad and had made many pilgrimages to Mecca. A whole school of Crimean poetry evolved around Abu Bakr—a school much influenced by contemporary Ottoman poetry, yet with a special Tatar subject matter and style.[23]

A second chronicle, the *Tevarih Deşt-i Kipçak*, written between 1623 and 1640 by a Crimean Tatar living in Kefe, emphasizes the separate identity and resulting sovereignty of the khans from time immemorial, and the fact that, because of their special traditions, the khans were able to deal with the sultans as genealogical equals. The real heroes of Crimean history, according to this chronicle, were those khans, such as Mengli Giray and Devlet Giray, who lived up to their independent heritage. (Devlet was the khan who sabotaged

the Ottoman campaign to regain Astrakhan in 1556 and who later made the
most famous of the devastating Crimean raids upon Moscow.)[24]

A chronicle from the early 1650s, *Uçuncu Islam Giray Khan Tarihi* by
Kirimli Haci Mehmed Senai, maintains the same emphasis on the Jingizid
origins of the Girays and the possession of the political attributes of the
former *hakhans* of the Golden Horde by the khans.[25] Finally, *Asseb'
o-sseiiar'*, a chronicle written by Seiid Mukhammed Riza in the 1750s, is the
most interesting and enlightening of those written during the khanate period.
By far the longest, and containing the most detailed information about Tatar
history and culture, it served as the basis for the two-volume Crimean history
by V. D. Smirnov. Riza emphasizes, to the point of slighting others, those
khans who acted according to the interests of the Jingizids—those who
followed a Crimean political policy separate from that of the Ottoman
overlords. His main hero is also Devlet Giray, who refused to endanger his
khanate's interests by taking part in the Ottoman campaigns. Riza uses the
provocative word *interference* when discussing Ottoman participation in
Crimean succession crises. He devotes the first quarter of the chronicle to the
period of Mongol-Tatar domination of the steppe, and presents the Crimeans'
history as one chapter in a unified Tatar history.[26]

It thus becomes clear that the Crimean Khanate, until its degeneration at
the end of the seventeenth century, operated internally and externally as an
early modern state with a lively cultural and economic life. Despite the fact
that the khans could not operate in an autocratic fashion because of the
divisions of power in the Crimea between the Girays, clans, clergy, and
Ottomans, they did provide effective and needed leadership in economic and
cultural life. It was in these areas that the Girays proved themselves
competent to rule. It would be only after the disappearance of Ottoman
financial support and the end of the lucrative slave trade, and with the
growing disillusionment among the Crimean cultural elite, that serious
questions were raised about the competency of the Girays.

5. The Crimean Role in Eastern European Politics

From the point of view of Muscovy, Poland-Lithuania and the Ottoman Empire, the Crimean Khanate played an important role in eastern Europe. It is a role that has been underplayed in the historiography of these states.

Importance in Ottoman History

For the Ottomans, the Crimean Tatars served as a necessary military element in their European policies and as suppliers of human and material resources. As a military force, the Tatars both provided the Ottomans with a supply of soldiers for their campaigns in eastern Europe and on the Caucasian front and acted as a military defensive buffer in the north. In the Ottoman army, the khans' troops served as *akinci*s (light cavalrymen) who prepared the way for the advance of the sultan's heavy infantry and cavalry forces. European opponents credited the effectiveness of the Tatar cavalry to their overwhelming numbers and sophisticated weapons. Yet Ottoman and Crimean historical sources show that the Tatar *akinci*s were neither numerous nor well armed in the European sense. Of the at most 50,000 light Tatar cavalry, it appears that only a small number were equipped with firearms. The Ottomans were the Tatars' only source of guns and munitions and they gave them only to the *sekban*s in the khan's personal guard. The strength of the Tatar cavalry was due to the extremely high quality of their campaign leadership and to the effective tactics they inherited from their years with the Golden Horde. Riding rapidly and quietly over the steppe (the most suitable terrain for their activities), the *akinci*s struck without warning. However, against fortified cities, the Crimeans proved practically useless. There, only well organized infantry with artillery could succeed, and the Crimeans had neither.[1]

The first Ottoman campaign in which the Crimeans took part occurred in 1484 against Akkerman. The Ottomans sent an "invitation" to the khan, accompanied by a quiver price of monetary gifts and ceremonial trappings. The money was sufficient to allow the khan to entice the clan leaders whose approval was needed for the khan's acceptance. Although the "invitations" were filled with such phrases as "assistance for the faith of Islam," and "for the brotherhood of the Ottoman dynasty," it is likely that the combination of the gifts with a promise of campaign booty was the deciding factor in Crimean participation.[2]

The Crimeans provided a second important military service: the defense of the empire's northern flank against attack and encroachment by Muscovite Russia and Poland-Lithuania. Numerous Tatar campaigns in the steppe region prevented this large area from being permanently settled until much later than would have been expected. It is no accident that the Russian appearance on the shores of the Black Sea (which brought about a sudden and serious deterioration of Ottoman power) could take place only after the Crimean Khanate had been tamed in the late eighteenth century.

The khanate was also important for the Ottoman Empire's economy. Agricultural commodities such as grain and meat, and condiments such as fish oil and salt that came from the northern shores of the Black Sea made up a critical portion of the Ottoman economy. In addition, the Crimea was an important source of slaves for the Ottoman military forces and for the imperial harems.[3]

Geopolitically, the Ottomans used the khanate as a buffer state, in the same way they used the Danubian Principalities. Yet there were major differences between the position of these provinces and the khanate. The latter was led by a Muslim dynasty that was in many ways independent of the Ottoman sultans. The khans were not appointees of Istanbul; they were not products of the Ottoman bureaucratic system. Correspondence between the Ottomans and the khans was in the form of invitations; diplomatic correspondence took place between sovereigns rather than in the form of the Imperial rescripts that characterized the relationships between the Ottomans and their other buffers. While the Danubian Principalities paid taxes and tribute to the Ottoman treasury, the khanate received financial rewards for its services.

Role in Muscovite History

What was gain for the Ottoman Empire was loss for Muscovy and Poland-Lithuania. Crimean control of the Black Sea's northern shores preserved the Black Sea solely for the Ottomans and denied Muscovy use of vital portions of the river transport routes upon which her internal trade depended. The mouths of the Don and Dniepr, two of the three most important Russian rivers, were located within the khanate. Until the Russians gained control of the khanate, grains grown in southern Russia were not readily available for foreign trade.

Prior to the taming of the khanate in the late eighteenth century, frequent Crimean raids in the steppe prevented the permanent settlement and government control of that area that allowed for such lucrative exports from that breadbasket in the nineteenth century. From the Russian perspective, it was a tragedy to be unable to use that area where the seasons were of sufficient length and the soil of sufficient quality to permit intensive agriculture. The effect on Muscovy's central regions was disastrous. Moscow had to depend on poorer regions to produce the foodstuffs necessary for her growing population. This meant that Muscovite agriculture became labor intensive during the period of its most important growth, and it certainly influenced the development of serfdom in Russia.

The instability of life in the steppe region caused many of the Muscovite peasants moving away from the increasingly difficult situation of serfdom in central Muscovy to migrate to the inhospitable climes of Siberia rather than to the south (which would have been warranted by the soil). Many of those who did choose the Ukraine and southern steppe found their ultimate homes in the Ottoman Empire, in Egypt, or elsewhere after being captured and sold by Tatar bands.

All of this is easily understandable. On the one hand were the needs of the Tatars to raid for economic gain and to save their open pastures; on the other hand was the deleterious effect of such raids on Muscovite agriculture and national development. What is difficult to explain, however, is Muscovy's reaction to the situation. Using Giovanni Botero's sixteenth-century observation that Muscovy's low population in relation to other eastern European states of the time was explained by the great numbers of Russians taken in Tatar slave raids, Professor Vernadsky argued that Ivan IV and his seventeenth-century successors should have realized that the Crimean Tatars were the greatest danger to Muscovite national development.[4]

Ivan IV's advisor on foreign affairs, Adashev, had tried to persuade Ivan IV that offensive operations against the Tatars and the creation of fortified bases in the south were the only ways to stop these raids. He said that either the khan should be persuaded to accept the tsar as his suzerain or Muscovy should try to annex the whole region. Russian historians, led by Kostomarov, said that Tatar raids not only threatened the *boyars'* interests but also presented to the Russians a "truly national task. . . . The first prerogative of Russia's welfare and prosperity was the subdual of these predatory nests and the annexation of their territory."[5]

Soviet historians have written that Muscovy recognized this need in the seventeenth century and acted on its behalf. Novosel'skii implied this recognition in his book title *The Struggle of the Muscovite State Against the Tatars in the First Half of the XVIIth Century.*[6] Yet his evidence gives the lie to his proposition. Until the end of the century, the Muscovite government did nothing that could be constructed as an active policy to remove the Crimean threat. In fact, Novosel'skii's own materials and all of the other available evidence leads one to conclude that Ivan IV and his successors realized that Muscovy was too weak in relation to the Tatars and Ottomans to mount an effective offensive in the south.

On the contrary, Muscovy continued to pay its onerous tribute to the khans until Tsar Peter I ended it early in the eighteenth century. Until that time, Moscow not only permitted, but actively encouraged, the appearance in its territory of Tatar merchants whose purpose was to offer Russian captives for ransom. The fact that Ivan IV ordered the collection of special funds for ransom rather than sending his army to free the captives by force is adequate evidence for the proposition that at that point he was not capable of a military solution to the problem. There were at least thirty-five Muscovite embassies to the Crimea and twenty-seven Crimean embassies to Moscow between 1474 and 1692. Both groups of embassies conducted diplomatic affairs in a normal way.[7]

Because of its other foreign concerns in the east in the sixteenth century and in the west in the seventeenth, Muscovy strove to assure a peaceful relationship with the Ottoman Empire whose strength it both feared and recognized. It was only Peter I who reversed this policy and undertook serious hostile actions against the Ottomans. The aggressive nature of Tatar policies in the steppe was not the major reason for this break; rather, it was Peter's desperate attempt to open a Black Sea route to the west and to gain recognition of Russia's strength in Europe.[8] There is no question, however, that Moscow's rulers found it frustrating constantly to be humiliated by a Muslim neighbor claiming connections with the Mongol tradition.

Crimean-Muscovite Competition

One episode in Crimean-Muscovite relations that deserves further explanation is the Muscovite annexation of the Kazan Khanate in the mid-sixteenth century. The competition between Muscovy and the Crimea for the former lands of the Golden Horde lasted throughout that century. Each side made important gains at the other's expense, yet neither succeeded completely. The prize was the immense region from Kazan on the Volga to Astrakhan at its mouth, and the steppe inhabited by Nogays and other Tatars in the south. The Girays achieved the first success by putting Sahib Giray on the throne in Kazan in 1521 and holding the throne until 1524 when he was forced to flee to Istanbul. Again in 1525, another Giray—Sefa—became the khan of Kazan. This success was short lived, and in 1532, Ivan IV was able to replace Sefa Giray with his man, Jan Ali, although this was not accomplished without a struggle. In the next year, the Crimean khan, Sahib Giray, conquered the Tatars of Astrakhan. His victory brought dominance over the Nogays living north of the Caucasian mountain ranges. In the 1550s, Ivan IV conquered Kazan once and for all and annexed it to his patrimony; in 1556, he wrested Astrakhan from the Crimean khan as well. The steppe Nogays remained Crimean vassals of an unreliable sort.[9]

In 1571, when Khan Devlet Giray mounted the most serious of all Crimean attacks against Moscow, he reached the suburbs of the city itself and set them afire. However, it was also during his reign that the Girays gave up pretentions to the complete heritage of the Golden Horde and their hope of reestablishing Jingizid rule in Kazan and Astrakhan. After this time, the khans concentrated their efforts on the steppe in Poland and the Ukraine.

But the lesson of the Muscovite annexation of Kazan was not lost on the Crimeans. Time and time again, Crimean leaders brought up the case of Kazan in connection with Moscow's plans and hopes. It was especially related to the fact that, with these conquests, the tsars considered themselves the heirs of the Golden Horde. The fact that the Crimean Khanate had been a part of the horde was warning enough of Muscovite ambitions. In the seventeenth century, Tatar dignitaries asked Bibikov, a Muscovite envoy to the Crimea, why the tsar was establishing several towns near the Crimea on the rivers Terek and Volga. Bibikov replied that "the peoples of Muscovy had multiplied and were cramped, and as the tsar was powerful, he built new towns." The Tatars responded, "Your ruler thus wishes to do as he did with Kazan; at first he established a town close by, then afterward seized Kazan; but the Crimea is not Kazan; in the Crimea, there are many hands and eyes; it will be necessary for your ruler to go beyond the towns to the very heart of the Crimea."[10]

Crimean-Polish Relations

The Crimean Tatars played a somewhat different role in Polish history. Although the Tatars made periodic raids into the Polish steppe where they seized captives for sale, Tatar policy had primarily economic rather than political motives. The Crimeans were not interested in making territorial claims at Poland's expense. From the khanate's beginning, there had been occasions when the interests of the Girays and the rulers of Poland-Lithuania had coincided against Moscow. As late as 1649, the Tatars concluded an alliance with Poland, in which the Polish king called Islam Giray II, "Khan of the Great Hordes of the Circassian, Nogay, Petcorian, Perikopian, and Crimean Tatars." Again in October 1654, the Poles and Tatars joined in a major attack against the Muscovite Ukraine, an attack that was followed by several others. These, incidently, showed that even at this rather late date the Tatar cavalry was superior to the Muscovites'. In 1661, after a joint Crimean Tatar–Polish/Lithuanian army had defeated the Russians, Muscovy was forced to forge an alliance with the Kalmyks whose cavalry was equal to that of the Tatars.[11]

However, Polish historiography emphasizes the hostility between the Poles and Tatars. Professor Baranowski, for example, discusses Tatar raids into Poland and the unfortunate Polish peasants who were carted away as captives. He quotes a Polish peasant proverb that states "O, how much better to lie on one's bier, than to be a captive on the way to Tatary."[12] But both the fact that Polish and Lithuanian envoys and ambassadors to the Crimea were well treated and the number of alliances these envoys concluded indicate that Polish-Tatar relations were as often good as they were hostile during these centuries.[13]

Cossack Hosts

Finally, the relations between the Crimean Tatars and the Slavic Cossacks are the most complex and least understood of eastern European affairs during the last half of the sixteenth century and the whole of the seventeenth century. Other than a few high points in these relations, such as the alliance between the Ottomans and Tatars on the one hand and the Cossack leader Hetman Hmelnicki on the other in 1648, and the alliance with Hetman Doroshenko in the 1670s, very little of a scholarly nature has emerged on these relations. It is clear, however, that the Cossacks played a political and military role in Slavic eastern Europe similar to the role played by the Tatars in Muslim eastern Europe. A major difference was the fact that the Crimeans had a state with governmental administration and urban centers while the Cossacks did not. Yet the efforts by both Tatars and Cossacks to maintain independence from their more powerful neighbors to the north and south gave to each a similarity of purpose.[14]

Crimean Khans

When speaking of the role of the Crimean Khanate during these two centuries, the quality of Tatar leadership that formulated and carried out this role must be mentioned. The Giray dynasty produced a number of rulers whose ambitions were matched in most cases by their skills and abilities. After the first two khans, Haci Giray and Mengli Giray, the reigns of four other khans stand out as among the most important of their time in eastern Europe: those of Sahib Giray, Devlet Giray, Gazi Giray, and Selim Giray. Of the four, three ruled during the sixteenth century; Selim Giray reigned in the late seventeenth and early eighteenth centuries.

Sahib Giray

Sahib Giray's activities have been noted in the Crimean relations with Kazan and Muscovy. He had acted as khan of Kazan from early 1521 until

1524 and then had spent eight years on the Giray estates in Istanbul. Sahib's relations with Sultan Suleiman I were close, and it was during Sahib's stay in Istanbul that Suleiman decided to use his help to increase his influence in the khanate.

After Mengli Giray's death in 1514, the great Crimean clans had chosen for khan first Mehmed Giray (from 1514 until 1523), then his son Gazi Giray I (from 1523 to 1524), and finally Saadet Giray (from 1524 to 1532). Ottoman participation in these choices had been perfunctory, only confirming the Karaçi *beys*' selection; this was a state of affairs not consistent with Suleiman's views of his imperial authority. He had planned to expand the theoretical and actual power of the sultan to include the political heritage of the steppe and the Jingizid authority there. But to accomplish this, he realized that the khanate would have to be placed in a position of tighter vassalage. Sahib Giray, in Istanbul, appeared as the person to accomplish Suleiman's goal. In 1532, the sultan sent Sahib to the Crimea as his choice for khan. The Crimean clans resented this innovation; they considered it illegal interference in their political prerogatives and refused to accept Sahib, selecting Islam Giray instead. They felt (and historical precedent was on their side in this dispute) that the Yasa of Jengiz Khan had dictated a horizontal line of succession requiring the choice of Islam as the oldest living brother of Mehmed Giray, although of course, when it had suited their interests in the past, the *beys* had conveniently ignored this dictum. Further, Islam's initial inclinations had shown him to be a follower of clan interests. An acceptance of Suleiman's choice would be a violation of Crimean traditions and would set a dangerous precedent.

The details of the struggle are not known, but Islam Giray seems to have succeeded in preventing Sahib from assuming power. Sahib, however, won Baki Bey, the Nogay chieftain, in the Deşt-i Kipçak, as an ally. In 1534, after two years of internal strife, Sahib Giray removed Islam from the throne and took it for himself.[15]

Sahib proved to be more than a spokesman for Ottoman interests. During his relatively long reign (until 1551), he pursued several policies aimed at strengthening Crimean power in the steppe against Moscow; he also tied the khanate economically and culturally more firmly to the Ottoman Empire. First, Sahib continued the struggle with Moscow for the inheritance of the Golden Horde. Having been in Kazan for a time, he realized that the Kazan Khanate had been an important key to power in the steppe. Accordingly, he sent his nephew, Safa Giray, back to Kazan as khan during the late 1530s and early 1540s. According to Tatar chronicles, Sahib made powerful attacks against Moscow. Surely his aggressive actions helped precipitate Moscow's final solution to the Kazan question: its total conquest and absorption by Muscovy in 1552.[16]

By tying his foreign policy to that of the Ottomans, Sahib found it necessary to take part in a growing number of Ottoman military campaigns, especially those in Hungary. Yet his primary attention was not in Europe but in the steppe and in the Caucasus—both areas of essentially Crimean rather than Ottoman interest. Four major accomplishments in these areas are attributed to his activities.

First, with his successes with Baki Bey, Sahib built a firmer relationship with the Nogays. From that time, the khan always used the Nogays to offset the power of the clans. They were not always dependable allies, but their connection became much closer.

In this regard, Sahib persuaded some Nogay tribes to settle in the peninsula, giving them the right to use lands in the Giray possessions. He moved others from the northern Caucasus and Volga region to the northern steppes of the Black Sea and to the shores of Bessarabia (the Bucak). While these movements served to increase the khan's authority and power, they also caused some turmoil in the steppe. The changes in existing power relationships left the steppe vulnerable to encroachment by Slavic Cossacks. Yet this result could not have been foreseen in Sahib's time.

Second, Sahib undertook a number of military campaigns in the Caucasus on his own. These campaigns brought several Circassian tribes under his political rule. When he died in 1551, his realm reached from Bessarabia to the northern Caucasus and represented a substantial increase in Crimean power in eastern Europe. These achievements, coupled with his efforts (though unsuccessful) in Kazan, certainly make of Sahib Giray a significant ruler, and not only in Crimean terms.[17]

Third, at home Sahib built institutions of power worthy of his grandiose foreign schemes. It is likely that it was Sahib who built the palace of the khans in Bahçesaray and moved the Great Portal from his former palace in Solhat. Mosques, public baths, and fountains were built or expanded during his reign. Cultural life flourished at the court. During his reign one of the most important Crimean chronicles was written—it described the scholars and artists whom Sahib patronized.

Fourth, Sahib succeeded in gaining primary authority for his administration over the port of Gözleve. This gave the Tatars a major outlet for trade and foreign relations independent of the Ottomans in Kefe.[18]

Devlet Giray

Sahib's successor, Devlet Giray, was also worthy of note. He ruled from 1551 to 1577 and is known for two major exploits closely related to the defense of Crimean power in the steppe. First was his participation in and eventual withdrawal from the Ottoman campaign to regain Astrakhan from Muscovite control. From about 1563, the Ottoman *divan* had considered various reactions to the Muscovite seizure of Kazan and Astrakhan; finally they had decided upon a direct attack on Astrakhan, the city farthest from Moscow. Coupled with this attack, the Ottomans planned to dig a canal that would connect the Don and Volga rivers and give the sultan a means of exercising and expanding his authority in the steppe. While the Crimeans favored the removal of Muscovy from those of the former Golden Horde now inhabited by Turkic peoples, they were not pleased with the prospect of further erosion of their authority in the steppe in favor of the Ottomans. The Tatars did not come to this conclusion in time to prevent their participation in the first part of the campaign, but in its midst, Devlet and his Tatar troops abandoned the Ottoman army near the Volga. This both brought an end to the famous Ottoman Don–Volga Canal project and assured Muscovite control of the entire length of the Volga River.[19]

Devlet's second exploit was his major assault on Moscow in 1571. There can be no doubt that this attack was closely related to the failure of the Astrakhan campaign. Here Devlet considered other means with which to inflict damage upon Moscow. In his attack, he successfully burned most of Moscow's suburbs, provided evidence of Ivan IV's inability to defend his capital against the Tatars, and took a large number of captives who were carried back to the Crimea for sale as slaves. In Crimean historiography, Devlet Giray's exploit earned him the epithet *taht-algan* ("the winner of the throne") and the Ottoman sultan granted Devlet the title "Emir of the Crimea, and sincere and loyal friend of our Throne."[20]

Gazi Giray II

For the Crimean Khanate, the period from Devlet's death in 1577 to the beginning of Gazi Giray II's reign in 1588, was a difficult one. Two major developments occurred. First, the Girays recognized that their dream of replacing the Golden Horde in the steppe and in the Volga region had been dashed by Ivan IV's successes. Consequently, Crimean attention turned from the north to both east and west—toward the Caucasus and Iran in one direction, and toward Hungary and the Danubian Principalities in the other. Attacks on Moscow for political reasons declined in importance and frequency although they continued for economic reasons—the collection of captives. Military campaigns against Iran and Hungary, with their promise of booty, assumed greater importance.

Second, there developed a much closer tie to the Ottoman Empire and its foreign policy; this closeness was manifested in several ways. Most important was more frequent interference in Crimean succession problems by the Ottomans. Slowly but surely, Ottoman practice began to overshadow the former Jingizid traditions. The Ottoman role grew more evident during Islam

Giray II's reign (1584–1588). At this time, the symbolically important mention of the sultan's name during the Friday noon prayers became normal procedure. This mention had been reserved for the khan as a symbol of his sovereignty. Now, with the sultan's name included, the khan's sovereignty was admitted to be severely limited. What had once been mere invitations to Ottoman campaigns now became orders. Any rejection brought about Ottoman attempts, often successful, to remove the khan and replace him with another.[21]

Gazi Giray II (1588–1608) proved a suitable khan to lead the Crimeans during the first years of this new Ottoman-Tatar relationship. Called Bora ("north wind") because of his reputed courage in battle, Gazi led Tatar armies against both Iran and Hungary and served the Ottomans in Anatolia against the Jelali rebels in the early seventeenth century. An Ottoman partisan who authored one of the Tatar chronicles called him "the perfect ruler." He claimed that the Crimea experienced its height in military and cultural affairs during Gazi's reign. But Crimean life and society would never be the same again. The loss of their connections with and aspirations in the direction of the Golden Horde and the steppe removed the major reason for their attempts at independent activity. From this point, the khanate really does become a vassal of the Ottoman sultan and plays an important role in Ottoman affairs.[22]

Selim Giray I

Finally, the reign of Selim Giray I (who ruled on four separate occasions: 1671–1678, 1684–1691, 1692–1699, and 1702–1704) should be mentioned. According to Tatar chronicles, Selim was distinguished by a high moral character, an ability to reconcile competing elements within Crimean society, and a cleverness that could please the Ottomans when necessary yet retain at least the semblance of Crimean dignity and independence. Whether the chroniclers were exaggerating is impossible to determine.

Selim was asked to step down at least three times, perhaps on all three occasions because of a reluctance to endanger Crimean interests for the benefit of Ottoman military campaigns. Twice during his second reign, his armies successfully defended the Crimea against Russian attacks led by Prince Golitsyn. Selim was also the khan who took part in the Constantinople Convention of 1700 that ratified Russian occupation of Azov and terminated the Muscovite tribute payments to the khans. On another occasion, he protected the Ottoman control of Bessarabia against Polish invasion. Professor Inalcik points out that it was Selim who was able to form "a constant defense for the Ottoman Empire during a period when there were constant changes of sultans and grand vezirs." This was especially important during these years, for the Ottomans had been badly defeated by the Habsburgs and had ratified the Treaty of Karlowicz in which, for the first time, they were the victims. Beyond these high points of Selim's life, however, little else has been discovered about his rule in the archives.[23]

By the end of the seventeenth century, in all areas of Crimean life—economy, politics, and cultural life—the khanate's fortunes were clearly on the ebb. This was due not only to a growing weakness within the state but also to the changing power relationships in eastern Europe. The decline of the Ottomans with their defeats at Karlowicz and Azov coincided with Muscovite growth. The eighteenth century brought about both the end of the khanate as an independent political and cultural entity and the Russian annexation of the Crimean peninsula and its Tatar inhabitants. As the following decades would show, this was to be an unmitigated tragedy for the Crimean Tatar people.

PART TWO

THE CRIMEAN TATARS
IN IMPERIAL RUSSIA

6. Russian Interest in the Crimea

With the Treaty of Karlowicz and Peter I's conquest of Azov at the end of the seventeenth century, the position of the Crimean Khanate as a powerful political entity in the steppe quickly came to an end. The combination of Ottoman weakness and Russian strength brought about a relatively sudden change in the balance of power in eastern Europe; with this change came a growing willingness of some elements in the Crimea to entertain Russian overtures. Russia's power received a strong impetus with the gain of control over the left-bank Ukraine and Kiev from Poland in the mid-seventeenth century. From that base of strength, the Russians were able to carry out their ambitions of southward expansion.

First Muscovite Attempts at Annexation

Aside from Adashev during Ivan IV's reign, the first individual to call for Russian military moves against the south and a possible annexation of the Crimean Tatar lands was not a Muscovite; it was the Croat, Iurii Krizhanich. When he visited Moscow in the 1660s, he asked for Muscovite protection for Ottoman Christians and drew up a proposal calling for Russian military action to free their Christian brothers who were under the Islamic yoke. Krizhanich pointed out that a state such as Muscovy should not tolerate an enemy infidel neighbor's incursions into its lands. Unless the tsar was willing to undertake strong military action against the Tatars, Tatar raids would continue. Muscovite subjects would remain in "heathen" captivity in the south and Muscovite honor would continue to be insulted.[1]

Muscovy's first real attempts to end the Crimean Tatar threat were the invasions of 1687 and 1689, which were led by Prince Vasilii Golitsyn. However, despite the shift in the balance of power, Muscovy was still too weak to succeed against the Tatars at this time. On both occasions, Crimean cavalry commanded by Khan Selim Giray I defeated the Muscovites in the steppe north of Perekop. It was only in 1696, when Peter I successfully exhibited new Russian power in his capture of Azov, that Russia gained access to the Black Sea and Tatar raids on Muscovy ceased. Tatar power was clearly on the decline.[2]

Ottoman records of relations with the Tatar khans in the early eighteenth century provide clear evidence of changing conditions in the khanate after the fall of Azov. In the first thirty-five years of the eighteenth century, the Crimean throne was occupied by eleven khans, each of whom proved incapable of effective leadership at home or in foreign affairs. The Ottomans deposed Crimean khans more frequently than before, now often at the request of one of the clan leaders. The khans, in turn, often sent Tatar armies into the Caucasus, against Iran, and into the Balkans at Ottoman request. But they often returned empty handed, having suffered great losses in men and horses.

During the first quarter of the eighteenth century, it was to the Crimeans' advantage that Russian rulers were preoccupied in European politics. Peter I was primarily interested in Baltic problems with Sweden and in making Russia a part of the European political system. Upon his death, St. Petersburg was thrown into domestic turmoil that lasted for a number of years. But during the reign of Tsarina Anna in the 1730s, Russian power was reestablished at home and abroad.

Anna provided clear evidence of Russia's intentions in world affairs when she intervened in the Polish succession crisis in 1733. At about the same time, Anna's military advisor, Count Münnich, counseled her on the benefits of eliminating the Crimea as a political entity. He succeeded in persuading her to make a major invasion of the khanate in September 1735 when Khan Kaplan Giray was off on a Caucasian campaign. In early 1736, a large Russian army entered the Crimean peninsula. It broke through the weak Tatar defenses at Perekop and reached Bahçesaray. Much of that city, including the khan's palace, was burned, and the fact that the khan was absent at the time persuaded the clan leaders in residence in the city that Kaplan Giray should be removed from power.[3]

One might have suspected that this invasion would have been the death blow for the khanate, but such was not the case. Because of disease and a shortage of supplies, the Russians were forced to evacuate Bahçesaray. Khans Mengli Giray II (1737–1740) and Selamet Giray II (1740–1743) made strenuous efforts to rebuild what the Russian army had destroyed. The khan's palace (now a museum) in Bahçesaray is the result of Selamet's effort. In less than three years, he reconstructed both the palace and the great mosque attached to it. This was an impressive feat for a defeated and practically bankrupt people.

With the reconstruction of the symbols of Giray power, the khan's ability to regain the confidence of the clans grew. Yet from then on, relations with the Russian Empire were completely changed. Selamet realized that, since the Ottomans were in no position to give the Tatars much support, total hostility toward Russia would only bring about a repetition of the events of 1736. With this in mind, he established both commercial and political ties with St. Petersburg. Following this, in 1740, the Russian governor of Kiev guberniia, Leont'ev, undertook a series of negotiations with the khan that resulted in periodic Russian embassies to the Crimea, the creation of a Russian consul in Bahçesaray, and the reception in St. Petersburg of several Tatar envoys.

Russian achievements in the Crimea must be credited to the astute policies of Tsarina Elizabeth (whose activities in domestic and foreign affairs have been underplayed by historians). She realized that her country could gain much from a closer association with the Tatars. She perceived that with an outlet to the Mediterranean Russia might achieve a more effective role in European politics, and that by stabilizing her southern frontier she would gain an enormous advantage in Polish affairs. Yet historians have assigned most of the credit in .this direction to her successor, Tsarina Catherine II, whose more forceful actions finally brought about the incorporation of the Crimea into the Russian Empire.[4]

There were both political and economic motives behind Russia's interest in achieving control in the Crimea. It is understandable that Soviet historians have given the greatest emphasis to the economic causes. They concentrate on the aspects of foreign trade with Europe that a warm water port on the Black Sea made more possible and on Russia's need to use the rich agricultural lands in the southern Ukraine that Tatar control prevented.

Yet there was also a political aspect to Russia's interest in the Crimea. This was partly psychological and partly real. Since the thirteenth century, Muscovy had suffered from both military incursions by and political subjection to the Tatars. The Tatars represented a hostile infidel force on Muscovy's frontiers. The elimination and consequent punishment of this enemy would do much to assuage this anger against and hatred of the Muslim Tatars.

Catherine II

At the beginning of Catherine II's reign, her close advisor on political matters, M. L. Vorontsov, prepared a long memorandum on foreign policy that gave careful consideration to the Crimean problem. He emphasized the "barbarous and savage" nature of the Crimeans and pointed out the long list of grievances Russia had against them. His recommendations were: (1) a line of strong Russian fortifications should be built along the border to prevent any future Crimean raids, and (2) the Crimean peninsula should be brought under Russian rule in order that the Crimean danger to Russia be removed.[5]

Catherine's foreign minister in the 1760s, Nikita Panin, was more interested in the north than Vorontsov. He persuaded Catherine to disregard Vorontsov's advice and to establish instead a consul in the Crimea. Catherine succeeded in this when Khan Kirim Giray accepted a Russian consul in Bahçesaray in 1763. This action implied both that the Tatars recognized that their future depended on Russian intentions and that the khan was trying to become more independent of the Ottoman sultan by reverting to the sixteenth-century Tatar traditions.[6]

The new Russian consul, Nikiforov, purchased an embassy building for himself in Bahçesaray. But by the end of 1764, his relations with the Tatar government were at an impasse. With the overthrow of Khan Kirim Giray by Selim Giray III, the consul's position was eliminated and Nikiforov was sent home. After this date, there is no evidence of any Tatar-Russian contact until the beginning of the great war in 1768.[7]

War of 1768–1774

The khan's military forces did not play a critical role in the major arenas of conflict of the great war. Their former close ties with Ottoman military policies had come to an end before the war, and there was little or no coordination between the Ottomans and the Tatars on the northern front. Although it is clear from both Russian and Turkish evidence that both sides were prepared for war, it was ironic that an event taking place in territory claimed by the khan was the initial cause for the conflict. In September 1768, a part of the Russian army fighting against the Polish Confederation of Bar passed through the town of Balta (from which the khan collected taxes and which he considered to be part of his patrimony) without any prior intention of aggression. The Tatars felt this to be an attack, however, and offered a spirited defense. As a result, Balta was destroyed and the townspeople were dispersed. In early October 1768, the Ottomans declared war on Russia, and the fateful period for the khanate began.[8]

From the beginning of the war in 1768 until early 1770, three khans ruled: Kirim Giray (1768–1769), Devlet Giray IV (1769–1770), and Kaplan Giray II (1770). Although Kirim Giray did lead one short campaign against Russian frontier settlements, the responses of the Crimeans to the war effort were weak and ineffectual. Kirim's mysterious death and Devlet Giray IV's inability to persuade the Tatar clans to send their forces to battle brought about negotiations with the Russians by an important part of the Crimean leadership. These negotiations, which took place during Kaplan Giray's short reign, were aimed at the creation of Crimean "independence."[9]

The most satisfactory account of these years is found in the nineteenth-century chronicle-history of Halim Giray Sultan. He found among some of the clan leaders, among the *beys* of the Nogays, and even in the Giray family itself "irresponsible actions" aimed at winning Tatar national identity—actions that began to call for Crimean separation from the Ottoman Empire. Halim Giray Sultan described three reasons for the khanate's collapse: (1) Russian cleverness, (2) the greed and ambitions of a small portion of the Crimean ruling elite, and (3) the growing inability of the Ottoman government to understand the realities of the shifting balance of power. Russian strength and Ottoman weakness were the primary reasons for the end of the Crimean Khanate; in my opinion, it is unfair to assign too much blame to the internal Crimean disintegration. However, Halim Giray Sultan did ignore the Nogays, and they were a major element in the khanate's demise.[10]

Russian Success with Nogay Tatars

During the early years of the war, Catherine's agents concentrated on the Yedisan Nogays who, under the leadership of their *serasker*, Can Mambet Bey, roamed the western shore of the Black Sea. By 1770, the Yedisan Nogays had signed a treaty of friendship with the Russian government. Can Mambet Bey, an important Russian supporter during the next fifteen years, declared in this treaty that his horde had "entered into eternal friendship and alliance with the Russian Empire . . . and will live peacefully under its protection."[11] Can Mambet Bey was granted both privileges and financial reward for his betrayal, and from 1770 on, his own agents operated to subvert the khan's authority.

The signing of this treaty was a decisive blow for both the Ottomans and the Tatars. The Yedisan territory was between the two Muslim armies. With the Russians controlling the area between the Dnestr and Dnepr rivers, it was only by sea that the khan could maintain relations with the Porte (Ottoman Empire). Further, the Ottoman navy was soon virtually destroyed in the Aegean by a decisive Russian naval strike at Çeşme. The Russians now used the Yedisan Nogay example in attempts to persuade other Crimean leaders to side with Russia.

Kaplan Giray

In June 1770, the Russian general Petr Panin, who had won the support of Can Mambet Bey, undertook a series of negotiations with the new Crimean khan, Kaplan Giray. He wrote to the khan, "the sultan has incorporated the

Crimeans and all of the Nogays within his authority, not by war or legitimate succession, but through the use of various tricks." Kaplan Giray saw the handwriting on the wall. The Ottomans could no longer protect the Crimeans against Russian expansion, and the time had arrived for an arrangement with the tsarina. Thus, in late 1770, the khan responded to General Panin: "We, the Crimean khan, and other leaders of the Crimean state, and the Şirin *mirza*s, instead of obeying the Ottomans, at the present time want to take an oath to a government such as yours that is friendly to us, and that will allow us to follow our ancient political traditions."[12]

There are two interesting parts to this statement. First is the mention of the Şirin *mirza*s; second is the mention of a return to ancient political traditions. It is ironic that the Şirins, who had been instrumental in the establishment of the Giray dynasty and in its subsequent submission to Ottoman suzerainty, would prove to be so important in its undoing. Yet there is every evidence that it was the Şirin action that actually forced the khan to accept this statement and to entertain the idea of a break with the Ottoman Empire. The Russians also showed themselves to be aware of the main issues of political conflict in the khanate. They mentioned ancient traditions that the Ottomans had increasingly violated during the eighteenth century. The Ottoman sultan had appointed and deposed khans without the participation of the Karaçi *bey*s. The Şirins and other *bey*s seem to have believed that the new Russian connection would return them to their former power.

The Ottomans quickly learned of Kaplan Giray's treason and ordered him replaced by Selim Giray III, who had been residing at the Giray estate in Istanbul. During the first half of 1771, Khan Selim Giray turned the tide against the growth of Russian influence. Both Kaplan Giray and the Şirin *bey* fled to an area under Russian control, and a Tatar army inflicted a defeat upon a Russian garrison near the rapids in the Dnepr River.

Russian Invasion

But in late spring of that year, Russian general Dolgorukii led a large army, in which there were elements of the Yedisan horde, into the Crimea through the weakened defenses at Perekop. He immediately issued in Catherine's name a manifesto that spread throughout the Crimea so quickly that there must have been Tatars there who were Russian sympathizers aiding in its dissemination. It promised that Catherine would "provide you with your former independence" if the Tatars "broke away from the slavery of the Porte."[13]

The Russians used both the argument of Ottoman interference in Crimean political prerogatives and a promise to return Tatar affairs to their former political traditions. And this manifesto, coupled with an invasion by a powerful army, seemed to be an unqualified success. By the end of 1771, the great majority of Giray and clan leaders accepted the Russian promises. This particular manifesto was written with the advice of a former Crimean official, Iakup Ağa, who after 1783 became one of the most important figures in the Russian administration of the Crimea.

In July 1771, General Dolgorukii took Gözleve, Bahçesaray, and Perekop. At the beginning of the month, his army entered Kefe and chased the Ottoman governor, Ibrahim Pasha, to Istanbul. On July 13, Selim Giray surrendered to the victorious Russian general. He pleaded that his subjects accept the new order, and asked the Russians to grant him the traditional symbols of sovereignty—the sword and the sable fur—which would show to all Crimeans that the Russians intended to abide by their promises to grant independence to the khanate.[14]

For reasons contemporary sources do not explain, Selim Giray changed his mind on the question of Russian influence and Crimean independence and abdicated in September. It is likely that remaining Ottoman partisans in the Crimea persuaded him that independence would be a sham and a temporary phenomenon, since Russian troops occupied all fortified places on the peninsula. Under Russian pressure, the clan leaders elected a new khan, Sahib Giray II. Sahib chose as his *kalgay* Şahin Giray, who during the following years became the primary Russian partisan in the Crimea.[15]

Other than the fact that his grandfather, Devlet Giray III, had ruled in 1716–1717, nothing is known about Sahib Giray before his election. Yet it was Sahib and his *kalgay* who were the architects of the new Crimean independent state that formally appeared in 1774. He succeeded in negotiating the return of the Nogay hordes to his authority. He also received a Russian promise of substantial military and financial aid in the creation of his new state.

Russian-Crimean Treaty

In late November 1771, a large delegation of Tatar dignitaries led by Kalgay Şahin Giray arrived in St. Petersburg to sign the formal agreement with the Russians that created the Crimean state. From the evidence of their relatively long stay in the Russian capital come some interesting details of the *kalgay*'s life. Şahin caught Catherine's attention immediately. According to a letter from the tsarina to Voltaire, Şahin was handsome and bright. There is no doubt that Catherine became infatuated with him at this first encounter. This infatuation prevented the tsarina from making wise judgments about his career during the years to come.[16]

The Tatar delegation returned to Bahçesaray in early 1772 with reports that the creation of an independent Crimean state under the rule of the Giray dynasty and the supervision and protection of Russia was near completion. In November 1772, the Russians and Tatars signed the Treaty of Karasu Bazaar, in the city of the Şirin clan. The main signatories were Lieutenant Shcherbinin for the tsarina, Khan Sahib Giray, the Şirin and Mansur beys for the Karaçi beys, and finally, led by Can Mambet Bey, representatives from each of the Nogay hordes that had accepted Russian protection.

The treaty established an "alliance and eternal friendship" between the newly created Independent Crimean State and the Russian Empire. It granted complete administrative power to the khan, who was to be chosen "according to tradition," without any interference by either the Ottomans or the Russians. The latter would maintain a presence in the areas that had comprised the Ottoman eyalet of Kefe.[17]

The full measure of this Tatar independence could not be realized, however, until the Ottomans ratified the treaty. So long as the Porte opposed it, those Tatars in the peninsula who did not accept the Russian presence had some hope of reversing the treaty. The Russian court and its partisans, Şahin and Sahib, realized this and made no effort to set up new independent institutions in Bahçesaray until the war came to an end. In Istanbul, there was a large and growing community of Tatar exiles. Many of the religious officials and mirzas had fled from Kefe with the defeated Turkish army in the middle of 1771. They exerted a great deal of pressure on the Ottoman government to intervene in the Crimea, but their hope was a fragile one and depended upon an Ottoman victory. By late 1773, there was no longer any question of the Ottomans' avoiding total defeat, and the question of the Crimeans was solved on the battlefield. This solution was merely ratified at the peace conference of Küçük Kaynarca, yet there the Ottoman diplomats showed themselves to be clever and astute politicians and avoided a complete loss of influence in the Crimea. They demanded the insertion into the final draft of the treaty of a clause granting the sultan religious suzerainty over the Tatar Muslims. This kept the door open for continued Ottoman interference in the Crimea.

From the Russian perspective, the treaty seemed to have solved the Crimean problem. Both the Russians and the Ottomans agreed to the creation of an independent state with the khan as its autocratic ruler. The Ottomans retained their influence only in religious affairs. The Russians gained possession of the important fortresses of Kilburunu in the west and Yenikale-Kerch at the opening to the Sea of Azov. What had been the sultan's virgin bride (the Black Sea) was now violated by the presence of infidel military forces.

The treaty signed in mid-1774 left unanswered some important questions—questions that threatened the continued existence of the independent state during the next few years. Most importantly, except for the mention of an autocratic ruler, the treaty did not spell out a form of administration for the new state. It gave no consideration to the political relations within Tatar society, the new state's economic basis, or the exact form of connection with the Russians. Most ominously, a peculiar event that took place in late 1773 left serious doubts about the state's future. For reasons not given by contemporary sources, in the midst of the negotiations at Küçük Kaynarca, Khan Sahib Giray suddenly ordered the Russian consul, Veselitskii, arrested and his property confiscated. Catherine was thus forced to reconsider the basis for Russian strength in the Crimea. For his own protection, Şahin Giray was removed to a more secure location at Poltava. With the Russian consul imprisoned, Khan Sahib Giray clearly losing interest in Russian protection, and Catherine's favorite, Şahin, in Poltava, the political arrangement was shaky. The independent Crimean state was off to a tenuous start.

7. The Crimean Independent State and Russian Annexation

Why Catherine II, in the face of her overwhelming victory over both the Ottomans and the Tatars, did not press for annexation of the khanate is one of the major questions of Crimean history. Most of her advisors had told her that annexation was the wisest course and would bring her empire the greatest benefits. Her victory had given her the opportunity her predecessors had lacked, yet it took nine years of strenuous Russian attempts to influence the direction of Crimean internal development before Catherine was convinced that her predecessors had been right. The annexation took place only in 1783.[1]

The leaders of almost all of the states interested in Russian expansion and the Crimean question expected the new political arrangements to be short lived. The Ottomans, seeing the treatment of Russia's Slavic brothers in Poland on the one hand and the conquest and assimilation of the Volga Tatars two centuries earlier on the other, saw no reason for a different course of events in the Crimea. The French (whose interference in Ottoman affairs in the 1760s had helped precipitate the war) foresaw that an independent Crimea placed between two powerful and hostile states could not avoid entanglements with one or the other. Great Britain was fearful that the Russian government would press its advantage into the Mediterranean and change the balance of power in southern Europe.

For the Crimean Tatars, these nine years of independence were a difficult and tumultuous period. Neither the Treaty of Karasu Bazaar nor that of Küçük Kaynarca provided clear guidelines for the reorganization of Tatar society and government that independence necessitated. Further, the fact that both Russian and Ottoman governments were to have a say in Crimean developments added to the difficulty. Catherine did not want the fruits of her victory to be dissipated in the Crimea. She forced Crimean governments from then on to abide by the spirit of the treaties that required "friendship" with her government.

The Ottomans were placed in an impossible situation too. They could make little sense of the treaty's permission for the continuance of their religious authority in the Crimea divorced from any political role. Finally, the fact that the Tatars could find no leader capable of forming a stable society that would preserve Tatar and Muslim traditions while at the same time creating an independent political administration was the final straw that brought about Russia's eventual annexation of the Crimea.

Crimean independence can be divided into three distinct periods: (1) the first two years, 1774–1776, during which the Crimean elite tried to determine what the degree of their independence would be (both the Russian and Ottoman governments tried their best to influence the elite's decision); (2) 1776–1778, when the Russian favorite, Şahin Giray, gained ascendancy with the help of Russian intervention (under Catherine's tutelage he tried to modernize the Crimean government along Western lines); and (3) 1778–1783, when Şahin destroyed many traditional Crimean institutions but proved unable to establish popular new ones. After this third period, Catherine II finally lost patience and ended the Crimean independent state.

Sahib Giray in Power

In 1774, after the Russian victory and its treaties, the Crimean elite was confused and demoralized. Both treaties demanded a reorganization of their society and government along lines alien to their traditions. This confusion had resulted in an initial attempt by the Crimean leaders and Khan Sahib Giray to reverse the treaty requirements and return to the prewar relationship with the Ottomans. Although in late 1773 Sahib had arrested the Russian resident in Bahçesaray and sent a petition to the Ottomans requesting that they "destroy the conditions of independence and return to the custom of appointing the khan from Istanbul," he did not remain in power for long. The Ottomans, living up to the spirit and letter of the Treaty of Küçük Kaynarca, refused to honor Sahib's petition.

Devlet Giray, whom the Ottomans had sent to the Kuban in the last years of the war, refused to accept the treaty signed by the Ottomans in 1774. He continued military operations against the Russians near Azov and led large groups of Caucasian tribesmen against Taman. In late 1774, Devlet crossed the Strait with his army, overcame the Russian defenses at Yenikale-Kerch, and occupied the city of Kefe. He met almost no opposition from either Sahib Giray or the Russian garrisons nearby. Devlet clearly intended to seize the Crimean throne for himself and to violate the terms of the treaty by requesting Ottoman support and recognition. Sahib Giray fled the Crimea to exile in Istanbul, where he spent the rest of his life.[2]

Devlet Giray Seizes the Throne

The Ottoman government was distressed to learn of these events. At this time the imperial *divan* was under the control of reformists who wanted to direct the government's attention from military to domestic matters; they saw great danger for their plans from any development that might require Ottoman intervention in the Crimea. Through a mix-up in timing, the Ottoman envoy sent to recognize Sahib Giray as khan arrived in Bahçesaray just as Devlet Giray appeared. Devlet seized the investiture and showed his Ottoman "acceptance" to the distrusting Crimean elite as proof that he was now their legitimate khan. However, Devlet was not foolish. His first major action was to free the Russian agent, Veselitskii. Devlet was going to try for Russian support as well.[3]

To everyone's surprise, Catherine II recognized Devlet as khan. The Russian consul, Shcherbinin, was ordered to address him as "your Excellency Devlet Giray Khan," and to present him with the official Russian papers evidencing Russian support for his regime. Yet in Russia, Catherine continued to work closely with her own Crimean favorite, Şahin. She was patient and permitted Devlet to rule until Şahin gathered enough support to regain the throne. It was not long, however, before Devlet made the same mistakes as his predecessors had made. The Nogay tribes in the north, whom Catherine had wooed away from the khanate in 1770, were Catherine's instrument in dislodging Devlet. The new khan made no effort to gain their adherence; he saw no need to impress the Nogays with the dangers of Russian involvement.[4]

In July 1775, Devlet sent a delegation of sixteen *mirza*s to Istanbul to ask the Ottomans to tear up the treaty and accept the Crimean Khanate as a vassal once again. The large number of Crimean exiles in Istanbul lent strong support for Ottoman intervention in the Crimea, demanding that Sultan Abdul Hamid I support the new Crimean government. However, the reformists, under the leadership of Ahmed Resmi, prevented Ottoman action. The Ottomans refused to provide the Russians with a motive for renewing the war. They were well aware that their own forces were so weak that war might bring about a complete collapse of their empire.[5]

Fearful that if Devlet succeeded in creating a viable administration she would lose what gains her diplomats and soldiers had made prior to 1774, Catherine II used her experience with the Nogay hordes to help Şahin regain the throne. She appointed him head of a Nogay government in the Kuban, with Can Mambet Bey in his administration. Catherine told this group that a few Crimeans had forgotten the harshness of the Turkish yoke, and that the Ottomans were continuing the struggle with no loss to themselves but at the expense of the Crimeans. This was persuasive enough that the Nogays accepted this movement across the Kerch Straits.

A full-scale rebellion against Catherine's autocracy, which was led by the Cossack, Pugachev, in 1775, severely limited her ability to act forcefully in the Crimea. Her hopes had to lie for the moment with Şahin Giray, Can Mambet Bey, and the Nogay hordes in the Kuban. Catherine had Şahin elected khan of the Nogays since "the khan and the Crimeans, in spite of the freedom granted them, continue to be stubborn in their intention to remain subject to the Porte."[6]

Throughout 1775, the Russians tried to persuade the Ottomans to deny all support to Devlet. At the same time, Catherine prepared strong military concentrations along the Perekop line under the command of General Prozorovskii. Although still relatively weak in numbers, these forces were the start of what would amount to a major buildup of Russian strength against Devlet.[7]

In the Crimean peninsula, Russian agents prepared the way for invasion. Catherine received information from Bahçesaray that Devlet was not having an easy time with the clan leaders, that he was in fact slighting the Mansur and Şirin clans because of their former support for Sahib Giray. She felt that, with the right sort of preparations, clan support for Şahin's candidacy might be forthcoming. One Turkish chronicler, discussing these events, speaks of the Mansurs as "sinners who attempted all sorts of tricks and devices," who provided the main impetus for handing the Crimea over to the Russians.[8]

Devlet maintained power for little more than a year. His main support came from the Crimean *ulema* and from Haci Ali Ağa, an Ottoman governor in Anatolia who acted against his orders from Istanbul in interfering in Crimean politics. Haci Ali Ağa sent a small army to the Crimea to help Devlet rid the peninsula of the last elements of the Russian occupation. But this was not enough. Devlet had almost no source of income. The revenues his predecessors had received from Ottoman dispensations or campaign booty were not available to him. He did not have the resources to maintain himself with a sufficient armed force to keep the Russians and Şahin out and the clans satisfied. It should have been apparent to Devlet that, unless he could gain support from the rest of the Crimean elite, his chances were poor.[9]

After Pugachev's defeat in mid-1775, Catherine could deal with the Crimean problem more forcefully. In early 1776, Alexandr Bezborodko presented to the empress a treatise about Crimean problems in which he emphasized the long history of Tatar cruelty against Russians. He wrote: "Tsar Ivan Vasil'evich IV knew well the customs of these treacherous and changeable Tatars. . . . He knew that the only means of ridding himself of the dangers of the Kazan Tatars had been to take their kingdom under his control."[10] The conclusion to be drawn from this observation was obvious. Yet Catherine was still willing to place her hopes in Şahin.

Second Russian Invasion

In November 1776, Catherine ordered an invasion of the Crimea and late in that month she captured Perekop, thus preparing the way for Şahin's entrance. With the aid of Nogay tribesmen, Şahin crossed the Kerch Straits in January 1777, and proceeded to move slowly toward Kefe and then Bahçesaray. In late March, Devlet finally realized that his ambitions were not going to be realized; no help had come from the Ottomans, and much of the necessary support in the peninsula was already in Şahin's camp. Devlet abdicated and sailed for Istanbul with some close associates. There he received belated aid from the Ottoman government in the form of a pension and a residence where he spent the next four years until his death.[11]

The Russians were pleased that all of this had been accomplished with so little expense. General Prozorovskii wrote to St. Petersburg, "Şahin's mounting of his throne . . . has brought union, peace, and quiet to this country." Nikita Panin, in an outburst of fantasy, congratulated Catherine on the outcome of this "legal election, one in which the Ottomans would be able to find no Russian interference." Panin said this action "preserved Crimean independence under their khan."[12]

But the Ottomans were not fooled. Sultan Abdul Hamid I is said to have exclaimed upon receiving the news of Şahin's victory, "Şahin Giray is a tool. The aim of the Russians is to take the Crimea."[13] His observation was accurate; the first period of Crimean independance had come to an inglorious end in 1776.

Şahin Giray's Policies

During his reign as khan, Şahin concentrated on four areas of reform: political, military, economic, and foreign affairs. After considering the basic institutions of Crimean society both during the heyday of Tatar power and in the last decades before the creation of Crimean independence, Şahin concluded that those very institutions that had given the khanate power in the sixteenth century were now the ones that made it weak.

In the sixteenth century, the khanate had combined the strength of the leadership of its khans with the great power of the clans. Each had an important stake in the other's success. However, this system had depended on weak northern neighbors whose human and economic resources could be taken by Crimean raiders. When the balance of power changed, the basic economic foundations of the khanate were lost.

In the eighteenth century, the clan leaders' right to choose the khan had led to increasing instability within the khanate. This instability had paved the way for the Russian victories in the 1760s and 1770s. Şahin realized that the khan had to win enough power to govern alone before the khanate could regain some of its former influence in eastern Europe. This meant the creation of a political system that resembled Russia's.

Thus Şahin first dealt with his lack of authority within the khanate. He believed that the only way to break the hold of the clan leaders was to eliminate their right of participation in the so-called election by the Karaçi *beys*. To this end, in the oath of allegiance that all *beys*, *mirzas*, and *ağas* had been required to take when Şahin entered Bahçesaray in late March 1777, he included: "since elections of khans in the future will undoubtedly cause division and quarrels among us, we wish that the ruling khan will choose from among his *sultans* ('sons') the one who will inherit the throne."[14] A modified form of vertical inheritance, this system permitted Şahin to rule without consideration of conflicting desires of the different clans or of the Muslim officials in the Crimea.

Şahin then moved to the primary institutions of his government including the *divan* ("state council"), and the representatives of the government on the local level (the *beys*). In the past, the *divan* had been an institution independent of the khan's authority; its purpose had been one of offering advice on important matters of state. Şahin, in convening a new *divan*, did not invite, as had been done in the past, all of the clan leaders; he invited only the Mansurs and Şirins, who had supported his entrance to power. No clergy was asked to participate in the *divan*. Şahin hoped that in this way he could make the *divan* an institution that would carry out his desires. The *beylik* problem was more difficult. Clans had considered the *beylik* lands their own, inherited from ancestors who were equal in legitimacy and tradition to the Girays. Former khans had had almost no influence or authority within the *beyliks*. Their officials could not even undertake the ordinary activities of tax collecting and judicial.affairs. At first, Şahin could not accomplish much. He began by renaming the *beyliks* as *kadiliks*. *Kadilik* referred to a political relationship between sovereign and official, not to the relationship between two sovereigns of unequal power that *bey* had implied.[15]

Finally, Şahin considered the construction of a new palace, one that would be more suitable for a modern, autocratic ruler of the late eighteenth century. He envisaged a building resembling Tsarskoe Selo in St. Petersburg, where he had spent some months at the empress's side, and he asked Catherine to send "some stonemasons who are familiar with Western architecture," to Bahçesaray.

The combination of these political reforms, the creation of a hereditary khanate with governmental institutions representing only his own interests, the stripping of independent local authority from the clans, and the construction of a new westernized palace were all intended to give him both the power and appearance of an autocratic ruler. If these were accomplished, Şahin believed he could make the Crimean khanate an independent state capable of surviving between the Russian and Ottoman empires.[16]

Şahin's military and economic reforms were closely related to his political innovations and were aimed at increasing central authority at the expense of other elements of society. Before, the foundation of clan power had been control of most military and economic resources in the khanate. Şahin decided that his "feudal" military forces would have to give way to a standing army that was under his own authority. He began to create such an army, which he called his *beşli* forces, and asked the Russians to send advisors and instructors to Bahçesaray to train them. He wanted his new army to look like a Western army with Western uniforms. (Like the Ottomans a decade later, Şahin mistook the Western armies' appearance to be the reason for their superiority on the battlefield.) To support the great expense of such an army, he tried to introduce a system of state taxation that gave the central government most of the funds the *beys* previously had had at their personal disposal. To accomplish this, Şahin needed many civil servants to determine and collect the taxes.

Crimean Opposition to Şahin

Although he had little chance for success without the backing of the clans (which he did not have), Şahin began to institute these changes. In the fall of 1777, he announced new state taxes, the schedule for drafting Crimean Tatar youths for his army, and the assignment of government officials to new positions in the local towns. He based his hopes for success on the promise of benefits the khanate would gain, rather than on the basis of an already strong local base of support. Even the Mansur and Şirin leaders were horrified at the implications of the khan's reforms and were unwilling to support a new regime that deprived them of their institutional influence.[17]

Two developments in late 1777 provided the spark for a revolt. First, the khan made the mistake of reversing Tatar traditional relations with non-Muslim communities in the Crimea. The large Christian and Jewish communities had been permitted to maintain independent judicial and local political administrations since the fifteenth century. They were subject only in a general way to the basic Islamic laws under which the Tatars lived. Unquestionably, the Tatars viewed both the Christian and Jewish subjects as legally inferior. They kept the infidel communities completely separate from their own. Yet there was no real persecution. Both sets of subjects had been able to coexist without the interreligious rivalry and violence found in Christian states.[18]

Şahin, not recognizing the mutual benefit of the separate nature of these communities, tried to make both subject to exactly the same laws. He wanted to grant equality of citizenship to all of his subjects. There was to be no distinction between Muslim and non-Muslim in taxation and military service. Judges who administered local courts were supposed to make decisions according to Crimean state law, instead of Muslim or Christian religious law. What was even worse from the Muslim point of view was that Şahin intended to change some of the foundations of the Muslim legal system by introducing infidel legal customs. The non-Muslim communities were mystified by these proposals, and the Tatars saw this as a scandalous departure from their religious faith, a faith they presumed to be Şahin's as well.[19]

Russian Colonization

A second development, and one over which Şahin had no control, was the beginning of organized Russian colonization of the Crimean peninsula. In late 1777, Catherine ordered preparations for the settlement in the Crimea of a number of Greek and Slavic emigrants from the Ottoman Empire. The new colonies were placed "under the control of the armed forces of Her Majesty" and were "for the purpose of strengthening Russia's position in the Crimea." At this early stage, only a few hundred such settlers were involved, but they were the beginning of what was to become a deluge. Bearing the Russian name *Albantsy,* the group settled near Yenikale on lands that had been seized from the Ottomans and retained by the Russian court.[20]

Şahin's popularity reached a new low when the appearance of the *Albantsy* was made common knowledge among the Tatars. He sent his new army against some rebels near Yenikale who refused to permit the members of the *Albantsy* free movement in the area. His army, however, deserted to the rebels, and save for a promise of Russian help, he was suddenly left without any internal base for support.

The rebels advanced quickly to Şahin's palace in Bahçesaray, where they dispersed the khan's few remaining supporters and set fire to his palace and its surrounding buildings. In less than two weeks, the revolt spread to the Kuban where those Nogays who had been the first to support Şahin also deserted and made overtures to the Ottomans.

In Istanbul the former khan, Devlet Giray, and the growing number of Crimean exiles in the city, spread rumors that the Russians were planning another invasion of the Crimea and that they were "carrying Şahin about in a cage and insulting every tenet of their religion." Under mounting public pressure, the Ottoman *divan* ordered a fleet bearing janissaries, under the command of Canikli Haci Ali Pasha, from Anatolia to the Crimean shores to protect "the integrity of the Treaty of Küçük Kaynarca." On January 2, 1778, the Ottomans appointed Selim Giray, leader of the exiles in Istanbul, as head of a new Crimean Tatar government.[21]

Third Russian Invasion

In February 1778, a Russian army joined with Albanian soldiers in Yenikale, and with Şahin, proceeded to bombard and capture the rebel towns. The damage inflicted on Akmeçet, Eski Kirim, and Kefe, was much greater than it had been in 1770–1772. According to one account, during the attack on Kefe a regiment under the command of General de Balmen burned almost all of the town to the ground and slaughtered all Crimeans found within.[22]

The Russians were completely in command of the situation by the time the Ottoman fleet arrived, giving it no chance to support the rebels. Şahin was back firmly in power in 1778; the revolt had been completely crushed and the Russian army was at his side. Yet Catherine was still willing to support him as the ruler who could make Crimean independence a reality.[23]

Şahin Giray's Reforms Begun Anew

During his second reign (1778–1783) Şahin had time to implement some of his reforms. But his task was complicated by an inexplicable decision Catherine made in 1778. She removed from the Crimean peninsula the Christian minority that was the one element of Crimean society that had some reason to support his reforms. Much has been written about this Christian exodus to a new settlement along the northern shores of the Sea of Azov and it need not be repeated here. For Şahin, the Christians had been an extremely important group. They had occupied almost all of the artisan and merchant positions in the Crimean economy, and the internal and external trade of the khanate had been in their hands. The Christians alone of the Crimean subjects had maintained contacts with foreign countries. Their loss was a critical one for the economy—one that neither Şahin nor (after the Russian annexation of the Crimea in 1783) the Tatars were able to overcome.[24]

In early 1779, there was one good piece of news for Şahin: the Ottoman government signed the Convention of Aynali Kavak with Russia. In this convention the Ottomans recognized Şahin as khan of the Crimea so long as he lived and promised not to intervene in Crimean affairs. They accepted the fact that the Crimea would not be subservient to the Ottomans even in religious matters.[25]

In the convention, the Russians also promised to remove their troops from the Crimea and to return the land around Özü (Ochakov) to the Ottomans. In turn, the Ottoman sultan recognized Russia's right to interfere in Crimean political affairs and agreed to accept a khan suitable for Russian interests. The Crimean Tatars, who had been completely demoralized by the Russian invasion of 1778, were even more so by the knowledge that they could no longer dream of a future Ottoman intervention on their behalf. Their future as Russia's vassal under the detested Şahin Giray seemed to be sealed. There was little they could do in the face of overwhelming military force.

Within the Crimea now, Şahin proceeded to complete some of the reforms he had begun in 1777. He reestablished his force of *beşlis*, now composed almost entirely of Nogays, mercenaries from Poland, Cossacks, and members of the *Albantsy* of Yenikale. Şahin was not going to make his survival dependent upon the fickle support of the Tatars. His circle of advisors became even closer and smaller than he had intended it to be in 1777. Only a handful of Tatars was admitted to his court in any political capacity. They represented no factions, merely themselves. For three years, Şahin enjoyed relative peace in the peninsula; the opposition to his rule could make no effective show of force.

But in 1781, trouble surfaced once again. Crimeans who could no longer stand the Russian influence around Şahin's court rose in rebellion. First it was the Yedisan Nogays who "elected" Murat Giray as their leader without the approval of Bahçesaray. Under Murat Giray, the Yedisans left the peninsula and crossed the Kuban River to the south. A few months later, the Cambuluk and Yediçkul Nogays refused to accept officials sent by the khan and declared themselves not subject to his or to Russian authority. The fragile rule that was holding the khanate together was coming apart.

In April 1782, a portion of Şahin's own army revolted against his commanders and joined the growing rebel force in Taman. In Taman, two of Şahin's brothers, Arslan and Bahadir, began secret negotiations with the rest of the Crimean elite; by the end of April, representatives of the main Tatar clans, the *ulema,* and the *kadi* of Kefe were openly plotting the khan's overthrow. In defending his policies, Şahin sent Arslan a note saying "This state is not a republic. Thus they [the clan leaders] cannot come to you for such discussions. You yourselves must come to Bahçesaray where we all can come to an agreement." This was obviously a trap and the dissidents refused to go.[26]

On May 14, 1782, a small rebel group led by Halim Giray attacked Kefe where Şahin and the Russian consul were discussing political matters with the *kadi.* After a short battle, Şahin and his *beşli* forces were completely routed. The next day, the khan and his few remaining supporters fled by ship to the Russian fortress at Kerch. The rebels immediately elected Bahadir Giray as khan and sent a delegation to Istanbul to receive the sultan's approval for the new election.[27] It was now clear to all that this third period of Crimean independence was nearly at an end. What would the Russian empress do in the face of three such failures in attempts to force the Crimeans to accept Şahin Giray as their autocratic ruler?

Throughout June and July of 1782, the revolt against Şahin's programs spread throughout the entire Crimean peninsula. Any of his officials who did not flee to safety were killed. The foundations of a new palace he had begun near Bahçesaray were destroyed. Offices and government buildings that represented his regime were also demolished.

Final Russian Invasion

Yet once again Catherine reinstalled Şahin on the throne, using military force to do so. General Grigorii Potemkin was placed in charge of the new Russian invasion. The army did enter Bahçesaray and was able again to disperse the rebels. Bahadir Giray and some of his supporters fled across the Kuban into Ottoman territory. Şahin reentered Bahçesaray under heavy Russian military guard.

But the usual manifestations of loyalty to the khan that the Russians had always been able to produce in past years were not forthcoming this time. The khan began to conduct a forceful repression of all of Bahadir's supporters. Iakup Ağa, who had become a Russian agent during Şahin's last reign, sent a worried note to Potemkin stating that Şahin was acting in a most irresponsible way — a way that would ensure the loss of all support in the Crimea. Catherine ordered the Russian advisor to force Şahin to cease "this senseless repression. As our generosity and kindness is not only meant for him, but for all of the Crimean peoples, he must stop this shocking and cruel treatment and not give them just cause for a new revolt."[28] Catherine's order was to no avail. Potemkin himself was not overly disturbed by the khan's actions, for he was already making preparation for the Russian annexation of the Crimea to take place during the next year.

Through Iakup Ağa, Potemkin learned that there were some elements in Crimean society who, tired and demoralized by the events of the past ten years, were not completely opposed to the idea of a Russian annexation. In late November 1782, Iakup Ağa reported a discussion with Şirin leaders about the "bliss" in which all of the peoples of the Russian Empire lived. "We discussed the happy situation of the Kazan Tatars and of all of the Muslim peoples who had freely entered the empire, and of the many benefits accruing to those Muslims who were subjects of the empress."[29] Potemkin must have been amused at the incongruity of this statement, but he was pleased to find that the Tatars themselves were considering entering the empire.

Russian Annexation

In March 1783, Potemkin returned to St. Petersburg intending to persuade the empress of the importance of annexing the Crimea in order to put an end to the great expense of maintaining an unpopular puppet ruler. In April, Catherine issued a manifesto proclaiming the annexation. In it she justified her act by saying that her empire had not been able to enjoy the fruits of its victories during the war of 1768–1774. Independence had failed, and the Crimeans had been ungrateful in not accepting Russia's gift. On the peninsula there was little immediate reaction to the annexation. Potemkin was ordered to place "posters in important locations to announce to the Crimeans Our receiving them as Our subjects."[30]

From among her advisors, Catherine received the greatest plaudits from Count Alexandr Bezborodko, one of Catherine's closest advisors, who had for a long time advocated this action. In his diary for that date he inscribed this justification for the annexation:

> The Porte has not kept good faith from the very beginning. Their primary goal has been to deprive the Crimeans of independence. They banished the legal khan and replaced him with the thief Devlet Giray. They consistently refused to evacuate Taman. They made numerous perfidious attempts to introduce rebellion in the Crimea against the legitimate Khan Şahin Giray. All of these efforts did not bring us to declare war. . . . The Porte never ceased to drink in each drop of revolt among the Tatars. . . . Our only wish has been to bring peace to the Crimea. . . . and we were finally forced by the Turks to annex the area.[31]

Of course almost none of this was true. The real opposition to the requirements of the Treaty of Küçük Kaynarca had never been in Istanbul; it had been within the Crimea. Şahin Giray and his policies of change under the direct influence and control of the Russians had left the Crimean elite little choice other than to flee or to provide opposition at home. The independence of the Crimea during this period was no more than a sham perpetrated and perpetuated by the force of Russian arms. It was a transitionary period between Ottoman suzerainty and Russian suzerainty. Again, the real question, which so far cannot be answered, is why Catherine preferred such a transition to outright annexation. There is no doubt that much less bloodshed, destruction, and turmoil would have resulted from annexation.

8. Reorganization of the Crimea

Catherine II, unlike many of her advisors, bore no malice toward the Crimean Tatars, nor was she prejudiced against her non-Russian or non-Christian subjects. Catherine's interest in the Crimea was economic and political rather than national or ethnic. In Russia's central regions, Catherine had taken great pains to improve the lot of her Muslim and Turkic subjects before 1783. She had reversed many of the policies of persecution and discrimination pursued by her predecessors, and as a result, had gained the active support of the leadership of these minorities. These changes should be kept in mind in order to place her actions in the Crimea after 1783 in a wider perspective.[1]

From the first major incorporation of Muslim subjects into the Russian Empire under Tsar Ivan IV until the mid-eighteenth century, official Russian treatment of these infidels had been harsh. Influenced by church doctrine and historical experience, the Russians had considered Muslim subjects dangerous to the state's internal security and a threat to its spiritual well-being. Ivan IV set the pattern for treatment of the Muslims with his two-pronged attack on Islam. He destroyed the institutional foundations of Islam in Kazan by destroying schools and mosques, and removing their educated elite and clergy. He forced many Muslims to convert to Christianity. A hundred years later, in the *Sobornoe Ulozhenie* (the law code of Tsar Alexei) of 1649, a special section was devoted to the problem of Russia's Muslims. There it was stated that the punishment for "proselytizing in the name of Muhammad was burning at the stake."[2]

Peter I was less concerned with religious distinctions between Muslims and Russians, yet he too pursued a policy, where possible, of destroying the Muslim intellectual and social elite. For example, he removed the status of nobility from all Muslim Kazan Tatars and put them in the social category of state peasants. An even more aggressive Orthodox mission among the Muslims occurred during the 1740s and 1750s, after the founding of the Kazan Office of New Converts. According to the edict creating the office, its purpose was to baptize, forcefully if necessary, all Muslims.[3]

Catherine II and Islam

It was a surprise to everyone when Catherine II closed the office of New Converts early in her reign. The use of forceful conversion was apparently distasteful to the enlightened Catherine. However, for several years she did continue to use other means to encourage baptism of her minority religious population. Catherine preferred to use financial incentives to achieve what force had failed to accomplish.

In 1773, Catherine instructed the Holy Synod to issue a "Toleration of All Faiths" edict. Although all faiths were mentioned in this document, it was particularly Islam that was discussed. The edict stated: "As God tolerates all faiths on Earth, Her Imperial Majesty will also permit all faiths, and desires only that Her subjects exist in harmony." The edict further prohibited "all bishops and all priests" from "destroying mosques" and ordered them "not to interfere in Muslim questions or in the building of their houses of worship."[4]

This edict set the stage for Catherine's experiments in the Crimea during its period of independence. From these experiments it is easy to see that Catherine viewed Islam as an impediment to social and political development, but not as a repugnant religion. She hoped that a forceful policy of modernization in the Crimea would show the Tatars the benefits and advantages to be gained by adopting the Russian model for their society. Her efforts in the Crimea had resulted in open Tatar hostility toward the Russian model, however, and one revolt had followed another. Independence had been rejected as a possibility by most of the Tatar elite, and annexation became the only possible solution for the empress. Catherine had been unable to perceive the fact that in an Islamic society, all areas of social, religious, and political life are closely related. The Muslim clergy, while not holding the top political offices, did maintain a firm hold over the population's allegiance, and the benefits of modern civilization could do little to change this. Something else had to be tried to gain the allegiance and support of the Tatar population for Russia.

The chief architect of the new policy was Baron Igel'strom, from Riga, a member of another Russian minority group, the Baltic Germans. His advice and innovations provided the method for Catherine's solution to this important problem in the Crimea, and later, in other Russian Muslim provinces. Igel'strom argued that any policy that ignored the Muslim leadership would be bound to fail. The Russian state had to utilize this Muslim leadership in order to be able to assimilate the Muslim masses by bureaucratic means. Further, Igel'strom believed that if this policy succeeded, these Muslims could be useful in furthering Russian imperialistic interests in central Asia. As a result, after the annexation of the Crimea, the government pursued a positive program toward the peninsula's Muslims. They incorporated the Islamic clergy into the ranks of the imperial bureaucracy and created Muslim institutions under the direct control of the government. It was against this background that the reorganization of the new Crimean province took place.

It must be remembered that fifteen years of disorders had left the traditional social bonds of Crimean society broken. The Christians had been removed from the peninsula; agricultural production had ceased, bringing Tatar peasants to a state of complete impoverishment; and the economic foundations of *mirza* power had suffered from the same disorders. Only the Muslim clergy had escaped relatively undisturbed. Gaining Tatar allegiance and support was not going to be easy for the Russians.

The annexation proclamation had promised: "solemnly and irrevocably for Ourselves and our successors to treat the inhabitants of this country as Our own subjects; to protect and defend their persons, their property, their mosques, and their religious traditions."[5] There is no question that Catherine fully intended that the annexation would bring few dislocations in Tatar social or religious life.

Prince G. A. Potemkin, who directed all of Russia's imperial policies in the south, had issued general orders to all Russian military officers in the Crimea stating: "On the annexation of the Tatar people to the sovereignty of Her Imperial Majesty, it is critical that property be respected and that our army turn toward the local inhabitants as brothers." Every instance of a problem with the local population was to be reported to him at once. Igel'strom was to see that his officers "protect the local inhabitants from harm by the soldiers, and that nothing should be taken without a voluntary sale." In response, Baron Igel'strom agreed that he would (1) uphold the Tatars' culture and religion; (2) make sure that no Tatars were recruited into the army against their will; and (3) see that the Russian officers were not "permitted to enter the Tatars' harems."[6]

Administrative Structure

This goal was to be accomplished with a minimum of political reorganization. First, the authority of the khan was replaced with that of the new Russian governor, who combined the khan's political and military authority with his own. The first such governor was Igel'strom himself, who acted under the direct authority of Prince Potemkin.

The rest of the Crimean administrative structure was to remain much as it had been before 1783. Political and military problems were to be separated, however, as both Catherine and Potemkin were uncertain of Ottoman intentions so soon after the annexation and wanted to be sure that Russian forces would be prepared if the Ottomans attempted to reverse the actions of 1783. This separation was accomplished through creation of a dual, and in many ways parallel, political structure on the peninsula. The civilian government was staffed almost exclusively by Tatar officials from previous

Crimean administrations, while the military regime was made up of Russian officers of the occupation army. Both administrations were under Potemkin's authority as represented by Baron Igel'strom.

The policy the Russians pursued from the beginning in the new Crimean province may be summed up easily. The tsarina simply incorporated the Crimea into the structure of the empire and did not consider it a *corpus separatum*. The keynote of this policy was a certain lack of interest in the Crimea as a special region different from the rest of the Russian southern frontier. Tavricheskaia oblast' in 1784, and then Tavricheskaia guberniia after 1802, included areas not historically part of any Crimean Tatar entity, and they served political and economic purposes that had nothing to do with those of their Tatar inhabitants. The peninsula lost its particular identity with the annexation; its Tatar population was diluted through territorial reorganization.

At first, Catherine made some efforts to bring Tatars into the administrative system on the peninsula. In 1783, a Crimean district government was established; it was chaired by the Şirin *bey*, Mehmetşa, who was given the Russian bureaucratic title of *namestnik*. Two of Şahin Giray's former officials, Gadini Kazi Ağa and the former *kadiasker*, Musledin Effendi, joined Mehmetşa as his chief deputies. These two were replaced by Rudzevich (the former Iakup Ağa) at the end of the year. The seat of the district government was Karasu Bazaar, the seat of the Şirin *bey* in years past.

By June 1784, the number of former Tatar bureaucrats who had offered their services to the new civilian government had risen to eleven. It was clear that for the time being Catherine and Potemkin were satisfied to use the government they had found at the time of the Crimean annexation.

The military administration was first headed by General de Balmen. However, it was soon discovered that he had been responsible for a number of outrages against the Crimean population during the last years of the war and was continuing to antagonize the Tatars. In late 1783, Baron Igel'strom was given that task too. By nature interested in and respectful of the Tatars, Igel'strom expected Tatar officials and his own military officers to act in concert. Documents from both institutions indicate that he was the guiding light of both. Mehmetşa and Rudzevich were both comfortable with Igel'strom and believed that any policy he suggested would be for the good of both Tatars and Russians.[7]

Re-creation of the *kaimakam* system first established by the khans was one of the first efforts of both institutions. Although in his reports to St. Petersburg Igel'strom preferred to use the Russian term *uezd*, within the Crimea itself he was satisfied to keep the Tatar name and form of this local institution. According to an edict issued by the district government and the military office, the *kaimakams* were to be directed by Tatar *kadis*—in most cases by the *kadis* who had served Khan Şahin Giray. They were granted a full range of political and police powers in their respective *kadiliks* (administrative units).[8]

Tax collecting was the one element of the former civilian Tatar government that was taken over by Igel'strom and the Russian colonial officials during the first year. It was assigned to Mavroeni, a former Cossack who had been the official in charge of the Kefe customs revenues under Şahin.

The major problem for the Russians was one of enlisting the support of the majority of the Tatar population who were controlled by the Crimean *mirzas*. The Russians found they did not know much about relationships between the nobility and the masses; furthermore, they did not know who the members of the nobility actually were. It was one thing to wish to treat the local population in a humane and enlightened way; it was another to understand the composition of the local population. Also, it was going to be necessary to make a complete analysis of the existing Crimean economic structure before the Russian goals of economic expansion and of integration of the new province into the empire could be satisfied.

The job of analyzing the Crimean economic structure was given to Igel'strom soon after creation of the dual administration had been completed. He was asked to find accurate information on the size, social distribution, and geographical distribution of the Crimean Muslim and non-Muslim populations. He was to learn what economic activities they took part in and what their incomes and revenues were. Igel'strom, realizing that this could best be learned from the Tatar leaders, requested the Crimean district government and its leader Mehmetşa to prepare a number of appropriate reports. For information on the non-Muslim population and their interests, Mehmetşa approached the leadership of the Christian and Jewish communities.

It soon became apparent that this information would be difficult to gather. The years of civil unrest and Russian invasion had destroyed the urban areas, and populations had moved away from the areas of conflict. In addition, most of the financial records of Şahin's administration had been lost.

Despite this handicap, reports began to appear in late 1783. By June of the next year they were complete. The questions they answered were: (1) How many *kadiliks* (judicial districts under jurisdiction of a *kadi* or judge) had there been in each of the *kaimakamliks* (the equivalent of the former *beylik* or administrative district) and which were they? (2) How many Tatar villages were in each district, and of these, how many were underpopulated or deserted? (3) How many Christian villages were in each *kadilik*? (4) How many mosques and churches existed in each *kaimakamlik* and which were damaged? (5) How many individual dwellings, empty and occupied, were there in each town, and which were Christian and which Muslim? (6) How much revenue had been assigned to the khan's government from each town? (7) What taxes on agriculture and on cattle production were customary from the villages? (8) How many officials, clerks, and translators were necessary for each *kaimakamlik*? and (9) How much salary was necessary for the upkeep of these officials? As one can see from this list, the information the Russians began with was scanty. The results of the survey were interesting.

First, the damage to the Crimean economy was greater than had been expected. Many Muslim and Christian towns were underpopulated. Thousands of homes and shops were deserted. Twenty percent of the homes in Kefe and 10 percent of those in Gözleve were in ruins as a result of de Balmen's outrages in 1778. Large, potentially productive agricultural areas were empty and fallow. No corner of the peninsula had escaped the ravages of war and insurrection. The job of returning the Crimea to its former economic productivity was enormous.

Based on this information, Igel'strom estimated the Tatar population of the entire peninsula to be a scant 53,616 males, giving an approximate total Muslim population of 150,000. Igel'strom was sure that this meant the population had declined by 50 percent in the years since 1772.[9]

Tatar Nobility

Igel'strom's second important task concerned the Tatar *mirza* stratum and their assimilation into the wider Russian *dvorianstvo* (nobility—the class). While Catherine intended to allow the Crimeans to pursue their own social customs as much as possible, she saw no contradiction in trying also to incorporate the various Tatar classes into Russian society. She was convinced that the *mirza*s would see that they had little to lose by accepting the Russian social ranks with their economic and social privileges.

Catherine's policy in the Crimea was closely related to her programs in other Muslim areas of the Russian Empire. In 1784, she ordered a full "rehabilitation" and restoration of "those rights the Kazan Tatars had once enjoyed" which had been removed by Peter I at the beginning of the century. In her typical style, Catherine's decree stated, "these *mirza*s for some time and for various reasons have not been able to profit from the properties they had inherited from their ancestors." Further, it stated, "It is Our desire that without regard to his nationality or faith, each *mirza* shall have the personal right to these lands and any advantages that will accrue from their use."[10]

In May 1784, Catherine instructed Potemkin to see to it that the Crimean *mirza*s "profit from the same favor of Our Imperial Majesty."[11] The next year, when the Charter of the Nobility instituted a major reorganization of all Russian noblemen into a type of caste system with limited self-government, the Tatar nobles were made members of the new Crimean Assembly of the

Nobility.[12] Catherine simply announced that the Crimean *mirzas* were the Tatar equivalent of the Russian *dvorianstvo* and were granted the privileges that had been acquired by their Russian counterparts in 1775 and 1785. But during the fifteen years that followed, it became evident that there were complications inherent in the application of these principles.

One of the major concerns of noble assemblies in Russia during the next several years was how to determine their membership. In the Crimea, this task was doubly difficult. While Russian *dvoriane* (nobles) could often present official documentation of their landholdings, or evidence of their ancestors' service and distinctions, the Tatar *mirzas* had difficulty in producing documents that satisfied the Russian officials. The very different division of lands between the Giray dynasty and the important clans, combined with the problems of lesser *mirzas*, meant that the Russian officials could not depend upon Russian models in judging claims of nobility.

Igel'strom felt it necessary to convene a special Tatar commission to decide on this issue. The commission, composed almost entirely of Crimean Tatars, discovered that most *mirzas* residing on lands of the Girays had no documents of any kind to prove their noble status. As a result, the commission was forced in most instances to accept verbal assurances. The commission disbanded in late 1785, at which time it announced the assignment of 334 Tatar *mirzas* to the rank of *dvoriane*.[13]

At first, and before large-scale Slavic colonization took place, the Tatar *dvoriane* were given a monopoly on ownership of Tatar serfs. The government decided that Russian *pomeshchiks* ("land owners" or "serf owners") should not have the right to enserf Muslim Tatars in the Crimea as this would only exacerbate already tense relations between the two nationalities. The government further decided that Tatar peasants residing on lands not under the control of Tatar *mirzas* should be assigned the rank of state peasant, which would ensure their "more equitable" treatment in comparison to their treatment as serfs.[14] This policy was to produce some major problems for peasants, *mirzas*, and bureaucrats during the next century because Tatar peasants living on lands of Russian *pomeshchiks* thus retained more freedom than those on estates of Tatar *mirzas*.

The results of this incorporation of the *mirza* stratum into the Russian *dvoriane* were mixed. On one hand, some Crimean nobles kept control of the lands and populations they had controlled before the annexation. This provided an element of continuity in land and social relationships that would have been disrupted by a complete Russification. On the other hand, the change brought about a Russification of those *mirzas* themselves. To work on an equal footing with their Russian counterparts, the *mirzas* found it necessary to adopt the Russians' habits, language, and ways of conducting class business. This was especially true of their participation in the local assemblies of the nobility. As Raeff points out, this Russification of a part of the elite without a corresponding change among the masses led to an inevitable split that was in many ways similar to that which had been taking place for a century in Russia.[15]

Crimean Clergy

The other important element of the Crimean elite, the Muslim clergy, received extraordinarily careful attention following the annexation. Before 1783, the greatest hostility toward the Russians had emerged from this class. Its ties to the Ottoman Empire had been close. Their belief in the constant struggle against the unbeliever who lived "beyond the frontiers of Islam" was as real in the eighteenth century as it had been in the sixteenth.

Yet it was in the upper ranks of this clergy that the Russian administrators eventually found their strongest native support. Such a victory for the bureaucrats must be credited to the ingenious policies begun by Igel'strom in the Crimea, and then continued in the Volga region. Igel'strom believed that it was only through the Islamic clergy that the common people could be won over. The Muslim clergy's control of the views and outlooks of the local communities was enormous, and if used in a sophisticated way, could be of great value to the Russians.

His plan was simply to recruit the clergy as the major instrument of tsarist control over the Tatars. His initial program ensured both that all of their social and economic privileges continued under the new regime and that no change would be introduced that could alter their position in religion, education, or local justice. Finally, they were put on the government payroll to receive extra financial benefits. The clergy, as well as the *imams* and *muezzins* of individual mosques, were given salary payments by late 1783. The evidence shows that most of the clergy accepted this privilege.

The Crimean clergy occupied many of the highest government positions at the time of the annexation: *mufti, kadiasker,* and many of the *kadis*. In the higher education system, the clergy kept control of teaching and administrative positions. In addition, their total numbers were high. In 1783, there were 1531 mosques with their staffs, 21 *tekkes* ("monasteries"), 25 *medresses* and 35 *mektebes* (higher schools and primary schools). The *mufti,* Musalar Efendi, and the *kadiasker,* Seit Mehmet Efendi, were assigned annual salaries of 2000 rubles. This placed them on a par with their Russian Orthodox counterparts.[16]

The vast landholdings of the Islamic clergy were also guaranteed by the Russian administration. *Vakifs*, which had grown in number and size in the last decades of the khanate, were not subject to Russian taxation and were denied to either Russian officials or newly arriving settlers. According to

Igel'strom's calculations, almost 30 percent of the productive land on the peninsula fell into this category. The Muslim clergy was also exempted from taxation and was granted the right to own serfs, a right denied their Orthodox counterparts. The combination of these policies gave the Russian colonial administration the possibility of achieving a peaceful transition from Muslim to Russian rule. It might have succeeded in the long run if these policies had not been reversed repeatedly during the nineteenth century. In fact, Igel'strom proved so successful that in 1785 he was transferred from the Crimea to the Volga region to institute his policies there.

Tatar Emigration

Other major problems surfaced soon after the annexation. These included a growing Tatar exodus from and the beginnings of Slavic colonization of the Crimea. It was only to be expected that, whatever the intentions of the Russian government, the presence in the Crimea of a large number of soldiers and low-ranking officers would bring about a disregard for orders from afar and produce Russian-Tatar enmity. The government's injunctions against mistreatment of the natives had to be repeated frequently. Reminders that the Crimea was not to be considered enemy territory were issued by Igel'strom's office almost weekly. Throughout the peninsula, however, there was still a certain amount of pressure applied by Russians against the Tatars. It brought about the beginning of what eventually became a large-scale exodus of Tatars to the Ottoman Empire.[17]

At first, those who left were mainly Tatars closely tied to Khan Şahin Giray who left with their deposed ruler. Additionally, among the 8000 Tatars who left in 1783 and 1784, there were many Ottoman subjects who had lived in Kefe. Potemkin had recognized that this would be the case and ordered his troops in the port cities not to interfere with any who wanted to leave for the Ottoman Empire.[18]

A much more serious emigration took place in the years 1785–1788; it culminated during the months after the signing of the Peace of Jassy between Russia and the Ottoman Empire in 1789, when the Ottomans permanently gave up any hopes of returning the Crimea to Muslim rule. Although some estimates suggest that as many as 100,000 Tatars left during these years, it is more likely that the number amounted to 20,000 or 30,000.[19]

Russian Colonization

By 1789, Russian colonization measures were underway, and for many Tatars it seemed the last opportunity to leave for a Muslim land and take some wealth. It is likely that some of the lower ranking *mirzas*, not receiving as many privileges as those admitted to the *dvorianstvo*, preferred to take their chances in Ottoman service. Rudzevich at the time claimed that some *mirzas* were saying in the villages that "it is against Islamic law to remain as subjects of Her Imperial Majesty."[20] Yet the fact that those emigrating were neither peasants nor clergy, but rather lower-ranking nobles and some urban inhabitants with trading interests in the Ottoman Empire leads one to disregard such a claim.

Since one of the main considerations of the Russian government had been the potential economic advantages of annexation, it was to be expected that everything possible would be done to encourage economic recovery and development. Yet in the years after 1783, it did not proceed toward this goal in a consistent or energetic manner. Only lands belonging to the ruling Giray dynasty and its closest associates were taken over by the state for its own exploitation. Most of the vast landholdings given away on a grand scale to Catherine's favorites came from this Giray land. Aside from areas saved for the construction of fortresses or harbor facilities, little or no land was confiscated from other Crimean subjects in the decade after the annexation. The lands vacated by the exodus of the Tatars in the late 1780s did not amount to what one might call vast landholdings either. Such contemporary sources as the account by Richard Willis in 1785, in which he spoke of the Crimea as being heavily settled by Russian serfs under the yoke of Russian administrators and landlords, cannot disprove the fact that, by the beginning of the nineteenth century, there were only 8746 Russian serfs (including children) on the peninsula.[21]

There were a few conspicuous examples of large grants of land made to Catherine's favorites or to other officials who took part in the administration. In 1784 alone, Potemkin dispensed more than 73,000 *desiatins* of state land to his officials and friends. To his ally, Bezborodko, he granted "a nice estate in Sudak" of 18,000 *desiatins*. Popov received over 32,000 *desiatins*. The Şirin *bey*, chairman of the Crimean district government, was granted over 27,000 *desiatins*, and so forth. But large-scale colonization and displacement of Tatars did not take place until the next century when one finds among the colonists "discharged soldiers, Cossacks, Greeks, Wallachians, Armenians, Germans, Bulgarians, and Jews."[22]

By 1793, according to Pallas, the population of the Crimean peninsula amounted to the following:[23]

	Male	*Female*
Tatar nobility	570	465
Tatar clergy	4,519	4,105
Common Tatars	48,484	99,280
Muslim slaves	343	405
Nogay Tatars	4,331	3,593

	Male	Female
Gypsies	1,664	1,561
Tatar merchants	1,780	1,048
Christians (non-Russian)	6,220	5,346
Servants	1,185	247
Russian household serfs	110	116
Russian colonists	4,861	3,397
Settlers newly established by the nobility	1,987	586
Cossacks	5,803	0
Christian clergy	89	33
Servants and Officers of the Crown and their families	382	270

Thus, by this date, those who could be classified as colonists or Russians who moved to the Crimea as a result of the annexation were not very numerous. With the changing government policy and the nineteenth-century reversal of many of the enlightened programs of Igel'strom and Catherine, this changed. Yet the annexation and the years immediately following seemed to offer the possibility of a peaceful transition for the Crimean Tatars.

9. Russian Administration of the Crimea in the Nineteenth Century

The nineteenth century is the most difficult to describe and evaluate in Crimean Tatar history. During the khanate period and after the Tatar rebirth that took place at the end of the nineteenth century, Tatar intellectuals and political figures wrote extensively about themselves. Foreign observers also left a great deal of evidence about the Tatars for both of those periods. But for the century that began with the annexation of the Crimea by Russia in 1783 and lasted until 1889 and the rise of a new Tatar culture led by Ismail Bey Gaspirali, historians have virtually no useful source material from Tatar or other non-Russian sources. Historical documentation from the government and from interested Russian observers of the area is all that is left. Although this evidence is weighty in quantity, its quality is not adequate to provide a complete picture of Crimean Tatar life during this time.

Russian administration during this period produced a number of important conflicts that hampered Tatar development. They derived in large part from the fact that the government was not very interested in the Crimean Tatars as a special group, and the region as such was not considered a colonial area. The following characterization of the Crimea at the end of the nineteenth century, written in 1951 by a Soviet apologist for the Tatar deportation that took place in 1944, might well have been the product of a nineteenth-century Russian writer expressing the generally held opinion about the Crimea at that time:

> In some historical works, the Crimea is considered at the end of the nineteenth century as merely an agrarian frontier, a colony of tsarist Russia. But this view is patently false. (1) The Crimea, measured by its economic development to the end of the nineteenth century was actually progressing as well as the central *guberniias* of our state; (2) The Crimea in no way may be considered a colony, because the Crimean land was from ancient times Russian land, and therefore the annexation of the Crimea to Russia was not the conquest of foreign land but was the reunification and reestablishing of the rights of the Russian people to its own land; (3) The economic development of the Crimea was accomplished by Russians, the towns were built by Russian workers, the fields were tilled in the great majority by Russian peasants.[1]

Throughout the nineteenth century, the Tatars experienced one of the most heavy-handed policies of Russification anywhere in the empire. Yet by the end of the century, a new movement developed among Tatar intellectuals, providing the basis for a national movement during the 1917–1921 revolutionary period and culminating in a relatively successful system of national communism emphasizing Tatar cultural and political identity. In this chapter and the next, the origins of this paradox will be discussed.

Administrative Organization

That the Russian government saw nothing special or peculiar about the Crimean Tatars is best evidenced by the territorial and organizational policies it pursued on the peninsula. From 1784 on, Russian officials viewed the Crimea as a part of the southern frontier zone. When Tavricheskaia oblast' was created in February 1784, areas not historically part of the khanate were included in the *oblast'* along with the peninsula. At first, the *oblast'* consisted of seven districts, four of which were on the peninsula (Simferopol', Feodosiia-Kefe, Evpatoriia-Gözleve, and Perekop, which was extended to Mariupol' north of the Sea of Azov), one on the Taman peninsula (Fanagoriia), and two in the northern steppe (Dneprovsk and Melitopol'). By including three non-Crimean districts, the government created an *oblast'* that was neither ethnically nor historically homogeneous, one that served political and economic purposes distinct from those of the Tatars.[2]

The first governor of the *oblast'* was Prince Grigorii Potemkin, who was aided by chief administrator, V. Kakhovskii. From 1784 until his death in 1791, Potemkin's interests in the south went well beyond any particular concern for the Crimea itself. Catherine II acted as the governor from 1791 until 1793, when she appointed her current favorite, Platon Zubov, as governor, which position he held for the remainder of her reign.[3]

Tsar Paul, who had no interest in the Crimea whatsoever, reorganized the southern frontier regions only as part of his total rejection of his mother's achievements. In December 1796, he incorporated Tavricheskaia oblast' and the *guberniias* of Voznezensk and Ekaterinoslav, into one super-*guberniia*, called Novorossiiskaia. He also combined the Simferopol', Evpatoriia, and Feodosiia districts into one very large district—that of Simferopol'. In the course of his undoing of Catherine's work, he gave back their Tatar names to all Crimean towns that had been given Russian equivalents in 1784. Thus Simferopol' became Akmeçet once again and Sevastopol' was replaced by Akhtiar. (This return to Tatar identities did not last beyond Paul, however.) For the Tatars, administrative changes at the end of the eighteenth century involved Tatarization on minor and Russification on major matters. In the new Novorossiiskaia guberniia, the Crimean Tatars had become only a small part of a largely Slavic frontier province.[4]

In 1802, Alexander I, as part of his return to the policies of his grandmother, Catherine II, returned the administrative organization of the southern frontier to what it had been in 1796. The abolition of Novorossiis-kaia guberniia and the re-creation of Tavricheskaia oblast', now given the title of *guberniia*, set the pattern for the Crimea's administrative organization until 1917. Once again, Tatar names were replaced with Russian ones.[5]

From the very beginning, Simferopol' (Akmeçet) was the *guberniia* center for the Crimea. It was the seat not only of the governors and their assistants but also of the Tatars who collaborated with the Russian regime. As the home of the former *kalgay*, Şahin Giray, and the residence of the Russian advisors for the last khan, Simferopol' was a logical replacement for Bahçesaray, whose ancient palace represented the independent past.

Governors assigned to the post in Simferopol' were a mixture of career bureaucrats and members of important and old Russian families. Such names as Miloradovich, Naryshkin, Pestel', Adlerberg, and Kavelin are representative of the latter, while Mertvago, Trepov, Kaznacheev, and Baronov represent the former.[6] Ironically, the only top administrative official in the Crimea who was well liked by the Tatars, and whose memory is important in their historical literature, was Armand Duc de Richelieu, who was never a governor of the Crimea at all, but was governor first of Novorossiiskaia and then of Khersonskaia guberniia in Kerson Province.[7]

In Simferopol', the provincial administration was divided into the regular *gubernskoe pravitelstvo* and the civil and criminal courts. The *gubernskoe pravitelstvo* was subdivided into two bureaus, both of which were staffed during the nineteenth century by Russian bureaucrats. The explanation for the exclusion of Tatars from these important branches of the local government was that "the Crimean Tatars do not know the Russian language and thus are unable to understand administrative matters that come before the bureaus."[8]

The fact that the Senate, responsible for the decree establishing the new *guberniia* in 1802, felt it necessary to justify this exclusion indicates that at least some members of the bureaucracy believed the practice to be irregular. Yet there is no evidence that there were any Tatars in these higher levels of the local bureaucracy at any time after 1802. At the provincial level, the only recognition of the Tatar problem was the creation of translation offices in each of the bureaus that had jurisdiction in the Crimea.[9] On the one occasion when a Russian law indicated that local inhabitants were to be represented in bureaucratic offices, it was specifically Russian peasants who were to have a say in the judicial administration.[10]

It was only at the district level that the Tatars were able to make any effort to influence Russian administrative policy. In the *uezd* courts, police administrations, and town governments, records mention an occasional Tatar member. Yet even at this level, Tatar participation was the exception.[11]

Probably as a result of this, the central government in St. Petersburg received a constant stream of information about misuse of authority, and corruption among Russian bureaucrats in the Crimea. In 1816, on the recommendation of Count Lanzheron, the military governor of Kherson military district, the Senate established a special commission to investigate the rising number of complaints reaching St. Petersburg about various acts of misbehavior by local Russian officials. Unfortunately, no accounts of these investigations or of any corrective policy on the part of the government have come to light.[12]

Tatar Mirza Class

Russian social policy in the Crimea during the nineteenth century was more complicated than its administrative program. The government pursued different policies toward the various Tatar social strata—the *mirza*s, the urban class, and the peasants—with a resulting increase in differentiation between the three as the century progressed. During the khanate period, the *mirza*s had controlled more land and wealth than any other group; on their lands, Muslim peasants had maintained their own personal freedom, limited only by financial responsibilities to their *mirza* landowners. The *mirza*s also had been accustomed to a high level of political participation through their assemblies (*kurultay*s) and the offices they had held within the khan's administration. The Tatar urban classes had been important, too, as artisans and merchants. Yet they had shared their position with large Christian minorities, almost all of whom lived in the Crimean cities.

The Russian government simply decided that the *mirza*s would become the Crimean equivalent of the Russian *dvorianstvo*. Both Catherine II and Potemkin had tried to incorporate the *mirza* class into its Russian counterpart, and by so doing, had hoped to ease the transition for the rest of the population. Yet it soon became apparent that the application of Russian rights for the Tatar nobility was neither automatic nor easy to accomplish. The years of war and invasion had so disorganized relationships between *mirza*s and land that the Russian governors could not decide which Tatars were nobles and which lands belonged to them. In addition, Tatar categories of nobility did not correspond to those of the *dvorianstvo*, and the *mirza*s, who found it difficult to adapt to the new *dvoriane* organization, could not always perform according to the rules and regulations of that class. They did not know Russian (which was used in all *dvorianstvo* proceedings), and they felt uncomfortable sitting beside their former enemies (a feeling that was reciprocated). Consequently, they resisted government attempts to fit them into new molds. Finally, the shifting administrative forms for the new territory, followed in short order by another reversal in 1802, confused all areas of government-*mirza* affairs. The Crimean Tatars were, in the face of these difficulties, fortunate to have as governors a group of officials who sympathized with their plight and tried sincerely to solve the problems in a fair manner.

Most important of these governors were Semen Zhegulin, who served from 1788 until 1797, Grigorii Miloradovich, who served from 1802 until 1803, and Dmitrii Mertvago, who served from 1803 to 1807.[13] In late 1794, Zhegulin requested a government reaffirmation of the rights of Tatar nobles "to the *pomesties* and all other privileges" to which their rank entitled them.[14] He reported that in previous years Tatar nobles had been continuously discouraged by a series of contradictory measures concerning these privileges. Yet even so, it seems that the real reason for these contradictory regulations was not so much malicious intention on the part of officials as it was insufficient knowledge about *mirza* status in the Tatar community.

With the reorganization of Tavricheskaia guberniia in 1802, the new governor, Miloradovich, requested and was granted the authority to establish in the Crimea a commission composed of both Russian bureaucrats and Tatar *mirza*s; its purpose was to attack these problems, to make some clear definition of Tatar nobility, and to apply the laws of *dvorianstvo* among the Tatars. The commission was to be chaired by Privy Councilor and Senator Lopukhin. Its Russian membership included the director of the survey department, Lanskii, acting state councilors Tumanskii and Kreiter, and Pavel Sumarokov. Representatives from Russian *pomeshchik*s, Tatar *mirza*s, and urban inhabitants. were included.

Tatar Landholding

The edict that established the commission repeated the promises of protection of the *mirza*s' land rights—promises that had been made first in the annexation manifesto and then in the edict of 1794. That the government issued edicts for the next ten years repeating these promises suggests that it was not an easy task to implement them.[15]

The commission was hampered by the fact that a number of developments that had taken place between 1783 and 1802 had confused the issues. Large amounts of land had already been granted to Russian *pomeshchik*s by Catherine. Much land vacated by *mirza*s emigrating to the Ottoman Empire had already been reassigned to various Tatars who were collaborating with the Russian government; many of these Tatars were not of traditional *mirza* rank. For example, Battal Bey, formerly an Ottoman *pasha* who had joined the Russian forces after 1783, was granted over 10,000 *desiatin*s in 1792.[16]

In early 1805, Chernov, a Russian *pomeshchik*, requested on behalf of some of the Russian members of the commission that the government ignore all Tatar complaints and demands for the restoration of land. Lopukhin, with the advice of Sumarokov, denied this request. But it showed that the various groups on the commission were not working toward the same ends. Finally, in 1807, the Crimean governor, Mertvago, asked the commission to make a simple determination about which of the Tatar *mirza* families belonged to the various ranks of Crimean nobility. Under threat of disbandment for failure to produce, after which decisions on these matters would be made by the governor alone, it took the commission only a few months to make some determinations; they simply decided that most of the Tatar nobility would be assigned the title of *dvoriane*.[17]

The commission's final report stated that those lands occupied at that time, as well as those that were empty and could be proven to have at one time been part of family patrimonies, would be registered as *pomestie* belonging to *mirza* families. No attempt was to be made to restore lands that had been seized from *mirza*s after 1783, and Tatars without land were to be excluded. In addition, Tatars who had entered Russian service and had received civil and military ranks would be made members of the *dvorianstvo* with all of its privileges—even if they did not belong to one of the traditional *mirza* clans. In 1810, after making these recommendations, the commission was disbanded.[18]

Yet in spite of these recommendations, the Tatar nobility's problems persisted. In the face of Slavic colonization and land seizure in the area, distrust on the part of Russian officials, and the loss of much of their own wealth after 1783, the *mirza*s' power and prestige steadily eroded.

Although Russian laws of that century give the impression that the rights and privileges granted to the *mirza*s after 1783 were preserved and constantly reaffirmed, the fact that one edict after another called for the introduction of *dvoriane* rights for them indicates that they either had not received or were unable to retain these rights. For example, in 1835 an edict permitted (as if for the first time) Tatar *mirza*s to take part in *dvorianstvo* elections—this, some fifty years after they were first admitted to that rank.[19] In 1839, for the first time, Tatar *mirza*s were given a right their Russian counterparts had enjoyed for more than a century. They could register their children in *dvoriane* rank before the children had performed any state service.[20] Then, in 1840, an edict stated (again as if for the first time) that Muslims living in Tavricheskaia guberniia had a right to achieve *dvoriane* rank.[21] Clearly, these rights, promised in the annexation manifesto and ratified in edicts of 1784 and 1794, were in the 1840s still privileges granted only by special governmental decree.

In addition, growing pressure on Tatar landholding was applied by an ever increasing Slavic population whose members were much better able to cope with the bureaucratic system. In Simferopol' in 1829 and 1830, new offices and commissions were opened for the purpose of assigning land and adjudicating disputes between Tatars and Russians. The Tatar nobility was asked to elect representatives to these commissions. These representatives were to be selected from those *mirza*s who could "handle the Russian language with ease."[22] But such acts did little to alleviate the growing impoverishment of the traditional Tatar elite.

Despite these difficulties, some of the Tatar *mirza*s adapted to Russian principles and served the state in both civil and military capacities. By the end of the eighteenth century, three Tatar *mirza*s had served as collegiate councilors: Mehmetşa Bey, as chairman of the Tavricheskaia oblast' Tatar nobility; Kazindar Mehmetağa, as a member of the district court; and Temir Ağa, as director of the Tatar section of the local civil court. In addition, there were five Tatar collegiate assessors: Kutluşa Ağa, Haci Gazi Ağa, Mehmetşa Mirza, Hamit Ağa, and Caum Ağa.[23]

Military Service for Tatars

Tatar participation in Russian military service was even more noteworthy. In 1784, Potemkin had created three Tatar regiments, which were commanded by former members of Şahin Giray's army. Trained before 1783 by Russian advisors, the Tatar officers and their troops took part in the Russo-Ottoman war that resulted in the capture of Ochakov. Platon Zubov, acting as governor of the Crimea in the last years of Catherine's reign, reported that the Tatars served well, were loyal, and deserved great praise from the government.[24]

With the outbreak of Russo-French hostilities in 1806, Murtaza Çelebi, the *mufti* of the Crimean clergy, asked Governor Mertvago to establish additional Tatar cavalry regiments. In 1807, four new Tatar regiments were created; they were commanded by Tatar officers. In May 1808, these regiments were sent to the front near Vilno where, according to a report of the Kherson district military governor, the "Tatar detachments were among the best." Again in 1812, they took part in the major battles on the Prussian frontier. Of the fifty Tatar officers who left the Crimea, twenty-five were killed in battle. As a result of their success, Alexander I re-formed the Tatar cavalry into regular cavalry regiments at the end of the war.[25]

Despite heavy emigrations of members of the Tatar elite after 1815, and although there continued to be substantial Russian opposition to their inclusion in the *dvoriane,* Crimean Tatar units continued to serve with distinction. In 1826, a Tatar Light Guard Squadron was created, one part of which was to serve in St. Petersburg as part of the royal light guard, the other part to remain on duty in the Crimea. In the Ottoman war of 1828, the St. Petersburg squadron was sent to Varna, where they put to rest any fears of continued Tatar support for their Muslim and Turkic brethren. This light guard squadron continued to serve the tsars until the military reforms of 1864.[26]

In 1837, apparently at the request of their leaders, the Crimean Tatar peasantry, which had been exempt from military recruitment since the annexation, were granted permission to apply for entry into the army. In spite of all these facts, Soviet accounts of Crimean history usually state that the Tatars were never loyal or trustworthy.[27]

The critical test for Tatar loyalty to the tsarist regime and for their utility as members of the Russian armed forces came with the Crimean War, which was fought on their own land against allies of their religious and ethnic neighbors. Even at this time, most of the Tatars served as loyal subjects. Although for security reasons, the local governor, Pestel, ordered the local civilian population transported from the coast and resettled inland, Tatar leaders did not put up any significant opposition. (This resettlement has been used by some historians as evidence of the government's mistrust of the Tatars.)

Tatar regiments on duty in the Crimea served with distinction against the French and British, while those stationed in St. Petersburg were assigned to guard duty at Kronstadt. In 1863, partly in recognition for their service during the war, a special Crimean cavalry convoy was created to serve the tsar himself.

Again, in the Ottoman war of 1877–1878, Tatar troops participated in front-line fighting, both in the Balkans and in the Caucasus. Thus there is no evidence to support the claim, often made and generally believed, that the Crimean Tatars in the nineteenth century were completely reluctant subjects. Large numbers of them participated in Russian military enterprises, and received deserved rewards for their service.[28]

Tatar Emigration

The Crimean War, though, proved to be the final straw for the great number of Tatar *mirzas* who had been unable to adapt to Russian service requirements: after the war a large number of the remaining Crimean Tatar elite emigrated to the Ottoman Empire. Herein lies the major tragedy of the Tatars in the nineteenth century. While estimates go as high as 80,000 for the number of Tatars who left the Crimea before the end of the eighteenth century, and it is believed that another 30,000 fled during the confusion surrounding the reorganizations of the Crimean territory between 1796 and 1802, the major exodus took place after the Crimean War.[29] It was apparently a result of a conscious government policy to encourage their exit.

Before the war, it had been the government's intention to discourage such emigration. While governor of Novorossiia, the Duc de Richelieu had inspected the Crimean peninsula and had concluded that any mass "exodus of the Tatars would have ruinous consequences for the area."[30] But after the Crimean War, the situation had changed. From Alexander II's point of view, the presence of the Tatars in the Crimea was a nuisance and a potential danger. He had received faulty information that the Tatars had collaborated en masse with the French and British, and based on this, he made the decision to facilitate and encourage their exodus in 1859. The tsar is reported to have remarked on the Tatar emigration: "It is not appropriate to oppose the overt or covert exodus of the Tatars. On the contrary, this voluntary emigration should be considered as a beneficial action calculated to free the territory from this unwanted population."[31] With this attitude held in the central government, it is no wonder that voluntary emigration turned into panic and mass flight. By the end of 1860, some 100,000 Crimean Tatars had left the peninsula. Ottoman sources corroborate the existence of large numbers of refugees from the Crimea in temporary housing in such cities as Sinop and Istanbul.[32]

During this period, the population of the Crimea dropped from an estimated 275,000 in 1850, to 194,000 in 1860; of these less than 100,000 were Tatar. This was clearly not the best way to increase agricultural and economic production on the peninsula. Somewhat belatedly, the government decided to discourage further emigration. By midsummer of 1860, no more passports were issued to Tatars, and it was threatened that any Tatars who left for any reason would be denied reentry. Yet the damage had been done.[33]

The tsar decided that those Tatars who remained should now be treated well so that they too would not panic and flee at the first opportunity. In November 1860, Count Totleben, an investigator for the government, recommended that the government "rid itself of the idea that the Tatars were enemies of the state, the notion which had helped trigger the emigration."[34] Yet the remaining Tatars had grown apprehensive about future government policy.

Crimean Cities

Soon after the annexation, Russian policies concerning the towns of the Crimea brought about massive changes and dislocations in their populations. Except for Bahçesaray and Karasu Bazaar, the Crimean cities had been turned over to Russian and other non-Tatar peoples. They became virtual Slavic and Greek/Armenian islands in a Tatar sea. It is not difficult to see why this happened.

Cities such as Kefe and Gözleve, which under Tatar rule had been important for the economic role they played in the southern trade, lost their function as the Russians built new port cities. The expansion of Sevastopol' and Balaklava as bases for the Russian fleet on the peninsula, of Kherson at the mouth of the Dnepr, and of Odessa further south along the coast, served to replace the old Tatar ports in importance. The new cities were built and populated by urban groups that had been introduced by the government for military and economic reasons. Kefe and Gözleve declined precipitously in size and economic life. The few remaining Tatar urban classes moved away, going especially to Bahçesaray, where there were large numbers of Tatars. Some Tatars remained in Simferopol', the peninsula's administrative center, but as the century progressed, the Tatar proportion of Simferopol's population continued to drop until by the end of the century, they accounted for scarcely a quarter of its total.[35]

In Bahçesaray, a restricted version of traditional Tatar urban society was maintained. Tatar artisans continued to organize their own administration based on the guild system. Haxthausen reported that during the year "every guild celebrates its own festivals, in which apprentices are discharged and declared masters of their respective crafts."[36]

Yet in all the other Crimean towns, Tatars were prevented from taking part in urban government. In Simferopol', Feodosiia, Staryi Krym, Evpatoriia, Militopol', Karasu Bazaar, and Perekop, there is no evidence of Tatar participation in urban government. A list of police commands in the towns of the Crimean province for 1891 shows that only in Bahçesaray were any Tatars represented in the bureaucracy. The only edict that recognizes non-Russian inhabitants of a Crimean town other than Bahçesaray is one from 1847, in which special permission was granted to fifty Tatar families to settle "in a special quarter" in Kerch, and to have a representative sitting on the town court.[37]

This development had a serious effect on Tatar culture. Before 1783, the Crimean towns had served both as meeting and communications centers for the *mirza* stratum of society, and as seats of Tatar consciousness. In the nineteenth century, without the catalytic effect of a Tatar urban life, the upper class found it increasingly difficult to maintain its own culture. Only toward the end of the century did a new Tatar urban class emerge in the old Tatar cities of Bahçesaray and Karasu Bazaar, bringing with it the reestablishment of a national Tatar culture that was quite different in form and content from what it had been before 1783.

Tatar Peasants

The Russians also had problems with the Tatar peasants who made up almost 90 percent of the peninsula's population. It was the ordinary Tatar peasant who had suffered most between 1768 and 1783. They had not taken part in political affairs during the last years of the khanate, or in public life during the period of independence, and they had resisted Şahin Giray's attempts at modernization. Influenced by the local Muslim clergy and centuries of tradition, they found it difficult to adjust to the new ways required by the Russian authorities. It was not long before the new Russian bureaucrats in the Crimea recognized this problem.

Individually, Tatar peasants had always been legally free. They owed certain duties and taxes to *mirzas* who held the right to use the lands on which the peasants lived. There had never been serfdom in any form in the khanate. Alexander I's land commission had found itself defending the free Tatar peasants against the Russian *pomeshchiks*' growing claims for the introduction of serfdom among them. It was particularly Sumarokov who prevented this from taking place. Although some of the Tatars claimed that, according to a long-standing Tatar tradition, the lands given to *pomeshchiks* should have been included in the land granted to the Tatar peasants, the commission decided that this would be going too far. It did decide, however, that the labor and dues the *pomeshchiks* could expect would be based on the principles that had prevailed among the Tatars before the annexation. The very same portions of peasant income that the khans and *mirzas* had received before 1783 was now to be taken by the Russian *pomeshchiks*.[38]

Catherine had determined that imperial interests would be best served if the peasants' free status were preserved, yet she found that she had to incorporate them into the Russian class of state peasants to do it. This created difficulties for Russian *pomeshchiks* who had been granted title to the peasants' lands. Governor Naryshkin noted in 1823 that the *pomeshchik*, "receiving land with Tatars living on it, did not have the right to consider it as his property. He could neither drive the Tatars away nor lay upon them duties as he wished."[39]

This policy hindered the government's anticipated expansion of agriculture in the Crimea. It also provided a motive for both *pomeshchiks* and certain bureaucrats to persuade Tatar peasants to leave for the interior where they would lose their legal status, and at the same time free up their old land for serfdom. Yet the Tatars who proved resistant found that many of the local governors could be counted upon to protect them from illegal *pomeshchik* pressure.[40]

When many peasants were removed from the coast during the Crimean War, *pomeshchiks* took advantage of the opportunity it afforded and made a great effort to prevent their return. They imposed higher taxes and duties on returning Tatars and seized village water supplies, forcing many peasants to remain inland, or as a last resort, to emigrate to the Ottoman Empire. By this time, the government's policy of protecting the peasants had eroded, and the growing weakness of the Tatar *mirzas* and the strength of the Slavic immigrants caused the peasants serious problems.[41]

The emancipation of the serfs in 1861 created new problems for the peasantry in the Crimea. How the government considered state peasants residing on *pomeshchik* lands and how it created new relationships that were in line with those existing in interior provinces are not fully known. There have been no studies that are based on archival sources and address these questions, and published sources provide only fragmentary and inadequate explanations of the results of the emancipation decree and the following peasant legislation as they concerned the Crimea.

Aside from Alexander II's encouragement of those wishing to leave the Russian Empire, the only documents uncovered mention the creation in the Crimea of a committee to oversee the changing conditions of *pomeshchik* peasants, the closing of all district land commissions and rural administrations, and the opening of the new *volost'* (local peasant community) governments. Yet until that collected by the *zemstvos* later in the century, there is virtually no evidence that helps to clarify the effects of the emancipation on the Tatar peasants or nobility.[42]

Russian Colonization

The greatest pressure applied on the Tatar population came from the growing Slavic colonization the government was encouraging. There can be no question that, from Catherine II's time, the administration viewed the Crimea both as a great potential economic resource and as an exotic place to live. Catherine had granted more than a tenth of the land on the peninsula to favorites and other officials; most of these grants were in parcels of from 500 to 2000 *desiatins*. The largest grant was over 20,000 *desiatins*. All of the land granted by the government during these first decades of Russian rule came from lands confiscated from Tatar owners who had emigrated after 1783 and from the khan's own holdings.

Certain parcels of the most valuable coastal property, which was useful for vineyard production, were assigned on contract to foreign businessmen. The first of these was a Frenchman, Josef Blanc, who received the right to use land near Sudak for wine production and for a vodka factory.[43]

The government found it difficult to persuade as many landowners and peasants as it wished to move to the Crimea. Some *pomeshchiks* preferred to use the Tatar peasants already living on the land. Of course they found it impossible to force state peasants to leave. One scholar estimates that, by 1793, Russian landowners had been able to bring only 226 male serfs to the Crimea, although they were more successful in settling the other areas of Novorossiia.[44]

Instead, the Russians were forced to import various other nationalities to fill up what appeared to be unnecessarily empty and unproductive land. Old Believers, Armenians, Greeks, Bulgarians, Germans, and even Swiss colonists were welcomed to the Crimea with handsome grants of land and financial privileges. A Swiss colony took root near Feodosiia, a German colony near Simferopol', and a Bulgarian one on the river Alma.[45]

Yet the total number of settlers and colonists in the Crimea by the end of the eighteenth century was disappointing. Sumarokov, on the basis of the findings of the land commission on which he served, estimated that by 1802, the total number of settlers amounted to 4500 and the total of *pomeshchik* peasants to only 8700. This was in a total population of more than 185,000.[46]

The government continued its policy of encouraging colonization and settlement by any possible means during the rest of the nineteenth century. Between 1820 and 1860, this policy was much more successful. On the southern coast of the peninsula, where both climate and land were superior to that in the north, village and town settlement intensified so that by 1854, out of a total population of more than 250,000, the Tatars accounted for only 150,000, the Russians accounted for more than 70,000, and Greeks, Armenians, Germans, and Jews made up the rest.[47]

After the Crimean War, a new set of privileges (financial and social) was promised to settlers coming to the Crimea. In 1862, anyone deciding to settle in a Crimean city or town would be given special privileges in the urban corporations not ordinarily available to newcomers. In the same year, money was set aside to pay for land purchase and living expenses for any foreigners coming to settle in the Crimea from the Ottoman Empire.[48]

The war with the Ottoman Empire in 1877 provoked another massive Tatar emigration, which continued on a more gradual basis until 1902. In a desperate attempt to counter this movement and to encourage some Tatars to return, the government took the unprecedented action of promising complete pardon and forgiveness to any Crimean Tatars who "ran away from their homes, and who now wish to return to their homeland." This proved unsuccessful, however, and by the 1890s, agricultural as well as urban labor shortages forced the government to import labor from interior provinces and the Caucasus.[49]

In summary, the social policies of the government during the first two-thirds of the nineteenth century compounded the ruin and uprooting of the traditional Tatar social structure that had taken place before 1783. The *mirza* class was decimated through emigration and Slavic displacement; the economic basis of their position had crumbled. Those Tatar nobles who had become fully *dvoriane* were essentially Russified, thereby satisfying official requirements for loyalty. Thus Alexander II could at the same time encourage deportation and emigration, and establish loyal Tatar military units for his own service. The Tatar urban class had diminished in size and importance and was isolated in the two central Tatar towns, both of which were outside of the mainstream of Crimean society. Tatar peasants, after an auspicious start, suffered a setback of major proportions as a result of the government's policies during the Crimean War. It became clear that if a Crimean Tatar national identity or movement were to appear, it would have to emerge from a new configuration of Tatar society.

10. The Crimean Tatar National Awakening

The emergence of a national movement among the Crimean Tatars took place in the last quarter of the nineteenth century. A part of an all-Muslim and all-Turkic awakening in the Russian Empire, it was a particularly Crimean movement as well. The national movement arose from two conflicts that were separate, yet related. On the one hand was the conflict between the Muslim population and the Russian government; on the other was a conflict within the Muslim community between the traditional clergy and a new Tatar intelligentsia that was striving for modernization and a new Tatar identity. The potential incompatibility of these two conflicts caused internal contradictions in the Crimean Tatar renaissance. How to become modernized without succumbing to the Westernized culture of the Russians was the most difficult problem the new Tatar leadership had to face. The policies pursued by the tsarist government since the end of the eighteenth century had caused this conflict to develop within the Tatar community.

Destruction of Tatar Architecture

Russian cultural policy toward the Tatars may be divided into two parts; one part deals with the Muslim cultural heritage and the other with strictly religious matters. Briefly, the Russians felt utter disrespect for the Muslim Tatar culture. Since they did not really consider the Crimea a Tatar province, most Russians considered monuments of Tatar culture that had survived the annexation to be reminders of a backward and uncivilized period. Most governors and bureaucrats made no effort to preserve any architectural reminders of the khanate period. Foreign visitors to the Crimea were horrified by the acts of destruction they were able to observe in all parts of the Crimea except for Bahçesaray. The cities, once the centers of Tatar cultural life, were now an exclusive preserve of non-Muslims who saw no reason to preserve useless buildings.

The first acting governor of the Crimea, V. V. Kakhovskii, ordered the destruction of many of the most priceless treasures of Tatar and Italian architecture. Later in the century, the traveler, Haxthausen, remarked that Kakhovskii had destroyed "the finest monuments of antiquity, amongst others a beautiful tower built by the Genoese, which had served as the minaret of the chief mosque in Kefe." In this regard, Professor Druzhinina wrote that "Kakhovskii was no better than his Mongol and Tatar predecessors."[1]

Edward Clarke, passing through the Crimea in 1809, wrote:

in Kaffa, the soldiers were allowed to overthrow the beautiful mosques, or to convert them into magazines, to pull down the minarets, tear up the public fountains, and to destroy all the public aqueducts for the sake of a small quantity of lead. . . .

In Karasu Bazaar, the Tatar cemeteries have been divested of their tombstones, and these have been broken or hewn so as to constitute materials for building. . . .

In Gözleve, its trade is annihilated; its houses in ruins; its streets desolate; the splendid mosques, by which it was adorned, are unroofed, and their minarets thrown down.[2]

Aleksandr Pushkin, who spent some time in the Crimea, described his impressions of Bahçesaray Palace, which had been converted into the residence of the Russian governor:

On entering the palace I saw a ruined fountain; water fell in drops from a rusty iron spout. I roamed about the palace, indignant at the carelessness with which it had been allowed to decay and at the half-European reconstruction of several of the rooms.[3]

Finally, Seymour, traveling in the Crimea in the 1850s, described the destruction that had taken place in Simferopol' in the 1830s:

In 1833, the Civil Governor, M. Kasnatchaief, in a most barbarous and ignorant manner, completed the work of destruction by attacking the great baths which had remained intact. He asked permission from Prince Vorontsov to enlarge the great square because it was too small for a parade ground. He received it, and set about destroying the mosque and the baths. In the space of a fortnight, by the aid of pickaxe and powder, both of these admirable monuments completely disappeared. In 1840, the great square was filled with their precious materials, which the local administration sold at the price of common stone. . . .

All the beautiful gardens, and the rich orchards, which surrounded the town in the time of the Tatars, have disappeared. One single winter was sufficient for two Russian regiments to annihilate every trace of the brilliant cultivation which formerly covered the hills. . . .

Tall and stately minarets, whose lofty spires added such grace and dignity to the town, were daily levelled with the ground, which, besides their connection with the religious establishments for whose maintenance the Russian Empire had been pledged, were of no other value to their destroyers than to supply a few soldiers with bullets.[4]

To put these events into perspective, it is worthwhile to quote some statements from a recent Soviet account of Crimean history. At the beginning of the nineteenth century, as Nadinskii wrote:

> the Crimea was a frontier region. The Tatars were still nomadic or semi-nomadic. . . . Only Bahçesaray and Karasu Bazaar retained their backward medieval characteristics. . . . In this century the Crimea was introduced to Russian culture. It became an integral part of the Russian state. By the mid-nineteenth century, the Crimea had stepped forward on the path of progress and civilization.[5]

Russia and Crimean Islam

On the other hand, the tsarist government paid extraordinarily careful attention to religious matters. Pursuant to Catherine's enlightened policy toward Islam throughout the empire, the new regime introduced no religious persecution. Despite the fact that they were living under a colonial regime in the Crimea, the Muslim dignitaries became a part of the regime itself. Regulated by the government, receiving much of their income from the Russians, they were supportive of the tsarist system. As a result of the annexation manifesto, which stated that "all Muslim clergy, existing in the time of Khan Şahin Giray, are to remain in their positions, and to retain their former authority," the government consistently pursued a policy of allowing much initiative to the Crimean clergy.[6]

Catherine had separated religious from civil matters, and had permitted religious governance to operate on different principles from those of social and political life. She had established a Muslim Committee of Muslim dignitaries to supervise religious matters and instructed Russian bureaucrats to keep their distance from strictly Muslim religious matters.

In 1791, with the death of Mufti Musalar Efendi, the stage was set for Russian involvement with the upper Tatar clergy. On the recommendation of the Crimean governor, the *kadiasker,* Seit Mehmet Efendi, took his place. The governor said that the new *mufti* was "a person filled with loyalty toward the Throne, faithful to his duty, intelligent, and just." On the new *mufti*'s advice, the governor reformed the *kadiasker*'s position into a new "spiritual office" consisting of six "well-chosen" members of the upper Crimean Muslim clergy, chaired by Abdurahim Efendi.[7]

One looks in vain through these early decisions and administrative acts concerning the clergy to find any clear exposition of duties and responsibilities, other than a call for continuation of procedures done as of old. Probably this was the result of general confusion in the imperial government about administrative procedures in all areas of the empire, confusion stemming from the absence of a cohesive legislative code to replace the outmoded Sobornoe Ulozhenie of 1649.

It was not until 1831 that comprehensive legislation was enacted putting the Crimean Muslim establishment into a form resembling other imperial institutions. Although much happened in the Tatar Muslim community during the ensuing seventy-five years, the 1831 edict survived with only minor revisions until 1914.[8]

First, the 1831 edict repeated Catherine's philosophy of separation of civil from religious governance and explained that the Crimean Muslim Religious Committee would retain all responsibility for matters bearing on Muslim religious life. Its competency would include the examination and resolution according to Muslim law, of all questions about "personal property, originating from inheritance, or from division of property among heirs; questions of marriage and divorce; questions of orphaned minors; questions of religious observances and punishments; and questions of assessments of religious fees and financial support levied upon the Muslim population." The clergy was exempted from all imperial taxes and levies so long as it upheld the regulations contained in this edict. Despite the fact that everywhere else the government was trying to rationalize the Russian legal system and to weed out local peculiarities, in the Crimea the government accepted and legalized those very differences.

Second, the edict defined and enumerated all of the positions within the Crimean clergy, including the *mufti,* the *kadiasker,* and the *imam*s, *mulla*s, and other mosque servitors in each parish. Finally, it listed the *muderris* and *hoca*s in the local Muslim schools.

The top officials were to be selected in elections supervised by the Department of Spiritual Affairs in Simferopol', and participated in by the upper level of the Muslim clergy, the marshal of the *guberniia* nobility, and the Muslim elders throughout the Crimea. The Muslim Committee on which these officials sat had within its jurisdiction all mosques and their schools and *tekke*s, as well as all *vakif* land.

This edict of 1831 was an unusual document because it provided for the maintenance of local particularism to a degree not pursued elsewhere in the empire. Its closest parallel was the Code of the Steppe of 1822, but the situation in the Crimea was not comparable to that in central and eastern Siberia. The main effect of the edict on the upper clergy was to tie it more closely to the interests of the throne—to recruit, in effect, the Muslim dignitaries as agents of the tsars in the Crimea. It likewise succeeded in creating a gap between the clergy and the Tatar *mirza*s, who were experiencing a policy of Russification on the one hand and exclusion from local politics on the other.

Later Russian legislation concerning the Crimean Muslim clergy merely refined the principles stated in the original edict. In 1832, the Simferopol' Muslim Committee was required to maintain a register of births, deaths, and marriages of Crimean Muslims. The next year, a decree prohibited Russian district courts from interfering in cases within the jurisdiction of the Crimean *mufti* and *kadi*s. In 1834, the government accepted the *mufti*'s recommendation for a method of registering parishioners in local mosques. In 1855, provision was made for appointment of an *imam* to travel with the Crimean Tatar Light Guard Squadron. Even as late as 1891, after the policy of Russification had been carried to an extreme by Alexander III, a decree from the State Council ratified the choice made by the Crimean Muslim community for a new *mufti* and a new *kadiasker*. In 1910, there were more than 1500 Crimean Tatar clergy registered with the Simferopol' Muslim Committee.[9]

Education

By allowing the Muslim clergy a monopoly over Tatar education, the government encouraged cultural traditionalism. Since tsarism had effectively wrecked the secular structure of Tatar society, this policy ensured that the Tatars had no social defense against Westernism. The Russians insisted that only a sense of traditional religious identity remain intact. When in the great reform period (1861–1876) the regime installed among the Tatars, as elsewhere, a *zemstvo* system and Western schools, the predictable result was the emergence of an intelligentsia free of the old social structures, but still consciously Tatar.

From the start, in order to compete with the Muslim schools for the loyalty of Tatar youth, the Russians offered schools in the Crimea in which the Russian language was taught.[10] But in the early years, these Russian schools were unsuccessful; they had little or no influence upon the Crimean Tatar upper classes until much later. In fact, in 1830, the decision was made to concentrate on the Russian education of Tatar children in Odessa, rather than in the Crimean peninsula.[11]

Demidoff reported that a "Tatar normal school," opened in 1828 in Simferopol', was tied administratively to the new Russian university in Odessa. "Turkish and Arabic and the Koran were taught. Upon leaving the school, the student had to serve the state for six years." He further wrote that Bahçesaray had three *medresse*s that were open to young Tatars "who are destined to be employed as civil servants or in the mosques. The *efendi*s teach the dogmas of religion to the students."[12]

Zemstvos

After 1860 the government stepped up its competition with Muslim schools, taking measures to increase the enrollment of children of lower-ranking Tatars in Russian schools. These schools increased greatly in number between 1877 and 1898, while they were under the direction of the new *zemstvo* organizations in the Crimea. But even here the vast majority were Muslim and Tatar in orientation, not Russian. Both their staff and the direction of their curriculum were controlled by the Muslim Committee in Simferopol'.[13]

The extension of the *zemstvo* reforms to the Crimea brought about important changes and innovations in Tatar society. The schools they established and funded became, in time, the source for a new Tatar intelligentsia. Tatars became represented in positions ranging from school staff members to sanitation workers and medical personnel, gained important experience in government and social service, and gradually replaced the old and weakened Tatar elite.

Veselovskii provides many statistics concerning *zemstvo* activities in the Crimea. After a close perusal of them, one is impressed with the rapid growth in expenditures in all areas of *zemstvo* activity, much of which benefited the Tatar population. In Simferopol' and Perekop districts, both heavily Tatar, *zemstvo* expenditures rose fourfold from 1877 to 1903. In the Feodosiia and Ialta districts, both almost exclusively non-Tatar in population, expenditures during the same period rose about threefold. This may have reflected greater need in the Tatar areas because of lower literacy rates (in Russian) and less advanced medical facilities. The breakdown on expenditures by percentage shows that in these two Tatar districts, medical outlays were significantly higher than in the more purely Russian districts.[14]

Yet by 1898, in Simferopol' district there was only one doctor for each 14,000 population while in Ialta district there was one doctor for every 7000 inhabitants. Even more telling are the figures for hospitals and usable beds. In Simferopol' there were three hospitals with a total of 9 beds. In Ialta, there were six hospitals with 70 beds, and in Dneprovsk district, ten hospitals with 157 beds.[15] Yet, all of this said, the Tatars had reason to be satisfied with those areas of *zemstvo* activity that touched their lives. It is no surprise that the next generation of Tatar elite would lavish great praise on the *zemstvo* movement.

The new Tatar intelligentsia that emerged from the *zemstvo* schools was not, however, revolutionary in outlook from the start. (Here lies the difference between the Tatar development and that in Poland, where the Russians encouraged the survival, until 1863, of the old social structure.) Indeed, because of the conservative clergy's control over Crimean schools before 1867, the first stirrings of reform originated outside of the Crimea. The first such ideas for change in Tatar Muslim education began in the 1850s in the Volga region among Kazan Tatars who were members of the urban bourgeoisie. The lack of such a group in the Crimea meant that such ideas did not easily find fertile ground there.

It was Shihabeddin Merjani, a Kazan Tatar, who started the movement for Tatar Muslim reform. A historian and educator, Merjani saw no contradiction between remaining faithful to one's Muslim heritage and learning Russian. He believed that the Turkic and Arabic languages, used by peoples and states hostile to Westernization and modernization, could not act as vehicles for the introduction of modern ideas into their societies. He knew of the advances that had been made in the first half of the century in Egypt under the tutelage of Muhammad Ali, who had found the French language to be an instrument of education among his Arab subjects. Merjani was not unfaithful to Islam; he was a firm believer who was convinced that Islam's survival depended upon its adaptation to the modern world.[16]

Gaspirali

In the Crimea, the initiator of the new Tatar intelligentsia was Ismail Bey Gaspirali (Gasprinskii), a student of the ideas of Merjani. Emerging from an impoverished Tatar *dvorianstvo* family, Gaspirali began his education in the traditional village *medresse*. With the encouragement of a friend in the city merchant guild, Gaspirali went on, first to St. Petersburg to learn Russian, then to Paris to learn French, returning five years later to the Crimea in 1866.[17]

In 1871, Gaspirali went to Istanbul; for the next four years he spent his time studying in Istanbul and in Paris. In Istanbul he learned of the activities of the Young Ottomans; in Paris he made contact with both liberals and socialists. Returning to Bahçesaray in 1875, he became acquainted with Merjani's ideas, and on the basis of his experiences in Europe, he concluded that Merjani's prescriptions for Islam were the paths Muslims should follow. The way to modernity for Russia's Muslims was inexorably tied to the Russian language and culture. This view of his has been a difficult one for Crimean Tatars in the twentieth century to accept.

Upon his return to Bahçesaray in 1875, Gaspirali was named instructor of the Russian language at the *medresse* there. He occupied this post for two years, during which time he studied some of the Russian Slavophiles, particularly Katkov, and began to develop the foundations for his nationalist ideas. In 1877, the Tatars of Bahçesaray elected him mayor of the city, a position he filled for five years. In 1881, he resigned to devote his time to education and journalism.[18]

Both his origins in the class that had suffered most during the nineteenth century and his training in traditional Islamic subjects, followed by his exposure to what must have appeared to his countrymen as a somewhat fantastic society in Russia and France, led him to introduce among the Tatars the first internal challenges to their inherited traditions. Convinced that his own Crimean society was in danger of complete internal collapse because its traditions were too weak to resist political and social assaults from Russian

Ismail Bey Gaspirali

pressure, he believed that only two options faced the Crimean Tatars—and indeed the whole of the Russian Islamic community. The first was their complete assimilation into Russian society via Russification; the second, a renewal of Islamic and Tatar society through an acceptance of Western (Russian) forms enclosing an Islamic and Tatar content.

Ironically, Gaspirali felt that assimilation would be the inevitable result of permitting the Muslim clergy a continued monopoly over Tatar education, since their extreme conservatism and outmoded curriculum could not prepare the Tatars to resist Russification. Only an adoption of Russian educational and cultural methods could form a class of Tatars that would be able to retain the best of their own traditions. This put him in the awkward position of advocating both the study of the Russian language and the introduction of Western (Russian) natural and social sciences into the curricula of Tatar schools. Only students who had mastered such skills, he felt, would be equipped to resist Russian encroachment upon their Islamic society.

These views placed Gaspirali in the company of such reactionary Russian officials and educators as the curator of the Odessa School District who, in 1870, had presented to Count Tolstoi a memorandum claiming that the government had been lax in its dealings with the empire's Muslims and that these latter must be required to learn Russian. Gaspirali realized the risk that such a policy incurred for the Muslims, a risk aptly reflected in Tolstoi's response that "the official aim of education for all natives must indisputably be their Russification and their merging with the Russian people."[19]

In 1881, Gaspirali published his first important book, *Russkoe musul-manstvo,* in which he called for the total and immediate modernization of Russian Islam. He believed that Russia "would be one of the greatest Muslim states in the world," that Russia was the heir to the former Tatar possessions, and that sooner or later Russians and Tatars would enjoy the same rights. He was convinced that the government would sooner or later abandon its idea of Russification. He wrote:

> I believe . . . that the Russian Muslims shall be more civilized than any other Muslim nation. We are a steady nation; give us the possibility to learn. You, great brothers, give us knowledge. The sciences should be admitted to the Tatar schools, and in the Tatar language. New schools should be erected in Baku, Tashkent, Kazan. The teachers should be graduated from a specially organized Russian Eastern university, in the same way as in India, where the pupils are educated in Indian schools, and in the Indian language. The Russians and Muslims shall come to an understanding in this way.[20]

Two years later, on April 10, 1883, Gaspirali introduced his journal, *Tercuman-Perevodchik.* In its editorial, Gaspirali wrote:

> Exactly one hundred years ago, on April 8, 1783, the small khanate, worn out by disorder and bloodshed, was made a part of the greatest empire in the world and received peace under the patronage of a mighty power and the protection of just laws. . . .

> Celebrating this day together with all the other peoples (of the Russian Empire) the Crimean Muslims cannot fail to recall all of those good deeds by which they have already profited for one hundred years.[21]

In the early issues of *Tercuman,* Gaspirali called for the modernization of Russian Islam, the equality of women in the Muslim world, the creation of a single Turkic language to be used in the press, and with it the establishment of a single Turkic educated elite uniting those in the Russian and Ottoman empires. In addition, he developed the idea that one Turkic language could serve all Turks. This was not a pan-Islamic theme but rather one of pan-Turkism. Indeed, "Turkness" was proclaimed as the one category to which all Turks belonged (Türkçülük).[22]

The only path to this revival was through education. In his own school in Bahçesaray, he began a new method for education, in which traditional Islamic subjects such as the study of the Koran and the fundamentals of Islamic law remained in the curriculum in Arabic; added to this base he introduced history, geography, and mathematics in Russian and Tatar. He wrote: ". . . Schools must open the way for our language and for our literature. It must bring us to a common understanding. The evolution of our languages has brought us to the point where we are unable to understand one another. . . ."[23]

The new language he called for was to be based on that called for by the Young Ottomans, a Turkic language purged of its many Arabic and Persian components. The slogan for his new-method education and for his journal *Tercuman* was *Dilde, Fikirde, Işte birlik.* ("In language, in thought, in work, unity.")[24]

At the start, *Tercuman* did not have a large readership, but it was widely spread throughout the Muslim world. In 1885, it had about 1000 subscriptions of which 300 were in the Crimea, 300 in the Muslim Volga region, 150 in Dagestan, 50 in Siberia, and 200 in central Asia; by 1907, its readership had increased to more than 5000 copies of each issue. In 1912, *Tercuman* had subscribers not only in the Russian Empire, but in Istanbul, Cairo, Kashgar, and India. The Soviet Orientalist, Samoilovich, wrote that its language in 1910 presented no great difficulties for the educated readers of Turkey, the Caucasus, the Transcaspian region, the Volga provinces, and Turkestan, indicating that, over the years, Gaspirali's efforts had had results.[25]

Gaspirali was always careful to direct his followers away from political opposition against the Russian government. Convinced that an attitude openly hostile to the imperial regime would be crushed quickly, he argued that there was no contradiction between supporting tsarism and striving for Muslim Tatar reform and national identity. Any struggle against Russia would be impossible and Islam would actually benefit from cooperation with Russia.

This view he expressed most clearly in 1896 in his essay entitled *Russkoe vostochnoe soglashenie,* in which he wrote:

> Muslims and Russians can plow, sow, raise cattle, trade, and make their livings together, or side by side. . . . We think that sooner or later Russia's borders will include within them all of the Tatar peoples. . . . If Russia could have good relations with Turkey and Persia, she would become kindred to the entire Muslim east, and would certainly stand at the head of Muslim nations and their civilizations, which England is attempting so persistently to do.[26]

With the old Tatar elite gone, and the clergy in the hands of the tsarist government, Gaspirali had to produce a new audience for these views. This he found among the Tatar youth attending or recently graduated from either Russian-Tatar schools or his own new-method *medresse.* Not all would accept his answers, yet all found it necessary to address themselves to the problems he voiced.

Gaspirali's Followers

Three chronologically different groups of Tatar intelligentsia emerged as a result of Gaspirali's efforts: Gaspirali's followers, the Young Tatars, and the Tatar nationalists. Not surprisingly, the first was closely tied to the master himself, and like him, was not revolutionary. It accepted his ideas and joined him in pressing for cooperation between Muslim and Russian. By 1905, this group had succeeded in establishing within the Crimea over 350 national schools, in which the languages of instruction were both Russian and the Turkic of *Tercuman*. These intellectuals were closely associated with the leadership of the Russian pan-Turkic and pan-Muslim movements that took advantage of the 1905–1906 disruptions to press for improvement for Russia's Muslim communities.

In March 1905, along with the Volga Tatar, Rashid Ibrahimov, Gaspirali called a meeting of a large number of Tatar intellectuals and social and economic leaders in Kazan to discuss problems of mutual interest and concern. This meeting produced a commitment to convene an all-Muslim congress later in the year. Also as a result of this meeting, a petition was sent to the government asking for elimination of many practices considered detrimental to the furtherance of Tatar and Muslim development. The government refused either to accept the petition or to permit the Tatars to hold their congress.

To take the place of the congress, Gaspirali planned an excursion on the Volga on the pleasure cruiser *Gustav Struve* to be convened in August 1905 near Nizhnii Novgorod. At this meeting, called "The Congress on the Waters," Muslim participants from all over the Russian Empire decided to organize a union (*Ittifak*) that would press for their mutual interests. Gaspirali was an important spokesman there for Crimean points of view. A second congress was held in St. Petersburg in January 1906. It created the *Ittifak* and organized Muslim activity in conjunction with forthcoming elections to the newly convened First Imperial Duma. This congress decided to unite their votes with those of the Kadet party.[27]

It was clear that this first group of Crimean Tatar intellectuals supported Gaspirali's desire to work within the Russian system and to participate in the new political institutions alongside of Russian liberals. Even the reactionary electoral laws issued for the Second Duma, which were aimed at reducing participation of non-Russians and workers and peasants, did not dissuade Gaspirali from retaining his hopes for a change of heart by the regime when times became calmer. But the law stated that "The State Duma, created to strengthen the Russian state, must be Russian also in its spirit."[28] And the Crimean clergy was putting more pressure on the government to remove even Gaspirali's relatively harmless group from circulation.

The Young Tatars

These attitudes persuaded a number of Crimean intellectuals that Gaspirali's dreams were unrealistic. This second generation of the new Crimean intelligentsia was more revolutionary in both form and content of their beliefs than Gaspirali, and they reacted against what they considered Gaspirali's political inaction. Even during the revolution, *Tercuman* had remained apolitical and did not provide either commentary on or suggestions about the revolutionary events. Thus it did not provide the sort of leadership that a growing leftist movement among Tatar intellectuals wanted. A liberal Kazan Turk, Abdullah Takac, articulated the four major criticisms of Gaspirali and his journal that represented the thinking of a growing number of Tatar intellectuals both inside and outside the Crimea: (1) *Tercuman* was written in the Crimean dialect, and thus was not understandable by other Tatars; (2) Gaspirali was a bureaucratic and monarchistic reactionary (he had sided with the bourgeois liberals represented by the Kadets who supported the idea of a continuation of the centralized Russian state); (3) he had shown himself too often amenable to the despotism of the Ottoman sultan; and (4) he was a scholastic writer and totally behind the times.[29]

In the Crimea this viewpoint was expressed by Abdurreşit Mehdi, from a peasant family of Perekop. Abdurreşit had been educated in a Tatar normal school, and he taught in a Russian-Tatar school in Karasu Bazaar. Concerned with neither pan-Islamic nor pan-Turkic ideas, his attention was directed toward the problems of the Tatars living in the Crimea. His political aim included an active struggle for the "national, social, and political liberation of the Crimean Tatar people," which would involve a "struggle against the statist autocratic system of tsarist Russia."[30]

Mehdi, though, had not removed himself so far from support of the Russian system as to reject his election as a delegate to the Second Duma, in spite of the harsh electoral law. In the Duma he served as secretary of the Duma Faction of the Union of Russian Muslims and led his own small group called the Young Tatars. The Young Tatars did not unite their activities with the Kadets, however, and found a greater affinity of views with the Socialist Revolutionaries. In a petition from the Young Tatars to the Duma, Mehdi declared:

> Our misery proves that our riches are in the pockets of others; the treasury, the financial interests. . . . Our people include 50,000 peasants without land — so that the lands of the *vakifs*, the state, and the proprietors of the crown remain unproductive, nourishing only a few privileged ones. All these lands have in the past belonged to the Tatar people; all have now passed into the hands of others.[31]

Both the Crimean delegation to the Second Duma and many Crimean Tatar members of the All-Russian Muslim movements in the next decade were more self-consciously nationalistic than Turks and Tatars from other groups who, until the end, continued to speak in terms of pan-Islam or pan-Turkism. Some historians have suggested that the preference for cultural rather than territorial autonomy expressed by the Volga Tatars at the Duma meetings was a function of their not having an easily defined territory of their own. Yet by this time the Crimean Tatars were a distinct minority in the Crimea too, and it seems that the differences in approach were rather a function of the distinctly different social and cultural policies of the tsarist regime in the two areas during the century.

With the dissolution of the Duma, Mehdi returned to the Crimea where he served as mayor of Karasu Bazaar until his death in 1912. Between 1906 and 1909, the Young Tatars published a newspaper, *Vatan Hadimi*, in Karasu Bazaar. As the bannerline of the journal, Medhi and the journal's editor, Hasan Sabri Ayvaz, chose the saying of Muhammad: "Love of the nation is love of the faith."[32]

An interesting series of documents from the chancery of Tavricheskaia guberniia, concerning the opening of the *Vatan Hadimi* and its editor, Ayvaz, was published by Krichinskii. From these documents it appears that the tsarist authorities were well aware of both the dangers inherent in the Young Tatar movement and the abilities of its leadership. Yet the paper survived for a surprisingly long time before the government suppressed it in late 1909.[33]

In reaction to the avowedly nationalistic aims of Mehdi and the Young Tatars, Gaspirali began publication of a second journal, *Millet* ("Nation"), in which he tried to regain the attention of Tatar youth. With a stroke of genius, he hired Ayvaz as editor of the new journal the moment the *Vatan Hadimi* was closed by the authorities. Gaspirali also tried to gain the support of the more radical Tatar leaders by publishing *Aslem-i Nisvan*, a journal for Tatar women. An illustrated literary review edited by Gaspirali's daughter Şefika, *Aslem-i Nisvan* continued the general striving for Muslim enlightenment for which Gaspirali had worked so hard. It, along with *Millet*, was finally closed down by the government in 1910.[34]

Tatar Nationalists

A third group of Tatar intellectuals emerged after 1907. This group, which developed in the midst of the Young Turk movement, was based in Istanbul. For some time, large numbers of Crimean students had continued their Muslim education in Istanbul after completion of their studies in Russian-Tatar normal schools. In 1908, under the influence of the Young Turks,

Crimean students founded a Crimean Student Society (Kirim Talebe Cemiyeti) with Noman Çelebi Cihan as chairman, Cafer Seidahmet as secretary, and Alimseyyid Cemil as treasurer. While this society remained a completely legal organization until its end in 1917, an illegal offshoot, called Vatan, appeared in 1909. Its unabashed goal was an independent Crimean state. Vatan's members engaged in continuous conspiratorial activity in the Crimea, and by the beginning of 1917, Vatan had succeeded in forming secret nationalist cells in almost all Crimean towns and villages. After 1910, Vatan issued proclamations against the tyranny of tsardom, and called for the introduction of ideas of *Tatarcilik* ("Tatarness") in the Crimea to replace Gaspirali's *Türkçülük*.

According to the Tatar historian/politician, Kirimal, "the interaction of these three streams of nationalist thought (Gaspirali, the Young Tatars, and Vatan) . . . gradually prepared the ground for a broad popular nationalist movement among the Crimean Tatars that came into the open in March 1917."[35]

By the beginning of World War I, the Crimean Tatar community bore almost no relation to that which had existed in 1783. With the large number of Tatar schools pursuing a curriculum modernized under the direction of Gaspirali, a new generation of Tatar leaders was coming of age. Participation in imperial political life in the Dumas and a close association with other Muslim groups in the empire, had given the leaders of the Crimean Tatars a broader horizon on which to view their own predicament. Yet they were not united. The fact that the Muslim clergy—those Tatar leaders most closely associated with the Tatar traditions—were tied to the interests and policies of the Russian regime, forced the new intellectuals to search in other directions for their new identity. And in this search, many fell victim to the quicksand of Western influences and rejected many elements of their past that were necessary for their national identity.

This does not mean that the Crimean Tatars were unsuccessful between 1917 and 1928 in creating the foundations for a national existence. Thanks to the peculiarities of tsarist policy in the first half of the nineteenth century, which did the work of destroying the Tatar old regime, Tatar society and its intelligentsia were more advanced in the national sense in 1921 than many other groups in old Russia.

But there was a degree of shallowness in Tatar political life during and after the revolutions of 1917; this was a direct result of the contradictions that a century of Russian policy in the Crimea had produced. The difficult questions Tatar leaders had to answer between 1917 and 1921 were not unlike those Professor von Grunebaum has identified as the stumbling blocks for Arab nationalists in the twentieth century:

Not the perfecting of potential or heritage was the objective of the admission of Western influence, but the removal of what was felt to be an inferiority . . . The question was not what to adopt, whence to select, but rather, what to retain, or perhaps even, was there in the traditional culture anything worth retaining.[36]

PART THREE

THE CRIMEAN TATARS AND THE USSR

11. The Russian Revolution and the Tatars

The First World War produced a crisis for the Crimean Tatars—in terms of both their identity and their loyalty toward the Russian government. The Tatars had been developing a national movement within the Russian system, participating in the Dumas, and leading various Muslim congresses. Their economic and cultural life had steadily improved after 1906. At the beginning of the war, there was no reason for the Tatars to oppose Russia's war aims against Germany and Austria; in fact, there was every reason for them to take part in the war in as effective a manner as possible in hopes of cultural and economic rewards.

However, war against the Ottoman Empire caused problems. These arose, not because of any special feeling of the Tatars toward the Ottoman government, but rather as a result of Russian policies against what they believed to be a potential Muslim fifth column supporting the Turks. The record of the leaders of the Crimean Tatar community during the war indicates that their movement for national separation did not begin until the war was almost half over. It emerged as an act of self-defense on the part of the Tatars and other Muslims in the face of a growing Russian hostility toward them.

Even as late as January 1912, the Crimean Tatar leadership was not in favor of the pan-Turkic movement then receiving strong support and encouragement in Istanbul. In a major dispute between Gaspirali and the pan-Turk, Yusuf Akçura, the Crimeans took the position that the Turks in the Russian

Empire had a historical destiny separate from those in the rest of the world.[1] In spite of this, the pan-Turks had sent a number of representatives to the Crimea between 1908 and the outbreak of the war, and their presence led Russian officials to fear a growth of possible sympathy toward the Ottomans once the war began.

In 1912, Crimean police arrested Haci Seyyid Haffa, a Muslim clergyman in Simferopol', for having Ottoman newspapers in his possession. In Simferopol' during the same year, a meeting of Tatars discussing the Ottoman war in the Balkans, was broken up by police and three Tatars were arrested. On both occasions, the provincial police were aided in their investigations and arrests by leaders of the Crimean Tatar clergy, who were also against close Ottoman-Tatar ties.[2]

During the first years of the war, regiments of Crimean Tatar cavalrymen were used on the western front. According to Russian records, they "stood up well in action."[3] But the administration in the Crimea was taking no chances; it pursued a policy of increasing suppression of Tatar cultural and national life. Police agents often interfered with Tatar religious and educational activities. Any discussion of historic Tatar ties with the rest of the Turkic world was prohibited. Newspapers and journals that had achieved such a sound foundation after 1906 were subjected to severe censorship and outright closings. Actions deemed favorable toward the Ottomans were magnified by the police into "intense agitation for the unification of all Crimean Muslims with the Ottomans."[4]

League of Non-Russian Nationalities

During the war years, the more outspoken defenders of Crimean Tatar rights were forced to flee the Crimea to avoid arrest. Among them were Çelebi Cihan and Cafer Seidahmet, both of whom became leaders of the 1917 Crimean national movement. Along with other Muslim exiles in the Ottoman Empire, these men formed the Committee for the Defense of the Rights of Muslim Turko-Tatar Peoples of Russia (*Rusya Musulman Türk-Tatarlarin hukukunu müdafaa komitesi*). This action played into the hands of the Russian administration, which was now given irrefutable proof of the absence of Turko-Tatar loyalty.[5]

In Istanbul, however, this committee found little support for its position, and it soon moved its center of activity to Switzerland. From this neutral base, the Crimean Tatars and other Russian Muslims presented their positions to both the German government and representatives of the Entente powers. The message to both sides was that the Muslim peoples within the Russian Empire were being systematically denied the right to their national and cultural development; that their minimal demands for an autonomous existence within Russia were being ignored; and that whatever the war's outcome, they needed the victors' help to gain these rights. In May 1916, the committee formed the League of Non-Russian Nationalities in Lausanne, and sent President Wilson of the United States a telegram that read:

> From the first days of the war, the Russians fostered an ardent patriotism that rendered any participation by non-Russians impossible. Congresses were convened that were hostile toward Islam. Priests delivered sermons and published proclamations hostile toward Muslims. In the hospitals, Russians distributed to wounded Muslims, in spite of their protests, Bibles in the Tatar languages, instead of the Koran. They even forced many Muslim soldiers to adopt Christianity. . . . We do not want vague promises. We adhere entirely to the declaration of the progressive bloc. We demand the following measures: . . . the total end to restrictions against non-Russian cults and religions. . . . Our participation in the army, administration, courts, liberal professions is prohibited. . . . since the war, there has not been even the shadow of justice; we have been persecuted and brutalized without cause. . . . Come to our aid! Save us from destruction!

Among the signers of this declaration were the Crimean Tatars Cafer Seidahmet, Negi Kuku, and Habibullah Timurcan Odabaş.[6]

By 1917, the Crimean Tatars were psychologically prepared to support any movement to eliminate the tsarist regime, and to remove from the Crimea Russian institutions representing centralized state control and authority. Yet up to this time, most Tatar leaders had not worked with or belonged to either the Social Democrats or the Social Revolutionaries, which were the Russian revolutionary groups. In the Dumas, the Crimean delegates, except for the Young Tatars, had usually worked with other Muslim representatives. There is no evidence that Tatar soldiers on the western front were susceptible to Social Democratic propaganda. In fact, almost all of the socialist discussions during the war had been aimed at problems that were not especially evident in the Crimea.

On the peninsula itself, the only revolutionary groups that had been organized by 1917 were located in the coastal cities of Sevastopol' and Odessa, and neither of these cities had more than a minimal Tatar population. In addition, the Russian military forces in the Crimea were almost exclusively non-Tatar. It was probably a result of growing fears of Turkish-Tatar collusion that the tsarist government assigned all Tatar forces to the western rather than the southern front. Thus when the revolution occurred, the Tatars were militarily at a disadvantage in the Crimea. The few Tatar troops that could be gathered to support the new movement proved to be no match either for the Russians of the Black Sea fleet or for the German invaders.

The Crimean nationalist movement passed through three phases during the revolutionary months of 1917: (1) following the February Revolution, from March 25 until the middle of May, the Crimean Tatars struggled to achieve cultural autonomy; (2) from mid-May until November, they pressed claims for territorial autonomy; (3) finally, following the November Revolution, they struggled to establish an independent state.[7]

Struggle for Cultural Autonomy

After the February Revolution, the new Provisional Government had to face the agrarian and nationality problems, both of which were extremely important and sensitive. The nationality problem concerned the Crimean Tatars directly. The Provisional Government's declaration of April 9, 1917, on one hand promised to pursue more liberal policies toward the empire's Muslim inhabitants, while on the other it refused to recognize the nationalities' right to establish their own governments. Despite this fact, in its last weeks the Provisional Government did plan a reorganization in the national, cultural, and religious fields that, if enacted, would have given the non-Russian nationalities more of an independent identity than they had enjoyed at any time during the tsarist era. In planning this reorganization, Kerensky's government recognized certain *faits accomplis* that had produced local autonomy in many areas of civil and military administration. Muslim military detachments had been formed in Kazan, Ufa, the Urals, the Volga, and the Caucasus, as well as in the Crimea.

In Simferopol' on March 17, 1917, the day the Provisional Government took power, the Crimean Tatars took part in a large demonstration led by the brothers Tarpi and Bekir Mehmed. The group adopted the motto "Freedom, equality, brotherhood, and justice" for the Tatar movement.[8] The leadership, which was composed of Tarpi, historian Abdulhakim Hilmi Arifzade, Mehmed Vecdi, Çelebi Cihan, and Cafer Seidahmet, announced the convening of a Crimean Muslim conference in Simferopol' on March 25.

At the Simferopol' meeting, the future of the Crimea was discussed. More than 1500 Tatar representatives from all parts of the Crimea adopted a series of measures designed to install on the Crimean peninsula an autonomous administration concerned with cultural and religious affairs. This was the forerunner of the nationalist organizations that appeared later that year.[9]

Electing Çelebi Cihan as the new *mufti* of the Crimea, and Cafer Seidahmet as director of a new *vakif* commission, the conference set the stage for the growth of a Crimean Tatar national identity that moved quickly in the direction of cultural and territorial autonomy. Both elected individuals had been leaders of the Vatan organization, the most radically independent group in the Tatar intelligentsia. Interestingly, the conference concentrated at first on religious offices. The conference decided to nationalize the *vakif* lands, to give the people control over the religious institutions, and to elect a Muslim executive committee that would proclaim cultural and national autonomy for the Crimean Tatars and take charge of "all national, cultural, religious, and political affairs."[10]

Two other political developments that paralleled (and harmed) the Tatar national movement took place in the Crimea. First, the Russian Provisional Government established its own institutions of authority in the Crimea, and from the beginning, they were not receptive to ideas of Tatar autonomy. These organizations included the Commissariat of the Tauride, chaired by V. Bogdanov, who was a Ukrainian Kadet and a Kerensky supporter. The tsarist urban *dumas* and town administrations were retained. Relations between Bogdanov and the Tatar leaders were strained from the start and the result was an open split that took place in July.

The second development to harm the Tatar cause was the organization in the coastal cities of revolutionary groups led by representatives of the Social Revolutionaries and the Mensheviks. The first revolutionary council was created in Sevastopol' in the first days after the February Revolution and it soon established branches in Kerch, Feodosiia, Evpatoriia, and Ialta. Although Soviet historians understandably emphasize Bolshevik participation in this, they admit that the Bolsheviks in the Crimea in early 1917 amounted to at most a couple of dozen members.[11]

Thus, although with the founding of their conference and the election of a central executive committee of forty-five members the Crimean Tatars were relatively successful in creating the bases for cultural autonomy, on the question of territorial autonomy their task was more difficult. Both the representatives of the central government and the leadership of some other important Muslim groups in Russia opposed the Crimean Tatars on this question.

Struggle for Territorial Autonomy

Soon after the tsar's abdication, the Muslims in the State Duma met and decided to convene a new All-Russian Muslim Congress in May 1917 in Petrograd. The Crimean Tatars were represented by twenty-five delegates, led by Seidahmet. Discussing various problems common to the Muslims, the conference soon broke down into two factions over the question of national and territorial autonomy. The Crimean Tatars, who were entirely supportive of the idea of federalism with territorial self-rule for each of the Muslim nationalities, were joined in their stand by the Azeris, the Bashkirs, and the Dagestanis. The Volga Tatars, who lived in a variety of dispersed areas and did not enjoy a particular territorial identity, could hardly be expected to agree with this position, and they did not. The final vote on the question adopted territorial autonomy rather than purely cultural autonomy by more than a two-thirds majority. The adopted proposal stated: "The form of government that is most capable of protecting the interests of the Muslim peoples is a democratic republic based on the national, territorial, and federal principles, with national-cultural autonomy for the nationalities that lack a distinct territory."[12] The Congress also created a National Consultative Council (*Shura*) to prepare the way for convening an All-Russian Muslim Constituent Assembly (*Kurultay*) to create organs of national and cultural autonomy.

In June and July, the latent hostility between the local organs of the Provisional Government and that of the Crimean Tatars broke into open conflict. The more radical leaders of the Tatar intelligentsia formed a national party called the Milli Firka. Most of its directors were products of schools in the Ottoman Empire and western Europe, and for this reason Soviet historians have branded them "Turkish and foreign agents."[13] Figures such as Osman Akçokrakli, a historian and archaeologist and the new editor of *Tercuman,* do not fit into the "foreign agent" category, though, and the primary purpose of the new party was to give political identity to Tatar aspirations for autonomy.

The Milli Firka's ideology was much more leftist than that of the Tatars who had been working closely with the Kadets, and by supporting the ideas of nationalization of the church and private property, opposition to the conservative clergy, breaking off from contact with Russian liberals, and a closer cooperation with the socialist parties, it became the first truly revolutionary Crimean Tatar party. Indeed, after the November Revolution, many of its members joined the Bolsheviks and became important party and government functionaries in the early 1920s.[14] Clearly the Kadet-dominated local commissariat of the Provisional Government found it difficult to pursue a hands-off policy toward these new Tatar developments.

Further, both the Central Executive Committee and the left wing of the Milli Firka began, in July, to publish Tatar newspapers that were consistently critical of the Provisional Government's nationality policies. *Millet,* edited by a former editor of *Tercuman,* Hasan Sabri Ayvaz, appeared in Simferopol' at the beginning of July. It was closely followed by *Golos Tatar,* which was published as the official mouthpiece of the Central Executive Committee. A few days later there appeared the first issue of *Kirim Ocaği,* edited by Veli Ibrahimov and Mustafa Kurtmehmed. Ibrahimov became an important Tatar Communist official in the 1920s.[15]

On July 23, under orders from Bogdanov, chairman of the Crimean Commissariat, government soldiers arrested Çelebi Cihan and Şabarov (the commander of the Tatar military forces) and took them to Sevastopol' to answer charges of treason and antigovernmental activities. Demands such as "The Crimea for the Crimeans," which these leaders and other Tatar officials had been making for national and territorial autonomy for the Crimea had been both dangerous and unreasonable from the point of view of the Provisional Government. After all, Bogdanov argued, the Tatars made up only slightly more than 25 percent of the population of his province, while Russians and Ukrainians accounted for slightly less than 50 percent.[16] (These figures, based on the census of 1897, were for all of Tavricheskaia guberniia, which included the districts along the northern steppe region and along the coasts of the Sea of Azov. None of the Tatar spokesmen ever included these Slavic areas in their definition of the Crimea.) The response of the Tatar community to these arrests was so violent that Bogdanov was forced to release both leaders unharmed on the next day. But from this time on, virtually no cooperation could be expected between the Tatar Executive Committee or the Milli Firka and the Petrograd representatives.

At the same time that the Crimean Tatars were organizing in their sphere, the Russian sailors stationed at Sevastopol' were becoming more revolutionary and organizing politically. By the early part of October, the sailors and the Tatar organizations were the only two effective forces in the Crimea. The strength and morale of the Provisional Government's forces were reaching a low ebb, and because of this, the Tatar leadership found it necessary to convene representatives from all elements of the Crimean Tatar population in order to strengthen their organization and prevent what the editor of *Millet* called a growing threat of anarchy and disruption. In the last week of October, Çelebi Cihan succeeded in having returned to Simferopol' two Tatar cavalry regiments that had been stationed in Kherson and Novogeorgievsk so that they could be used by the Central Executive Committee if needed.[17]

The Kurultay

The Tatar National Constituent Assembly (Kurultay) was called to meet in the palace of the khans in Bahçesaray on November 24, 1917. Its delegates were chosen "on the basis of a broad franchise of all adult male and female Tatars."[18] After some understandable delay in electoral procedures, the Kurultay was opened on December 9 and continued to meet until December 26, when it accepted a new constitution for the Crimean state. On that day, too, the Kurultay transformed itself into a national parliament and elected from its delegates a Crimean national government led by Çelebi Cihan.

The adopted constitution included the following sections:

1. The Kurultay recognizes the right of all nationalities to determine their own cultural form.

2. The Kurultay proclaims that the realization of national ideals can occur only through the use of legislation that is the expression of the will of the nation, and concerns itself with all areas of Tatar life. It deems indispensable the

continued existence of a national parliament elected on the basis of universal suffrage.

3. The Kurultay proclaims that only those laws representing the will of the people are viable and declares that the parliament must be reelected each three years. This Kurultay recognizes that, in the present difficult situation, elections have offered great problems and this Kurultay will thus become the first parliament to sit for one year.

4. The parliament will have legislative authority over the following matters: national education, religion, justice, military questions, finances, political affairs, and eventually, questions relative to commerce, industry, and agriculture.

5. The Kurultay, recognizing full liberty and independence of the executive, legislative, and judicial branches, proclaims the separation of powers.

6. The national Crimean government will be composed of the following directors: of education, of religious affairs, of finance and *vakifs*, of justice, of foreign affairs, and the chairman of the Council of Directors.[19]

The first members of this Crimean Tatar Directorate were as follows: Çelebi Cihan, both chairman of the directorate and director of justice; Cafer Seidahmet, director for foreign affairs and military organization; Seidahmet Şukru, director for religious affairs; Ibrahim Ozenbaşli, director for national education; and Seidcelil Hattat, director for finance and *vakif*s. On December 27, the directorate established its residence in Simferopol' and immediately issued a "proclamation to all inhabitants of the Crimea" in which it promised full equality and freedom for all who lived on the peninsula, and a return of law and order in the difficult times of anarchy spreading throughout Russia. The directorate and the Tatar parliament were, however, to have only a few short weeks of existence before a combination of pressures—from the Sevastopol' revolutionaries and from the Germans from the north—extinguished both.[20]

Bolsheviks and Nationalities

The Bolsheviks' nationalities policy, first officially stated by the faction's Central Committee in 1913, had been ambivalent on the question of self-determination and national autonomy. Although in the early 1920s much was made in the foreign press of the extremely liberal national policies of the Bolshevik leaders, there were elements of their ideology that should have warned even the most optimistic observer of their ultimate intention to eliminate national self-determination within the Soviet state while supporting its development elsewhere.

In 1913, the special resolution of the Bolshevik Central Committee stated that "the right of all nationalities forming part of Russia freely to secede and form independent states must be recognized. To deny them this right or to fail to take measures guaranteeing them its practical realization is equivalent to supporting a policy of seizure and annexation." Even the most ardent nationalist could subscribe to this, yet the "operative" element of the resolution which followed stated:

> But it must also be said that the right of nationalities to secede must not be confused with the expediency of secession of a given nation at a given moment. The party of the proletariat must decide the latter question quite independently in each particular case from the standpoint of the interest of social democracy as a whole and the interests of the class struggle of the proletariat for socialism.[21]

In November 1917, the Bolsheviks announced a "declaration of rights of the people of Russia," stating:

> The right of the peoples of Russia to govern themselves has already been proclaimed by the First Congress of Soviets in June 1917. The Second Congress of Soviets in October 1917 confirmed this right in a way more decisive and precise than before. Executing the will of the Soviets, the Council of Commissars of the people in its declaration of November 15, 1917, has resolved the national question on the following bases: (1) the equality and sovereignty of the peoples of Russia; (2) the right of the peoples of Russia to direct their own future, including the right of secession and constitution of an independent state; (3) the suppression of all restrictions and privileges in the area of religion or nationality; (4) the free development of national minorities and ethnic groups in the Russian territory.[22]

Two extremely important documents were issued over Stalin's signature on December 12, 1917. The differences between the two are striking. The best known, the "Proclamation to all the Muslims of Russia and the Orient," promised great changes in Muslim life and in the relations between the Muslims and the new Soviet government:

> Muslims of Russia, Tatars of the Volga and the Crimea, Kirgiz and Sarts of Siberia and Turkestan, Turks and Tatars of Transcaucasia, Chechens and mountaineers of the Caucasus, and all you whose mosques have been destroyed, whose beliefs and customs have been trampled underfoot by the tsars and the oppressors of Russia. Your beliefs and usage, your national and cultural institutions are henceforth free and inviolable. Organize your national life in complete freedom. You have the right. Know that your rights, like those of all the peoples of Russia are under the powerful safeguard of the revolution and its organs, the soviets of workers, soldiers, and peasants. Lend your support to this revolution and its government.[23]

This proclamation clearly was aimed at the public in the Muslim areas in a blatant attempt to gain their support for the revolution. On the same date, however, Stalin issued another statement relative to this subject. Not for public consumption, it stated:

> It is necessary to limit the principle of free self-determination of nations, by granting it to the toilers and refusing it to the bourgeoisie. The principle of self-determination should be a means of fighting for socialism.[24]

In the next year, Stalin added to this statement:

> There are occasions when the right of self-determination conflicts with . . . the right of the working class, that has assumed power, to consolidate its power. In such cases—this must be said bluntly—the right to self-determination cannot and must not serve as an obstacle to the exercise by the working class of its right to dictatorship. The former must give way to the latter.

Again, at the Tenth Party Congress in March 1921, Stalin made crystal clear his views on the rights to secession that had been alluded to in the declaration to the Muslims three and a half years earlier:

> We are for the secession of India, Arabia, Egypt, etc., because this would mean liberation of those oppressed countries from imperialism. We are against the secession of the border regions of Russia, because secession in that case would mean imperialist bondage for the border regions, and a weakening of the revolutionary might of Russia, and a strengthening of the position of imperialism.[25]

Bolsheviks in the Crimea

It was not long before the Bolsheviks were in a position to apply their principles to the problem of Crimean secession. In October and November of 1917, at the same time that the Tatar nationalists were convening their first conference and making plans for their national Kurultay, Russian and Ukrainian liberals in Simferopol' were establishing a new provincial assembly. This was followed within two weeks by elections to a Constituent Crimean Assembly. There were about 550,000 eligible voters, of whom 54 percent took part in the election. In the final tallies, the Socialist Revolutionary Party received a clear majority, while the bourgeois nationalist Milli Firka Party received only 31 percent. The remainder went to the Kadets. P. Novitskii was appointed chairman of the assembly.

According to Nadinskii, at the end of November 1917 there were thus two "counter-revolutionary governments" in the Crimea: the Tatar National Directory and the Crimean Provincial Assembly. In neither were the Bolsheviks represented or supported. In the face of growing revolutionary activity among the sailors and soldiers of the Sevastopol' command, and with news of growing anarchy and violence in the central Russian regions, the leaders of these two governments agreed to establish a Crimean General Headquarters to coordinate their activity. Both shared a strong desire to oppose the Bolsheviks, even though they disagreed on the question of secession and the nature of the future Crimea. The chairman of the Headquarters was Cafer Seidahmet; the vice-chairman was tsarist army officer Makukhin.[26]

In December 1917, the only pocket of strength the Bolsheviks had in the Crimea was located in the garrisons in Sevastopol'. There, on December 15, 1917, they succeeded in seizing control of the local government and installing a "Soviet of Workers, Peasants, and Soldiers," although it must be added that at first there were no representatives of either workers or peasants in the soviet. The inevitable conflict between these two centers of power was openly initiated by the Crimean General Headquarters. Fearing that military forces on the peninsula not under control of the Headquarters could not be trusted in the future, it used troops from the Tatar directorate to disarm the naval academy cadets in Evpatoriia. On December 28, 1917, the Sevastopol' soviet revkom (Revolutionary Commissariat) sent an ultimatum to Seidahmet demanding that the Crimean General Headquarters relinquish all claims to military control of the peninsula within twenty-four hours, and that the soldiers of the directorate submit themselves to disarming by representatives of the soviet. The confrontation was coming. No quarter or concession would be forthcoming from either side.[27]

The Bolsheviks' fears of Tatar-nationalist-led Crimean secession from the newly proclaimed soviet state were well founded. Although virtually none of the inhabitants of the Crimea favored the Bolshevik revolution or Lenin's government (the soldiers and sailors in the garrisons were exclusively non-Crimean in origin), non-Tatars could be expected to do everything in their power to prevent a secession and to further the revolutionary aims within the Crimea. In the third week of January 1918, naval squadrons under the control of the Sevastopol' soviet landed at Feodosiia and Kerch and began marching toward Bahçesaray and Simferopol'.[28]

With this serious threat to their continued authority, the members of the Tatar directorate split over the question of what policy to pursue toward the Bolsheviks in Sevastopol'. The left-wing members of the directorate, led by its chairman, Çelebi Cihan, argued on behalf of a rapprochement with the soviet, even going so far as to suggest creation of an all-Crimean government that would include representatives of the soviet. Not surprisingly, word came from the Bolsheviks that they were interested in such negotiations. They were sure of their own military strength and eager to encourage division in the nationalist ranks. But in a vote of the directorate, Çelebi Cihan lost by forty-three to twelve and resigned from the Executive Committee. He was replaced by Seidahmet.[29]

With no hope of achieving their aims through negotiation, the Sevastopol'
Bolsheviks decided to terminate both the Tatar and liberal governments in
Simferopol'. They marched on the capital on January 25, 1918. The
Bolsheviks met units of the Tatar cavalry at the village of Suren, on the road to
Simferopol', and easily defeated them. They entered the Crimean capital the
next day and met only minor opposition. The Kurultay disbanded and most
of its leadership escaped into the mountains or fled to Turkey.[30]

Çelebi Cihan, former chairman of the Executive Committee, did not
escape, however. Still preferring to try for a compromise with the Bolsheviks
and hoping to develop on the part of the soviet some understanding of the
interests of the Tatars, he remained in Simferopol'. Realizing the importance
of eliminating all traces of Tatar nationalist leadership, the Bolsheviks
ordered him arrested and removed to Sevastopol'. There in the first week of
February, he was executed and "his body thrown into the sea."[31] Thus the
Bolsheviks eliminated the most intelligent and effective of Tatar leaders—and
the one most willing to cooperate with the new Soviet government. In the
months to come, with the rise and fall of successive Soviet governments in the
Crimea, it should have been no surprise that the remaining Tatar leaders were
not as conciliatory as Çelebi Cihan had been. The overwhelming strength of
the bourgeois nationalist representatives in the Tatar leadership was in part
the result of this Bolshevik policy of eliminating Tatar nationalists.

From the perspective of the Crimean Tatars, the short period from
November 1917 to January 1918 is the only period since 1783 during which
their nationalist desires ever became a reality. Under the next few governments (between January 1918 and October 1920), it can surely be said that the
Crimean Tatars were not masters in their own house, nor did they experience
the benefits of an autonomous cultural existence.

The first Bolshevik administration in the Crimea lasted from January 27
until April 25, 1918, at which time the German occupation forces destroyed
their government. That is a period Soviet historians prefer to gloss over, for
the behavior of the new Crimean soviet leaders was nothing to remember
with favor. The leaders of the Sevastopol' soviet were completely unequipped
to handle administration of the entire peninsula. They had no knowledge of
the local inhabitants and their customs, and they were totally insensitive to
the problems occasioned by the restoration of order and government. Not
only were the soviet leaders unable to govern effectively; they lost control
over their own forces as well.

During the months of February and March, soldiers and sailors presumably under the command of the Sevastopol' soviet ravaged the countryside
and towns. They killed literally thousands of the local Slavic and Tatar
population. In the towns of Bahçesaray and Simferopol', the result of Soviet
government in this period was quite simply mass slaughter. The economy

ground to a halt. The local population found it necessary to unite (in a fashion their leaders had been unable to inspire in November) to oppose "legitimate" requests and demands from the "lawful" Soviet authorities, and more importantly, to defend themselves against the rampages of leaderless and anarchic elements of the Soviet Crimean garrisons. It is difficult for even the most sympathetic observer to accept the Soviet characterization of this self-defense as "counterrevolutionary behavior." When the Germans arrived in May 1918, they reported finding near Simferopol' several mass graves containing more than 1500 bodies each. There can be no historical justification for these events. Soviet historians find it more comfortable merely to ignore them.[32]

The historian must admit, however, that the Peace Treaty of Brest Litovsk, signed on March 3, 1918, had completely undercut the foundations of Soviet authority in the Crimea. From this date on, local Crimean Bolsheviks were able to expect no economic or military support from Petrograd. This knowledge may well have encouraged the Bolshevik troops in the Crimea to act with less restraint than they would have otherwise. On March 6, 1918, the Bolsheviks established a new Sovnarkom (Soviet Peoples' Commissariat) in Simferopol'. They invited token representation from the left-wing Tatar members of the former national directorate. In the government that was created, there was to be a commissariat of Crimean Muslim Affairs, but they could find no Tatar willing to accept the post. On March 21, 1918, the Sovnarkom proclaimed the formation of the Soviet Republic of the Crimea. It received immediate recognition from Petrograd. Chicherin, in fact, sent a telegram to Berlin claiming that this new republic was now in no way connected with the Soviet government and thus would not be bound by the Brest Litovsk Treaty. He argued that Germany should recognize its existence as an independent state.[33]

In the elections of delegates to the Sevastopol' soviet held in early April, the Bolsheviks found themselves heavily outpolled by both the Socialist Revolutionaries and the Mensheviks. In similar elections throughout the Crimea, the Bolsheviks were unable to elect delegates. It was clear that among the local population of the Crimea, support for the Bolsheviks was virtually nonexistent. If they were to succeed in establishing control over the Crimea and over the new "Soviet Republic," they would have to do it by armed force. But without substantial help from Petrograd, this task was beyond their capabilities.

In mid-April, a number of Tatar revolts occurred in the Crimea; these resulted in the removal, and in some cases the killing, of local Bolshevik officials. The Sovnarkom left Simferopol' entirely, but its members were found by Tatar and Russian forces and taken to Ialta where they were all executed in late April. Among those executed were N. G. Slutskii, chairman of the Sovnarkom; A. Koliadenko, commissar of finance; S. P. Novosel'skii, commissar of the interior; and Ia. Tarvatskii, chairman of the Simferopol' town soviet. This act coincided with the appearance of German forces in the Crimea in early May. [34]

Meanwhile, hoping to persuade the Germans to consider the Crimea within their sphere of influence, the Tatars sent Cafer Seidahmet to Rumania and other delegates to Turkey and Germany. Their representations succeeded. On March 29, 1918, in an agreement with Austro-Hungary, Germany decided to include the Crimea within her Ukrainian and South Russian areas of control. In Rumania, Seidahmet joined with former general Sulkiewicz of the Russian army (a Lithuanian Tatar) to form a Muslim Corps. This corps was to be used in clearing the Crimea of Bolshevik troops. [35]

Without the presence of the Sovnarkom leadership, Bolsheviks in the Crimea could offer only token resistance to the German advance from the Ukraine. Acting as an advance troop for the German army, Sulkiewicz's Muslim Corps and the two cavalry squadrons under the command of the Kurultay helped clear the peninsula of Bolshevik forces. The Tatars, by taking part in the liberation of the Crimea, were counting on gaining considerable independence from the Germans, even if the Crimea did ultimately remain within the German sphere of influence. And at first, it seemed that was exactly what the Germans intended to do.

Within a week of the complete occupation of the Crimea by the German army under General Kosch, the Tatar leadership negotiated for the reconstruction of the national Kurultay and for as wide a national autonomy as possible. On May 12, 1918, Cafer Seidahmet returned from Istanbul and was chosen as the Tatar prime minister. He chaired the first session of the Kurultay on May 16. Using such phrases as "We now are free to belong to the Turko-Tatar world," and "Crimea for the Crimeans," Seidahmet stated the most extreme desires of the Tatar nationalists—desires that soon proved to be too radical for the German command. Kosch refused to recognize Seidahmet as prime minister; yet he agreed to allow the Kurultay to function as an assembly for the Tatar population, provided its officers were acceptable to the Germans and to other elements of the Crimean population.

Sulkiewicz Regime

After a considerable amount of bickering and negotiation, the Tatar leaders and the German command agreed on creation of a new Crimean national government that was to be subject to the requirements of the German occupation forces. Suleyman Sulkiewicz was chosen as its leader. Having served as a Russian general on the western front, he seemed a good choice to represent all Crimean parties. In addition, V. I. Polivanov, a Russian, was chosen minister of justice; Salomon Krym, a Crimean Karaim, became finance minister; Mustafa Kipçakski became minister of agriculture; and M. Bekirov, minister of communications. There is no doubt that the Germans considered this government a pliable one. On the other hand, its officers were preponderantly from the Tatar and non-Russian communities. Its ability to survive as constituted depended on support from the German command since the Russian and Ukrainian population of the peninsula had been alienated by being excluded from its leadership to such an extent. On June 5, 1918, this government held its last session. It was finally reconstituted to represent more accurately the various nationalities in the Crimea.[36]

Understandably, Soviet accounts of these months are extremely hostile toward this Crimean government. It is called traitorous, a puppet of the German occupation forces, a band of reactionaries, and so forth. And there is some truth to these claims. Yet Nadinskii's statement that the Tatars and their German superiors intended to reestablish a Crimean Khanate is absolutely untrue. Although by this time Seidahmet represented a centrist position in the Tatar political community, there is no justification for the claim that he was in favor of bringing back the pre-1783 form of government, with its khans, its Giray dynasty, and its autocratic power. The Tatars wished for reestablishment of an independent Crimean Tatar state with a Kurultay ("parliament") that represented the voices of the people.[37]

That the German forces were opportunistic and concerned with furthering German interests needs hardly be said. Between themselves, the Germans spoke of the Tatars as natives, with all of the negative connotations possible in that term. They viewed the Crimea as an important strategic area and a potential economic resource. Germany was satisfied with whatever form of government would best serve her interests. Thus, when the first formulation of the Crimean national government under Sulkiewicz was not able to satisfy enough desires of the non-Tatar population to permit easy German control, German forces quickly dissolved it and forced the appointment of a number of non-Tatars as officials.

On June 5, 1918, Sulkiewicz, whom the Germans still believed to be the most acceptable figure to all Crimean groups, was ordered to form a new cabinet. His task was "to end the struggle between Tatar and Russian politicians." To this end, he announced the following government on June 19: Sulkiewicz, premier and minister of war; V. S. Nalbandov (Armenian), a wealthy landowner, minister of interior; Keller (German Crimean), minister of education; Freemann (German Crimean), minister of commerce; Count Golitsyn (Russian), minister of agriculture; Count Tatishchev (Russian), former director of the Moscow Union Bank, minister of finance; Charikov (Russian), former ambassador to Istanbul, minister of foreign affairs; and

Gendre (French), minister of the marine. This cabinet was as heavily weighted in favor of reactionary Russian officials as the first had been with Tatars.

The Tatar leadership protested strongly enough to force Sulkiewicz to restructure the cabinet again within the week. Sulkiewicz remained premier, but added the ministries of the interior, war, and marine to his portfolio; Seidahmet was made minister of foreign affairs; Achmatowicz (Polish Tatar), minister of justice; Nikitin (a Russian moderate), minister of commerce; Tatishchev retained his post; T. Rapp (leader of the Crimean German community), minister of agriculture; Nalbandov, minister of education; and Freemann remained as before.[38] Thus, it appears that the first crucial weeks of the Crimean government were spent on relatively unimportant political reshuffling rather than on attending to critical matters of state.

This last cabinet was noteworthy for its lack of political partisanship. Sulkiewicz sincerely tried to give the cabinet direction that would avoid creating conflict and rancor between the various national groups. Popular especially with the Tatar community, the government's activities were chronicled in a diary kept by Nalbandov.[39] On June 25, Sulkiewicz issued a "Declaration," signed by his cabinet, setting forth the aims and directions he would pursue. First of all, Russian was to be the primary language of the government, but both Tatar and German would be secondary languages, and all government business would be published in all three. The state flag would be the former flag of the Kurultay, and the seal would reproduce both the eagle of the Milli Firka and the owl of the former Crimean Independent State. A commissariat would become the central political institution; state *duma*s and rural assemblies would remain as they had been before 1917. The Tatar writer of the period, Arslan Krichinskii, wrote that this government was "humane and democratic. . . . It refused to permit the hegemony of one people over another."[40]

In July 1918, Seidahmet and Tatishchev went to Berlin for the purpose of lobbying for special treatment for the Crimea. Their proposal included absolute separation of the Crimea from the Ukraine. At that time Ukrainian leaders were making claims to authority over the Crimea. In addition, the Crimean proposal sought both creation of special economic ties between Germany and the Crimea that would benefit them both, and as much self-government as they could bargain for. The two diplomats were remarkably successful. In August, the Germans granted a substantial loan to the Crimean government. Further trade arrangements were formalized for the export of Crimean foodstuffs to Germany in return for industrial equipment (much of which had been seized by the German occupation forces in other western parts of Russia). Finally, the cabinet was allowed to create organs of local government throughout the Crimea without German interference.[41]

It is strange to find in both Soviet and Western scholarly works on this period a variety of claims that contradict this evidence. One Soviet work says:

> Tatar nationalists, appearing as the true lackeys of the German occupation forces, acted completely against the interests of the local Crimean population. . . . The agreements took from the people bread, cattle, and so forth, for shipment to Germany. This created enormous hardships for the workers and peasants. . . . Workers and peasants were taken from the Crimea as slaves (*rabi*) to Germany.[42]

A recent Western account reads:

> Sulkevich's regime . . . was a puppet government. It was out of touch with the Tatar and Russian population. . . . It assisted the occupants to ship food from the Crimea to Germany. . . . Germany refused to surrender any authority to the Tatars.[43]

Kirimal admits that the Achilles heel of the Sulkiewicz regime was its failure to control and strengthen its own military force. It depended on the support of the German army. In this respect, it can be at least partially described as a puppet regime. But it was quite successful in pressing for and gaining consideration for Crimean Tatar and Crimean Russian interests. This is most clear in the sticky negotiations that were necessary in the face of the new Ukrainian government's attempts to extend its own authority into the Crimea.[44]

In April 1918, Lubinskii, foreign minister of the new independent Ukraine, proclaimed that the Treaty of Brest Litovsk had assigned the Crimea to his state. He argued that his state required an exit to the Black Sea, and that it needed not only Odessa but also the Crimean peninsula ports. The Central Rada (the chief administrative institution of the new Ukranian state) had established a Ukrainian Marine Central Secretariat that in March had announced the creation of a Ukrainian state fleet. In April, one brigade of Ukrainian troops actually entered the northern Crimea following immediately behind the Germans. In May, the German command said that it would respect the integrity of the Crimea; thus it forestalled for the moment any Ukrainian attempt to annex it. But in July, the government of Skoropadskii established a Committee for the Steppe Ukraine, by which was meant the entire Crimea. This issue was one of the most important discussed by Seidahmet and Tatishchev in Berlin. Finally the problem was solved, again in favor of the Crimeans, with the September announcement in Berlin of the "recognition of an integral Crimean State." Turkey soon followed suit in giving recognition. But the issue was to be raised again in mid-October.[45]

The Tatars received favored treatment from the German administration with its recognition of the importance of the Kurultay. The Kurultay was permitted to exist during this entire period, and it had three long sessions between late May and mid-October. Since there was no equivalent Russian institution for the Crimea, it was allowed to act as a sort of national parliament representing the interests of all national groups. Yet it must be admitted that the Tatars controlled its activities. As a high officer in the Kurultay, and later as minister of education in the Sulkiewicz regime as well, Krichinskii was an important link between the two institutions. The Kurultay appointed a new national directorate, which was also recognized by the Germans; Abdulhakim Hilmi was its premier.[46]

Salomon Krym

The Sulkiewicz regime and Tatar self-rule fell as a result of increased pressure from the Ukraine, a change of heart by General Kosch, and the growing number of Russian army officers and landowners arriving in the Crimea following unsuccessful military activity against the Bolsheviks. On October 17, 1918, an entirely Russian gathering called the Assembly of the Urban, Agricultural, Professional, and Socialist Parties of the Crimea met in Simferopol' and demanded a complete reversal of German policy. For example, the assembly refused to accept the existence of the Kurultay and its claim to represent the non-Tatar elements in the Crimea, refused to admit the principle of a separate and independent Crimea, and rejected the makeup of the Sulkiewicz regime. The assembly felt that Sulkiewicz's government was heavily weighted against the Russian and Ukrainian elements on the peninsula.[47]

The German command acquiesced to the assembly's demands, hoping to gain as much support from the local Russian population as possible in the face of a growing threat of invasion from the powerful White forces in the northern Caucasus. The White forces' intention was to struggle not only against the Bolsheviks, but also against the German occupiers of Russian territory. They had both moral and physical support from the Entente. Sulkiewicz resigned barely a week before the Germans began to evacuate the Crimea.

The Russian and Ukrainian political leaders of the assembly established a new government on November 16, 1918. It was a government controlled by Russian liberals, particularly members of the Kadet Party, and led by Salomon Krym, a Crimean Karaim who had been a Kadet deputy to the First State Duma. In addition, Bogdanov was to be minister of the interior and Maksim Viniaver the foreign minister. One of the most important proclamations of the new government stated that Sulkiewicz's separate and independent Crimea was no longer a goal. The Crimea now was to be considered part of a "Great and Indivisible Russia." Further, Krym's administration was not to be so amenable to Tatar interests as the former had been. Under its first election law, districts that were drawn gave little voice to the Tatars. Their areas were to have a much higher ratio of voters to deputies than those of Russians and Ukrainians. In addition, Krym canceled the open invitation to return to the Crimea that Sulkiewicz had issued for all Crimean Tatars living abroad. Krym also strove, unsuccessfully, to absorb into the Crimea three Ukrainian districts of the former Tavricheskaia guberniia in order to dilute Tatar influence.[48]

Civil War in the Crimea

On November 22, 1918, Krym's government was given added support when the first elements of the White "Volunteer Army" crossed the Kerch Straits and arrived in Ialta four days later. So far as the Tatars were concerned, none of these developments was acceptable. Throughout December, mass protests were organized in Ialta, Evpatoriia, Feodosiia, and Simferopol'. The Kurultay tried to call a national boycott of all political and economic relations between the Tatars and the government. A special meeting of the Kurultay formulated a series of demands that their representatives delivered to Krym. These included: (1) the government was to remain neutral on the question of the independence of the Crimea until a decision could be reached at a European peace conference; and (2) each nationality in the Crimea was to be represented in the government by a number of officials equal to its proportion of the population.

The Tatars received satisfaction on neither request. Yet it must be said that Krym tried to placate Tatar sensitivities as much as he could in nonpolitical arenas. He encouraged publication of Tatar newspapers. Both *Millet* and *Krym* continued to appear and their nationalist orientation underwent no government censorship. Tatar schools continued to flourish and the newly founded University of Simferopol' continued to be Tatar in orientation. Yet there can be no doubt that the hopes of Tatar politicians for an independent Tatar-controlled regime were out of the question so long as Krym and the Russians were in control. The Tatar response to this was to attempt to influence the Entente powers, especially France, which had received responsibility for the Crimean region, to support their demands.[49]

During these months of the Russian Civil War which lasted from 1918–1921, the Crimea became a major arena for struggles between conflicting positions and groups. In these disputes the Crimean Tatars had virtually no say, and the basic issues being fought over were of little immediate concern to them. Neither the Bolsheviks nor the Whites evidenced respect for Tatar sensitivities or interests. Neither camp was prepared to consider an independent Crimea, least of all one controlled by the Tatar minority. For both, the concept of a "Great and Undivided" Russia (albeit with different political forms) was the goal. With the ebb and flow of White and Bolshevik power in the Crimea, from January 1919 until late 1920, the Tatars were bystanders. They were interested, but they could not participate.

This state of affairs encouraged division among the Tatar politicians. They searched for support in a variety of camps. The moderate element of the Milli Firka (the whole party was termed "extreme right wing" by one Western scholar) chose to support as best it could the administration of Salomon Krym. This group included Tatar landowners and teachers as well as the editors of the two major Tatar newspapers. The right wing nationalist element of the Milli Firka refused to consider Krym's government as theirs and continued to struggle for the concept of an independent Tatar Crimea. It eventually made a request to the League of Nations for recognition. The leftist elements of the Milli Firka, led by Veli Ibrahimov, saw their best chance for success in linking up with leftist Russian groups in the Crimean towns. Ibrahimov's faction eventually developed contacts with the Bolsheviks.[50]

A Second Bolshevik Government in Crimea

In April 1919, a Bolshevik army entered the Crimea and defeated General Denikin at Kerch. By April 30, this army had succeeded in occupying the entire peninsula. It proclaimed the creation of the Socialist Soviet Republic of the Crimea. Lenin's brother, D. Ulianov, was appointed chairman of the Crimean revkom. On June 1, the Crimean Republic joined a military union with similar Soviet republics of Russia, the Ukraine, Belorussia, Lithuania, and Latvia. It seemed as though the Crimean Tatars were about to enter into a new era of political life.

The new Bolshevik government was far friendlier to Tatar interests than the earlier Bolshevik regime had been. This time, members of the leftist faction of the Milli Firka had helped them succeed, and many government positions were offered to these Tatars. A new Bolshevik newspaper was founded; it was published in Tatar and represented Tatar interests. But soon after this new Soviet government was organized, the army of General Denikin arrived again and put an end to it.[51]

This time the White regime actively repressed all Tatar activities. It pursued the goal of a "Russian United and Indivisible," and curtailed all nationalist groups. On June 28, 1919, the Tatar National Directory was dispersed. The Milli Firka Party was prohibited. In August, all Tatar journals were closed, and their printing offices were seized by the government.

Denikin's actions forced the Milli Firka to join the Bolshevik underground in the Crimean cities almost en masse. Although a recent Soviet account of these months claims that all Tatar nationalists supported Denikin (and thus when discussing the Bolshevik underground makes no mention of Milli Firka support), the exact opposite was true. No members of the Milli Firka helped Denikin: they were not permitted to join him.[52]

At the beginning of 1920, Denikin's administration was replaced by that of Baron Wrangel, who recognized the mistakes in nationality policy on the part of his predecessor. He did what he could to redress some of the Tatar grievances. He reinstated some Tatar newspapers and allowed a new one, *Krym Musulmanlari Seasy* ("The Voice of the Crimean Muslims"), to start in Simferopol'. In addition, Wrangel promised religious and cultural autonomy in the future. But this time the military and economic pressures were so great against the Whites that Wrangel was not able to accomplish much in the way of this policy before his government fell under another Bolshevik invasion.[53] In October, the Bolsheviks occupied the Crimean peninsula for the third time. This time they stayed until the German invasion in 1941. The new era for the Crimean Tatars had finally arrived.

12. The Crimean ASSR (1921–1941)

Just prior to the establishment of Soviet power in the Crimea for the third and last time, the Bolsheviks made strenuous attempts to create an institutional base that would be attractive to nationalities yet still serve to unify the state. This was difficult for several reasons. The chief benefits that many national groups would gain from the fall of the tsarist regime were not social or economic but national. Nothing the leaders of the national groups had seen during the years of the civil war had led them to believe that the Bolsheviks were interested in decentralizing the government.

Yet the Bolsheviks found Stalin to be an imaginative and shrewd politician who was able to present a series of plans aimed at persuading the national groups that becoming part of the Soviet state was their most effective way of achieving autonomy. Although it is easy now to see that Stalin never considered that to be of great importance, at the time it was difficult to perceive his long-range goals—or those of the government to which he belonged. During the Russian Civil War, when the leaders of the White Guards were doing their best to suppress any vestiges of national autonomy in their regions, the Bolsheviks issued a series of statements and decrees dealing with regional, national, cultural, and political autonomy. Pointing to Stalin's first major statements on the national question before World War I, the Bolsheviks could justifiably say that they had always been interested in the legitimate national aspirations of the peoples of the Russian state. They added that their criticisms of the colonial and national policies of the tsarist government were sincere and that they had a good deal to offer on the national questions. In November 1917, the Bolsheviks proclaimed that the "peoples of Russia are equal and sovereign." They stated that these peoples "have the right to manage their own affairs up to separation and the establishment of an independent state." That same month, in their proclamation to "the Muslims of Russia and the Orient," the Bolshevik leadership promised rectification of all tsarist repressive measures concerning the Muslims' cultural, religious, and national life.[1]

In December 1917, the government restored to the Muslim world the "sacred Koran of Osman," which had been removed from Samarkand to the national library in St. Petersburg. Finally, in January 1918, the Bolsheviks created the Commissariat for Muslim Affairs to take care of Muslim nationality questions. The commissar, Mullah Nur Vakhitov, a Tatar and former member of the administration of the province of Kazan, had as his assistants Galamjan Ibrahimov, a Tatar and delegate from Ufa to the Constituent Assembly, and Sharif Manatov, a Bashkir and delegate to the same assembly from Orenburg.[2]

Commissariat of Nationalities

However, by May 1920, as the civil war was ending, Stalin and other Bolsheviks felt the time had come to reorganize national institutions concerned with nationality questions. More emphasis was put on government centralization and less on national autonomy. On May 19, 1920, Stalin announced the reorganization of the Commissariat of Nationalities to bring about closer central control of nationality affairs. The emphasis was now on "fraternal collaboration among all the nationalities" and on the cultural development of the various ethnic groups. One of the most important tasks set before the commissariat, one that would have great consequences in the years to come, was: "the study and application of all measures necessary to guarantee the interests of minorities that live in the territory of other nationalities of the Soviet Federation of Russia."[3] Since by 1920 there were important Slavic minorities in all of the non-Russian regions, this gave the central government a wedge with which to interfere in the internal affairs of these areas in order "to protect the interests there of the minorities" (the Russians and Ukrainians).

Perhaps the most important characteristic of this reorganized Commissariat of Nationalities was that its members were to be chosen according to region, not according to nationality. Those nationalities without an autonomous region or republic would be denied representation. But those regions having important minorities (such as Russians and Ukrainians in central Asia) would be represented by a delegation chosen to reflect their national diversity. The electoral procedure was stacked against the possibility of non-Slavic nationalities having too great a say in the commissariat's affairs. In addition, Stalin reserved the right to approve or reject any delegates sent to represent a given region. This concept was spelled out in the clearest fashion in the political journal for the Red Army, on December 18, 1921:

> The Soviet power recognizes no national autonomy; on the other hand it completely favors the desire of the nationalities to enjoy a regional autonomy. By regional autonomy the Soviets mean the granting the right of autonomy to the workers of a region, a province, a country, whatever their nationality. It will never be, therefore, a question of according to one nationality autonomy to the detriment of another. The Soviet power will not favor a nationalist movement along the lines of those that appeared in the Caucasus, in the Ukraine, in the

Tatar Republic. These forms are essentially bourgeois and have no goal other
than that of reducing to slavery the native working classes.[4]

Despite these facts, it must be pointed out that in comparison with other
multinational states or colonial empires of the time, the reformed institutions
of the Soviet government still appeared far more receptive to national and
cultural autonomy than the others.

The Chekha in the Crimea

For the leadership of the Crimean Tatars, these developments had little
immediate impact. Unlike many other regions of tsarist Russia, in the Crimea
Bolshevik party members had been from the start almost exclusively Russians
or Ukrainians. For the Tatars, the attempts by the Bolsheviks to establish a
revolutionary government had meant the imposition of yet another Russian-
dominated, Russian-oriented administration that would not be representative of Tatar national interests. Execution of several Tatar leaders and open
hostility toward others were not encouraging signs of Bolshevik intentions.
The execution of Çelebi Cihan, the leftist leader of the Milli Firka, likewise
appeared to show that the Bolsheviks were not interested in brotherly
collaboration with the Tatars. Of course, if the new third Bolshevik government in 1920 had altered these earlier policies, some members of the Tatar
leadership would have been willing to cooperate with them.

In an official note from the Milli Firka to the Bolshevik leadership in the
Crimea, the Tatars stated that the goals of the Milli Firka and the Communist
party were similar. The note said the Milli Firka differed "not in principle,
but only in timing, place, and means of the realization of socialism." In other
words, the modernization of Tatar life was the ultimate goal of both parties.
The Tatar party leaders were naive to believe that the Bolsheviks were
concerned with the "life of the Tatars."[5] Indeed, as Essad Bey wrote, "the
last soldier of Wrangel's had not left the Crimea before Comrade Bela Kun,
chief of the Chekha (Bolshevik secret police), arrived with the mission to
eliminate both the bourgeoisie and the anarchists." With Kun came Nikolai
Bystrykh who had been appointed by the Crimean revkom as commissar of a
special section of the Crimean Chekha.[6]

Bystrykh was in charge of weeding out all remaining elements who were
opponents of Soviet power, and the numbers of those eliminated testify to his
efficiency. This took place in November 1920, and according to several
contemporary sources, as many as 60,000 representatives of the above-
mentioned groups perished in a period of less than six months. A Soviet
account brands these elements "bandit sheikhs, White Guardists, and Tatar
nationalists, who had tried to prevent the establishment of Soviet power."

Early in December, Lenin himself stated that in the Crimea "there are now over 300,000 bourgeoisie who must be dealt with."[7]

Between November 1920 and the summer of 1921, Bystrykh's Chekhists established centers of operation in Odessa, Simferopol', and Sevastopol', and carried on an armed struggle against the native inhabitants of the Crimea— both Tatars and Russians. They succeeded in removing a good number of those hostile to the establishment of Soviet power. The Tatars who had been organized to oppose the governments of Denikin and Wrangel, continued their armed partisan operations, now against Kun's forces. Led by Ismail Nazal, the Crimean Tatar partisans took the name "Green Forces." Operating primarily out of the mountain regions of the peninsula, they succeeded in making Kun's task extremely difficult. By summer of 1921 neither side had won a convincing victory. The Bolshevik leadership in Simferopol' thus decided to introduce another tactic, that of gaining cooperation from the Tatar leadership at the cost of promising both a good deal of national autonomy for Tatars and participation by Tatars in the new government.[8]

Sultan Galiev and the Creation of the Crimean ASSR

Early in 1921, the Soviet government sent the Volga Tatar Communist leader, Sultan Galiev, to the Crimea to investigate the situation and to report on the reasons for the growing opposition there to Soviet rule. His report was not good news for Moscow. Criticizing the activities of Bela Kun and the Chekha, Galiev reported that Communist officials were administering the Crimea "as a colony" and were not interested in the sensibilities of the local Tatar population. His recommendations, in direct contradiction to the wishes of the Crimean Communist officials, were: (1) that the Crimea be reformed into an autonomous Soviet republic; (2) that the land reform that had been going badly be stopped for the moment; and (3) that a major effort be made to attract Tatars into Party membership.[9]

In late July, the Bolshevik administration in Simferopol' announced a broad program of amnesty for all Tatar nationalists who had opposed Bolshevik victory in the Crimea. This was an attempt to gain acceptance of the new regime by the Tatar partisans and by the Milli Firka leaders, many of whom had gone underground during the Bela Kun terror. In return for this gesture, the Milli Firka announced that it was again willing to negotiate with the Soviets. Although in the long run most of their demands were not met, the Bolsheviks were willing at this point to listen to Tatar requests, including those for full autonomy, and for Tatar control of all religious and educational institutions in the peninsula. On September 23, 1921, an assembly of representatives from both Tatar and non-Tatar communities in the Crimea met in Simferopol'. For a short time at least, Tatar and Russian Communists, Milli Firka members, and non-Party leaders all met together to discuss the Crimea's future. The outcome of this meeting was the October 18, 1921, announcement by the Sovnarkom (Council of Peoples' Commissars) of the Russian Soviet Federated Socialist Republic (RSFSR), of the formation of the Crimean Autonomous Soviet Socialist Republic (Crimean ASSR), to be an integral part of the RSFSR.[10]

The decree announced that Simferopol' was to be the administrative center of the new republic. The Crimea would be divided into the Djankoy, Evpatoriia, Kerch, Sevastopol', Simferopol', Feodosiia, and Ialta districts. Each district was to be administered on the local level by a district council, and the entire Crimean ASSR would be presided over by a Central Committee of the Council of Commissariats of the People of the Crimea. Twelve commissariats were created to handle internal Crimean matters. The Moscow government reserved control over the leadership of these commissariats and required that all their activities be in accord with practices in the RSFSR. All matters dealing with foreign affairs and communications remained in the hands of the Moscow central government. Likewise, the important port cities of Sevastopol' and Evpatoriia were not subject to the jurisdiction of the Crimean republican government. In fact, only the commissariats of the interior, of justice, of education, and of health retained any sort of autonomy, and even these were responsible both to the Central Committee and to the Council of Commissariats in Moscow.[11]

According to Castagne, these measures did not satisfy the demands of Tatar nationalist leaders, who saw through the facade of this autonomous republic and recognized it as being an integral part of the RSFSR, with regional autonomy only in nonsensitive governmental areas. As a result, the Tatars sent a delegation to Moscow to plead their case. They promised full support for the Soviet government if the Milli Firka would be accepted as a legal political arm of the Tatar people and if its leaders would be assigned to many of the Crimean administrative positions in the new government. In addition, they asked for autonomy in political matters. On January 10, 1922, apparently as a result of this delegation's activities (and this is related only by Castagne), the Simferopol' government issued a proclamation stating:

> The government in Moscow has recognized, in principle, the right of independence of the Crimea. We have enumerated the maximum number of privileges for the Crimean Tatars that the government in Moscow has approved: (1) recognition of the complete independence of the Crimea; (2) the Crimea has its complete independence in both internal and external affairs; (3) the Tatar language will be the only official language for the Crimea, but the Tatar government will promise to continue the instruction of Russian in its schools; (4) the frontier of the Tatar government of the Crimea will be

determined according to ethnic bases after a delay of six months; (5) the Tatar government promises to consider the government in Moscow as an allied and friendly government, and to take no actions against the interests of Russia.[12]

If this proclamation was actually issued, it is a remarkable document. Virtually no writer on Crimean or Soviet history has mentioned its existence, and in view of contemporaneous Soviet policy, it makes little sense. Yet soon after the alleged publication of this document in Simferopol', a Tatar delegation left for negotiations with the new Turkish government in Ankara, apparently fulfilling the promises for complete Tatar control of their own external affairs. Further evidence for this visit of the delegation to Ankara was the Soviet government's receipt in Simferopol' of a telegram from Ali Fuad Pasha, ambassador for the Turkish Grand National Assembly to the Soviet government. It "affirmed that toward the beginning of February the Crimean delegation would leave for Ankara, where it would negotiate a friendly accord with the nationalist government."[13]

Stranger still was a note published in January 1921 in *Poslednii novosti*, the Russian newspaper in Paris. It was claimed to be the text of the accord between the Crimean government and Moscow. It read:

1. The government in Moscow recognizes the Crimean constitution written by the Kurultay in November 1917, that is, before the advent of the Bolsheviks.

2. For the organization of political power, Moscow assigns to Simferopol' 150,000 rubles.

3. The Republic of the Crimea has the right to conclude economic accords with all countries.

4. Amnesty is granted to all the members of the Kurultay who had taken part in the struggle against Soviet power in December 1918.

5. The Red Army is evacuating the Crimea. It will be replaced by the national Tatar army, whose officers will be chosen from among the Russian officers who know Tatar. The former Tatar cavalry division will be reconstituted.

6. The Crimea will have the right to build railways; these for both export and import of economic goods.

7. The Tatars will occupy the official posts of ministers of agriculture, finance, and education. The administrations will be under the control of Tatar functionaries.[14]

All in all, one must say that the provisions of these documents are unusual. If implemented, the Crimean Tatars would have received real autonomy. Yet from the beginning, most of these provisions never became reality. Actual political autonomy had to be won by the efforts of various Tatar leaders within the Crimean Bolshevik administration; their leader was Veli Ibrahimov. More than anyone else, Ibrahimov was responsible for the creation of what Tatar exiles now refer to as the Golden Age of the Soviet Crimea, which lasted from 1923 to 1928.

From 1921 until 1954, the Crimean peninsula was included within the RSFSR. For the Tatars, this was better than their possible fate had seemed in the early days of the revolution. As Professor Potichnyj has pointed out:

> Between 1917 and 1920 various Ukrainian national governments asserted their claims to the Crimea, and even Communist Ukrainian leaders were loathe to relinquish Ukrainian demands. From the standpoint of the Crimean Tatars, there were distinct advantages associated with not being subordinated to the Ukrainian Republic. . . . more autonomy to be enjoyed from a government located afar.[15]

Administrative Organization

According to the decree establishing the Crimean ASSR, its administration was made up of the Republican Council of Workers, Peasants, and the Black Sea Fleet; a Crimean Central Executive Committee; and the Council of Peoples' Commissars. The Republican Council of Workers, Peasants, and the Black Sea Fleet had basic political authority. In its makeup, this council heavily favored the urban and more revolutionary population. The Workers' Council had one delegate representing each 500 urban inhabitants, and the Council of Peasants had only one delegate for each 2500 members of the rural population. The Crimean Central Executive Committee, which consisted of fifty members, was selected from the Council of Workers, Peasants, and the Black Sea Fleet. Finally, the Council of Peoples' Commissars, which consisted of twelve members was at the top; it was chosen by the Executive Committee and approved by Moscow.[16]

The Land Question and Famine

It is clear that, at the beginning, this government did not reflect either Tatar interests or sensibilities. Seizing almost half of the cultivatable land on the peninsula, and laying the groundwork for a series of large collective farms, the policies of the new republican government precipitated a famine in the Crimea. The Crimea did not suffer this calamity alone; indeed, the famine that struck the central regions of the Soviet state during the winter of 1920–1921 was in most respects as bad as that in the Crimea. According to one estimate, as many as 27 million people in the state suffered from starvation by the fall of 1921. The Crimea, however, suffered especially, since the Soviet government seized Crimean foodstuffs and shipped them to the "more important" central regions to ease the effects of the famine there.[17]

However, the republican government's first acts on the land question cannot explain the disastrous effect that Soviet rule had on the Crimean economy during these early months. On October 23, 1921, the Council of Peoples' Commissars in Simferopol' abolished private property "to satisfy the land needs of the peasants." This land was reorganized on paper into several hundred large state farms. But there is every evidence that virtually none of this reorganization was accomplished by the fall of 1921, when the harvests were due, or by the spring of 1922. The only possible explanation for the distress in the Crimea must be the refusal of the rural Crimean population to provide their harvests for distribution in the towns, coupled with the growing demands for this produce in other areas of Russia. Indeed, the gravest effects of the famine were felt in the Crimean cities. Estimates of a mortality rate as high as 50 percent (in Bahçesaray) have been recorded for that winter. Evidence of Soviet intention to use the famine as a road to complete Tatar submission is Soviet confiscation of Turkish grain in Sevastopol' and its transfer to the central regions. The Simferopol' government also rejected Italian Red Cross aid to the Crimea.[18]

The famine had terrible effects on the Crimean population. In the primarily non-Tatar city of Sevastopol' more than 11 percent of the population died. The entire peninsula's population decreased by more than 21 percent. This figure includes some 50,000 who fled across the border, many of them Tatars moving to Rumania, and as many as 100,000 who died of starvation. Of this latter figure, only some 60 percent were Tatars. Thus the results were not felt solely by the Tatar population.[19] A contemporary description of life in Evpatoriia at this time portrays the situation:

> Bands of gypsies live in the suburbs of the city, dying of hunger. Robberies are innumerable during the night. The soldiers of the Red Army, in rags and bare feet and dying of hunger, attack the inhabitants at nightfall and steal their clothing. The Communists are not exempt from these attacks. The lack of fuel requires that doors, windows of houses are used for heating. . . . The commissar of health in the Crimea, Semachko, in order to purchase the necessary medicines, has decided to sell abroad "useless toys" including bronzes, paintings, furniture, and objects of art from the Crimean palaces.[20]

Almost all industrial production that had survived the war was shut down for lack of fuel and raw materials. The fishing industry ceased to operate because of "a serious shortage of line and other necessities for fishing, as they had been requisitioned by the Bolsheviks and taken to Russia."[21] Schools were closed because professors and students had left for lack of food. The price of a loaf of bread climbed from 90,000 rubles in October 1921 to over 150,000 rubles in May 1922. According to a report published in *Izvestia* on July 15, 1922, by Kalinin, who had traveled to inspect the Crimean disaster, the number of starving in the Crimea had reached 302,000 persons in February of that year. Of this number, 14,413 had died. In March, 379,000 were starving and 19,902 died; and in April, 377,000 were starving, and 12,754 died. By any measure, these are grim statistics.[22]

Faced with serious shortages in every necessary commodity, and with the projection of further economic deterioration, the Bolshevik government concluded that drastic measures were needed. Of course, similar, if not so serious problems were occurring elsewhere in the Soviet state. The Crimean problem was not Lenin's only one. Yet there is no question that the situation in the Crimea was worse than elsewhere in the state. A new economic policy was needed.

N. E. P. and Veli Ibrahimov

As they had found Sultan Galiev in the Volga region, the Bolsheviks found a Crimean Tatar Bolshevik, Veli Ibrahimov, to take charge of reconstruction in 1923. Veli Ibrahimov had been one of the editors of *Kirim Ocaği* in Simferopol' in July 1917 and a member of the Tatar National Directory in October 1918. He had been a member of the leftist faction of the Milli Firka and had pressed for collaboration with the Bolsheviks at the end of the White Guard occupation. Now a committed Communist, he nevertheless had strong Crimean Tatar nationalist tendencies. During the period when he occupied the positions of chairman of the Crimean Central Committee and chairman of the Crimean Council of Peoples' Commissars, he strove to implement Tatar national culture and political life. He was the perfect individual to implement Lenin's New Economic Policy in the Crimea, a policy that would bring with it a liberalization of agricultural and economic policy, and a loosening of political and cultural restrictions.[23]

It is remarkable that Lenin and the Bolshevik leadership were willing to give in to the desires of the Crimean Tatars. The makeup of the Crimean population in 1923 was as follows:[24]

Russians and Ukrainians	306,000	49.1%
Tatars	150,000	25.0
Jews	50,000	8.0
Germans	40,000	6.4
Armenians	12,000	2.0
Bulgarians	12,000	2.0
	623,000	

Party membership in 1921 was:

Workers	49.8%
Peasants	23.1
Others	27.1

Of the 5875 members of the Crimean Bolshevik party organization in 1918, only 192 were Crimean Tatars. By 1925, the total membership had risen to 6450 and included 333 Tatars. At that time, the party was composed of:[25]

Workers	63.0%
Peasants	17.3
Others	19.7

Yet in the face of these numbers, the Bolshevik leadership strongly advocated utilizing Veli Ibrahimov in the Crimea. Because of his earlier work for the Crimean newspapers and his early participation in the Crimean National Government, government leaders should have expected Ibrahimov's interest in national goals. But, as Professor Bennigsen has wisely noted: "The Muslims were deluded into thinking that they could take advantage of the new regime in finally implementing their reformist movement; and the Bolsheviks entertained falsely the hope that they would be able to reeducate their fellow travellers and make them in the long run into good Marxists."[26] The Bolsheviks also hoped that Socialist or Communist Tatars would see the errors in a nationalist policy that opposed the centralizing nature of the Soviet state.

Veli Ibrahimov's policies took several forms. First, he introduced Crimean Tatars into all levels of government in the Crimean ASSR. He drew especially from the Milli Firka party. This party had been outlawed in early 1921 and so its operations remained underground and illegal. Yet as most Tatars will admit, the Milli Firka exercised considerable influence both in Crimean affairs and on the leadership of Veli Ibrahimov. Lemercier-Quelquejay has remarked that, until 1927, the Crimea was "one of the few Muslim territories of Soviet Russia where the political importance of the native element was greater than its numerical importance."[27]

Second, Ibrahimov returned much of the Crimean economic structure to those who had held it before 1918. That is to say, lands went back to their former landowners and peasant villages, and industrial enterprises were returned to their former management if it could be found. Much of the land had been owned by absentee Russian landowners and most of that land was transferred directly to the Tatar villagers who occupied and utilized it. A conscious effort was made to give total amnesty to all Crimean Tatars who had fled abroad during the revolution and to encourage their participation in the Crimea's economy. Ahmed Ozenbaşli, one of Ibrahimov's chief ideologues of this period and a theorist of national communism, wrote:

The Soviet regime, resting on the dictatorship of the working class alone, is justified in central Russia, where industrial capital has already touched the peak of its development. . . . But when this regime is applied to nomadic Muslim masses, or to those who have only just entered the era of merchant capitalism, it fails to be viable. We wish then for assistance in passing through the stages of economic development normally. We do not wish to skip such development so as to plunge into forms of government that we can neither understand nor assimilate. . . . In the Crimea, the principle of national government must be adopted, not the principle of class government.[28]

Third, and most important for the Crimean Tatar intelligentsia, Ibrahimov pursued a cultural policy of Tatarization of the Crimea. This included reopening national Tatar-run schools, scientific institutes, museums, libraries, and theaters. As Kirimal points out, this policy (which lasted until 1927) went a long way toward creation of a new Crimean Tatar national intelligentsia. Graduates of these schools were prepared to enter national life in the areas of the press, literature, and the government. The Crimean Tatar language was recognized with Russian as the state language of the Crimean ASSR. A number of books on Crimean Tatar history and culture were published. In Simferopol', scholarly journals were begun, and they offered frequent contributions from members of the former nationalist Tatar intelligentsia such as Bekir Çobanzade, Hasan Sabri Ayvaz, Osman Akçokrakli, and Ahmet Ozenbaşli. In 1924, in Simferopol' (which was now allowed to be called by its former Tatar name, Akmeçet) Tavrida University was opened; at that time it had a science faculty and, after 1925, an Oriental institute. There the language and literature of the Crimean Tatars were taught and studied. Crimean Tatar teachers' schools were established in Kefe, Bahçesaray, Ialta, and Simferopol'.[29]

Yet with all of this development, there is no evidence that either Veli Ibrahimov or the vast majority of his supporters and officials ever intended complete independence for the Crimean Tatars. They seemed more than happy to work within the contours of Soviet policy. However, in 1928, the dream ended with the elimination of Ibrahimov and his associates. A vast purge of the Tatar intelligentsia who had been pursuing the course of national communism followed.

Stalin and Ibrahimov's Removal

A seemingly minor issue precipitated Veli Ibrahimov's removal, but it coincided with a change in Moscow's political direction. Stalin's decisive victory in which he took direction of the Party after Lenin's death made him ready to put an end to the "lax policies begun with the N.E.P. [New Economic

Policy]" and to destroy the national communist movements throughout the Soviet Union. The issue in the Crimea was, on the surface, one of land use and appropriation. One of Ibrahimov's primary intentions had been to open new areas of the northern steppe to agricultural settlement and production. In the years 1925–1927, two dozen new settlements and villages were peopled with southern Tatars and Tatars returning from Rumania. Then in late 1927, perhaps because the Soviets did not want them elsewhere, the government ordered Ibrahimov to make room on the southern coast of the Crimea for some 3500 Jewish families from Belorussia. Ibrahimov complained about Moscow's interference in internal Crimean affairs. He pointed out that this involved moving some 3000 to 3500 Tatar and Russian families from their homes to make room for the newcomers, and he felt that the whole project was without merit.[30]

Moscow's response, signed by Stalin himself, was terse, and in January 1928, Ibrahimov was arrested and accused as a bourgeois nationalist. His trial took place in the spring, and on May 9, 1928, he was executed. In the next year, the Communist party in the Crimea as well as government organizations "tinged with Veli Ibrahimovism" were purged. This affected at least 3500 Tatars. Some were executed, others imprisoned and exiled. It is clear that Moscow's policy in this period was not merely a response to Ibrahimov's protest; rather, it was a frontal attack on Tatar national communism. Moscow's policy was a part of a much larger program of "Sovietization" of local Communist parties, which in the Crimea took on the character of Russianization.[31]

A recent Soviet account ignores the Jewish problem entirely and merely criticizes Ibrahimov for his social and economic policies. "He pursued a program of helping the *kulaks* [rich peasants] in the Crimea. Together with the *kulaks* and the bourgeois nationalists, Ibrahimov worked against the poor."[32] (Of course, that had been Lenin's policy too.) In Ibrahimov's place, the Bolsheviks named another Tatar, Mehmet Kubay, chairman of the Crimean Central Committee. The first (1937) edition of the *Great Soviet Encyclopedia (B.S.E.)* describes Veli Ibrahimovism and the "bourgeois nationalist deviation" in the Crimea thus: "The Milli Firka continued to resist, sowing national discord. Nationalist feeling in the Communist party itself now became acute, as well as armed struggle against the revolution in the form of banditism."[33]

Sovietization of Crimean Society

Sovietization of Tatar society took several forms. First, all educational institutions were given new leadership. In some cases, this resulted in a change of Tatar directorship. Tatars whose education had long preceded the revolution were removed and replaced by the "new Soviet Tatar intelligentsia." In other cases, the Tatars were replaced by Russians or Ukrainians. Editorial boards of newspapers and journals, directors of Tatar national theaters, and writers and poets were removed from their posts. Many were tried on charges of bourgeois nationalism or anti-Soviet activity and sentenced to exile in the Urals and western Siberia. One observer noted that "virtually the entire prerevolutionary Tatar intelligentsia was eliminated in the year after Ibrahimov's removal."[34]

There was a Latinization of the Tatar alphabet. Although it must be admitted that some of the Tatar intelligentsia were in favor of this move, and several, among them Çobanzade, worked with the Turcologist, Samoilovich, in planning this reform, it had a disastrous effect upon Tatar language and literature. The forced introduction of this new alphabet cut off the new generation of Tatar students from the wealth of prerevolutionary and even early postrevolutionary Tatar literature that had been written and published in the Arabic alphabet. The reform gave the government an easy method of selecting what Tatar literature they would permit the younger generation to read—they allowed only certain works to be translated and republished in Latin characters. In fairness, it should be noted that the very same reform, with the same results, was taking place at the same time in Atatürk's Republican Turkey. And it must be further noted that the Latin alphabet is a better conveyor for the Tatar language than either the Arabic or the Slavic alphabet. (Cyrillic is as unfit for this purpose as Arabic was.) Chirva admits that "the Tatar nationalists and clergy were opposed because it would weaken their ideological position and their influence. Thus the reform of Tatar literacy was not only of cultural but also of political impact."[35]

Struggle Against "Bourgeois Nationalism"

The Soviet attack on Crimean Tatar "bourgeois nationalism" did not stop with their culture. In 1928–1929, "bourgeois elements and *kulak*s" in the Tatar economy were also ruthlessly removed. They either disappeared or were sent to various labor camps and settlements in Siberia. The figures on the number removed from the Crimea during these two years vary from 35,000 to 40,000. They must have accounted for a substantial percent of those peasants and farmers on the peninsula.[36]

According to an article in *Revoliutsiia i natsionalnosti,* in 1930, the problem was that:

in the Crimea . . . the power of former landlords and *kulak*s is still preserved. Their land has not yet been properly nationalized; the village poor have not been given land, they remain oppressed and exploited by the *kulak*s. The

Soviet and cooperative organizations were infested with alien elements, and the villages had no representation. It was only after an investigation by the Central Committee of the CPSU [Communist party of the Soviet Union] that an end was put to this disgusting state of affairs. . . . In the Crimea, it was the group of Ibrahimov that opposed and resisted the agrarian revolution; not only the feudal and capitalist elements, which is natural, but at times also a section of the party and soviet apparatus that defends and represents the interests of those elements.[37]

The struggle against the *kulak*s left a broad swath through the Crimean rural population. Many, if not most, of those removed to central Asia and Siberia could in no way be considered to have been powerful or rich farmers. One eyewitness to the collectivization of Crimean agriculture described it:

They gathered thousands. . . . People who had grown up in the mild climate of the south and had never left the mountains or sea shores were made to emigrate to the taygas and tundras so that they perished in the early stage of the emigration. This was not some kind of a general measure but mass extermination, the ruthless and meaningless extermination of a whole nation.[38]

Of course this was an exaggeration. There were still many Crimean Tatars to remove to central Asia in 1944. Yet the results of the policy were clear, and they should be kept in mind when considering the reaction of many Crimean Tatars to the German invasion in 1941.

Tatar Resistance and Collectivization

There is evidence of at least one uprising by Crimean Tatar peasants in response to these policies; it took place in Alakat, on the south coast of the Crimea in December 1929 and January 1930. But the peasants were no match for the massed force of the Soviet authorities. According to an eyewitness, Omar Mustafa Oğlu, on January 18, 1930, the government sent both army and navy against Alakat, arrested all members of families in the region, and shot many of them on the spot. Forty-two elders of the village of Uskut were executed in Simferopol' on March 24.[39]

There were other sorts of resistance to the forced collectivization too. According to a Soviet account, many peasants in the Crimea killed their livestock rather than turn them over to the new state farms. "In the Karasu Bazaar region in 1927, there were 9309 horses and 65,000 sheep, while in 1930, there were only 4835 horses and 26,000 sheep." These actions were dubbed counterrevolutionary activity. In supporting the degree of force required for the collectivization in the Crimea, Khazanov wrote: "the Tatar nationalists had relations with the capitalist elements in Turkey. The Tatar bourgeois nationalists and right-wing opportunists claimed that in the

Crimea there was no class struggle, and among the Tatars there were no
kulaks."[40]

The primary result of the forced collectivization in the Crimea (which
consisted of removing the most productive agricultural population, sending
them to the east, and seizing lands from villages and rural settlements) was a
recurrence of the terrible famine of 1921–1922. This time, the period of
famine lasted from 1931 until 1933. What made the situation far worse than
before was that even in the months of the most severe food shortages, the
Soviet authorities confiscated food which they exported in return for foreign
currency needed for industrialization. The peasants did not have control of
their own villages and thus could not hold back enough for subsistence.
Aleksandrov, who witnessed these years in the Crimea, later wrote:

> During the dreadful famine years of 1931–1933, when bodies were piled in the
> streets of villages and towns, foreign ships were incessantly loading golden
> wheat in Crimean ports, and unfermented wine was being poured through
> pipes into the holds of tankers. The terrible famine mowed down all who had
> stayed behind. Foodstuffs were deliberately not imported into this area,
> deprived of its own produce.[41]

The situation reached such a state that Mehmet Kubay, chairman of the
Central Committee of the Crimean ASSR issued a strong protest to Moscow
in which he courageously wrote, "Moscow plunders the Republic of the
Crimea and exports all her natural resources, while leaving no food to the
people starving to death."[42]

Soviet figures for production during these years are instructive about the
disastrous effect of the policy of collectivization—especially in 1932, the year
of the first annual harvest under the new system. The production of fruit
products in 1932 was only 33 percent of that of 1931; production of grapes
declined 30 percent and tobacco declined 50 percent.[43]

With one known exception, Moscow authorities were completely insensitive to the problems being encountered by the Crimean Tatars. That
exception is a peculiar notice that appeared in the journal *Revoliutsiia i
natsionalnosti* in 1934. It stated that the local Crimean Communist authorities
were acting in an irresponsible way in deciding which Tatar peasants to call
kulaks:

> The Soviet apparatus of that district (Karasu Bazaar) is obviously in a bad state,
> in that not only the village soviets are utterly indifferent to the complaints,
> but also the District Executive Committee itself. Again and again the soviets in
> that district were giving the peasant plaintiffs fictitious, utterly unjustifiable,
> and even fantastic classifications (such as the ownership of 400 hectares of land,
> or of 200–300 head of cattle, employment of twenty farm laborers, and so
> forth). But the checkups revealed that the households were always those of

working peasants, and that not even the grandfathers and great-grandfathers of the plaintiffs had ever owned such an amount of land or cattle.

The telling conclusion to this report, however, was that nothing was being done to rectify the situation. Crimean peasants continued to suffer great injustices.

> It should be pointed out that the Crimean Executive Committee does not struggle hard enough against this kind of irresponsibility on the part of the local Soviet officials. In spite of many letters from the secretariat of the chairman of the All-Russian Central Executive Committee, nothing decisive was done in Karasu Bazaar and other districts in order to regularize the handling of the complaints.[44]

By 1933, the Crimean Tatar community had suffered a number of devastating blows. They had seen the Sovietization of their cultural and educational life, which had removed all Tatars deemed untrustworthy from their posts; they had seen the removal of their most effective Crimean Tatar communist leader, Veli Ibrahimov, and those who had worked with him during the Crimean "Golden Age"; and they had seen the famine caused by the attempted destruction of Tatar agricultural life. Between 1917 and 1933, approximately 150,000 or 50 percent of the Crimean Tatars had either been killed or forced to leave the Crimea. Those who left went to central Asia for resettlement or to labor camps, or they went abroad to Rumania and Turkey. The vast majority of Crimean political and cultural leaders were among these groups. Those leaders who remained (at least until 1933) were considered politically safe for the Soviet regime. Yet even they found it impossible to remain silent and to acquiesce in a policy aimed at the destruction of the Crimean Tatar community. These leaders were dealt with by the Soviet authorities during the period of the "Great Purges," which took place between 1933 and 1939.

The Purges in the Crimea

Kubay was removed and executed after his protest about the famine. He was replaced as chairman of the Crimean ASSR Central Committee by Ilias Tarhan and as chairman of the Council of Peoples' Commissars for the Crimea by Ibrahim Samedin. From 1933 to 1936, whether reluctantly or not, these two officials presided over the virtual elimination of all of the remainder of the Crimean intelligentsia. Among those tried for "bourgeois nationalism and anti-Soviet activity," were a variety of "nationalists, counterrevolutionaries, traitors, anti-Soviet elements, *kulak*s, and Trotskiites."[45]

On October 5, 1936, the Simferopol' newspaper, *Yani Dunya,* noted the purge of the Pedagogical Institute of the Crimea. This included Çobanzade (who had been instrumental in introducing Latinization of the alphabet), Hasan Ayvaz, Osman Akçokrakli, and the novelist, Latifzade. At the same time, the Faculty for Tatar Language and Culture in the Tavrida University was eliminated. Those executed included historians Hilmi, Akçokrakli, and Aziz; Turkologists Çobanzade, Ayvaz, Liman, Odabaşli, Cemalettin, and Tanabayli; professors of medicine Osman, Abdullah, and Omer; University and Institute directors Hasan, Çeşmeci, Aleksandrovich, Şumin and Bekir; journalists Sukuti, Turpçu, and Murgaza; and poets Biranbay, Latifzade, Şimzade, Kadir, Camanakli, and Cavtobeli. An interesting sidelight to this policy was the account on Tatar literature that was given in the 1937 edition of the *B.S.E.* which states that "talented writers in the Crimea had grown up in the struggle with the remnants of bourgeois nationalism," and offers no other details or explanation.[46] At this point the anti-Tatar campaign reached into the Muslim clergy for the first time since 1921. Almost all mosques and clerically controlled schools were closed. Clergymen were deprived of positions and forced to leave for central Asia or abroad.[47]

To complete their Sovietization of the Crimea, Bolshevik authorities needed to destroy the Tatar contingent in the Crimean Communist party and introduce a policy of Russification of Tatar culture. Both of these occurred in the years 1936–1940: the last remaining Tatar members of the party who could be considered even slightly interested in nationalist deviations, were removed and the Crimean ASSR was reorganized in such a way as to make the title "Autonomous" meaningless. In November 1936, at the Eighth Congress of Soviets, Stalin had said specifically about the Crimean ASSR, "Take the Crimean Autonomous Republic for example. . . . But the Crimean Tatars . . . are a minority. Consequently it would be wrong and illogical to transfer the Crimean Republic to the category of Union Republics."[48]

The new Soviet Constitution of 1936 brought with it major changes for the Crimean Republic—changes in line with Stalin's thoughts on the Tatars' minority position. First of all, the Crimean ASSR was more closely bound to the RSFSR. The Crimean soviet was not to be permitted any final action without prior approval of the RSFSR authorities. Internally, the Crimean administration was divided according to legislative and executive authority. The legislative organ became the All-Crimean soviet, which was to be chosen by election every four years. Its members came from within the Communist party and represented workers' unions, professional unions, state farms, and youth organizations. The executive power was in the hands of the Council of Peoples' Commissars, twelve members of which were chosen by the All-Crimean Soviet and one member chosen by the Central Committee of the CPSU. All elections were subject to supervision by RSFSR authorities; none of the Crimean institutions could act without RSFSR approval.[49] There was to be no question of any policy of autonomous activity. Finally, during the purges, Ilias Tarhan, Samedin, and all members of their government were removed, arrested, and either deported or executed.[50]

Russification of Tatar Culture

In the cultural area, Sovietization meant Russification. With the loss of most of the native creative intelligentsia in the purges, the Crimean Tatar cultural community had no leadership with which to face the onslaught of Russification. In 1938, the Latin alphabet was replaced with the Cyrillic. At the same time, most existing Tatar literature was declared to be politically unacceptable ("nonproletarian and non-Soviet"). The number of journals and newspapers published in the Tatar language dropped from twenty-three in 1935 to nine in 1938. Arabic, Persian, and Turkish words were excised from the Tatar language, and Russian words and grammatical rules were introduced.[51]

Finally, in 1937–1938, the Communist government in the Crimea embarked on a policy of sheer terrorism in the Tatar countryside. The official justification for this activity was the need to reform the social and family customs of the Crimean Tatars so as to allow them to conform with Soviet (Russian) standards for social behavior. The result of this activity was predictable. Villages resisted any official intrusion into their family matters. The Soviet response to this resistance was the use of heavy force. Hundreds of peasants were arrested by agents of the NKVD (Peoples' Commissariat of Internal Affairs). One of the residents of Karasu Bazaar writes of a night in December 1937:

> Sixty were arrested. I was also included among them. Meanwhile all of our Muslim clergy were in the Karasu Bazaar prison. Among them, one of the most outstanding clergymen and educators of the Crimea, Sheik Mehmet Hoca Ahmet Vecdi, who was seventy years old; Sheik Şeyzade Abdulmecit, aged seventy-five; Kafadar Haci Muzaffer, aged eighty, and so forth.

Another wrote: "In 1937, seventeen Tatars were arrested in the Kilchoi village of Ichky Region, which contained forty-five Tatar and forty-five Russian dwellings. Out of those who were arrested, only two ever returned. Others perished in the prisons."[52]

The story of the Crimean Tatars during the interwar period is bleak. Yet there exist a few pieces of evidence that do not fit into this picture of total persecution. First of all, there are the above-mentioned reports from Moscow about the admitted misbehavior of local Crimean Communists. Moscow made at least a minimal effort to correct these actions. Also, there was the recognition in 1930 that, to that time, Soviet policies in the Crimea had not succeeded in bringing enough Tatars into the political and economic life of that Soviet Autonomous Republic. Again, published in *Revoliutsiia i natsionalnosti,* in 1930, we read that:

> The picture of the indigenization of the central apparatus in the Crimea is as follows: in the Peoples' Commissariat of Finance, only 7 of the 107 officials are Tatars; in the Peoples' Commissariat of Agriculture, 46 of 606 officials are Tatars; in Soyuzkhleb, only 2 of 66 employees are Tatars, and both are . . . messengers. In the other central institutions, too, we get almost exactly the same picture. Matters are no better regarding the development of cadres from the indigenous proletariat: the Crimean industries employ 27,210 workers, but these include only 1806 Tatars. The metallurgical plant (the largest undertaking in the Crimea) has only 416 Tatars (5.3 percent) among its 8103 workers.[53]

Thus, although this evidence further substantiates the Tatars' complaints about not being able to participate fully in their own national life, government authorities were aware of the problem and were not satisfied with the results of their policy. Of course, there is no evidence that either of these reports had any verifiable impact upon either Crimean society or Soviet policy.

A second peculiar event, for which there is no explanation or justification, occurred in 1934, when the Crimean ASSR became the first autonomous republic to receive the Order of Lenin—for "great contributions in economic and cultural construction."[54]

Third, in 1935, the report by the Committee for Economic Planning for the Southern Shore of the Crimea was published. It emphasized, throughout, the poor treatment of the Tatars by the Russians, from 1783 until 1935, and promised to try to rectify the situation on the southern shore. It made such statements as "under the slogan 'orthodoxy, autocracy, and nationality' the best land was taken from the local Tatar population and distributed to the eternal use of new *pomeshchiks*," and "the cruel policies of the government forced more than a quarter million Tatars to emigrate."[55]

This committee's recommendations were not remarkable for the effect they had on the Tatar population, yet they evidenced real concern for the Tatars' economic plight. They proposed that a much higher proportion of the workers in the Crimean health resorts be taken from the local Tatar population rather than "importing from central regions workers who have plenty of work already." In an admission of a racist attitude, the report stated that Russians coming to the Crimea must be forced to give up the idea that "only Slavs should serve them here." In addition, the report proposed that Tatars who had either voluntarily or through coercion left the Crimea be "persuaded to return" since the region was distinctly "underpopulated at the present time."[56]

Finally, the article on the Crimea published in the 1937 edition of the *B.S.E.* gives an historical account of the Crimean Tatars that is remarkable for its objectivity. It includes such statements as:

> After 1783, the weight of the heavy colonial yoke forced many Crimean Tatars to emigrate. After 1802, continued Russification of this frontier forced the emigration to continue. . . . The movement of the Tatars away from the coast during the Crimean War conveniently allowed the Russians to seize the best lands. . . . By the end of the century, the Russian government's policy was characterized by economic, cultural, and legal inequality.

This article even discussed the Tatar political development prior to 1918 in a relatively direct and honest fashion, leaving only the Soviet period—and especially that of Veli Ibrahimovism—for the customary diatribes against bourgeois nationalism.[57]

The year 1941 ushered in a new period for the Crimean Tatars. These years brought the defeat of the Soviet army in the south and the German and Rumanian occupation of the peninsula. The behavior of the Crimean Tatars during this period proved to be the cause of the final disaster of 1944. In approaching this subject, several facts must be remembered. First, the activities of the Soviet government between 1928 and 1939 had resulted in the destruction of the Crimean Tatar native political and cultural leadership to an extent not experienced by any other Soviet nationality. Almost half of the Tatar population had already been destroyed or deported. Second, the Tatar masses, that is the peasants, had not experienced a single verifiable benefit from Soviet rule. They had suffered the same fate as their leadership. As Lemercier-Quelquejay wrote: "It was an enfeebled and exhausted Tatar community that encountered the final tragedy, German occupation, and later, deportation."[58]

13. The Crimean Tatars in World War II

In October 1973, the Jewish poet and teacher Ilya Yankelevich Gabai committed suicide by leaping from the balcony of his eleventh floor apartment in Moscow. This was far more than a personal tragedy. Gabai had been the most prominent Jewish dissident in the Soviet Union to struggle for the rights of other repressed nationalities and cultural groups, especially those of the Crimean Tatars. Arrested, tried, sentenced to years in labor camps, incarcerated in psychiatric asylums, Gabai personally suffered for his beliefs and for his actions on behalf of both Jews and Tatars. Why should a Jew have taken such interest in the Muslim Crimean Tatars? Gabai had been convinced that the suffering of Jews and Tatars after World War II derived from the same source, namely a continuing prejudice against them on the part of the Russian element in the Soviet Union. He believed there could be no other explanation for the treatment of the Crimean Tatars after 1944.

To Western ears, this argument sounds strange. We have been told by Soviet politicians and historians as well as by most Western scholars interested in Soviet affairs that the Tatars were punished for blatant acts of collaboration with the German occupation forces in the Crimea. While their punishment was harsh, it has been said that it was well deserved.

Yet on the basis of recently revealed evidence from a variety of sources, our beliefs about the Tatar "treason" during the war need to be revised. Even in his secret speech to the Twentieth Party Congress in 1956, Chairman Khrushchev suggested that Stalin's claims about the collaboration of certain nationalities with the Germans had been wrong.[1]

Yet Khrushchev refused at that time to include the Crimean Tatars in his exoneration. But in 1967, in the face of a growing mass movement among the Crimean Tatars in their places of exile (primarily around Tashkent), the Soviet government issued a decree containing a partial rehabilitation in which it said that in 1944 charges had been "groundlessly leveled at the whole Tatar population of the Crimea."[2] This decree was published only in the Tashkent area, and most Soviet citizens are still ignorant of it today. The Tatars are still denied the right to return to the Crimea. Yet the mere publication of such a decree gives us an indication of how false the original charges may have been.

There are three different accounts of the activities of the Crimean Tatars during the Second World War, and at first glance they are mutually exclusive.

The first account is by Soviet historians (the account generally accepted in the West) of traitorous behavior by the Crimean Tatar people from 1941 until 1944. It includes charges of (1) active Tatar collaboration with the German and Rumanian occupation regime in both political and military affairs, (2) armed Tatar opposition to the efforts by Soviet partisans in the Crimea, and (3) Tatar participation in German self-defense battalions. First-hand accounts of Soviet partisan leaders in the Crimea document these charges. From this come the explanation and justification for the group punishment levied upon the Tatars after the war.

A second account, and one that has been discussed only in recent years, is by the Germans; it is based on German wartime documents. Here one meets a decidedly different emphasis—one that dismisses the Tatars as Orientals and as a prime example of *Untermenschen,* who were not important subjects for German consideration during the war. Much of the German documentation expresses the view that eventually the Tatars were to be removed from the Crimea to make way for the more racially and historically worthy Germans. Other Soviet nationalities are consistently mentioned as more trustworthy supporters of the German occupation regime than the Tatars, and not much is said about the active collaboration or great support the Russians say the Crimean Tatars gave to the Germans. On the basis of the German evidence, the Soviet treatment of the Tatars becomes much less justifiable.

Finally, the third account, provided by the Crimean Tatars themselves and supported by documents from other Soviet dissidents in the Samizdat press, emphasizes four points: (1) as a result of the purges in the 1930s, there was no able Tatar leadership in the Crimea on the eve of the war; (2) difficulties experienced by the Tatars during the war included economic and political repression from the Germans as well as reprisals and terror from the Soviet partisans; (3) the Tatars attempted to recreate their national life, which had been destroyed after 1928; and (4) Tatars were shocked and surprised at the complete elimination of their nationality in 1944 for reasons they still are unable to understand. It is a difficult task for the historian to recreate a picture of the years 1941–1944 that is true to the evidence provided by all three of these accounts.

Nazi Plans for the Crimea

Although the Crimea was on the southern border of the Soviet Union, the Germans had already planned in April and May of 1941 to invade and occupy the peninsula. At the beginning of April 1941, Alfred Rosenberg, the director of the foreign bureau of the Nazi Party, issued a memorandum that contemplated division of the Soviet Union into seven regions, one of which was to be "the Ukraine and the Crimea." Here there was no thought of a separate Crimean entity. Indeed, Alexander Dallin points out, "the inclusion of the Crimea as well as the Russian Cossack territories west of the Volga meant the award of extensive alien areas to the Ukraine." Later, Rosenberg clarified his position on the Crimea by stating that, although "it was to be part of the future greater Ukraine under the name of Taurida," it would be kept under "direct German rule."[3]

Even before the German advance toward the east, German military and political planners left no doubt that there would be no room for Tatar inhabitants in the Crimea once it had been absorbed by the Reich. According to early Nazi racist theory, "Mongol, Tatar, and Kirgiz were all considered synonyms for subhumans. It was the Asiaticization of Russia that had destroyed its racial purity." In a propaganda piece published for home consumption as late as 1943, the Germans spoke of "Tatar types" and "Asiatic backwardness" being replaced in the Crimea by the "better race."[4]

At a policymaking conference on July 16, 1941, Hitler decided that the Crimea "was to become a purely German colony, from which all foreigners were to be deported or evacuated."[5] Among the foreigners he included the Crimean Tatars. Hitler viewed the Crimea as the future German Gibraltar in the Black Sea. During the next year, the Germans were to consider the transformation of the Crimea into a German *Gotenland*; Simferopol' would receive the historic name of Gotenberg and Sevastopol' would become Theodorichhafen. Germans living in Rumania and in the South Tyrol would be moved there. Hitler is reported to have said at the time, "I think the idea is an excellent one. . . . I think, too, that the Crimea will be both climatically and geographically ideal for the South Tyrolese."[6]

There were other considerations that inclined the Germans toward the Crimea. First, the German command believed that sufficient pressure could be brought upon the Turkish government to bring it into the war on the side of the Axis. After all, the Turks had long been friends of the Germans, had fought alongside Germans in the First World War, and had realized that the Soviet government never really abandoned the desires of their tsarist predecessors to expand southward. But this meant that the Germans had to handle the Crimean Tatar question delicately, for of all the Soviet nationalities, the Crimean Tatars had excited Turkish interest the most intensely. For this reason and no other, the German officials decided against early transfer of the Tatars out of the Crimea. In fact, Von Papen, the German ambassador in Ankara, pleaded with his government after the completion of the Crimean campaign, to establish there an administration in which the Crimean Tatars would participate. This, he felt, would have a strong political effect in Turkey.[7]

Finally, Hitler and his general staff realized that control of the Crimea was essential for two strategic reasons: (1) it was a southern guarantee of control over the Ukraine, and (2) in Soviet hands, it could become "a Soviet aircraft carrier for attacking the Rumanian oil fields." Also, denial of the Crimea to the Soviet government would inflict heavy economic damage upon their war effort by depriving them of its contributions of industrial and agricultural production.[8]

German Invasion

Despite the fact that such plans had been in the works for months and the fact that the Crimean invasion did not occur until three months after the outbreak of the German-Russian war, the Soviet administration in the Crimea was completely unprepared for the German takeover. Between the time of their first appearance at Perekop in September and November 30, the German and Rumanian divisions led by General Manstein captured the entire peninsula with the exception of Sevastopol'. This occurred even though they were heavily outnumbered at the time. It was only in the cities of Odessa and Sevastopol' that the Nazis met serious resistance. (For this reason these two cities were later assigned the title of Heroic City of the USSR.) In late December, the Soviet command succeeded in landing new forces at Kerch and Feodosiia, but in a relatively short time, they too were forced to evacuate. After a furious series of battles, Sevastopol' fell to the Germans in July 1942, with heavy loss of life on both sides.[9]

Between September and December of 1941, two events took place in which the Crimean Tatar leadership set the stage for future collaboration with the German regime. First, in most Crimean cities the German advancing army was met with jubilation and calls of "liberators" from the local Tatar population. This was no surprise. Little that had occurred in the 1930s had given the Tatars to think that they were living in anything other than a Soviet (Russian) colonial appendage to the USSR. In the last years before the outbreak of war, the purges and the destruction of the Tatar national leadership had been especially severe. By 1941, most of the leading Tatar officials were either dead or in Soviet labor camps in western Siberia, and the Tatar Communist leadership had been greatly depleted as a result of Stalin's efforts to eliminate all traces of national communism in the USSR. Thus, what could have been expected from the Crimean Tatars when a foreign army entered their homeland with the announced purpose of removing that "hated Soviet leadership" other than the jubilation that provided the Soviet government with one more justification for the Tatars' group punishment.[10]

The second event involved three Crimean Tatar leaders from the exile community in Turkey and Rumania: Cafer Seidahmet, Mustecip Ülküsal, and Edige Kirimal. Ülküsal had been the editor of the Crimean Tatar journal *Emel* in Rumania for ten years and had been one of the leading Tatar politicians in the exile community after the abolition of the Crimean A.S.S.R. Negotiations between Cafer Seidahmet and the German ambassador in Ankara, Von Papen, produced an invitation for Ülküsal and Kirimal to go to Germany to assist in the formulation of Nazi policy towards the Crimea and the Turkic peoples of the Soviet Union. In late November, 1941, these two Tatar leaders left Istanbul for Berlin where they became Crimean Tatar representatives in Germany and acted as lobbyists for the Tatar cause. Among other things, they asked for special treatment for Crimean Tatar prisoners who had been captured along with other Soviet soldiers in the first months of the war. Although they accomplished very little on behalf of the Tatars, Rosenberg is reported to have responded positively to this request out of consideration for Turkey.[11]

Soviet Evacuation

The behavior of Soviet officials evacuating the Crimean peninsula did nothing to encourage Tatar support for the anti-German struggle. In the first place, the NKVD (Peoples' Commissariat of Internal Affairs) forces in Simferopol' solved the problem of what to do with the large number of prisoners held in the Crimea by executing them all before they left. According to one eyewitness account:

> On the eve of the evacuation of Simferopol' on October 31, 1941, the NKVD shot all the prisoners in the cells under the NKVD building and the city prison. . . . After the departure of the Bolsheviks, the bodies of women and infants were discovered among the multitude of corpses in the cellars of the Simferopol' NKVD building. . . . On November 4, the NKVD shot all of the prisoners in the Ialta city prisons.[12]

It is likely that this was repeated in all of the Crimean cities. One must remember that many of the prisoners held by the NKVD in the Crimea had been charged with various "national deviations" and were political, not criminal prisoners.

In the second place, Soviet administrators preparing to evacuate the Crimea tried to prevent the Germans from receiving a windfall in supplies and industrial plants. From the perspective of the Soviet government, which was in a life-or-death struggle with Germany, whatever policy would further the Soviet war effort and at the same time hinder the Germans was the correct policy to pursue. Unfortunately, from the perspective of the Crimeans, both Tatar and non-Tatar, Soviet policies were seen in a hostile light. The Bolshevik politicians and economic managers ordered the destruction of all industrial capacity that could not be removed, burning of all warehouses that contained foodstuffs (necessary for the approaching winter months), dynamiting of water and sewage facilities, and tearing down of electrical and telephone lines. In every case, these acts of destruction made little difference to the Germans and Rumanians who continued to import all necessary supplies or to seize what they needed from the already hard-pressed local population; they did, however, make life exceedingly difficult for the Tatars and other Crimeans during the first months of the German occupation. By the next summer, virtually all Crimeans, both Russian and Tatar, saw these acts as aimed against themselves rather than against the Germans. As Kirimal has written: "the reign of terror during the retreat provided evidence (to the Tatars) that in the event of the return of the Bolsheviks to the Crimea, the Crimean population would again be subjected to persecution."[13]

German Administration of the Crimea

Once firmly in military command of the Crimean peninsula, the Germans left no doubts about their intention to rule it without sharing any significant political authority with any local representatives. The German Crimean administration was divided into three parts, each operating fairly independently of the others. First was the military command, under the direction of General Manstein, whose chief concern was the maintenance of order and the prevention of a resurgence of Soviet power in the area. Manstein tried to operate his administration in such a way that a minimum of German troops were necessary in the Crimea, thus freeing as many as possible for action on the front. Because of this overriding desire, Manstein did everything within his power to foster cordial relations with the Tatar population and tried his best to encourage the Tatars to form their own self-defense battalions, to work against partisan activity on the peninsula, and to prevent disturbances by a dissatisfied local populace. Political and racial problems were of little interest to Manstein; only those developments that influenced the German military capacity merited his attention.

Manstein was relatively successful in his attempts to gain active support from the Tatars. According to both German and Tatar evidence, the Germans persuaded between 15,000 and 20,000 Tatars to form self-defense battalions that were partially armed by the Germans and sent into the mountains to hunt down partisan units. Mühlen points out that the Crimeans wre not the only Soviet people to participate in such units—the Volga Tatars contributed between 35,000 and 40,000 volunteers; from the various Caucasian peoples over 110,000 volunteers were recruited; and the Kalmyks provided about 5000 volunteers. The irony is that it was the Kalmyks and the Crimeans, with their relatively small number of military collaborators, who were so severely punished after the war, while the Volga Tatars, with many more, escaped such group punishment entirely. Of course, the Slavic nationalities of the USSR participated much more numerously in the Nazi occupation regime than any of the Soviet oriental peoples.[14]

In order to gain Tatar support in the Crimea, Manstein realized that he had to act cautiously, particularly since the Tatars constituted barely one-fourth of its population. Thus it is no surprise that, while he consistently favored a liberal policy toward the Tatars' religious and cultural interests, Manstein steadfastly opposed granting them any political or administrative power in the Crimea. Early in the occupation, Manstein remarked: "the passivity of numerous allegedly anti-Soviet elements must yield to a clear decision in favor of active cooperation against the Bolsheviks. Where it does not exist, it must forcibly be brought about by appropriate means." Further, he said that strict "respect of religious customs, especially of the Muslim Tatars," must be maintained. During the occupation, Manstein was responsible for the granting of what rights and privileges the Tatars received.[15]

A second branch of German authority in the Crimea was that of the political command, which was under the authority of Erich Koch, Reichs-kommissar for the Ukraine. Koch's Crimean representative was Alfred Frauenfeld, General Commissar for the Crimean peninsula. Descriptions of Frauenfeld's character vary from one historian to another. Dallin argues that he was a "fanatical Nazi and an obsessed bigot," one interested solely in the "Gothic origins of Crimean culture."[16] Luther, quoting a memorandum from Professor Mende, a German Orientalist connected with the Ostministeriums, says that, although Koch had little understanding of nationality problems, Frauenfeld, an Austrian who had been supporting the Anschluss, was receptive to both cultural and national problems of minority peoples: "In contrast to Koch, Frauenfeld pursued a policy of 'fraternization' between the personnel of the occupation administration and the civilian administra-tion. . . . He was responsible for the opening of national schools and theaters."[17] Tatar sources from the period agree more with Dallin's view of Frauenfeld and believe that Manstein and the military officers were respon-sible for the "new order" relating to Tatar culture and religion.[18]

A third German administration was conducted through the offices of the police, the SS, and the Einsatzstab, under the direct authority of Rosenberg in Berlin. This administration, perhaps unintentionally, succeeded in under-mining the activities of the other two by acting in a particularly chauvinistic, even racist, manner. This branch, led by Ohlendorf, was responsible for the liquidation of as many as 130,000 members of the Crimean population, including virtually all of its Jewish and Gypsy inhabitants (the former including the Karaims and the Turkic Jewish Krymchaks) and numerous partisan and other anti-Nazi elements. Not satisfied with the elimination of these "sub-humans," Ohlendorf ordered the confiscation of Crimean li-braries, museums, and bookshops. He destroyed everything that bore traces of Soviet ideology and transferred to Germany everything with artistic and material value.[19]

Tatar Administrative Units

Although most accounts claim that the Crimean Tatars were unduly privileged during the German regime, there is much evidence to the contrary, and the German leaders' conception of the Tatars as *Untermenschen* makes this an odd idea. The decision to tolerate the presence of the Tatars during the war was a practical one not based on any principle of liberality. As early as late November 1941, the German administration granted to the Tatars the right to establish Muslim Committees in various towns in the Crimea as a symbolic recognition of some local governmental authority. Yet these committees were never given any political power. They were to concentrate their attention exclusively upon religious and cultural affairs. In July 1942, Frauenfeld permitted Kirimal to announce that he was now recognized by the German staff as the representative of Crimean Tatar interests. Yet here too, Kirimal's competence was limited to economic and national questions. As Mühlen points out, all political decisions "were retained by the German administration."[20]

Crimean Tatars entrusted with the control of the cities' Muslim Committees were largely those members of the earlier intelligentsia who had returned from exile in 1941. They had formerly been leaders in the Milli Firka party. Among them was Ahmet Ozenbaşli, who was elected Chairman of the Muslim Committee of Simferopol' in mid-1942. Ozenbaşli was a strong opponent of the German occupation regime and used his position on the committee to work toward the goal of increased Tatar national and political rights. He found himself often at odds with Kirimal on the matter of relations with the Germans, since Kirimal, in Berlin, had a much more restricted field of activity. There is some evidence that Ozenbaşli retained contact with the Soviet underground in Simferopol', and provided strategic and political information to the Soviets.[21]

Ozkirim points up the limited role in Crimean affairs allowed the Muslim Committees: "According to the instructions given the Simferopol' committee in its first days, it was to concern itself solely with the repairs of mosques, to make propaganda against communism, to provide religious services for the Tatar 'self-defense' battalions, and to give material aid to these 'volunteers' ' families." Abdulhamitoğlu concludes that their prescribed functions allowed the Muslim Committees no influence in Crimean affairs.[22]

Although most historical accounts repeat that it was only the Tatars who were allowed even the semblance of local self-government by the German authorities, there were, in fact, a number of governmental institutions made up of local inhabitants that were not under the control of the Tatars. During the occupation, the mayor of Simferopol' was Kamenskii, who was a Russian; his chief deputy, Sevastianov, was also Russian. The director of the educational ministry in Simferopol' was Granovskii. The Simferopol' police chief, Fedov, was salaried by the German police command.

A Soviet partisan wrote in a recent memoir that the Crimean self-defense battalions had Slavic as well as Tatar members and that their local commander was Lieutenant Iablonskii, who had received the Iron Cross. Earlier, Iablonskii had been a tractor driver for and then a deserter from the Red Army. It appears, in fact, that of all of the Crimean leaders who occupied positions of authority within the German occupation regime, only Tohtaroğlu, the minister of cultural affairs, was a Tatar. The Muslim Committees had no Crimea-wide authority and could not be considered examples of political collaboration at all. The main political collaborators in the Crimea appear, on the evidence, to have been its Slavic population.[23]

The Crimean Tatars were not unique in receiving benefits from German policies. In religious affairs, the Tatars were not allowed to choose their own *mufti,* although the Orthodox were permitted the choice of their bishop. In most official communications, only German and Russian were used as languages; even street names were posted only in German and Russian. The official radio of the Crimea broadcast primarily in Russian and German with only one and a half hours on Friday devoted to religious programs in Tatar. Favoritism toward the Tatars seems nonexistent in these areas. It appears that cultural activities where the Tatars were allowed relatively free rein were initiated after strenuous efforts by the Muslim Committees and without German encouragement. It is true that the Germans often accepted what these committees proposed—primarily on the advice of General Manstein.[24]

The Crimean Tatars were permitted to restore their former national development in two main cultural areas denied them since the 1930s. First came the reestablishment of the Crimean National Theater company in Simferopol'. It began to perform a number of prerevolutionary plays as well as plays written in the 1920s. Second, the Tatars reopened a truly national newspaper, *Azat Kirim,* in Simferopol'. Although under strict censorship by the German authorities who had a number of Tatar-speaking officials in the Crimea, *Azat Kirim* succeeded in keeping Tatars abreast of Crimean and world affairs. Plans were also made for opening a new university in Simferopol', and a Tatar rector, Ahmet Ozenbaşli, was appointed. However, the university was not opened before the collapse of the German war effort in the east.[25]

During the occupation, the Germans removed a substantial number of Tatars from the Crimea and sent them to Germany to work in various labor camps and on various industrial projects. While Soviet historians describe this group of Tatars as volunteers, most Tatar and German evidence points to an unwilling participation on their part. Along with the tens of thousands of Soviet soldiers captured in the first months of the war, there were some 500 Tatar prisoners of war also held in detention in Germany throughout the war. Despite attempts by Kirimal in Berlin to have these Tatar prisoners returned to the Crimea, there is no evidence he succeeded. It seems that most of them returned to the Soviet Union only at the end of the war, as part of the general policy of repatriation. Toward the end of the war, some of the Tatar prisoners were assigned to the units of General Vlasov, but their numbers were few.[26]

Soviet Partisans

Tatar hostility to the activities of Soviet partisans in the Crimea was the major reason given for their deportation by the Soviets after the war. A number of books have been written on the Soviet partisan movement in the Crimea, and until recent years, authors have dealt with the Tatars in a hostile manner. The commander of the partisans during the first year of the war was A. V. Mokrousov, who throughout his long career was both a government official and a professional soldier. Having fought against Denikin and Wrangel as a partisan, Mokrousov later participated in the Spanish Civil War of 1936–1937. Beginning in the early years of the Soviet regime, his opinion of the Crimean Tatars had been extremely hostile. In the first months of the German occupation, Mokrousov refused to allow Tatars to join the partisan groups under his direct command. According to an account of a Russian participant, Mokrousov had actually ordered the shooting of some Tatars who had arrived at the partisan center to volunteer. Indeed, it was only after the instigation of his removal by the Soviet government that any Tatars were permitted to join the Soviet partisans in the Crimean mountains.[27]

Both the accounts of Ekaterina Shamko and Ivan Kozlov, who were partisans in the Crimea, mention Tatar members of their units only in the guise of informers.[28] Soviet underground leaders in the Crimea used such slogans as "Remember that you are Russian people, and Russian people never betray their native land" to appeal to Russian nationalist feeling in the Crimea while dissuading Tatars from answering the call.[29]

There is no question that large numbers of Tatar villagers as well as the six organized Tatar self-defense battalions fought hard against the Soviet partisans. As Shamko has written in a recent account: "The Fascists found in the Crimea some social support from the Tatar bourgeois nationalists— former *kulaks*, criminal figures, and other antipopular elements. The traitors knew well the local inhabitants and turned over all suspicious characters (often the patriots) to the German police."[30]

An SS report of December 15, 1941, acknowledged that the most valuable information the Germans received on partisan locations and identity was from "statements from the local population, statements made by partisan deserters, and statements made by relatives of the partisans."[31] But this is not the whole story. A Crimean partisan, Ivan Genov, noted in his diary both that the Soviet partisans expected the Tatars to turn them in to the Germans, and that the Germans were offering from 50 to 150 rubles for each partisan identified; for the partisan leader Mokrousov a value was set at 10,000 rubles. "But up to now," Genov wrote, "they [the Tatars] have not brought the Hitlerites into the forests."[32]

The major question to be asked is why this happened. First, there was Mokrousov's refusal to admit Tatars to his units. Second, the partisans often acted in extremely arbitrary fashion, raiding and sometimes destroying Tatar villages in the mountains in the hopes of provoking German retaliation. German documents verify this state of affairs. A report of February 1942, stated: "On 9 February, 150 partisans attacked the village of Stzlia which was plundered. The village of Kasanli had been occupied by partisans a few days earlier, and some time later 500 partisans attacked Baksan, and 220 partisans raided the village of Beshui." A report to Major Stephanus, chief of antipartisan warfare in the Crimea, said: "The commander of a fighter group informed us over the phone that he had with him the Soviet mayor of 'L' who had told him that partisans were invading the village day and night, taking cattle away and forcing young lads to go with them. The partisans had threatened the mayor with hanging."[33]

Tatar Anti-Nazi Activities

On the other side of the ledger, there were numerous Tatars who did fight against the German occupation forces. One Tatar group, known as the Tarhanov movement, was comprised of 250 Tatar partisans who fought the Germans throughout 1942 until they were completely destroyed.[34] From 1967 to 1969, the Tashkent Crimean newspaper, *Lenin Bayragi,* published a series of documents and articles about Tatar partisan activity and reported that near Kerch there had been discovered many catacombs and caves containing the remains of Tatar units that the Germans had succeeded in liquidating. In its July 31, 1967, issue, it said: "More than eighty Tatar villages had been destroyed by the Germans in their antipartisan operations. Quite a number of Tatars were among the Soviet partisans executed by the Germans during the war, including Ema Bekirov, Nuriye Devletov, Zahide Halilov (all women), and Ibrahim Bosnayev, Tahi Suleyman, Seyit Veli Arifov, and others."[35] Likewise, Soviet Samizdat literature contains numerous accounts by Crimean Tatars in Uzbekistan who wrote about their own or their parents' participation in the partisan organizations. I. Osmanov reported that his father had been on the command staff of the partisans after Mokrousov's removal in late 1942.[36]

Recently, a Soviet collection of documents concerning the wartime Crimea has now admitted the participation of large numbers of Crimean Tatars in the struggle against the German occupation regime. These documents include the stories of Ibraimov, who was largely responsible for the evacuation of Simferopol' in late October 1941; Cemilev, who was on the governing staff of the underground Sovnarkom in Sevastopol' in early 1942; Kulibaba, who was commissar of the defense battalion of Sevastapol' in June 1942; and Osmanov, partisan commissar of the First Crimean Region in late 1942.[37]

In this collection, Document 152, of July 7, 1942, reports the problem of relations between the partisans and the local population. In attempts to maintain friendly relations, the partisan Obkom published newspapers illegally in both Russian and Tatar. The document admits that much support for their activities (in the form of volunteers and supplies) came from the Tatars, "But there were *some* [my italics] Tatar villages, a *part* [my italics] of the Tatar population. . . . that not only did not help the partisans but actively helped the German-Rumanian occupation regime."[38]

This is of course a far cry from all or even most of the Tatar population. Document 195, of November 3, 1943, shows "an address of inhabitants of several villages to the Partisans," coming from such Tatar villages as Kizil-Koba, Cafar-Berdy, Beirat, Mamak, and Efendikoy; the essence of the message was "Death to the Germans."[39] Finally, toward the end of the war, such Tatar anti-Germans as Mustafaev and Selimov, commissars of partisan movements in the south, are mentioned in the collection.[40] Thus, we now have evidence from Soviet sources of the meaning of "and many others" in Shamko's 1959 statement, "Among the partisans were Russians, Ukrainians, Belorussians, Georgians, Armenians, Azeris, Uzbeks, and many others."[41]

Finally, one must mention that there were many Crimean Tatars who served in the Soviet army on other fronts and who avoided capture by the Germans. According to Pisarev, "nearly 20,000 Crimean Tatars fought on the front during the war; thousands were given orders and medals of the USSR. Eight were called Heroes of the Soviet Union, and one Crimean Tatar pilot, Ahmet Khan Sultan, was twice awarded the order of Hero of the Soviet Union." And in the most recent issue of *The Chronicle of Current Events*, information about the full extent of Crimean Tatar participation in the Soviet war effort has been given:

It is shown that out of the total population (302,000) before the war, there were 95,000 men over 18 years. 53,000 fought in the army and 12,000 in the resistance and the underground. 30,000 participants in the war perished.

Summing up the conclusions from the data of the census, the document charges that the Soviet people have been deceived by the press and other forms of propaganda which have kept quiet about the part played by Crimean Tatars in the war and about their bravery (40% were decorated with orders and medals, including nine as Heroes of the Soviet Union) and sacrifices.[42]

The Crimean Tatar novelist, Cenghis Dagci, in exile in England, has written a number of novels about Tatar life under German occupation. None of these unfortunately has been translated from the original Turkish. In a recent interview, Dagci, in discussing his *O Topraklar Bizimdi ("Those Lands Belonged to Us"),* said:

> The tragedy did not start only after the war (deportation), it had its beginnings in the thirties. Thousands of Crimean Tatars were deported between 1930 and 1936. These people were not opposed to the regime, they were only interested in cultivating their land, their vineyards, and orchards. They were simple, innocent people living in an agricultural community. . . . The charge that the Crimean Tatars betrayed their Russian comrades during the war was nothing but a pretext, a deliberate slander. Among all the people of the Soviet Union, including the Russians, the Crimean Tatars collaborated the least.[43]

The Red Army Advance

As the German war effort in the Soviet Union began to collapse in 1943, the Germans made one last desperate attempt to gain the support of Muslim peoples, particularly those in Turkey and the Arab world, by reestablishing the Muslim position of *mufti* in the Crimea. They tried to use this position as propaganda, purporting to show their great concern for Islam as a counterweight to the newly appointed Soviet *mufti* in Tashkent. The Tatars in Berlin were enthusiastic about this decision which would ensure "the presence of a trustworthy personality through whom the Tatar population could be influenced." The choice was to be Ozenbaşli. According to Dallin, the army in the Crimea, which had from the very beginning opposed the election of a *mufti*, was not impressed with these arguments, and a German army spokesman replied, "of late, the Tatars have proved extremely unreliable."[44] Ozenbaşli, himself, when learning of this proposal, fled the Crimea to join the Crimean Tatar exile community in Rumania. He had been opposing the Germans all along, and could not accept serving them for reasons of propaganda.

By November 1943, the Soviet army had advanced from Stalingrad as far as Perekop, the "key to the Crimea." In April 1944, they entered the Crimea from the north and in May, the Germans were completely routed. During the first two weeks of Soviet military presence in the Crimea, the Soviet officials conducted a reign of terror over the Tatars who were left behind. Any Tatar charged by at least two persons with having collaborated with the German regime was executed without trial. Eyewitnesses report that in Simferopol' the streets were lined with corpses hanging from tree branches and telephone poles. In addition, the entire population of a number of Tatar villages—men, women, and children—was executed without trial or formal charges. One witness wrote: "After the Soviet army entered the Crimea, according to a general order from the Commander, all of the Tatar population was subject to arbitrary actions of the NKVD detachments. Unrestrained soldiers raped women and children. Defenseless people were plundered and hung. For two weeks, the Tatars were tortured, attacked, and killed."[45]

These outrages were influenced by two causes. The Soviet soldiers had been exhausted by the battle for Stalingrad and were in a vengeful state of mind. Most of them had been led to believe that the Tatars, more than any other Soviet nationality, had participated in the extermination of non-Tatar Soviet citizens in the Crimea. While he was in Leningrad during the tough months of 1942, Alexander Werth reported that many Soviet officials were talking of the Crimean Tatars' collaboration:

> I remember a significant conversation on the subject with Konstantin Oumanskii on July 24, i.e., on one of the blackest days of the Black Summer of 1942; "I must say I am a little worried about the Caucasus. . . . Even when a Russian or a Ukrainian is not particularly pro-Soviet, he still remains patriotic; he will fight for a united Russia, or the Soviet Union, or whatever you like to call it. But the Tatars in the Crimea are, to a large extent, disloyal. They were economically privileged by the wealthy tourist traffic before the revolution, and now they have not been so well off. But they never liked us. It is well known that during the Crimean War they gladly 'collaborated' as we'd now say, with the English and the French. And, above all, there are religious factors which the Germans have not failed to exploit."[46]

Although much of what Oumanskii said was untrue (especially about the Crimean War), there is no reason to think that he did not believe what he was telling Werth. His view seems to have been a widespread one. Werth later wrote that when he was in the Crimea in the days just after the Soviet reoccupation, he learned from Yefremov, mayor of Sevastopol', that: "the Crimean Tatars . . . had played a particularly cruel game in hunting down disguised Russian soldiers." Werth accepted his judgment and concluded: "Altogether, the Tatars' record was as bad as could be. . . . They had formed a police force under German control, and had been highly active in the Gestapo."[47]

There was also a good deal of personal distaste for the Tatars, distaste that had national, historical, and cultural underpinnings. As Levitin wrote in 1969, on the occasion of the arrest of General Grigorenko:

> My father was, before the revolution, a judge in Baku; he had the common colonial psychology of an official and so did his underlings. He was possessed of Great Russian chauvinism accompanied with scorn for the non-Russians.

He had a special scorn for the Tatars, and this I inherited from him. I remember with what disgust I looked upon the director of our school because he was a Tatar.[48]

After all the evidence is in, it appears that the charge against the Crimean Tatars was not wholly groundless. But equally, it was not wholly true, and there were more than a few extenuating circumstances. Given the pervasiveness of Soviet Russian hostility toward the Tatar population before, during, and after the war, one is forced to ask whether the deportation was just the result of Tatar collaboration.

14. The Deportation of the Crimean Tatars and Their Struggle for Rehabilitation

A little more than a month after the Soviet reoccupation of the Crimea and barely two weeks after the period of NKVD and military terrorism against the Tatars, the ultimate punishment against the Crimeans was carried out. On the night of May 18, 1944, in a well planned and executed operation, literally all Crimean Tatars were collected for forcible removal from their homeland. Under Marshal Voroshilov's supervision, the deportation was conducted by forces under the command of Ivan Serov, First Deputy Peoples' Commissar for Internal Affairs in the USSR.[1]

Serov had had a varied and interesting career. His experience and ability made him a perfect choice for carrying out both this deportation and those of the various Caucasian peoples who would soon follow the Tatars. His career had begun in the 1930s with a post in Stalin's personal secretariat under Malenkov's direction. In 1939, he began his activities as a highly skilled "mover of people and material," when he formulated the plans for the liquidation of anti-Communist elements along the Baltic coast and for the mass deportations from Latvia, Estonia, and Lithuania. In February 1941, Serov became the first deputy minister for State Security, and in July of that year, when Beria combined the NKVD with the KGB (State Security Police), he was appointed first deputy people's commissar for internal affairs.

In this capacity, he directed the removal of industrial equipment from Stalingrad in 1942 and 1943. Much of that experience was useful to him for his next major assignment—the deportation of the Crimean Tatars, the Chechen Ingush, the Kalmyks, the Volga Germans, and the Mesketian Turks to other regions of the USSR. One might say that Serov had by this time become a professional "mover," one who seemed uninterested in the political or ethical questions involved in such actions. His superiors had little reason to be dissatisfied with his performance; for the success of these last movements, Serov was promoted to Colonel-General, awarded the title "Hero of the Soviet Union," and granted an Order of Lenin.[2]

The Deportation

Descriptions of the Tatar deportation have been given by both victims and perpetrators. Grigorii Burlitskii, who was one of the NKVD officers in charge of the actions in the Crimea and the Caucasus and who fled to West Germany in the early 1950s, gave a full account of these events in 1952. Similar evidence has appeared in a number of petitions and open letters from Crimean Tatars in exile. Ann Sheehy quotes from an "Open Letter from the Russian Friends of the Crimean Tatars," of 1968 or 1969, that stated that many Tatars received only a few minutes' notice to collect some belongings and to assemble:

> It was not to be shot. It was a journey of lingering death in cattle cars, crammed with people, like mobile gas chambers. The journey lasted three to four weeks, and took them across the scorching summer steppes of Kazakhstan. They took the Red partisans of the Crimea, the fighters of the Bolshevik underground, and Soviet and Party activists. Also invalids and old men. The remaining men were fighting the Fascists at the front, but deportation awaited them at the end of the war. And in the meantime, they crammed their women and children into the trucks, where they constituted the vast majority. Death mowed down the old, the young, and the weak. They died of thirst, suffocation, and the stench. . . . On the long stages, the corpses decomposed in the huddle of the trucks, and at the short halts, where water and food were handed out, the people were not allowed to bury their dead and had to leave them beside the railway track.[3]

Burlitskii reported that the methods used were:

> the same that had been applied in the Chechen Ingush Republic in the Northern Caucasus, that is to say, all of the Turkic people, without any exceptions, were all of a sudden and at the same moment arrested by the NKVD detachments that had been sent into the Crimea for that purpose. Those who were arrested were forced into the closed wagons of a freight train and sent out of the Crimea. . . . The Tatars were taken by surprise so that they could find no opportunity to resist. . . . They were packed into the wagons like sardines, the wagons were locked and sealed and put under guard of military detachments.[4]

Even those Tatars who had fought long and hard for Soviet victory—those who had been in the first ranks of the Soviet Communist party, as well as those in the partisan and regular Red Army units—were swept up in the vast deportation net. This fact has never been explained satisfactorily by Soviet historians. Commissars Ahmetov and Isaev, Tatars in the Fifth Partisan Brigade as late as April 1, 1944, whose unit greatly aided the advance of the Red Army into the Crimea, were removed from their unit in May and deported with the rest.[5] Ahmed Ahmedovich Abdulaev (director of the partisan medical corps) as well as Major Mahomed Hamzalov, Sergeant Mahmet Duliev, and Sergeant Mundin Khasafov (all in the Soviet Crimean partisan movement) met the same fate, despite the fact that these four had been among those awarded the title "Hero of the USSR," on November 17,

1943, for their participation in the Soviet landing at Kerch.[6] The local Crimean Tatar Communists and their families, and the chairman of the Central Executive Committee of the Crimea, Menlibari Khaurullah, who "had fought actively against the German army alongside of the Soviet partisans, and who had called upon the Crimean Tatars to take up arms against the Germans," were deported too. All in all, some fifty Communist Tatar writers and journalists, "who had distributed anti-German proclamations and newspapers in Tatar during the war," met this fate.[7]

In his novel, *Those Lands Belonged to Us,* Cengiz Dagci describes the experience of a young Tatar partisan who returned to his village just after the deportation had taken place and found it empty, save for a former friend Alim:

"Tell me, Alim, what's happened in Chukurdja?"

Alim stared at him in silence like a dumb man.

"Who is here in Chukurdja, Alim?"

Alim shrugged. "Nobody."

"What about Bilal Agha?"

Alim turned his eyes on the ground and began to speak in an anguished voice. "Two days ago the Russians came to the village. They hanged Grandpa Djavit and Kaytaz on the tree by the mosque. They shot fifteen people including Hassan Agha, lining them up against the mosque wall. They killed some others too, but this I didn't see. Then they gathered the people in the village square. I stood near Bilal Agha. He whispered in my ear, 'You run away, Alim. Run away to the mountains, look for Selim, find him and tell him what you've seen. Tell him to stay in the hills. You too stay there, don't come back to the village. Because this village isn't ours now.' "[8]

Abolition of the Crimean ASSR

On June 30, 1945, a year after the deportation, the Crimean ASSR was abolished and transformed into the Crimean oblast' of the RSFSR. It was not until June 28, 1946, when it was published in *Izvestiia,* that the announcement of both the Tatars' deportation and the creation of the Crimean oblast' appeared.[9] The text of this decree explains these changes:

During the Great Patriotic War, when the peoples of the USSR were heroically defending the honor and independence of the Fatherland in the struggle against the German-Fascist invaders, many Chechens and Crimean Tatars, at the instigation of German agents, joined volunteer units organized by the Germans and, together with German troops, engaged in armed struggle against units of the Red Army; . . . meanwhile the main mass of the population of the Chechen-Ingush and Crimean ASSRs took no counteractions against these betrayers of the Fatherland.

In connection with this, the Chechens and the Crimean Tatars were resettled in other regions of the USSR, where they were given land together with the necessary governmental assistance for their economic establishment.

On the proposal of the Presidium of the Supreme Soviet of the RSFSR, the Chechen-Ingush ASSR was abolished and the Crimean ASSR was changed into the Crimean oblast' by decrees of the Presidium of the Supreme Soviet of The USSR (June 28, 1946).[10]

The portion of the Criminal Code of the RSFSR that applied to this justification was article 58-1a, which stated:

> Treason to the Fatherland, that is, actions committed by citizens of the USSR, to the detriment of the military power of the USSR, its state independence, or the integrity of its territory, such as espionage, betrayal of military state secrets, defection to the side of the enemy, escape or flight across the frontier, are punishable by the highest measure of criminal punishment—shooting, with confiscation of all property, or, in the case of extenuating circumstances, by imprisonment for a term of ten years with confiscation of all property.[11]

It is difficult to imagine that the authors of this article had envisioned its application to an entire nationality.

Until today, this official justification for the resettlement has been accepted by most observers of Soviet affairs. Yet this explanation requires further analysis. There can be no question that a large number of Soviet officials believed that the charges made against the Crimean Tatars were in fact true; this is evidenced by the opinions quoted by Werth and others cited in chapter 13. Perhaps they believed that the Tatars had been worse traitors than any other Soviet nationality. Yet this cannot explain the deportation of all of the Tatars—even those who had fought with the Soviet army and partisans—as well as those who had served in the Soviet underground as commissars and political instructors during the occupation.

Explanation of the Deportation

There must have been other reasons, though Khrushchev, in his famous speech to the Twentieth Party Congress, said that Stalin, if he had had the opportunity, would have deported the entire Ukrainian population, too, for their collaboration with the Germans.[12] The fact remains that such nationalities as the Volga Tatars and the Turkestanis provided many more military and political collaborators than did the Crimean Tatars, yet there appears to have been no attempt at group punishment for these nationalities at all.

The answer to this perplexing question may be found, perhaps, in Stalin's foreign rather than domestic policy. Recently the deportation of the Meskhetian Turks has come to light. This has never been officially announced or admitted by Soviet authorities, and with good reason. The Meskhetian Turks, who formerly resided in a region of Soviet Armenia along the Turkish border, did not collaborate at all with the German invaders; in fact, they had no contact with them at all. Yet when the Chechens and the Crimean Tatars were removed, these people were deported to the Soviet East, primarily to Uzbekistan. In a recent article, Wimbush and Wixman offer the intriguing suggestion that the Meskhetian Turks were removed from the Turkish border and replaced by Soviet Armenians just at the time when Stalin was making strong claims to increased Soviet influence in the Turkish Republic and angling for control of the Straits. These authors suggest that Stalin wanted to be sure that no fifth column of Turkic nationals would stand in the way of such pressure being applied on the Soviet-Turkish border.[13]

Might not the same reason hold true for the Crimean Tatars as well? Evidence for this possibility emerges from an analysis of the *Geographical Atlas of the USSR,* published in 1950, which shows that all of the other non-Slavic minorities (save the Armenians) were removed after 1944 too — this included Greeks and others who as a group had not aided the Germans in any way. They were replaced by both Russians and Ukrainians.[14]

It is interesting to consider the dates of Soviet demands upon Turkey for joint control of the Straits in the light of the dates of the deportation of the Tatars and Meskhetian Turks. In Moscow in March 1945 (after the deportation and the first major immigration of Slavs was completed), Molotov informed the Turkish ambassador, M. Selim Sarper, that the USSR was renouncing the Turco-Soviet Treaty of Neutrality that had been signed in September 1925, since "this treaty no longer corresponds to actual conditions and to changes brought about by the war that require significant alterations in our relations."[15] On July 7, Molotov informed Sarper that the USSR requested the right to establish military and naval bases on the Straits. In the same conversation, Molotov also raised the question of the northeastern Turkish provinces of Kars and Ardahan, which had been "ceded to Turkey at the end of the First World War at a moment when the Russian weakness left them no alternative to acceding to Turkish demands." These provinces were now to be returned to the USSR.[16] It is no coincidence that the Meskhetian Turks had lived on the border of the province of Ardahan.

The Soviet demands for the Turkish Straits, it seems to me, related very closely to the decision to remove the Crimean Tatars from the region and to replace them with Russians and Ukrainians. These demands were repeated by Stalin at Ialta (ironically in the, by now, purged Crimean peninsula) and later at Potsdam.[17] It seems likely that these claims against Turkey had as much to do with the Soviet decision to liquidate the Crimean ASSR as did the Tatar collaboration with the Germans. Although the Soviet authorities have never mentioned this particular connection, publications appearing in the USSR in recent years emphasize with greater frequency the Crimean Tatars who heroically defended the Soviet state during the war, thus admitting indirectly that the explanations of 1944 and 1946 were not complete.[18]

The reasons made little difference to the Tatars at the time, although in recent years, as they have formed their civil rights movement, they are returning to discussions of these most critical questions. For many of those deported (Tatar figures claim 46 percent while official Soviet government figures claim 22 percent), the deportation itself was their last problem: they died—either en route or during their first months in their new places of settlement. A large proportion of those in the second category had been sent to concentration camps in the Sverdlovsk region in the Urals; others were shipped to camps in the Tashkent area where the largest number of those now surviving reside.[19]

First Experiences in Exile

Placed under the jurisdiction of the *Glavnoe pereselencheskoe upravlenie* ("Main Resettlement Administration") within the NKVD, the facilities available for the Tatars at their settlements were inadequate to say the least. According to the "Open Letter":

> The act of deportation had ended, yet the wholesale destruction of the people was just beginning. Because of propaganda which government agencies made among the local population, the Tatars met a hostile welcome. Unaccustomed to the heat, the malarial fevers, above all the water so much less clean than in the Crimea, the Tatars became sick and weak, and many died. At first they were housed in stables, dungeons, and sheds. Later on, those who had survived the first phase, built special houses through hard work, but this occurred much later. As for the years 1944–1945, the people suffered heavy casualties.[20]

According to the account of Yusuf Suleymanov, in 1969:

> They took us and unloaded us in Urta-Aul like cattle for slaughter. Nobody paid any attention to us. We were hungry, dirty, and ill. People became even more ill, and started to swell from hunger, and began to die in families. I want to say that from our village, where there were 206 people, 100 died. I myself buried 18. Out of seven households of my relatives not one remained.[21]

In the "Open Letter," there are such statements as:

> Thirty families from our village were brought, of these only five families survived with some losses. . . . My niece, Menube Şeyhislam with her eight

children were deported and all died from hunger in Uzbekistan. This was despite the fact that her husband remained behind with the Red Army and died on the front.[22]

A large number of Crimean Tatars were to join those in exile later. All Tatars in the Red Army remained in uniform until the end of the war. It was only then, as they prepared to return to their homes in the Crimea, that they learned of the tragedy that had befallen their families. They were forced to join their people in Uzbekistan and in the other places of Tatar resettlement. This last group of Tatars numbered about 5000.[23]

For the Tatars who had fallen prisoner of war to the Germans and for those who had been forced to move to Germany to work during the war years, the situation was even worse. Together with the Crimean soldiers who had been evacuated with the Germans to Rumania and Hungary, and who had been placed in the Waffen SS Division of the Eastern Turks (this group also included Azeris, Volga Tatars, and Turkestanis), they were forcibly returned to the USSR by the victorious allies at the end of the war. Many of these people were not sent to the new places of Tatar settlement; they were either executed for wartime treason or confined in corrective labor camps in the Urals. Nothing has been heard of this group since.[24]

One interesting sidelight to the arrival of the Tatars in the Tashkent region has been provided by A. Krasnov Levitin, who wrote:

> On May 1, 1944, I went to a rest house near Tashkent with a correspondent of the Uzbek radio committee. The administration accepted me well and located me in a room with the head of one or another important enterprise. This is what this person spoke to me about. "The worker strength that I am able to use is poor. Completely bad. The place is without water, damnation! Dry. What to do? I was finished, until the Crimean Tatars have now rescued me!"
>
> "What! How?"
>
> "Yes! They brought in several groups of them. Peasants, grandmothers, old gents, little children! I tell them: 'Come to work.' But it didn't work out. They refused. So I didn't give them anything. Then about half agreed to work for me. My requirements were fulfilled. I received an Order for my successes."[25]

Eradication of Tatar Identity in the Crimea

Meanwhile, in the Crimean oblast', the Soviet authorities proceeded to remove all historical, cultural, and even linguistic traces of the Crimean Tatars. In a petition signed by 115 Crimean Tatars and presented to Soviet authorities in 1968, we learn that "they destroyed the graves of our fathers, grandfathers, and children, and destroyed the monuments of our ancient Crimean culture. Is it possible to forget such things? By destroying such monuments one cannot prove that our culture ever existed."[26] And again, in the "Open Letter," we read, "Everything was done to destroy all traces of the national life of the Tatars and the very memory of their existence. . . . Everything written and printed in Crimean Tatar was burnt—from ancient manuscripts to the classics of Marxism-Leninism inclusive."[27]

Immediately following the deportation, there were wholesale changes in place names on the peninsula. These included: Küçük Uzun to Malorichens'koe; Demerci to Luchiste; Biia Sula to Verkhorichia; Karasu Bazaar to Bilogirs'k; Islam Terek to Kirovs'ke; and Büyük Onlar to Oktiabrs'ke.[28]

The written history of the Crimean Tatars met the same fate as their historical monuments. First, a special session on Crimean history was held in early 1948, in Simferopol'; it was subsequently covered in *Voprosy istorii*. At this session there were a number of papers delivered on such subjects as ancient civilizations in the Crimea and the relationship between the Crimea and Kiev Rus. There were also a paper by S. Ia. Lur'e on early Greek inscriptions and one paper on the nineteenth century, "Questions on Crimean history in Pushkin." The final paper, that of P. N. Nadinskii, entitled "The Bolshevik Party in the Struggle against Tatar Bourgeois Nationalists," is described in the report as "a first and very successful attempt to illuminate several difficult sides of the history of the Soviet Crimea. He concluded that the survival of capitalism in Crimean Tatar society was the cause of their opposition to the Soviet State during the Great Fatherland War."[29] The period from the eleventh century to the nineteenth century was totally ignored.

Likewise the new edition (second) of the *B.S.E.* (1953) removed all traces of the Crimean Tatars and their civilization save for the claim that they had been primarily brigands and raiders and an advance guard for Ottoman expansion into Slavic lands. In the article, "Krymskaia Oblast'," the population is given as Russian and Ukrainian. In the historical portion of the article, the peculiar statement is made that "the annexation of the Crimea to Russia had a great progressive meaning for the socio-economic and cultural development of the Crimea," as though it were an animate object itself devoid of human inhabitants. Although it discusses the formulation of the Crimean ASSR in 1921, it gives no reason for it; there is no mention of the Tatars after the statement that along with Mensheviks, Social Revolutionaries (S.R.s), and Germans, they had fought against the establishment of Soviet power in the Crimea. In an article on the Second World War, the Crimean Tatars were mentioned only in the role of treacherous traitors.[30]

Even the eminent Soviet medievalist, B. D. Grekov, was enlisted in the struggle against the Tatars' past. In an article in *Pravda* on the problem of Crimean history, he said:

There are erroneous judgments and views on Crimean history and literature that must be completely revised by Soviet historical science. Bourgeois historians of various countries, refusing to accept the fact that for centuries the Crimea had the sole object of carrying out the aggressive plans of Russia's enemies, have worked to distort the history of the Crimea with the intention of carrying out the hostile plans of their masters. Russian historical science, Russian Soviet historians must struggle against the foreign falsifiers of the history of the Crimea.[31]

Crimea Given to the Ukraine

The final disposition of the Crimean peninsula was made on February 19, 1954, when the Crimean oblast' was removed from the RSFSR and placed in the Ukrainian SSR by a decision of the Presidium of the Supreme Soviet. Presumably this was an award to the Ukrainian Republic on the three hundredth anniversary of its union with Moscow, although Voroshilov, chairman of the Presidium, stated "that the Crimea was strategically important, and that its transfer to the Ukrainian Republic showed Russia's trust in its Ukrainian partner."[32] Potichnyj also points out that "by transferring the Crimea to Ukrainian jurisdiction, the Soviet leadership made the Ukrainians responsible for the Crimean Tatar problem whether they liked it or not."[33]

There was little reaction to this act in foreign countries. Virtually no response came from the West, or even from the Republic of Turkey, which might well have shown some interest. On May 12, 1954, a group of Ukrainian exiles in West Germany, constituting what they called the "Third Congressional Session of the Ukrainian National Assembly," issued the following statement:

First of all, the right of self-determination of the Crimea belongs to the Crimean people and not to Moscow. Only the free self-determination of all the native Crimeans who lived in the Crimea before the compulsory deportations will be able to determine the future status and future welfare of the Crimea. Secondly, another proof of the intrigue and deceit of the Moscow government is the fact that while solving the Crimean problem, Moscow has not considered the return to their homeland of some of the people forced into exile from the Crimea, the Crimean Turks.[34]

One likely reason for this statement was the fact that, by 1954, the Crimean oblast' had a substantial majority of ethnic Russian inhabitants, and the last thing that Ukrainian nationalist leaders wanted at that time was a further dilution of the Ukrainian nature of the Ukraine. This was a far cry from the demands made by those very same Ukrainian politicians during the Second World War, or for that matter, by their predecessors during the German occupation in World War I.[35]

In addition, two important immigrations into the Crimea had taken place by 1954. The first began in September 1944, (indicating that plans for the Tatar deportation must have been formulated well before April 1944) and lasted to the end of 1949. These settlers came primarily from the regions of Voronezh, Kursk, Briansk, Rostov, and Tambov; they were established on 190 newly founded collective farms in the region between Aluşta and Bahçesaray, on lands seized from former Tatar villagers. The second immigration lasted from early 1950 to August, 1954 and involved Ukrainian settlers who had been given 12,000 rubles each on which to establish themselves in the Crimea.[36]

The "Special Settlement" Regime

From their deportation in 1944, until after Stalin's death in the mid-1950s, the Crimean Tatars in exile lived in extreme difficulty. They lived under special settlement restrictions which meant that they were denied the right to move about freely, not only in the USSR, but even in the republic in which they resided. They were forced to report personally to the local NKVD office once every two weeks. In an account provided by Il'ia Liuksemburg in 1973, we learn of the details of their day-to-day life:

> In the 1950s, I studied at the agricultural technical institute in Tashkent with one of them named Selik. He was intimidated and cautious in word and deed. From him I learned a lot of details about events. The Crimean Tatars were not taken into active military service; they were excluded from peasants' work; they had to live in outlying districts. They had no passports. Why? From what arose such persecution of an entire people?

> On one beautiful day, my friend Selik disappeared from the institute. Without caution, he had snapped out with an especially sugar-and-honey phrase at an instructor of political economics. That was in 1957. Then they didn't dare to raise their heads.[37]

In 1954, for some unexplained reason, some of the restrictions levied upon the Tatars were lifted. This was done only for those who could prove that they had actually fought with the partisans or the Red Army; two years later, in April 1956, this lifting of restrictions was applied to the rest of the Tatar community. This was done by an unpublished decree; no other members of Soviet society would learn of it. But the new decree retained some of the parts of the decree of 1944: The "property of the Crimean Tatars confiscated at the time of their deportation will not be returned, and they do not have the right to return to the Crimea."[38] It has been assumed by scholars that the decree of 1956 permitted the Tatars to move about freely in the USSR, but as future events showed, the fact of the unpublicized nature of this decision made it extremely difficult for Tatars to find acceptance elsewhere. The official propaganda against the Tatars from 1944 on had been too effective.

Khrushchev and the Tatars

At the Twentieth Party Congress in 1956, Khrushchev discussed the problem of the deportation of nationalities in his "Secret Speech," and he did mention directly several of the deported peoples—all but the Volga Germans, the Meskhetian Turks, and the Crimean Tatars. He said:

> The Ukrainians avoided this fate only because there were too many of them. . . . Otherwise he [Stalin] would have deported them also. Not only no Marxist-Leninist, but also no man of common sense, can grasp how one can make whole nations responsible, including women, children, old people, Communists, and komsomolists, and expose them to misery and suffering for the hostile acts of individual persons or groups of persons.[39]

Why did commonsensical Khrushchev ignore the other deported nationalities?

In the next year (1957) the Soviet government publicly absolved all of the deported nationalities (except for the Tatars, Volga Germans, and Meskhetian Turks) from the charges of treason, and restored to them their "autonomous regions."[40] Of course, no such charges had ever been made against the Meskhetian Turks. For the Tatars, however, there was nothing except the permission to begin the publication in Tashkent of *Lenin Bayragi* ("The Flag of Lenin"), the first Crimean-Tatar-language newspaper since 1944. As Sheehy points out, the fact that much of the official improvement in the life of the Crimean Tatars was accomplished without national publicity led to the remarkable fact that as late as 1966, after this newspaper had been operating for nine years, the leading Soviet linguists were unaware of its existence. They wrote in 1966 that the Crimean Tatar language was "in the category of languages without a written form."[41]

First Tatar Petitions and Trials

Both of these events had great consequences for the Crimean Tatar people. The lifting of the restrictions on movement and the right to publish their own newspaper (albeit under close supervision by Uzbek authorities) allowed the Tatars to begin organizational activities aimed at gaining both the right to return to the Crimea and national rehabilitation. For the next ten years, the Crimean Tatars in Uzbekistan pursued a program of action that resulted in the application of so much pressure upon the Soviet government by 1967 that it was forced to react in a partially satisfactory way. That the Tatars were able to bring this pressure to bear is all the more remarkable since they had virtually no help from spokesmen abroad, though within the Soviet Union a growing number of non-Tatar Soviet intellectuals had begun to become interested in their cause.

The first action that the Tatar leaders took was the sending of a petition to the Supreme Soviet in June 1957. The petition, with over 6000 signatures, asked for rehabilitation and the right to return to the Crimea, "in the light of Leninist nationality policies." It was made in response to a report of a speech given by Secretary A. F. Gorkin of the Supreme Soviet Presidium, published in *Izvestiia* on February 12, 1957, that called for a return to Leninist nationality policies.[42] During the next four years, four other petitions followed, with the number of signatures rising to 18,000. Finally a massive effort produced a petition with over 25,000 signatures that was delivered to the Twenty-second Party Congress in October 1961.[43]

Probably as a response to this last petition, two Tatar leaders were tried and sentenced in Tashkent for producing and distributing "anti-Soviet propaganda," and "stirring up racial discord." One of them, Şevket Abduramanov, a production supervisor of the Board of Works in Tashkent, received seven years in a strict labor camp. The other, Enver Seferov (aged thirty-seven), a manager of a social labor organization in Leninabad, received a five-year sentence.[44]

In 1962, a second trial resulted in the sentencing of two more Tatars to a four- and a three-year sentence. One of the Tatar leaders, Mustafa Cemilev, described the reasons for their arrest:

> In 1962, late February, when I was working in the rare books section of the Tashkent public library, on the subject of the history of the Crimea and the Crimean Tatars, I met two other of my nationality interested in the same subject. After a few weeks I decided to give a short lecture to a small group of thirty or forty Tatars. . . . It was the beginning of a small movement. We established a center not far from Tashkent. A few months later, we called it the Union of Crimean Tatar Youths, and its goal was the return to our homeland. . . .
>
> In April, I learned of several arrests by the KGB, of Murat Omerov, a worker in a tractor factory; of Refat Hocenov, a physics student in Tashkent University; of Seit Amza Umerov, a student of law; and Ahmed Asanov, the owner of the house where we had been meeting. On August 10, 1962, began the trial of Murat Omerov and Seit Amza Umerov for being in the "anti-Soviet organization," "Union of Crimean Youth."[45]

Tatar Community Committees

Between 1962 and 1966, the Crimean Tatars expanded their efforts in two directions. First, in each Tatar settlement they organized committees whose aim was to instruct the Tatars about the truth of their past, the facts of life under the German occupation, and the injustices of their deportation and subsequent existence. Second, Crimean Tatar delegations from these committees were sent to Moscow (this was perfectly legal both according to Soviet law and under the special provisions of the decision of 1956), to deliver petitions signed by members of the Tatar communities and to present their case to Soviet authorities.

These movements which took place in the Tatar settlements and in the community-at-large, were a great nuisance to Soviet authorities, since they were within the law. According to accepted Soviet practice, it was incumbent upon the government to accept and consider petitions from Soviet citizens on any subject whatsoever. They, of course, could not recognize the legitimacy of the "lobbyist" nature of the delegations since, as Potichnyj points out, the "Soviet government does not recognize such special interest representation."[46]

Just how impressive the Tatars' actions were is well described by Ann Sheehy: "[on the eve of the Twenty-third Party Congress] 14,284 letters as well as numerous telegrams were sent to various party and government bodies. A petition to the Congress, signed by more than 120,000 Crimean Tatars (i.e., virtually the whole adult population) . . . was handed into the Central Committee."[47] Although Georgadze, secretary of the Presidium of the Supreme Soviet, agreed to meet with some of the representatives, no result or satisfactory response was forthcoming. In June, the Moscow authorities tried to bar the entry into Moscow of more Tatar representatives; arrests and trials followed.

In 1965 and 1966, arrest of Tatar leaders seemed to be the only way the Soviet leaders could deal with this almost unprecedented movement for civil rights for an entire nationality; this was particularly true, since the Tatars did not resort either to terrorism or violence, but pursued their course completely within the Soviet legally accepted methods. In 1965, in the Uzbek SSR, the following arrests and subsequent sentences occurred: Esvet Abdullacev (age twenty-seven), a student, for complaining to the Party leaders in Fergana—three years; Çatiçşe Cahiretdinova (age forty-one), for complaining to Soviet authorities in Moscow—one year; Eskender Cemilev (age thirty-eight), a teacher, for hooliganism—one year; and Refat Seidametov (age twenty-four), a driver, for hooliganism—one year.[48]

In 1966, the arrests and trials continued. In February, two were arrested and given two-year sentences; in June, four were arrested, including Muhsim Osmanov, a sixty-year-old invalid who had been wounded as a Soviet partisan. All were given three-year suspended sentences. In September, Osmanov was arrested again—for the same offense of hooliganism. The Soviet government hoped that this form of harrassment would discourage the Tatars so they would give up their embarrassing struggle in Moscow itself.[49]

In September 1966, a final, almost desperate, attempt by the government to stop this Tatar activity resulted in the addition to the criminal codes of the republics where Tatars resided of new articles aimed primarily at making illegal the sort of activities that the Tatars had been undertaking legally. These activities included "the dissemination of deliberate fabrications defaming the Soviet state and social system," and "the organization of or active participation in group actions violating public order."[50] It was on the basis of these new articles that a number of celebrations organized by the Tatars in Uzbekistan to celebrate the forty-fifth anniversary of the creation of the Crimean ASSR were broken up. As a result, eighteen Tatars (including three party members) were arrested and received two-year sentences.[51]

Yet, surprisingly enough, the Soviet authorities' response did not dampen the spirits or intentions of the Tatar leadership. Despite the constant harassment and arrests, the number of Tatar representatives in Moscow actually increased during the last months of 1966 and the early part of 1967. Like the problem of the sorcerer's apprentice, for each Tatar arrested, the local communities sent three replacements, until by mid-1967, there were over 400 Crimean Tatars resident in Moscow as official delegates of the Tatar village and community committees. Threatening to demonstrate in Red Square if necessary, these representatives finally received word that a group of top-ranking Soviet officials would listen to their complaints. On July 21, 1967, the chairman of the KGB, Andropov; Secretary Georgadze; USSR Procurator General Rudenko; and the minister for the preservation of public order, Shchelokov, met with a representative group of the Tatars in the Kremlin. Promising eventually to recommend to the Central Committee that the Crimean Tatars be rehabilitated, and committing the party leaders to reconsider the question of return to the Crimea, the Soviet leaders sent the delegates back to Uzbekistan with the "good news."[52]

But in the month of August, the Tatars learned that there had been "some break in communications between Moscow and Tashkent," and the local Uzbek authorities again arrested large numbers of Tatars who were announcing the decision they had received in Moscow the month before. Some 130 Tatars were arrested and 18 received either two- or three-year sentences on charges of "organizing mass disorders and resisting the authorities."[53]

Partial Rehabilitation

In time, the Soviet leadership made good on part of its promise. On September 9, 1967, over the signatures of N. Podgorni and M. Georgadze, a decree that partially rehabilitated the Tatars was issued and published in newspapers in the Tatar areas.

Decree of the Presidium of the Supreme Soviet of the USSR, on citizens of Tatar nationality formerly resident in the Crimea: After the liberation of the Crimea from Fascist occupation in 1944, accusations of the active collaboration of a section of the Tatars resident in the Crimea with the German usurpers were groundlessly leveled at the whole Tatar population of the Crimea. These indiscriminate accusations in respect of all the citizens of Tatar nationality who lived in the Crimea must be withdrawn, the more so since a new generation of people has entered on its working and political life. The Presidium of the USSR Supreme Soviet decrees to: (1) Annul the section of the relevant decisions of State organs which contains indiscriminate accusations with respect to citizens of Tatar nationality who lived in the Crimea. (2) Note that the Tatars formerly living in the Crimea have taken root in the territory of the Uzbek and other Union Republics; they enjoy all the rights of Soviet citizens, take part in public and political life, are elected deputies of the Supreme Soviets and local Soviets of deputies of working people, work in responsible posts in Soviet, economic, and party organs, radio broadcasts are made for them, a newspaper in their national language is published, and other cultural measures are undertaken. With the aim of further developing areas with Tatar population, the councils of ministers of Union Republics are instructed to continue rendering help and assistance to citizens of Tatar nationality in economic and cultural construction, taking account of their national interests and peculiarities.[54]

15. "The Right to Return"

Prior to 1967, when making their demands for redress of grievances, the Crimean Tatar leadership had concentrated on three areas: (1) complete rehabilitation of their nationality, to be officially announced by government authorities; (2) restoration of property illegally seized at the time of the deportation; and (3) the right to return to their homeland in the Crimea, with the re-creation of the Crimean ASSR. In their euphoria just after the issuance of the decree in September, the Tatars temporarily forgot these demands. But not for long. It did not take a high degree of sophistication to realize that the wording of the "rehabilitation" left two of their demands completely unanswered and only partially dealt with the third.

First, the decree reaffirmed the portion of the 1956 decree rehabilitating the Tatars who had fought with the partisans or had served in the Red Army that specifically denied their demand for restoration of property seized in 1944. While admitting that the Soviet authorities had made a serious error in charging the entire people with treason, the decree did nothing to compensate the victims of that error.

Second, the decree of 1967 did not speak of Crimean Tatars at all, but rather of "Tatars resident in the Crimea," or "citizens of Tatar nationality who lived in the Crimea." This implicitly denied the existence of their nationality itself. Thus, there could be no need to return to the Crimea—a people without a nationality has no homeland to which to return. In addition, the decree described the Tatars as having taken root in the areas to which they had been deported, implying that they did not want to return. Although the decree mentioned their national language, this reference clearly meant the language spoken and read by Tatars in general, not by those of the Crimea in particular.

Finally, and perhaps most ominously, the decree was not published widely and loudly as originally promised by Andropov; it was published selectively, in those regions of the USSR where the Tatars had "taken root." For the vast majority of Soviet citizens, nothing had changed, and the views about the Tatars with which they had been indoctrinated for twenty-three years remained unrevised. In the years that followed, this fact caused the Tatars untold harm, for they were unable to persuade many non-Tatar Soviet citizens of the justness of their cause.

Since 1967, the Crimean Tatar leadership has concentrated its efforts in four areas. First, convinced that the rehabilitation decree had appeared not because of internal Soviet self-criticism, but rather as a response to the heavy pressure that they had applied themselves, the Tatars decided to continue this pressure in the hopes that eventually the rest of their demands would also be met. As a result, their lobbying efforts in Moscow continued as forcefully as before 1967. In Uzbekistan, where most of them resided, pressures were applied to the local Soviet authorities. Second, an organized effort was made to persuade some Tatar families to return to the Crimean peninsula, with or without official permission. Third, the Tatars strove to connect their movement with the larger movement of Soviet intellectuals for the introduction of civil rights within Soviet society. And fourth, taking advantage of the promised expansion of Soviet authorized cultural activities for Tatars in Uzbekistan, they used their newspaper, their publishing house, and their positions in universities and other cultural institutions to revive Tatar national consciousness. Unlike their Jewish cosufferers, the Tatars could not operate in a fifth direction, however, since any hope of foreign interest in their cause has not been encouraged. The Republic of Turkey, the most logical foreign state to respond to their appeals, has so far ignored their plight.

Some Tatars Try to Return

The Tatars soon learned just how seriously the authorities took the decree's statement that the Tatars had "taken root" in Uzbekistan and other union republics. In 1967 and 1968, several thousand Tatars and their families, acting on their own, arrived in the Crimea to look for housing and employment. Although nothing in the decree specifically denied the Tatars this right, it had stated that they would be permitted to live anywhere in the USSR "in accordance with the existing legislation on employment and the passport laws." This meant that only a citizen who had been officially registered in a district would be allowed to find employment and accommodation there.

The Soviet officials in the Crimea clearly had been ordered to deny registration to any returning Crimean Tatars. According to Sheehy,

> up to December 1967, out of the 6000 or so Crimean Tatars who arrived, only three single men and two families succeeded in getting registered. The remainder were either forcibly deported or, their funds exhausted after months of vain efforts to get registered, were eventually compelled to leave of their own accord.[1]

One report describes the fate of two such Tatars in early 1968:

> Two Crimean Tatars from Uzbekistan, Idris Kaytaz, and Kara Izzet, set out on the road to the Crimea. Kaytaz took his seventy-eight-year-old mother with him. They went to Uskut, a village in the Crimea. The village leader informed

them that there was no place for them, not because they were Tatars, but because all houses were full. Then Idris and Izzet together went to the neighboring kholkoz asking for work. These requests were forcefully denied. They tried to get permission to register at the kholkoz pension, again refused. The next morning, a struggle with eight policemen ensued, and they were ordered to leave. . . . Yet they remained in the village for ten days, living in tents and apparently not interfered with by the villagers. On the eleventh day, the police came, tore down their tents, placed the two families in trucks and took them to Simferopol'. . . . The City Municipal Commissar's assistant, A. P. Derkach, informed them that the "1967 edict did not give the Crimean Tatars the right to return to the Crimea. We will never let you back. . . . Get out!"[2]

Many such stories have emerged from Crimean Tatar *samizdat* ("unofficially published") literature in the years since.[3]

The two most serious incidents that occurred in 1968 involved several hundred Crimean Tatars in the area of Simferopol'. First, on May 17, a large group of Tatars gathered on Lenin Square demanding consideration of their requests for residence permits and employment. They were photographed by the KGB and then ordered to disperse. The KGB commander reportedly said, "We fought against the Germans and against you too." The Tatars were forcibly removed from Simferopol' and returned to Uzbekistan.[4] A second incident took place on May 26, when about a hundred Tatars who had pitched tents along the river Salgir near Simferopol' were violently dispersed by the KGB and the local militia. The next day, about forty of them were placed on a bus bound for Baku, and in Baku on a boat for Krasnovodsk and Tashkent. A further eleven persons were arrested and imprisoned for fifteen days for acting "in a manner contrary to public order."[5]

Aside from responding to these attempts at Tatar immigration, Soviet authorities pursued two courses of action. They tried to intimidate Tatars in the Tashkent area to sign statements renouncing forever their intentions to return to the Crimea and expressing satisfaction with their new homeland in central Asia. This was a futile exercise, for no amount of forceful persuasion could make many Tatars sign such documents. As Sheehy points out, "although the authorities resorted to blackmail, deception, and intimidation, they managed to collect only 262 signatures."[6]

A second tack was the attempt to soften the Tatar demands by holding out the promise that at some time in the future such a return would be permitted, provided the Tatars behaved themselves while the authorities considered "all the ramifications of such a decision." There is not one shred of evidence, however, that the Soviet government ever really intended to make good on this promise. Potichnyj concludes that "the 'legal and orderly way' of returning to the Crimea was nothing but a bureaucratic subterfuge to discourage, if not completely bar, the Tatars' return."[7]

Although one later Soviet justification for the reluctance to permit the Tatars' return was the argument that there was a real need for them in Uzbekistan, and an "already sufficient population" in the Crimea, all of the evidence points to just the opposite situation in both areas. On the one hand, the authorities in Uzbekistan consistently refused to use the majority of Tatars in those fields of endeavor for which they were trained, and on the other, reports of a shortage of population in the Crimea, attempts by the authorities to encourage both Russians and Ukrainians to immigrate there, and of a rather sluggish return of the Crimean economy to its mid-1920s level continue to emerge from the Crimea even today. The case of I. Balbekov, a tractor specialist who went to the Crimea from Samarkand in May 1968, and applied at the Soviet Raikom in Simferopol' for work, exemplifies the situation. "He received the runaround, and this response from the director of the local tractor station: 'We have much work, we need more people. But we are not permitted to take on Crimean Tatars.' "[8]

Again in June, two Tatars—Bekirov Lepur and Seidaliev Hursent—went to the construction bureau of the town of Saki in the Crimea and requested work. The director of the bureau, Okunev, agreed to assign them a job. "But in a few days, the local police discovered this act, ordered Okunev to dismiss them, and criticized him for accepting Crimean Tatars in his establishment."[9]

In 1968–1969, about 900 Tatar families successfully settled in the Crimea. Of these, approximately 250 were allowed to return through an official labor recruitment campaign, a response to a continued labor and population shortage on the peninsula. Although this campaign remains in effect today, it ceased for the Tatars at the end of 1969.[10]

One recent scholarly account suggests that a reason for this Soviet recalcitrance might be connected with the exchange of Polish and Russian populations at the end of the war. Many of the individuals brought into the Crimea after 1945 to replace the deported Tatars were Ukrainians displaced from the portions of Galicia left to Poland. One of the officials directly responsible for the adverse decisions on Tatar requests was Nikolai Podgornyi, whose task it had been to handle this population exchange in the first place. "These Ukrainians, forcibly evacuated from their homes in Poland, may have been especially fearful of a second displacement following the return of the Tatars."[11] Yet it was also true that the Tatars were not rejected by the local populace in the Crimea—only by the political and police officials.

In Simferopol' in late 1972, "People's Judge Mironova demanded that the Crimean Tatars clear out of the Crimea and live in the places to which they had been exiled, or else the most brutal measures would be used against them."[12]

Recent information emerging from the Soviet Tatar community indicates that some gradual improvement in Tatar settlement in the Crimea is taking place. About twenty to thirty families a year are invited to return, with fares paid and a new home and a job guaranteed. According to Enver Ahmetov, however, "We regard the scheme as a way of lulling the rest of us to stay in exile, waiting the turn that will never come." Ahmetov also warned that the Soviets have established, in 1973, a "purely Tatar region in Uzbekistan around the town of Dzhizak." The region has a Tatar theater, a Tatar newspaper, and Tatar language schools. Clearly this is a move to encourage the Tatars to stay in Uzbekistan.[13]

Tatar Pressure in Moscow

Another form of Tatar protest against the 1967 rehabilitation has been the continuation of their lobby in Moscow, coupled with a series of political and cultural demonstrations in Uzbekistan. The Soviet authorities refused to recognize the legitimacy of a permanent Tatar lobby in Moscow and used all of their powers of arrest and persecution to prevent its continuation, but without success.

One of the Tatars who had met with Andropov in July 1967 and who succeeded in getting the government to issue the rehabilitation two months later was harrassed and persecuted by the authorities for the next several years. Professor R. I. Muzafarov, a professor of philology, was dismissed from several institutions of higher learning after his participation in the Moscow delegation. His scholarly works were denied publication—this despite the fact that he was the only Crimean Tatar who specialized in philology and who had an advanced degree in the subject. As reported in the *Chronicle of Current Events:*

> One of his books had already been typeset for the Kazan University Press, but did not appear because it was based on Crimean Tatar materials. . . . For over three years now (1972) the manuscript of his third book on Crimean Tatar proverbs, favorably reviewed, has been lying unopened in the chief Editorial Office for Oriental Literature in the Nauka publishing house. . . . On April 12, 1972, the paper, *Trud,* published an article by Yu. Baranov entitled "the Professor gets a Fail" in which Professor Muzafarov was depicted as a "rolling stone" with a "colorful biography" and an "ignoramus" who had not written "a single article" for several years.

Muzafarov, finally driven to desperation, wrote a letter to Brezhnev:

> I would like to hope, respected Leonid Ilich, that the Central Committee will not only share my indignation at the whole of this shameful story—a story of the unprecedented victimization of a Soviet scholar for his public activities, which were aimed at the realization of the Leninist principles of our nationalities policy, but will also take certain practical steps. I beg to be

guaranteed the opportunity to pursue without hindrance my scientific and pedagogical work in my chief speciality—Crimean Tatar philology—and I request that the conditions necessary for this be created. . . . I expect the Central Committee to oblige the editor of *Trud,* A. M. Subbotin, to allow me the opportunity publicly to refute Yu. Baranov's slanderous article.

As the *Chronicle* points out, the response of the government was the "entirely unprovoked dismissal of Professor Muzafarov from the Kishinev Institute of Art, where he was working at the time, and where he had spent only two months."[14]

In Uzbekistan, in the months just prior to the announcement of the rehabilitation, another young Tatar intellectual, Reşat Cemilev, had been among those who organized the Tatar demonstrations that took place in Tashkent on June 6, August 27, and September 2. After the last, he was arrested, and on December 13, 1967, was tried in the Tashkent City Court and sentenced to a year of corrective labor.[15]

Demonstrations in Uzbekistan

The first major demonstration resulting in a violent Soviet response was the famous Chirchik Affair which occurred in Uzbekistan in April 1968. In order to celebrate both Lenin's birthday and their annual spring festival on April 21, several hundred Tatars gathered at Chirchik, not far from Tashkent, where they listened to speeches calling for a return to Lenin's nationality policy and the restoration of the Crimean ASSR, which Lenin had been responsible for. Since the local authorities had refused repeated requests to permit this gathering, it was deemed illegal, and both police and military forces were called in to disperse the crowd.

This time there was a violent response as the Tatars were no longer in a mood for passive acceptance of Soviet repression. Many Tatars were arrested, though only a dozen were actually charged with disturbing the peace and subsequently sentenced to relatively short terms. As a result of this event, the Tatar leadership decided that the time had come to appeal to world opinion, to make their plight known more generally throughout the USSR and the West. Accordingly, they sent and delivered petitions to Moscow, increased their representation of lobbyists in the capital, sent notices and appeals to foreign institutions, and increased their contacts with leaders of other Soviet dissident movements.[16]

Immediately after the Chirchik Affair, the Tatars from Tashkent selected a delegation comprised of more than 800 representatives and dispatched them to Moscow to present a formal complaint. The Deputy Procurator of Moscow, Stasenkov, replied, "Your problem has been fully and finally settled and will be given no further consideration." *The Chronicle of Current Events* described their arrests: "Crimean Tatars were arrested in hotels, private apartments, on railway stations, in squares, and at other points in Moscow, were bundled into a mail and goods train and sent under escort to Tashkent."[17]

The text of their complaint is worth repeating, because of its muted tones and because there was nothing in it that violated any published Soviet statutes:

> We wished to have a solemn and festive celebration honoring the birthday of V. I. Lenin who is especially dear to our people because he sponsored the creation of the Crimean ASSR. Notice of the fete was given to the Gorkom First Secretary, V. G. Yakubov, who opposed the event. He told our representatives that he would not permit the Crimean Tatars to observe Lenin's birthday in any way. [Had Lenin suddenly become a dangerous hero of the past?] "If you gather together for a mass outdoor fete you will be forcibly restrained." Major General Sharaliev of the Ministry of Public Order who was present at the time, telephoned to Tashkent and gave the order "send up troops to the city of Chirchik." On April 21, autos began approaching Chirchik bringing Crimean Tatars from various settlements in Tashkent oblast' to join in the celebration. Reinforced details of militia that had been stationed along all the routes forced the passengers out of the cars and took away the drivers' permits. The people who had gathered saw that there was no place to hold a celebration because all available space had been taken up by militia and troops. The gathering then proceeded to the city park still wishing to have some sort of observance of the birthday of the great Lenin. By one in the afternoon, the celebration was in full swing; national dances and games were begun. Then suddenly the park was surrounded by troops and police and the inconceivable began to happen. Streams of some sort of poisonous liquid were aimed at the merrymakers from pressure hoses that had been brought up by the police. The streams knocked people off their feet, leaving white spots wherever the liquid came into contact with their clothing. . . . The police were equipped with gas masks. People were also directly assaulted by police who twisted their arms, beat them up, and brutally shoved them into police vans. Some of the people, especially women who were mistreated, tried to put up resistance, but most of the celebrants, having broken through the police cordon, formed a street procession. When it approached the local party office, a delegation of eight persons left the column to go and register a complaint with the Gorkom against such arbitrary treatment. The delegation was not received, and again powerful streams of liquid were directed at the demonstrators, who were also attacked by police. In spite of this, the demonstrators refused to be driven away, and until nightfall troops and police were battling with people expressing their indignation at such reprisals.

> Late at night, the daytime violence was followed by arrests carried out in people's homes. Even persons who had not taken part in the celebration were arrested. According to incomplete records, 300 arrests were made.

We are certain that this violence was carried out with the knowledge of the party and government leadership of the Uzbek SSR inasmuch as, in addition to those mentioned before, Gorkom Secretary Yakubov, and Major General Sharaliev, Deputy Procurator of the Uzbek SSR Bocharov, and representatives of the Uzbek SSR KGB were also directing the activities in question.

Viewing these activities as a discredit to the Soviet society and govenmental structure and as a provocation against our people, we demand in the name of the latter and at their behest:

1. the immediate release of all those arrested;

2. the formation of a special party-governmental investigation committee that should include freely elected representatives of the Crimean Tatar people but should not include representatives of the local authorities, since they were indirectly responsible for the reprisals. The committee should be charged with conducting an immediate public investigation of the events that took place . . . and with exposing and punishing all responsible.[18]

Since the only response that the Soviet government found itself able to give to this protest (which was itself within Soviet law, if not accepted practice) was further repression and govenment-directed violence, the Tatar leadership decided upon the ploy of pleading to world opinion. Believing that the rest of the world was largely uninformed about the problems of the Tatars since 1944 and recognizing that even the scholarly public in the West was in agreement with Soviet judgments on Tatar disloyalty during the war, this appeal summarized the history of the persecution since 1944 and repeated the official judgment of 1967 exonerating the Tatars from the charges. This "Appeal by Representatives of the Crimean Tatar People to the World Public, June 21, 1968," said:

During the twelve years after 1944 we lived as exiles and were discriminated against. Our children, even those born in exile, were branded as "traitors"; slanderous stories were published about us and are to this day still being read by Soviet people. . . . Every day dozens of people are summoned to appear at their local KGB offices and there pressured by blackmail and threats to renounce returning to our homeland. In the course of our struggle, a total of more than three million signatures on letters have been sent by our people to the Soviet government. This means that each adult Crimean Tatar has affixed his signature to them at least ten times. . . . Not a single party or governmental body has ever once given us a reply; not a single Soviet newspaper has ever once referred to our fight. We appeal accordingly to the world public. We appeal to all the peoples of the Soviet Union as a small independent people appeals to brother peoples.[19]

Over the next year, the Tatars sent dozens of letters, petitions, and news items to representatives of foreign institutions as well as to virtually all relevant Soviet agencies. These communications included an *informatsiia* signed by ten Tatars and sent to all political organs of the USSR in October 1968; a protest to the CPSU Central Committee, the Supreme Soviet of the USSR, and the Council of Ministers of the USSR and Soviet society on January 31, 1969; and a note from the International Youth Help Committee for the Movement of the Crimean Tatars in Tashkent, sent to the Politburo on May 15, 1969, a copy of which was forwarded to the United Nations Human Rights Commission.[20]

From the perspective of Soviet law (at least those portions of it that have been published), the Crimean Tatars believed their complaints so just and their demands so reasonable that they were bewildered by the response they received from Soviet legal and political authorities. Believing that their plight was caused by malicious individuals within the system rather than the system itself, they continued to try to inform all important Soviet officials of their situation in the hopes that somewhere there existed an authority that would hew to the letter and spirit of Soviet law.

Thus, in June 1969, the Tatar leaders decided to make public the total list of the complaints in the best possible forum they could find—Moscow during the World Conference of Communist and Workers' parties. Led by five of the most vocal Tatar representatives, Zampira Asanova, Enver Ahmetov, Reşat Cemilev, Aider Seitulayev, and Ibraim Kholopov, they "unfurled banners at the foot of the Mayakovsky memorial with the slogans 'Hail to Lenin's Nationalities Policy' 'Communists, give the Crimea back to the Crimean Tatars!' 'Stop Persecuting the Crimean Tatars!'" According to the report of this demonstration in the *Chronicle of Current Events,* a crowd of several hundred gathered to watch silently: "no one asked the demonstrators to disperse. The policemen on traffic duty left their posts, signaled to about ten bystanders who supposedly expressed the anger of the people, and fell upon the demonstrators using physical violence. There were some shouts of 'They shouldn't have betrayed Russia!'" They then were "driven off to 38 Petrovka Street where they were interrogated by investigators of the Ministry of the Interior" although they were not at that time charged with a crime. Their arrests came later.[21]

Use of the Soviet Legal System

Despite the fact that not even this protest and petition brought any response except arrest and violence, the Tatar leaders did not give up their attempts to achieve through normal legal Soviet channels what they considered to be justice. On September 24, 1969, another protest was forwarded to the Politburo; on June 24, 1970, a petition signed by 456 Tatars protesting illegal arrests and detentions of Tatar leaders was sent to the Supreme Soviet.[22]

On June 18, 1971, "Tatar Information Bulletin No. 101: To the Crimean Tatar people and the CPSU Central Committee" was issued; it contained lists of petitions and documents handed in to "the highest party and governmental organizations between February 16 and March 4, 1971," including:

> Seventy-two collective letters, with 461 signatures from Chirchik; a letter from 233 Crimean Tatars about the book *300 Dnei v tylu vraga* by Zarlyk Saginbayev, published in Frunze, 1969, which propagates "the line of discrimination against our people"; 164 volumes of documents containing appeals from young people with 4125 signatures; and telegrams to L. Brezhnev, M. Suslov, Kosygin, Podgorny, and Ya. Nasriddinova (president of the Supreme Soviet's Council of Nationalities) requesting them to petition the Presidium of the Twenty-fourth Party Congress for the return of the Crimean Tatars to their homeland and the restoration of Crimean Tatar autonomy.[23]

Of course there was no positive response to this bulletin or apparently to any of the documents or petitions turned in to the authorities.

At the time of the meeting of the Twenty-fourth Party Congress, the Tatars submitted another petition, this time signed by more than 130,000 people; it pleaded:

> The Central Committee of the Communist Party is well aware of the existence in the USSR of the national movement of the Crimean Tatar people for a return to their homeland in the Crimea and the restoration of Lenin's historic decree on the autonomy of the Crimea. Hundreds of thousands of Soviet citizens are participants in this movement. The Crimean Tatar people sends thousands of its representatives, messengers from the people, to the central authorities, in Moscow—to the Central Committee alone they have handed hundreds of thousands of letters from individuals and 163 volumes of various documents on which a total of more than three million signatures have accumulated over the years—and all without result.
>
> Our people appealed to the Twenty-fourth Party Congress; the Presidium of the Congress was sent an appeal that more than 130,000 people had signed; yet our question was not raised at the congress. Our situation as a nation is intolerable. For we do not ask for ourselves anything exceptional. We wish to be an equal people among the equal peoples of our country. We have faith that the party will solve the problem. . . .
>
> With great bitterness we inform the Congress that the numerous letters and appeals sent by Crimean Tatars . . . over a number of years remain unanswered, are passed over in stubborn silence and ignored, despite the legal obligation to reply to us.
>
> Moreover, our problem, from a matter for consideration by party and legislative bodies, has been turned into a matter for the agencies of security and internal affairs, at which our people expresses its deep indignation.

The Crimean Tatar people angrily condemn the deeply disturbing atmosphere that has been created in the Crimea with regard to its original inhabitants and to citizens of Crimean Tatar nationality who arrived to take up residence there after the promulgation of the decree of 1967. . . .

Appealing to the great forum of the Communists of our country, we ask you: (1) to sanction an organized return of the Crimean Tatars to their native land—and to create the necessary conditions for their successful development as a people and as a nation; (2) to renew the validity of Lenin's decree of 18 October 1921, on the formation of the Crimean ASSR; (3) to reinstate in the ranks of the party all those expelled from it for taking part in our national movement; (4) to call to account the falsifiers of the history of the Crimean Tatar people.[24]

This appeal was repeated again in late summer 1972 and sent to the Presidium of the USSR Supreme Soviet, the Council of Ministers, and to the Politburo of the CPSU Central Committee. At the same time, an appeal by "Crimean Tatar youth" with thirty-three signatures was sent to the editors of *Komsomolskaia pravda.*[25]

Soviet Responses

The protests and petitions continue without end, despite the fact that time and time again the leaders of the Tatar movement have been subjected to arrest and trial resulting in severe sentences. The Soviet government apparently decided that, together with the rehabilitation decree, a hard clamping down on the Tatar leadership would bring about the movement's end. Beginning in the year after its issuance, the authorities began a campaign of arrest and trial of most of the Tatar leaders, as well as of a selected number of ordinary Tatar protestors. Of the latter, they had literally thousands from which to choose. In April 1968, Enver Abdulgaziev, born only in the year of the German invasion of the Crimea, and a successful engineer in Tashkent, was arrested together with Said Abchairov (an engineer), Ibrahim Abibulla-cev, Reşat Alimov, Refat Ismailov, and five others for helping to organize the Chirchik festival; all received sentences of two and a half or three years at hard labor.[26]

In May 1968, ten Tatars were arrested in Moscow for delivering an unwanted petition to the Party Central Committee, and were sentenced to up to one year at hard labor.[27] The first important public trial of a Crimean Tatar, that of Omer Bayev, was held in Simferopol'. Arrested in Novorossiisk on August 29, 1968, and charged with agitation and dissemination of anti-Soviet propaganda, Bayev was tried on April 28, 1969. The prosecutor claimed that he had sent to official Soviet authorities a number of anonymous letters filled with slander about the treatment of the Tatars. Even worse, he had written a letter to Professor Senichkina of the Marxism-Leninism Institute in Leningrad claiming that the "nationality problem in the USSR has not yet been solved," and that letter had found its way into the hands of the KGB. For such slander and damage to the social and political well-being of the USSR, Bayev received a sentence of two years of corrective labor.[28]

Important Trials of Tatars

A second major trial and, according to Sheehy, the most important of them all, took place in Tashkent during July and August of 1969; this was the famous "Case #109," the trial of ten leading Tatar figures. According to Sheehy, the ten "represented a typical cross-section of the leading campaigners in that they were predominantly from the younger generation who could only just remember the deportation and included workers and members of the intelligentsia."[29]

From oldest to youngest they were: Ridvan Gafarev, (born in 1921), an electrician and a war invalid who had fought with the Red Army against the Germans; Ismail Yaziciev (born in 1925), a teacher, a poet, and at that time a bricklayer, who had received the title *Hero of the USSR* during the first years of the war; Riza Omerev (born in 1926), a Soviet partisan in the Crimea, now a construction worker; Izzet Khairov (born in 1938), a Communist party member and physical engineer; Rolland Kadiev (born in 1940), a physicist of some reknown in the USSR and abroad for his work on problems of relativity; Reşat Bayramev (born in 1941), an electrician in Melitopol'; Ruslan Eminev (born in 1941), a construction worker in Samarkand; Haydar Bariev (born in 1943), a tractor operator in Chirchik; Svetlina Ahmet (born in 1943), a registered nurse; and Munire Halil (born in exile in 1946), also a nurse.[30]

The evidence against these ten included "bulletins from the Moscow representatives and republican Action Group meetings"; letters from members of the Soviet movement for human rights; a document, written by Bayramov, entitled "Genocide in the Policy of the Soviet Government"; and "also entries in the visitors' book of the Simferopol' Museum complaining that it contained nothing about the Crimean Tatars, and in particular about the Tatar heroes of the Revolution and Second World War."[31]

While the trial was open and lasted for more than five weeks, it consisted primarily of charges and evidence presented by Soviet authorities and witnesses claiming: that the Tatars' demands were silly and unjustified, that they had committed treasonous acts during the war, and that the edict of 1967 was really more than they deserved. Thus we can see that the wording of the rehabilitation had not even reached the eyes of the chief political and legal authorities in the Uzbek SSR by 1969![32] Kadiev and Bayramov were sentenced to three years in "ordinary regime" camps for their especially criminal behavior; the others received from one to one and a half years.[33]

It should have been clear after this trial that, while the Soviet authorities were not willing to exceed the sentencing norms of Soviet law, they were willing to expend a great deal of time and effort to close down the Tatar movement. In January 1970, a third major trial took place in Tashkent—the trial of two other thorns in the sides of the authorities, Il'ia Gabay and Mustafa Cemilev. Although Gabay was a Jewish activist interested in the Tatar cause, his trial was combined with that of Cemilev because their charges were identical—slandering the Soviet social and political system. Mustafa Cemilev, born during the German occupation in 1943, had been arrested and had served time in prison on two prior occasions. The earlier charges had been for hooliganism. This time, the charges were more serious, and he was given a three year term in a "special regime" camp. Gabay had been living in Moscow and had been active in the preparation of documents about the persecutions since 1944. At the time of his arrest, the police found 137 volumes of such documents that he had planned to present to the government authorities himself, along with a petition for redress of grievances. In his last words before sentencing, Gabay stated that the actions of the Soviet government toward the Tatars and other small nationalities in the years since 1944 had amounted to a clear case of genocide. For his efforts, he received a three-year sentence to a "special regime" camp.[34]

Throughout 1970, trials of various Tatar leaders and intellectuals continued. On January 8, 1970, Nuri Abdurrahim was sentenced to two years for collecting information concerning the treatment of Crimean Tatars; in Tashkent, in June of that year, Tatar engineer Nurfet Marahaz was sentenced to two years for disseminating false information about Soviet treatment of national minorities.[35]

In September 1970, Sinie Mustafayeva, born in 1952, was "sentenced to three years of ordinary regime corrective labor camps for putting up black flags on the premises of the police and district Executive Committee of Tio-Tiube Settlement on May 18 of the same year (anniversary of the deportation)."[36]

Finally, according to tables compiled by Lewytzkyj, during the year 1970 one Tatar was tried in Moscow, and in Tashkent, Ruslan Eminev was sentenced to a six-month term and Muarrem Martynov, a poet, to two years.[37] As reported in the West, the trials that took place in 1971 include those of Ibrahimov, who tried to settle in the Crimea, and of Aişe Seitmuratova, a history lecturer at Samarkand University. They were charged "with the preparation and circulation of material slandering the Soviet social and political system. . . . and sentenced to three years and two years respectively."[38]

The latest information about the repression through the judicial system concerns the trial of Ceppar Akimov and of Reşat Cemilev. Akimov's biography is an interesting one. Born in 1909 in the Crimea, he began his career as a teacher, then was assigned to the Peoples' Commissariat of Education of the Crimean ASSR. He also served as editor of the Crimean State Publishing House in Simferopol'. In 1939, he joined the party. After the German invasion, he edited the partisan newspaper *Kizil Kirim* and published Tatar leaflets for the Soviet partisans. In 1944, he was deported to Bekabad in Uzbekistan where, until 1948, he served as deputy head of the Farkhad railway. In 1968, he was expelled from the party.[39]

At Akimov's trial in Tashkent in November 1972, the indictment included the following statements:

Akimov and other representatives of initiative groups knowingly make false assertions that . . . dozens of Crimean Tatars are allegedly languishing in prisons up to the present day. . . . false aspersions are cast on the position of the Crimean Tatars in the USSR to the effect that their national equality has allegedly been violated . . . slanderous fabrications are cited about how after the deportation of the Tatars from the Crimea "there started a nightmarish life in reservations and exile."[40]

On his own behalf, Akimov declared:

The documents signed by me express the will and aspirations of the Crimean Tatars, their content does not distort Soviet reality, but merely reflects a situation that actually exists concerning the national question. . . . This movement is legal and inevitable; I therefore consider the charges brought against me to be unfounded and illegal.

He received a sentence of three years.

In the trial of Reşat Cemilev in Tashkent in April 1973, the charges included those of "compiling documents that defame the Soviet system and also a breach of public order" (the Mayakovskii Square demonstration in 1969). In July 1973, a Tatar group appealed Cemilev's sentence of three years stating that he was:

one of those activists of the national movement who have understood that the solution of the national question of the Crimean Tatars is inseparably linked with the problem of democracy in the country, and that the tragedy of the Crimean Tatar people is not only a result of the evil deeds of individual personalities like Stalin, Beria, and Voroshilov, but a product of the totalitarian system as a whole.[41]

The most recent events of a judicial nature center around the trial (again) of Mustafa Cemilev, in Omsk, on April 14 and 15, 1976. The trial was held in Omsk rather than Tashkent where the alleged crimes took place, because

foreign correspondents may not travel to Omsk. It was only because Andrei
Sakharov and his wife attended and were subsequently brutalized by the local
police that the Western press found the event interesting (there can be no
doubt that this was Sakharov's reason for going). Cemilev was sentenced to
two and a half years in a labor camp on the familiar charge of anti-Soviet
slander, this despite the fact that the only prosecution witness withdrew his
testimony, claiming it "had been extorted from him." On April 19, Soviet
historian Aleksandr Nekrich, called upon his colleagues to give up their
"shameful silence" on Cemilev and other persecuted Soviet dissidents. On
May 25, 1976, the Supreme Soviet refused to overturn Cemilev's conviction,
even though it had to admit that the prosecution was left with no viable
evidence.[42]

The "Struggle for Human Rights" Movement

In early 1968, the Crimean leadership made the decision to relate their
movement to the more general "Democratic" and "Struggle for Human
Rights" movements among the Soviet intelligentsia. As a result of this
decision, several important dissident leaders have adopted the Tatar cause as
their own; likely, the growing interest in the Tatar problem in the West is
directly related to this fact. It is, in fact, only after such spokesmen as
Sakharov, Kosterin, Grigorenko, Franko, Lisenko, Yakir, Volpin, and Pisarev
have publicized the Tatars' plight that Western observers have been willing to
change their opinions that the Tatars "received more or less what they
deserved."

The first of the dissidents who took up the Tatar cause was the writer
Aleksei Kosterin, who had been a member of the Communist party. He had
long been known for his support of other small Soviet nationalities (particularly those that had been deported) and had inundated governmental
authorities with letters requesting a change in policy. In February 1968, he
had written:

> The national question in our country looks particularly unattractive at present.
> I am thinking of the policy of genocide toward a series of small nations, begun
> under Stalin and continuing to this day. The Volga Germans and Crimean
> Tatars . . . to this day do not have the right to return to the land of their
> forefathers, . . . and in effect are condemned to forcible assimilation. This
> situation is particularly vile against the background of our "defense" of all
> those oppressed and persecuted in Greece, Spain, . . . America, and Africa.[43]

As the result of the Chirchik repression, Kosterin sent a letter of resignation
from the party, dated October 24, 1968, in which he wrote:

> The label *antiparty* was wantonly attached to my letters. I had already been
> reproached for defending the Tatars of the Crimea. . . . I should have been

reproached for having defended with arms, in the first years of the Revolution, the Leninist policy of nationalities and the right of minorities to national equality.[44]

Piotr Grigorenko

Although Kosterin was seriously ill, a large number of Tatars held a seventy-second birthday party for him in Moscow. At the party, ex–Major General Piotr Grigorenko, who was not himself a Tatar, spoke on behalf of the Tatars. His speech is rightly considered to be the most important event in the early years of the Tatar-dissident cooperation. Grigorenko demanded that the Tatars themselves step up their campaign, utilize all legal methods sanctioned by published Soviet law, force the Soviet authorities either to grant them their rights or to break their own laws instead. Reading first from a note of appreciation from the Tatars, Grigorenko began:

> I thank Comrade Kosterin for everything he has done for our people and for other minority peoples whose rights have been violated by the evil forces of the country. Comrade Kosterin held out a helping hand to us in a time of cruel repressions against the representatives of our people who demanded recognition of the Crimean Tatars' sovereign rights—first of all, the right to a homeland—and in a time of grim struggle by our people for the right to exist.

Then Grigorenko proceeded to advise the Tatars about the future of their movement:

> The great mass of the Soviet people, who had been widely informed at one time that the Crimean Tatars had sold out the Crimea, was never told that this "sellout" was nothing but a figment of the imagination. . . . You were formerly subjected to repressions as Crimean Tatars, but, since the "political rehabilitation," it seems that there is no such nation. The nation has disappeared, but discrimination remains. . . . What basis is there for placing your people in a position of such inequality? Article 123 of the USSR Constitution reads: "Any direct or indirect restriction of the rights . . . of citizens on account of their race or nationality is punishable by law." Thus the law is on your side.
>
> . . . you underestimate your enemy. You think that you are dealing only with honest people. This is not so. . . .
>
> You address yourselves to the leadership of the party with meekly written pleas, which pass through the hands of those who are against your struggle for national equality. . . .
>
> . . . as long as you request . . . your case is not moving forward. . . . In order to put a stop to this abnormal situation, you must learn that what is prescribed by law should not be requested; it should be demanded!
>
> . . . do not limit your activity to the writing of petitions. Strengthen your

demands by all means that are available to you under the Constitution—make use of the freedom of speech and of the press, of meetings, street processions, and demonstrations.[45]

Alexei Kosterin died on November 10, 1968.[46] At the funeral which was held at the mortuary of the Botkin Hospital in Moscow, twenty-three Tatars representing various Tatar settlements attended, as did several Soviet dissidents. One Tatar poet, Muarrem Martynov, delivered a eulogy in Tatar:

> To A. Ye. Kosterin
> O, Democrat Kosterin! You have left us forever.
> Whom will we look to now for support—we the exiles, the Crimean Tatars!
> You did not die a natural death—they killed you.
> Having suffered in prisons and camps, faced with repression wherever you turned.
> You did not close your eyes to arbitrariness, you met the enemy head on.
> Following Lenin's tradition, you took the offensive against the enemy yourself.
> "Let our party be just and then there will be no nationalism," said our leader Lenin.
> Sleep peacefully, most honorable of Russia's sons.
> You will always be in the hearts of the Tatar people.
> Farewell, farewell, our faithful friend!
> Oh, Aleksei Yevgrafovich! You are like a son to our people!
> In mourning clothes you have dressed us, the deserted ones.
> The eyes of the Tatar people you have today filled with tears. We will cherish your legacy as the light of our lives.
> We will keep your ashes forever.
> The Crimean Tatar people are eternally grateful to you.
> They are ready to become the kind of fighter that you were.[47]

At the end of the funeral, Grigorenko summed up by saying, "It was no accident that he left his ashes to the Crimean Tatars. And we will abide by his last wishes and take the urn holding his ashes to the Crimea as soon as autonomy is restored to the Crimean Tatars in the land of your ancestors. . . . There will be freedom! There will democracy! Your ashes will be in the Crimea!"[48]

Grigorenko took up where Kosterin left off. For the rest of 1968 and early 1969, the ex-general sent to party and government organs one letter and protest after another on behalf of the Tatars. Their tone did not please the authorities. In December 1968, he sent USSR General Procurator Rudenko a letter entitled "KGB—Organ of Caste Lawlessness," complaining against the Chirchik repression. Then in March 1969, he wrote and sent to the Politburo a pamphlet entitled "Who are the Criminals?" In it he said, "Sometimes

Stalinism suddenly rears its ugly head." Of the indictment of the "Tashkent Ten" he wrote:

> Here is what is written, for example, on page 10, of the indictment: "this letter casts aspersions on the policy of the CPSU and the Soviet government toward national minorities. The resettlement of the Crimean Tatars in 1944 is represented by the writers of the letter as a 'barbarous crime.' Well, this brutal deportation of 1944—that was part of the policy of the CPSU and the Soviet government toward national minorities, and those who call it a 'brutal crime' must be tried for slandering this policy."

It was clear to Grigorenko that the authors of the indictment were in fact accepting Stalin's policy toward the deported nationalities—a change of emphasis at least from the position of the writers of the rehabilitation decree two years before.[49]

Before setting out to attend the trial in Tashkent, Grigorenko wrote: "Genocide was one of the terrible products of the two accursed führers of the twentieth century. But the frenzied Adolf fell at once upon nations numbering hundreds of millions, while the 'Marxist' Stalin preferred to 'get a little training' on the small nations. Among these nations, fate included the Crimean Tatars."[50] It was at this trial that Grigorenko himself was arrested, and thus began his ordeal of trials, arrests, and commitments to psychiatric hospitals.

Other Soviet Intellectuals and the Tatars

By no means were all Soviet intellectuals willing to take on the authorities or to support the causes of the dissidents. In either late 1968 or early 1969, an anonymous letter was sent "to the representatives of the Crimean Tatars," presumably from a number of intellectual "friends" of the Tatars; it warned them against dealing with one having such "dangerous mental problems" as General Grigorenko. Addressed to "Our Dear Fellow Citizens," it stated: "Already in March 1969, our group discussed the new situation and strongly emphasized that the leadership of the so-called Crimean Tatar national movement has become infected with adventurism and hostile ideology. And it is taking on a more and more anti-Soviet character. It is beginning to work with other anti-Soviet troublemakers like P. G. Grigorenko." The letter warned the Tatars that such activities as Kosterin's funeral were extremely dangerous for their well-being and their future, and advised that they return to "lawful behavior," that is, to accept the position that the authorities had assigned to them.[51]

Other Soviet dissidents included the Tatar problem in the general set of problems they faced. In the Ukraine, Taras Franko and Maria Lisenko sent a petition to the Supreme Soviet of the Ukrainian SSR on July 26, 1970, asking that it consider reestablishing the Crimean ASSR.[52] When Grigorenko was arrested, A. Levitin-Krasnov wrote a moving essay, "A Light in the Window," in which Grigorenko is compared "to the Good Samaritan of the parable, who did not pass by the man who had fallen among thieves." In it, Levitin-Krasnov wrote, "The struggle for the return of the Crimeans to their homeland—this is only part of one great problem. The problem is the struggle for democracy and humanitarian behavior in our country."[53]

Major Henrikh Altunyan, a resident of Kharkov and a military friend of Grigorenko's who had joined him at the trial in Tashkent, complained bitterly to the authorities in Moscow about Grigorenko's treatment and about the Tatar problem. On June 30, 1969, Altunyan met with Nikolai Madrasov, a representative of the Central Committee of the party, and a few days later he met with Georgii Denisov, an alternate to that committee. Altunyan told Madrasov:

> in my estimation, it is necessary to solve this Tatar problem quickly. From the perspective of politics, they [the Tatars] have been cleared. All that remains is their right to return to the Crimea, which should not be such a difficult thing to arrange. Sooner or later they will return, and will re-form their autonomous republic.

Madrasov responded, "There is no work for the Crimean Tatars in the Crimea; basically they are not asking to return." In the meeting with Denisov, Altunyan learned that:

> he [Grigorenko] had fallen under the influence of enemies of the Soviet state. You do not know anything about this matter. The Crimean Tatars have no intention of going anywhere. That they want to return is a lie. I live in Moscow and have heard nothing about this. What do you know? You live in Kharkov.[54]

It is inconceivable that responsible Soviet authorities could respond in such a manner. But they did.

Finally, Nobel Laureate Andrei Sakharov has lent his support to the Tatar cause. In his *Reflections* (1968), Sakharov said:

> Nationality problems will long continue to be a reason for unrest and dissatisfaction unless all departures from Leninist principles that have occurred are acknowledged and analyzed, and firm steps are taken to correct all mistakes. . . . Is it not disgraceful to continue to restrict the civil rights of the Crimean Tatar people who lost about 46 percent of their population . . . in the Stalinist repressions?[55]

He mentioned the Tatars in his speech upon receiving the award of the International League for the Rights of Man, on December 5, 1973:

> The Crimean Tatars, the Volga Germans, and the Meskhi Turks, resettled under the Stalinist tyranny, cannot return to their homelands. Such a key

problem for our country as that of assuring freedom of emigration is still unresolved.[56]

It has been largely through the work of such prominent figures that Western observers have become interested in the Tatar question, though it still is not very widely discussed in the West and Western governments have not shown the official interest in the Tatars they have shown in the Soviet Jews.

A New Tatar National Consciousness

In addition to stepping up their protest, petition, and demonstration activities, and linking their cause with those of other dissidents, the Tatars have also been concentrating their efforts on reviving Crimean Tatar national consciousness through the press, literature, and education in their places of exile. Without question, the most important development in this effort has been the use of *Lenin Bayragi,* the Crimean Tatar language newspaper in Tashkent. Since 1967, *Lenin Bayragi* has published articles concerning the truth about Tatar life in the Crimea during the German occupation, examples of Tatar literature, and general news about the Tatar movement. Edited for most of this period by I. Islamov, the role of this newspaper is, in the opinion of Kirimal, important enough to warrant comparison with *Tercuman.*[57]

Since August 1969, *Lenin Bayragi* has carried a special column entitled "Nobody Is Forgotten and Nothing Is Forgotten," in which reports of Crimean Tatar war heroes are given. Among those so honored were Nuri Nuftullayev, a naval pilot killed during the defense of Leningrad; Ilyas Karirov, a Tatar commander of an artillery division in Belorussia; and Ava Muslimova, a fearless woman partisan.[58] In 1970, it introduced another column entitled "Immortal Soldiers of the Revolution," which discussed the activities of Tatar Bolshevik revolutionaries during the years 1916–1920, many of whom were killed during Wrangel's occupation.[59]

Tatar educators and writers, both from the older group of intelligentsia surviving from the pre-1944 period and from a younger generation born in exile have worked hard to preserve the written Crimean Tatar language through their publications and research. In 1969, a member of the older generation, poet Eşref Şemizade, wrote: "The Crimean Tatar language is the language of our people, and over the course of thousands [sic] of years it has played a great role in cultural development. . . . A nation can exist only under the condition that it has its own literary language." He continued by saying that Crimean Tatar children who attend Uzbek, Kazakh, and Russian schools now have the opportunity to study their own native language because a textbook on the Crimean Tatar language has been written by the "well-known teachers Memet Umerov and Yusuf Bolat."[60]

Another article in *Lenin Bayragi,* written by Tatar linguist B. Gafurov, appealed to the young Tatars "to emulate Bekir Çobanzade, a prominent poet and scholar who loved his native language and literature, and who perished during the Stalinist purges in the late 1930s."[61]

Aside from *Lenin Bayragi,* the Department of Crimean Tatar Language and Literature at the Nizami Tashkent Pedagogical Institute, "where the students are mainly Crimean Tatars who have taken courses in their native language in Uzbek secondary schools," is another center for the maintenance of Tatar culture. Related to this department is the section for Crimean Tatar publications in the Gafur Gulam publishing house in Tashkent; headed by the Tatar poet, Çerkes Ali, with Seitomer Emin as poetry editor, in 1969 this section published more than twenty works in the Tatar language. Not only works by contemporary Tatar writers, but also those by a number of prewar and even prerevolutionary Tatar intellectuals are being published. Such figures as Gaspirali, Çobanzade, and the poet Çergiyev, who died in a Stalinist camp, are now represented in the firm's publications.[62]

Despite the fact that the Crimean Tatars are permitted an increasing amount of cultural freedom in Uzbekistan and other places of exile (a further Soviet concession to their protest movement) the authorities seem no nearer to a decision to allow the Tatars to return to their homeland. Without the interjection of help and interest from the outside, particularly from Turkey, it seems doubtful that such a return would ever be permitted. It is true that the authorities are more careful than they were three or four years ago to refrain from repeating charges of Tatar infidelity during the war as the reason for their continued denial of Tatar demands. For example, in the third edition of the *B.S.E.,* while the statement that the "annexation of the Crimea had a progressive significance," is repeated, no mention is made of any Tatar treason during the occupation.[63]

Today, the population of the Crimean Tatars is primarily located in Uzbekistan: Tashkent has 64,000; Tashkent oblast' another 139,000; Samarkand has 70,000; Andijan, 54,000; and Fergana, 51,000. Also, in the Kirgiz area there are 38,000 Crimean Tatars and in Osh oblast' there are 38,000.[64] Fewer than 1200 Tatar families have succeeded in gaining registration in the Crimean peninsula.

The question still remains: "Why are the Soviet authorities so adamant about refusing to permit the Crimean Tatars to return to the Crimea?" There is no easy answer. Reddaway believes "fears doubtless exist that the Tatars could, under certain circumstances, be more loyal to their ethnic and cultural kin in Turkey than to the USSR. . . . Probably even more important is the leadership's fear that if it yields to the demands of one aggrieved group, a hundred others will press their claims with renewed energy."[65]

Yet the fact remains that the Soviet government has already yielded to many of the Tatar demands—by their rehabilitation, which in 1967 could have served no visible political purpose, and by permission to expand cultural and educational activities in the Tatar language, thus implying that the Crimean Tatars do constitute a nationality. It may be true that there are still a great many officials who were so intimately connected with the deportation and later persecutions, and who still believe in their correctness, that to undo such a policy would be too painful an admission of error.

Regardless of what happened in the 1940s, is there still an excuse for the continuing forced exile of these people? After the accord at Helsinki, not even the Soviet government still accepts the doctrine of collective guilt. An anti-Soviet propagandist might find grounds on which to suggest, on the basis of current Soviet policy toward the Tatars, that maybe Russian chauvinism actually did account for the deportation in 1944.

Glossary

Ağa—a Turkish and Tatar title meaning gentleman, given to many officials

Akinci—a corps of light cavalry in the Ottoman army

Albantsy—the name given by the Russian government to settlers coming to the Crimea from the Balkans after 1774

Beşli—the new army formed by Khan Şahin Giray along Western models

Bey—in the Crimean Khanate, a title held by the leader of each Tatar clan; in the Ottoman system, a title inferior to *pasha* and superior to *ağa*

Beylik—in the Crimean Khanate, the name given to the lands of each Tatar clan, presided over by the *bey*

Boyar—in Muscovy, a hereditary noble and member of one of the most prestigious families

Caliph—head of the Islamic community; regarded as a successor to Mohammed

Caravan-serai—an inn on a caravan route

Central Rada—the parliamentary institution in the independent Ukraine, after 1917 and before the Ukraine was incorporated into the Soviet Union

Cingiziye—an epithet indicating descent from Jengiz Khan

Cizye—poll tax on Christian subjects in the Ottoman Empire

Code of the Steppe—law code written by Michael Speransky in 1822 for the Siberian provinces of the Russian Empire

CPSU—Communist Party of the Soviet Union

Dervish monastery—in Turkish, a *tekke*, in which live members of Muslim mystic orders; in the Crimean Khanate, these were often Muslim missionaries

Desiatin—a Russian measure of land, smaller than an acre

Divan—in the Crimean Khanate, the council of advisors to the Khan; in the Ottoman Empire, the council of state

Duma—in the Russian Empire, a parliamentary institution, introduced in 1906, that existed both on the national level as the State Duma, and on the local level in provinces and towns

Dvoriane—Russian noblemen

Dvorianstvo—the Russian noble class

Emir—a chief or commander

Eyalet—in the Ottoman Empire, a province

Gazi—one who fights for Islam

Golden Horde—the portion of the Great Horde of Jengiz Khan that included the Russian principalities and the steppe west of the Volga River

Great Horde—the empire of Jengiz Khan; in the mid-fifteenth century, the name given to that portion of the Golden Horde not included in the khanates of Kazan or the Crimea

Great Yasa—the law code developed by Jengiz Khan for his empire

Green Forces—rebels, usually peasants, against the introduction of the Soviet system in various areas of the Russian Empire

Guberniia—a province in the Russian Empire

Gubernskoe pravitelstvo—the administrative institution of a *guberniia*

Hakan—an oriental potentate

Han—an inn or large commercial building; also the Turkish name for "sovereign," equivalent to khan

Hoca—a Muslim religious teacher

Horde—at first, a division of the empire of Jengiz Khan; later applied to each separate remnant of that empire; also used to name the various Nogay Tatar groups

Imam—in a mosque, the leader of prayer

Ittifak—Turkish word for "union"; the name given to the Union of Russian Muslims during the Duma period

Janissary—from the Turkish *yeni çeri* or "new army"; the elite corps of troops in the Ottoman army

Jingizids—descendants of Jengiz Khan

Kadets—the Constitutional Democrat Party, liberals, in the Duma period

Kadi—a Muslim judge

Kadiasker, sometimes *kazasker*—originally the chief military judge; later a high official in the hierarchy of the Muslim judiciary

Kadilik—a Muslim judicial district, presided over by a *kadi*

Kaimakam—in the Ottoman system, a governor of an administrative district; in Şahin Giray's administration, an acting representative of the khan

Kaimakamlik—the district of a *kaimakam*

Kalgay sultan—a member of the Giray dynasty; theoretically the heir apparent of the reigning khan

Kalmuk, sometimes *kalmyk*—a Mongolian people remaining from the Golden Horde, residing in the lower Volga area

Kanun law—in the Ottoman system, law originating from the sultanate, not necessarily from Muslim law

Kapikulu—in the Crimean Khanate, a noble who received his title directly from the khan; it was not a hereditary title as was that of *mirza*

Karaçi beys—the four or five most important clan leaders who, meeting together, represented the interests of the clans in Crimean politics

KGB—Soviet state security police

Khan—the head of state in the Crimean Khanate; also heads of state of other khanates

Khanate—both the state itself and the form of government in the Crimea before 1783

Kulak—in the Soviet Union, a derogative term for rich, capitalist peasant; in practice, used by the Soviet government for all rural opponents of the regime

Kurultay—in the khanate, a gathering of all clan leaders for legislative purposes; later, the parliament of the Crimean state in the revolutionary period, from 1917 to 1921

Medresse—a traditional Islamic upper school, usually attached to a mosque

Mensheviks—a faction of the Social Democrat Party in the prerevolutionary period in Russia; opponents of the Bolsheviks in the same party

Millet—(1) in the Ottoman Empire, a community organized according to religion; at various times there were millets of the Greek Orthodox, Armenian Orthodox, Jewish, Roman Catholic, and Protestant faiths; (2) a Crimean Tatar journal, published until the outbreak of World War I

Milli Firka—a Crimean Tatar nationalist party during the period of World War I, the Revolution and Civil War, and existing illegally during the Soviet period until 1928; in Turkish and Tatar, it means "National Party"

Mirza—a hereditary Crimean Tatar noble

Muderris—a professor; also a grade in the Muslim clerical hierarchy

Muezzin—in a mosque, the one who calls the faithful to prayer

Mufti—a senior Muslim religious official

Mulla—a member of the Muslim hierarchy; often used in the twentieth century in a derogatory way for a Muslim religious figure who is opposed to all change and modernization

Namestnik—in Muscovy, a governor representing the tsar; in the Russian Empire, often used for a representative of the central government on the local level

N.E.P.—the "New Economic Policy," introduced by Lenin in 1921; in reality a partial return to capitalist economics in the face of massive failures in collectivization of land and nationalization of industry; phased out in 1924

NKVD—Soviet state security police

Nogay Tatar—nomadic Tatar, at times subject to the Crimean Khan, organized in various hordes, and dwelling in the steppe north of the Crimea and in the northern Caucasus

Nurredin sultan—in theory the second heir to a ruling Crimean Khan; a member of the Giray dynasty

Oblast'—in the Russian Empire, a district in a *guberniia,* or province

Padishah—the sovereign in the Ottoman Empire, also called the sultan

Pasha—in the Ottoman Empire, the highest title of civil and military officials under the padisha

Peace of Jassy—signed by the Ottoman Empire and the Russian Empire in January 1792, granting the Russians the port of Ozi and forcing the Ottomans to renounce all claims to sovereignty in the Crimea

Polovtsy—a Turkic nomadic people who lived in the southern Ukrainian steppe in the ninth to twelfth centuries

Pomeshchik—a Russian landowner

Pomestie—the land held by a Russian *pomeshchik*

Porte—a term used by Europeans for the Ottoman Empire, sometimes called the Sublime Porte; from Babiali ("sublime porte"), the Ottoman name for the door of the foreign ministry

Rehin—the Turkish word for "hostage"; used for a Crimean Tatar prince remaining in the Ottoman Empire as a "hostage" to ensure the khan's good behavior

Revkom—revolutionary commissariat

RSFSR—Russian Socialist Federated Soviet Republic

Samizdat—in the Soviet Union, an unauthorized publication

Sancak—in the Ottoman Empire, a subdivision of an *eyalet* (province)

Sekbans—in the Crimean Khanate, the elite military guard of the khans

Serasker—in the Ottoman Empire, a military commander; in the Crimean Khanate, a representative of the khan in the Nogay Hordes and, at times, among the Circassians

Sheikh—head of a Muslim religious order

Sobornoe Ulozhenie—a Muscovite law code issued in 1649

Soviet—in Soviet Russia, a council—on local, republic, and national levels

Sovnarkom—Council of Peoples' Commissars in the Soviet Union

S.R.—Socialist Revolutionary Party, a competitor of the Bolsheviks in Russia between 1912 and 1921

Steppe—the prairie north of the Black Sea and the Caspian Sea

Sultan—in the Ottoman Empire, the head of state; in the Crimean Khanate, a Giray prince

Tatarcilik—a word coined by Ismail Bey Gaspirali meaning "Tatarness"

Tekke—a Dervish monastery

Tercuman—the newspaper founded by Ismail Bey Gaspirali; in Turkish and Tatar, it means "translator"

Timar—a kind of fief granted by the Ottoman sultan to his retainers

Türkçülük—Turkishness

Turkic—a linguistic and ethnic subdivision of Altaic; includes Turkish, Turks, and Tatars, among others

Turkish—the language spoken by the Turks in the Ottoman Empire and Turkey; also an adjective referring to the Turks of the Ottoman Empire and Turkey

Uezd—in the Russian Empire and the Soviet Union, a district that is a subdivision of an *oblast'*

Ulema—in the Crimean Khanate, the intellectual class, made up of theologians and religious lawyers

Uluhane—In the Crimean Khanate, a mother of a khan

Untermensch—German word meaning "subhuman"

Vakif—in Islam, a pious foundation; property held by any Muslim institution, exempt from state dues

Vali—in the Ottoman Empire, a governor of a province

Volost'—in the Russian Empire, a subdivision of a *uezd*

Votchina—in Muscovy, inheritable land

White Forces—also called White Guards, or Whites; opponents of the Bolsheviks in the Russian Civil War, usually supporters of the monarchy

Yarlik—in the empire of Jengiz Khan and in the khanates of Kazan and the Crimea, a patent of authority from the khan

Yasa—the law code of Jengiz Khan

Young Tatars—in the Crimea, a group of Tatar nationalists taking their name from the Young Turks, a similar group in the Ottoman Empire

Yurt—in Tatar and Turkish, "homeland"

Zemstvo—begun in 1864 in the Russian Empire, an institution on both the national and local level whose responsibilities included education and social welfare

Abbreviations

B.S.E.	*Bol'shaia Sovetskaia Entsiklopediia*, 1st ed., Moscow, 1937; 2nd ed., Moscow, 1953; 3rd ed., Moscow, 1973.
Cahiers	*Cahiers du monde russe et soviétique*, Paris, 1960–.
Chteniia	*Chteniia v imperatorskom obshchestve istorii i drevnostei rossiiskikh pri moskovskom universitete*, Moscow, 1846–1918.
E.I.	*Encyclopaedia of Islam* (new edition), Leiden, 1950–.
ITOIAE	*Izvestiia tavricheskogo obshchestva istorii, arkheologii i etnografii*, Odessa, 1866–1916.
ITUAK	*Izvestiia tavricheskago uchennago arkhivnago kommissii*, Odessa, 1874–1917.
P.S.Z.	*Polnoe sobranie zakonov rossiiskoi imperii*, 3 series, St. Petersburg, 1830–1917.
SIRIO	*Sbornik imperatorskogo russkogo istoricheskogo obshchestva*, St. Petersburg, 1867–1916.
ZhMNP	*Zhurnal ministerstva narodnago prosveshcheniia*, St. Petersburg, 1846–1917.
ZOOID	*Zapiski imperatorskago odesskago obshchestva istorii i drevnostei*, Odessa, 1844–1916.

Notes

1. The Origins of the Crimean Tatar Khanate

1. P. N. Nadinskii, *Ocherki po istorii kryma*, pt. 1 (Simferopol', 1951), pp. 58–59, shows the existence in Mangup of a Slavic population with diplomatic and family ties to the Muscovite principality as late as 1474, when Ivan III's son married the daughter of a Mangup prince.

2. N. A. Smirnov, *Rossiia i turtsiia v XVI–XVII vv.*, 2 vols. (Moscow, 1946), vol. 1, pp. 16–17.

3. Ibid., pp. 18–28; Ahmed Dede Münecimbaşi, *Münecimbaşi Tarihi* (Istanbul, 1973), vol. 1, pp. 273–74.

4. V. D. Smirnov, *Krymskoe khanstvo pod verkhovenstvom otomanskoi porty do nachala XVIII veka* (St. Petersburg, 1887), pp. 30–33.

5. V. D. Smirnov (1887), pp. 34–47, 88–89; Ananiasz Zajaczkowski, ed., *La chronique des steppes kiptchak: Tevarih-i Dešt-i Qipčak* (Warsaw, 1966); Anatolii L. Iakobson, *Krym v srednie veka* (Moscow, 1973), p. 108.

6. V. D. Smirnov (1887), pp. 89–93.

7. Ibid., p. 146; Halil Inalcik, "Kirim Hanliği," *Islam Ansiklopedisi* (Istanbul, 1955), vol. 6, p. 746.

8. V. D. Smirnov (1887), p. 227.

9. O. Akçokrakly, *Tatarskie tamgi v Krymu* (Simferopol', 1927), p. 12.

10. H. Inalcik, "Hadjdji Giray," *E.I.*, vol. 3, pp. 43–45.

11. Akdes N. Kurat, *İV–XVIII Yüzyillarda Karadeniz Küzeyindeki Türk Kavimleri ve Devletleri* (Ankara, 1972), p. 210.

12. Inalcik, "Hadjdji Giray," p. 44; V. D. Smirnov (1887), p. 236.

13. Inalcik, "Hadjdji Giray," p. 44.

14. Henry Howorth, *History of the Mongols from the 9th to the 19th Century* (London, 1880), vol. 2, pt. 1, p. 451.

2. Ottoman Hegemony in the Crimea

1. Halil Inalcik, "Yeni Vesikalara Göre Kirim Hanliğinin Osmanli Tabiliğine Girmesi ve Ahidname Meselesi," *Belleten* 8, no. 31 (1944), pp. 185–229, upon which this discussion is based.

2. Inalcik, "Kirim Hanliği," p. 747.

3. F. Khartakhai, "Istoricheskaia sud'ba krymskikh tatar," *Vestnik evropy* 2 (1866), p. 201; Howorth, pp. 456–57; M. de Peysonnel, *Traité sur le commerce de la Mer Noire* (Paris, 1787), vol. 2, pp. 228–30; Inalcik, "Yeni Vesikalara," p. 223.

4. Inalcik, "Yeni Vesikalara," *passim*.

5. Ibid., pp. 226–27.

6. Ibid., p. 219.

7. I discuss this in my "Crimean Separatism in the Ottoman Empire."

8. Feridun Bey, *Münşeat-i Selatin* (Istanbul, 1849), vol. 1, p. 502.

9. I have elsewhere examined these financial ties in greater detail; see my article "Les rapports entre l'Empire ottoman et la Crimée: l'aspect financier."

10. Dilek Desaive, "Le Khanat de Crimée dans les Archives Ottomanes," *Cahiers* 13, no. 4 (1972), pp. 560–83, for examples of notes that indicate a growing Ottoman interference.

11. "Istoricheskoe i diplomaticheskoe sobranie," *ZOOID* 4 (1863), pp. 277–78, 379–80; S. Belokurov, *O posol'skom prikaze* (Moscow, 1906), pp. 78–79.

12. See Mehmed Mubarek, *Meskukat-i Kirimiye* (Istanbul, 1900), a catalogue of surviving examples of Crimean coinage in the Topkapi collection; and Petrun', "Khanski Iarliki na Ukrains'ki zemli," *Skhidnie Svit* 2 (Kharkov, 1928), pp. 170–87.

13. See P. N. Nadinskii, *Ocherki*, vol. 1, pp. 58–65; N. A. Smirnov, *Rossiia, passim;* and A. A. Novosel'skii, *Bor'ba moskovskago gosudarstva s tatarami v XVII veke* (Moscow, 1948) for negative judgments about Crimean Tatar legitimacy.

14. H. Inalcik, "Giray," *Islam Ansiklopedisi* (Istanbul, 1948), vol. 4, p. 786; B. Spuler, *The Muslim World* (Leiden, 1960), vol. 2, p. 95.

15. N. L. Ernst, "Bakhchisaraiskii Khanskii dvorets i arkhitektor vel. kn. Ivana III friazin Aleviz Novyi," *ITOIAE* 2 (Simferopol', 1928), pp. 39–54.

16. Inalcik, "Kirim Hanliği," p. 755; Kurat, *IV–XVIII Yüzyillarda*, p. 227.

17. Kurat, *IV–XVIII Yüzyillarda*, pp. 223–24.

3. The Political System of the Crimean Khanate

1. Kurat, *IV–XVIII Yüzyillarda*, p. 226.

2. A. Skal'kovskii, "Zaniatie kryma v 1783 g.," *ZhMNP* 30, no. 2 (1841), p. 3.

3. [V. Tiapkin], "Perevod s shertnyia gramoty," *Drevniaia Rossiiskaia Vivliofika*, vol. 15, p. 1.

4. Ozalp Gökbilgin, *Tarih-i Sahib Giray Han* (Ankara, 1973), pp. 175–76.

5. F. F. Lashkov, "Istoricheskii ocherk krymsko-tatarskago zemlevladeniia," *ITUAK* 23 (1895), pp. 71–72; Khartakhai, p. 143; Gökbilgin, *Tarih*, p. 185.

6. Khartakhai, pp. 108–9; Lashkov, "Istoricheskii ocherk," pp. 76–78.

7. A. Fisher, "Les rapports," for lists of Ottoman payments to Giray sultans.

8. See Barbara Kellner-Heinkele, *Aus den Aufzeichnungen des Said Giray Sultan* (Freiburg, 1975), pp. 1–92, for the best discussion of the Girays; Inalcik, "Giray," pp. 783–89.

9. Kellner-Heinkele, pp. 93–148; Khartakhai, pp. 210–13; Inalcik, "Kirim Hanliği," p. 755.

10. Kellner-Heinkele, *passim.*

11. A. Bennigsen and Chantal Lemercier-Quelquejay, "La Moscovie, L'empire Ottoman, et la crise successorale," *Cahiers* 14, no. 4 (1973), p. 453–87.

12. I. F. Aleksandrov, "O musul'manskom dukhovenstve," *ITUAK* 51 (1914), pp. 207–10; Gözaydin, *Kirim* (Istanbul, 1948), p. 38.

13. F. F. Lashkov, "Arkhivnyia dannyia o beilikakh," *Arkheologicheskii S'ezd: Trudy* 6, no. 4 (1889), pp. 96–110.

14. "Istoricheskaia spravka ob obrazovanii v tavricheskoi gubernii tatarskikh dvorianskikh rodov," *ZOOID* 23 (1901), p. 42; Inalcik, "Kirim Hanliği," p. 753.

15. Lashkov, "Arkhivnyia dannyia," pp. 107–8; Lashkov, "Istoricheskii," p. 80; Khartakhai, pp. 219–21.

16. Inalcik, "Kirim Hanliği," p. 753.

17. Gökbilgin, *Tarih*, pp. 156–57.

18. Lashkov, "Istoricheskii," pp. 86–87.

19. Ibid., pp. 91–93; Khartakhai, p. 228, says the origin of this term is *emir zade* (the heir to the position of *emir* or *bey*).

20. Lashkov, "Istoricheskii," pp. 92–93; Inalcik, "Kirim Hanliği," pp. 754–55.

21. Lashkov, "Istoricheskii," pp. 99–100; Peysonnel, II, p. 281; A. L. Iakobson, *Krym v srednie veka* (Moscow, 1973), p. 143.

22. Inalcik, "Kirim Hanliği," p. 752; A. Sergeev, "Nogaitsy," *ITUAK* 48 (1912), pp. 7–11; I. Iurchenko, "Opisanie Perekopskikh," *ZOOID* 11 (1879), pp. 479–86; O. Gökbilgin, *1532–1577 yillarda arasinda Kirim Hanliğinin Siyasi Durumu* (Ankara, 1973), pp. 27–29.

23. Inalcik, "Çerkes: Ottoman Period," *E.I.*, vol. 2, pp. 24–25.

4. Economic and Cultural Life in the Khanate

1. Iakobson, *Krym*, and Novosel'skii, *Bor'ba*.

2. See Charles Verlinden, *L'Esclavage dans l'Europe médiévale* (Brugge, 1955), vol. 1; Verlinden, "La colonie vénitienne de Tana," *Studi in onore di Gino Luzzatto* (Milan, 1950), vol. 2, pp. 1–25.

3. A. Fisher, "Muscovy and the Black Sea Slave Trade," *Canadian-American Slavic Studies* 6, no. 4 (1972), pp. 575–94.

4. Bohdan Baranowski, *Chlop polski w walce z tatarami* (Warsaw, 1952), pp. 49–56; Novosel'skii, *Bor'ba* p. 436.

5. M. Dragomanov, *Pro ukrainskikh Kozakiv, tatar ta turkiv* (Kiev, 1876), pp. 17–19; M. Hrushevsky, *A History of the Ukraine* (New Haven, 1941), p. 160–61.

6. Solov'ev, *Istoriia rossii*, vol. 4, pts. 7–8, p. 140.

7. Ibid., p. 83; M. A. Alekberli, *Bor'ba ukrainskogo naroda protiv turetsko-tatarskoi agressii* (Saratov, 1961), p. 124.

8. Zbigniew Wojcik, "Some Problems of Polish-Tatar Relations in the Seventeenth Century," *Acta Poloniae Historica* 13 (1966), pp. 87–102.

9. Anatole de Demidoff, *Travels in the Krimea*, (London, 1853).

10. P. S. Pallas, *Travels Through the Southern Provinces of the Russian Empire, in the Years 1793 and 1794* (London, 1812), vol. 2, pp. 208, 249–50; W. Barthold, "Ak Masdjid," *E.I.*, vol. 1, p. 312.

11. Pallas, vol. 2, p. 19; H. D. Seymour, *Russia on the Black Sea and the Sea of Azof* (London, 1855), pp. 34–35.

12. Seymour, p. 38; Iakobson, *Krym*, p. 145; Pallas, vol. 2, p. 33; A. Fevret, "Les tatars de Crimée," *Revue du monde musulman* 3 (1907), p. 97; B. Spuler, "Baghče Saray," *E.I.*, vol. 1, pp. 893–94.

13. N. Ernst, "Bakhchisaraiskii Khanskii dvorets i arkhitektor vel. kn. Ivana III friazin Aleviz Novyi," *ITOIAE* 2, pp. 39–54.

14. N. Ernst, "Bakhchisaraiskii . . . ," p. 43; M. Bronevskii, "Opisanie Kryma," *ZOOID* 6 (1867), p. 344.

15. Pallas, vol. 2, pp. 29–31; Seymour, p. 39; John Parkinson, *A Tour of Russia, Siberia, and the Crimea, 1792–1794* (London, 1971), pp. 193–95; all give interesting descriptions of the palace.

16. Fevret, pp. 98–99; See P. I. Sumarokov, *Dosugi krymskago sud'i ili vtoroe puteshestvie v Tavridu* (St. Petersburg, 1803–1805), 2 vols., for many well done diagrams of the palace as it appeared at the beginning of the nineteenth century. The Tatar history is that by Halim Giray Sultan.

17. B. Adler, "Die Krim-Karäer," *Baessler Archiv* 17 (1934), pp. 103–33.

18. See A. Fisher, "The Administration of Subordinate Nationalities,"; Khartakhai, "Istoricheskaia sud'ba," p. 143; Peysonnel, *Traité,* vol. 1, p. 13, and vol. 2, p. 322; Baron de Tott, *Mémoires* (Hamburg, 1785), vol. 2, p. 129.

19. Seymour, pp. 41–45; Pallas, vol. 2, pp. 34–36; A. Samojlovic, "Beiträge zur Bienenzucht in der Krim im 14.–17. Jahrhundert," *Festschrift Georg Jacob,* pp. 270–75, has discovered a khan's charter granting to the Karaims of Çufut Kale a monopoly on honey production.

20. Feridun Bey, vol. 2, p. 404.

21. H. Inalcik, "Eyalet," *E.I.,* vol. 2, pp. 721–24. A typical misrepresentation of Ottoman presence in the Crimea and confusion of Crimean and Ottoman identities is found in V. A. Golobutskii, *Zaporozhskoe kazachestvo* (Kiev, 1957), p. 37, where he says "After 1475, the Ottomans built forts at Perekop, Gözleve, Kefe, Yenikale, Arabat, and others."

22. Fevret, p. 95; Kurat, *IV–XVIII Yüzyillarda,* p. 224; and Iakobson, *Krym,* who gives the account by Dortelli.

23. Gökbilgin, *Tarih,* especially pp. 20–21, 221.

24. Ananiasz Zajaczkowski, ed., *La chronique des steppes kiptchak* (Warsaw, 1966) and by the same editor, " 'Letopis' Kipchakskoi stepi, kak istochnik po istorii kryma," in A. S. Tveritinova, *Vostochnye istochniki* (Moscow, 1969), vol. 2, pp. 10–28.

25. Kirimli Haci Mehmed Senai, *Historia Chana Islam Gereja III,* Olgierd Gorka and Zbigniew Wojcik, eds., (Warsaw, 1971).

26. Seiid Mukhammed Riza, *Asseb o Sseiiar' ili Sem' Planet'* (Kazan, 1832); V. D. Smirnov (1887), and V. D. Smirnov, *Krymskoe khanstvo pod verkhovenstvom otomanskoi porty v XVIII stoletie* (Odessa, 1889).

5. The Crimean Role in Eastern European Politics

1. Akdes N. Kurat, *Türkiye ve Idil Boyu* (Ankara, 1966), pp. 83–84; Inalcik, "Kirim Hanliği," p. 755.

2. Fisher, "Les rapports," for a complete discussion of these gifts and other financial arrangements; also Ozalp Gökbilgin and Dilek Desaive, "Le khanat de crimée et les campagnes militaires de l'Empire Ottoman," *Cahiers* 11, no. 1 (1970), pp. 110–17; Inalcik, "Giray," p. 786.

3. C. M. Kortepeter, "Ottoman Imperial Policy and the Economy of the Black Sea Region in the Sixteenth Century," *Journal of the American Oriental Society* 86 (1966), pp. 86–113; A. Fisher, "Azov in the Sixteenth and Seventeenth Centuries," *Jahrbücher für Geschichte Osteuropas* (1973). The role of these slaves has not yet been studied by historians. This author is in the midst of a full study of the Black Sea slave trade.

4. G. Vernadsky, *The Tsardom of Moscow 1547–1682* (New Haven, 1969), pp. 10–12; quote from Giovanni Botero, *Relationi Universali* (Brescia, 1599).

5. Vernadsky, pp. 88–89, 91–92.

6. Novosel'skii, *Bor'ba.*

7. F. F. Lashkov, *Pamiatniki diplomaticheskikh snoshenii krymskago khanstva s moskovskim gosudarstvom* (Simferopol', 1891); A. N. Zertsalov, *Ob oskorblenii tsarskikh poslov v krymu v XVII veke* (Moscow, 1893).

8. Fisher, "Azov,"; Fisher, "Muscovite-Ottoman relations in the 16th and 17th centuries," *Humaniora Islamica* 1 (1973), pp. 207–17.

9. See the excellent study by Jaroslaw Pelenski, *Russia and Kazan: Conquest and Imperial Ideology* (The Hague, 1974); Kurat, *IV–XVIII Yüzyillarda,* pp. 231–33.

10. Solov'ev, vol. 7, pp. 264–65.

11. Vernadsky, pp. 500, 552; Zbigniew Wojcik, "Mediacja tatarska miedzy Polska a Turcja w roku 1672," *Przeglad Historyczny* 52, no. 1 (1962), pp. 32–50; Howorth, p. 549.

12. Baranowski, *Chlop Polski w walce z tatarami* (Warsaw, 1952).

13. [M. Litvin], "Izvlechenie iz sochineniia Mikhaila Litvina," *Memuary otnosiashchiesia k istorii iuzhnoi rusi,* no. 1 (Kiev, 1890), pp. 4–5.

14. Dmitrii Bantysh-Kamenskii, *Istoriia maloi rossii* (Moscow, 1822), 2 vols. Nadinskii, vol. 1, pp. 80 ff.

15. Inalcik, "Kirim Hanliği," p. 748.

16. Ibid.; Kurat, *IV–XVIII Yüzyillarda,* p. 233.

17. Kurat, *IV–XVIII Yüzyillarda,* p. 232, says that Sahib's expansion of Crimean power should give him the reputation of the most ambitious and successful of Crimean khans. Yet, most accounts of Crimean history scarcely mention him.

18. Ibid., pp. 231–35.

19. Kurat, *Türkiye ve Idil Boyu, passim.*

20. Alexander Bennigsen and Chantal Lemercier-Quelquejay, "Les expéditions de Devlet Giray contre Moscou en 1571 et 1572," *Cahiers* 13, no. 4 (1972), pp. 555–59; Kurat, *IV–XVIII Yüzyillarda,* pp. 236–42; Inalcik, "Kirim Hanliği," pp. 748–49; Inalcik, "Dawlat Giray," *E.I.,* vol. 2, pp. 178–79; Vernadsky, pp. 131–32.

21. Bennigsen and Lemercier-Quelquejay, "La Moscovie," pp. 453–87.

22. Kurat, *IV–XVIII Yüzyillarda,* pp. 245–54; Inalcik, "Kirim Hanliği," p. 749; Inalcik, "Ghazi Giray II," *E.I.,* vol. 2, pp. 1046–47; C. M. Kortepeter, *Ottoman Imperialism during the Reformation: Europe and the Caucasus* (New York, 1973).

23. Inalcik, "Kirim Hanliği," p. 750; Kurat, *IV–XVIII Yüzyillarda,* pp. 255–58.

6. Russian Interest in the Crimea

1. Iurii Krizhanich, *Politika* (Moscow, 1965), pp. 382–83, 435, 482; M. N. Berezhkov, "Plan zavoevaniia Kryma, sostavlennyi Iuriem Krizhanichem," *ZhMNP* 127 (1891), pp. 483–517, and 128 (1891), pp. 65–119.

2. Fisher, "Azov,"; B. H. Sumner, *Peter the Great and the Ottoman Empire* (London, 1949).

3. Francis Ley, *Le Maréchal de Münnich et la Russie au XVIIIe Siècle,* (Paris, 1959); Inalcik, "Kirim Hanliği," p. 750. The important Tatar library of Khan Selim Giray I was totally destroyed too—it held many of the most important Tatar chronicles and manuscripts.

4. N. Borzenko and A. Negri, "Bakhchisaraiskaia, arabskaia i turetskaia nadpisi khanskago dvortsa," *ZOOID* 2 (1848), pp. 491–94, for evidence of those portions of the surviving palace rebuilt by Selamet Giray. M. Mironov, "K istorii pogranichnykh nashikh snosheniia s krymskim khanstvom," *Kievskaia starina* 11 (Feb. 1885), pp. 339–56.

5. M. L. Vorontsov, "Opisanie sostoianiia del vo vremia Gosudaryni Imperatritsy Elizavetu Petrovny," *Arkhiv Kniazia Voronstova* 25 (Moscow, 1882), pp. 308–10; A. Sergeev, "Doklad Imperatritse Ekaterine II-oi po vstuplenii Eia na Prestol, izobrazhaiushchii sistemu Krymskikh Tatar," *ITUAK* 53 (1916), pp. 190–93.

6. V. Ulianitskii, *Russkiia konsul'stva za granitseiu v XVIII veke* (Moscow, 1899), vol. 1, pp. 445–50.

7. A. Fisher, *The Russian Annexation of the Crimea 1772–1783* (Cambridge, 1970), p. 28, for a discussion of this Turkish document and Nikiforov's exit.

8. I. H. Uzunçarşili, *Osmanli Tarihi* (Ankara, 1956) vol. 4, pt. 1, p. 370.

9. This campaign has been discussed in detail by most historians of the Crimea because of one chance event. A French agent, Baron de Tott, accompanied the khan in this battle and left a colorful account of it.

10. Halim Giray Sultan, *Gülbün-i Hanan, passim.* Fisher, "Crimean Separatism."

11. A. Skal'kovskii, "O Nogaiskikh tatarakh," p. 153; E. I. Druzhinina, *Kiuchuk-kainardzhiiskii mir 1774 goda: ego podgotovka i zakliuchenie* (Moscow, 1955), p. 108.

12. Boris Nolde, *La formation de l'empire russe* (Paris, 1952–1953), vol. 2, p. 59; Necati Efendi, "Zapiski Mukhammeda Nedjati Efendi," *Russkaia starina* (March 1894), p. 132.

13. "Politicheskaia perepiska Imperatritsy Ekateriny II," *SIRIO* 97, pp. 245–46.

14. "Bumagi Imperatritsy Ekateriny II," *SIRIO* 13, p. 129; Fisher, *Russian Annexation,* pp. 40–43.

15. Halim Giray Sultan, p. 183. Selim Giray's tomb is in the cemetery of the mosque of Ayas Pasha in Istanbul, and on the stone he is described as "a patriot," Howorth, pp. 596–97.

16. Fisher, *Russian Annexation,* pp. 45–47.

17. Ibid., pp. 49–51.

7. The Crimean Independent State and Russian Annexation

1. See Fisher, *Russian Annexation,* where no satisfactory explanation of this question emerges.

2. Ibid., pp. 57–60.

3. Ibid., p. 61.

4. Ibid., pp. 60–63; "Arkhiv voenno-pokhodnoi kantseliarii grafa P. A. Rumiantseva-Zadunaiskago," *Chteniia* 56, pp. 16–18.

5. Fisher, *Russian Annexation,* pp. 62–64; Nolde, vol. 2, pp. 123–25, claims that the Ottomans sent Devlet on this mission and aided his administration. There is no evidence for this in the Turkish sources.

6. "Diplomaticheskaia perepiska Imperatritsy Ekateriny II," *SIRIO* 135, p. 266.

7. "Diplomaticheskaia perepiska," p. 441.

8. Ahmet Cevdet, *Cevdet Tarihi* 2nd ed. (Istanbul, 1854), vol. 1, p. 131.

9. N. F. Dubrovin, *Prisoedinenie kryma k rossii* (St. Petersburg, 1885–1889), vol. 1, pp. 56–78, for a series of reports on Devlet's problems; Cevdet, vol. 1, pp. 124–25.

10. N. Grigorovich, *Kantsler Kniaz A. A. Bezborodko, SIRIO* 26, p. 369.

11. Fisher, *Russian Annexation,* pp. 73–81.

12. "Arkhiv . . . Rumiantseva Zadunaiskago," p. 116; "Pis'ma grafa N.I. Panina k Imperatritse Ekaterine Velikoi," *Arkhiv kniazia vorontsova* 26 (1882), p. 153.

13. Uzunçarşili, vol. 4, pt. 1, p. 446.

14. Dubrovin, *Prisoedinenie,* vol. 1, pp. 498–99; Fisher, *Russian Annexation,* pp. 82–84.

15. F. F. Lashkov, "Shagin-Girei," *Kievskaia starina* (Sept. 1886), p. 57; Skal'kovskii, "Zaniatie kryma," pp. 9–11.

16. Dubrovin, *Prisoedinenie,* vol. 1, p. 654.

17. Fisher, *Russian Annexation,* pp. 86–90; Karaim Rabbi Azaria Iliia, "Sobytiia sluchivshiiasia v krymu," *Vremennik imperatorskago moskovskago obshchestva istorii i drevnostei rossiiskikh* 24 (1854), pp. 103–14.

18. Fisher, "Administration . . . Empires," *passim.*

19. Azaria Iliia, *passim.* A. L. Bert'e-Delagard, "K istorii Khristianstva v krymu," *ZOOID* 28 (1910), p. 66.

20. N. F. Dubrovin, "Bumagi Kniazia . . . Potemkina-Tavricheskago," *Sbornik voenno-istoricheskikh materialov* 6 (1893), pp. 26–29.

21. Uzunçarşili, vol. 4, pt. 1, p. 447; Inalcik, "Çerkes," pp. 24–25.

22. Dubrovin, *Prisoedinenie,* vol. 2, pp. 4, 92; S. Safonov, "Ostatki grecheskikh legionov v rossii," *ZOOID* 1 (1844), p. 218.

23. Grigorovich, p. 93.

24. On the Christian exodus, see Marc Raeff, "The Style of Russia's Imperial Policy and Prince G. A. Potemkin," in G. N. Grob, ed., *Statesmen and Statecraft of the Modern West* (Barre, Mass., 1967), pp. 1–52; Fisher, *Russian Annexation,* pp. 100–105; Nolde, vol. 2, pp. 140–52; Gavriil arkhiepiskop, "Pereselenie grekov iz kryma," *ZOOID* 1 (1844), p. 197.

25. Dubrovin, *Prisoedinenie,* vol. 2, pp. 92–93.

26. Ibid., vol. 4, p. 508.

27. Ibid., p. 512.

28. "Bumagi Imperatritsy Ekateriny II," *SIRIO* 27 p. 232.

29. Dubrovin, *Prisoedinenie,* vol. 4, pp. 931–32; "Bumagi . . . Ekateriny II," *SIRIO* 27, pp. 222–23.

30. *P.S.Z.* series 1, vol. 21 no. 15,707, p. 897.

31. Grigorovich, pp. 530–32.

8. Reorganization of the Crimea

1. See A. Fisher, "The Administration of Subordinate Nationalities," and Fisher, "Enlightened Despotism and Islam," for fuller treatments of this subject.

2. Chantal Lemercier-Quelquejay, "Les missions orthodoxes en Pays Musulmans de moyenne—et basse—Volga, 1552–1865," *Cahiers* 8, no. 3 (1967), pp. 369–403.

3. *P.S.Z.,* series 1, vol. 11, no. 8664, pp. 719–20; E. A. Malov, *O novokreshchenskoi kontore* (Kazan, 1873).

4. *P.S.Z.,* series 1, vol. 19, no. 13,996 (1773), pp. 775–76.

5. Cafer Seidahmet, *La Crimée: Passé–Présent* (Lausanne, 1921), p. 39; see also M. Raeff, "The Style of Russia's Imperial Policy," pp. 1–52, for an excellent analysis of Russian motives underlying its imperial regime in the south.

6. E. I. Druzhinina, *Severnoe prichernomor'e v 1775–1800 gg.* (Moscow, 1959).

7. F. F. Lashkov, "Statisticheskiia svedeniia o Kryme, soobshchennyia kaimakamami v 1783 godu," *ZOOID* 14 (1886), pp. 91–93; *P.S.Z.,* series 1, vol. 22 nos. 15,924, 15,925, 15,975, 15,988, 15,989, 16,081, 16,531 (the edicts creating all of the new Crimean institutions).

8. Lashkov, "Statisticheskiia svedeniia . . . ," pp. 92–93.

9. Ibid., pp. 94–98, includes lists of empty towns or portions thereof; F. F. Lashkov, "K voprosu o kolichestve naseleniia Tavricheskoi gubernii v nachale XIX stoletiia," *ITUAK* 53 (1916), pp. 158–76.

10. *P.S.Z.,* series 1, vol. 12, no. 15,936 (February 22, 1784), p. 51.

11. "Rasporiazheniia . . . Potemkina-Tavricheskago . . . ," *ZOOID* 12 (1881), p. 304.

12. Raeff, p. 14.

13. Raeff, p. 15.

14. Druzhinina, *Severnoe prichernomor'e v 1775–1800 gg.* (Moscow, 1959) p. 97; Lemercier-Quelquejay, "The Crimean Tatars," p. 17; Nadinskii, *Ocherki,* vol. 1, p. 103.

15. Raeff, p. 15.

16. I. F. Aleksandrov, "O musul'manskom dukhovenstve," *ITUAK* 51 (1914), pp. 207–20. There was one instance of a contrary policy being followed, namely the conversion of a mosque in Sudak to a church. See Seidahmet, *La Crimée,* p. 39.

17. Raeff, pp. 13–14.

18. Lemercier-Quelquejay, "The Crimean Tatars," p. 18; Druzhinina, *Severnoe,* pp. 118–19.

19. Lemercier-Quelquejay, "The Crimean Tatars," p. 18, gives these high figures saying it left in the Crimea only "60,000–70,000 Tatars . . . living in the stricken countryside." See Fisher, *Russian Annexation,* pp. 145–46, for counter-arguments. Since she says that, in 1804, there were 120,000 Tatars in the Crimea and the exodus had continued, the earlier figures seem defective.

20. Druzhinina, *Severnoe,* p. 119; Arsenii I. Markevich, "Pereseleniia krymskikh tatar v turtsiiu," *Izvestiia AN SSSR,* series 7 no. 4 (1928) pp. 375–405.

21. Nadinskii, *Ocherki,* vol. 1, p. 100.

22. Lemercier-Quelquejay, "The Crimean Tatars," p. 17; Nadinskii, *Ocherki,* vol. 1, pp. 100–101; Raeff, p. 15.

23. Pallas, vol. 2, pp. 343–44.

9. Russian Administration of the Crimea in the Nineteenth Century

1. Nadinskii, *Ocherki,* vol. 1, p. 168.

2. *P.S.Z.,* series 1, vol. 22, no. 15,920, on the formation of Tavricheskaia oblast', 1784.

3. Raeff, *passim;* Nadinskii, *Ocherki,* vol. 1, p. 96.

4. *P.S.Z.,* series 1, vol. 24, no. 17,634; Nadinskii, *Ocherki,* vol. 1, p. 96; Druzhinina, *Iuzhnaia,* p. 174.

5. *P.S.Z.,* series 1, vol. 27, no. 20,449; ibid., series 2, vol. 13, no. 11,080; ibid., series 3, vol. 4, no. 2077.

6. V. P. Laskovskii, "Praviteli tavridy," *ITUAK,* vol. 35 (1903), pp. 24–26. From the re-creation of Tavricheskaia guberniia in 1802, the governors were: Grigorii Miloradovich (1802–1803); Dimitrii Mertvago (1803–1807); Andrei Borozdin (1807–1816); Andrei Lavinskii (1816–1819); Andrei Baranov (1819–1821); Nikolai Perovskii (1822–1823); Dimitrii Naryshkin (1823–1829); Aleksandr Kaznacheev (1829–1837); Matvei Muromtsov (1837–1843); Viktor Roslavets (1843–1845); Vladimir Pestel' (1845–1854); Count Nikolai Adlerberg (1854–1856); Grigorii Zhukovskii (1856–1871); Andrei Reitern (1871–1873); Aleksandr Kavelin (1873–1881); Andrei Vsevolozhskii (1881–1889); Petr Lazarev (1889–1901); Vladimir Trepov (1902–1903).

7. Cafer Seidahmet, *La Crimée,* p. 51.

8. *P.S.Z.,* series 1, vol. 27, no. 20,449, p. 290.

9. The following decrees concern administrative reorganization in the Crimea: *P.S.Z.,* series 1, vol. 27, no. 20,643; ibid., series 3, vol. 11, no. 8115; vol. 12, no. 8539; and vol. 14, no. 11,033. Translators are discussed in: ibid., series 1, vol. 27, no. 20,449 (section 16); ibid., series 2, vol. 30, no. 28,947 and vol. 34, no. 35,102.

10. *P.S.Z.,* series 3, vol. 12, no. 8741.

11. Ibid., series 1, vol. 22, no. 16,557; vol. 31, no. 24,610; ibid., series 3, vol. 16, no. 13,589 and vol. 12, no. 8741.

12. "We learn that some officials are seizing harvests from Tatars without legal justification." *P.S.Z.,* series 1, vol. 33, no. 26,254.

13. Lashkovskii, *passim.*

14. *P.S.Z.,* series 1, vol. 23, no. 17,265.

15. Ibid., vol. 27, nos. 20,270 and 20,276, which created the commission; vol. 28, no. 21,275; vol. 29, nos. 22,002 and 22,203 repeated the earlier tasks; vol. 30, no. 23,325, created the St. Petersburg committee; vol. 31, no. 24,349, closed the commission.

16. F. F. Lashkov, "Sbornik dokumentov po istorii krymsko-tatarskago zemlevladeniia," *ITUAK,* 26 (1897), pp. 28–29, 90–102.

17. Lashkov, "Arkhivnyia dannyia," pp. 96–110.

18. Lashkov, "Sbornik dokumentov," pp. 24–154, lists and discusses all known Crimean Tatars who had become military or bureaucratic officials with the rank of *dvorianstvo* by 1808.

19. *P.S.Z.,* series 2, vol. 10, no. 8676.

20. Ibid., vol. 14, no. 12,419.

21. Ibid., vol. 15, no. 13,304.

22. Ibid., vol. 4, nos. 2617 and 2808; vol. 5, no. 3761.

23. Izmail Muftizade, "Ocherk voennoi sluzhby krymskikh tatar s 1783 po 1889 god," *ITUAK* 30 (1899), pp. 1–2.

24. Muftizade, pp. 3–6; G. K. Kirpenko, "Ordera Kniazia Platona A. Zubova," *ITUAK* 26 (1897), pp. 1–10.

25. Muftizade, pp. 6–13; G. S. Gabaev, "Zakonodatel'nye akty i drugie dokumenty o voennoi sluzhbe krymskikh tatar," *ITUAK* 51 (1914), pp. 137–39; *P.S.Z.,* series 1, vol. 30, nos. 22,772 and 23,778.

26. Muftizade, pp. 10–17; *P.S.Z.,* series 2, vol. 12, no. 10,862.

27. Arsenii Markevich, "Tavricheskaia guberniia vo vremia krymskoi voiny," *ITUAK* 37 (1905), pp. 6–8.

28. *P.S.Z.,* series 2, vol. 38, no. 39,667; Muftizade, pp. 17–18.

29. Lashkov, "K voprosu," p. 160, for eighteenth-century figures. Mordvinov, "Mnenie Mordvinova otnositel'no kryma," *Arkhiv grafov mordvinovykh* 3 (St. Petersburg, 1902), p. 195, for the 30,000 figure. *P.S.Z.,* series 1, vol. 23, no. 17,265, which discusses vacated Tatar lands, does not hint at such numbers however, and Ottoman sources are silent on the matter.

30. Mark Pinson, "Russian Policy and the Emigration of the Crimean Tatars," *Güney-Doğu Avrupa Araştirmalari Dergisi 1* (1972), pp. 37–38.

31. Lemercier-Quelquejay, "The Crimean Tatars," p. 19.

32. Pinson, p. 47.

33. Lemercier-Quelquejay, "The Crimean Tatars," p. 19; Pinson, pp. 50–55; *P.S.Z.,* series 2, vol. 36, nos. 35,063 and 35,126 on Tatar passports and empty lands.

34. Pinson, p. 49.

35. Seymour, p. 247, says in 1854 that "under Russian dominion, Kaffa has sunk again in size. . . . It has no more than 4500 inhabitants." He describes Karasu Bazaar (p. 241) as "reserved for the Tatars. It retains a strictly oriental character." On Bahçesaray, he says (p. 37) "Like Karasu Bazaar, Bahçesaray keeps much of its eastern character." On pp. 34–35, he writes: "Simferopol's streets are enormously wide. The houses in the rich part are built in a bad kind of bastard Italian style. . . . The town has a population of 8000 souls of whom 5000 are Tatars."

36. Baron von Haxthausen, *The Russian Empire: Its People, Institutions, and Resources* (London, 1856), vol. 2, pp. 127–28.

37. *P.S.Z.,* series 3, vol. 11, no. 7826. The lists of these police commands are found in the section of tables at the end of the volume. For other edicts on town government in the Crimea, see *P.S.Z.* series 1, vol. 20, no. 14,252; vol. 23, no. 17,348; vol. 29, no. 22,101; vol. 39, no. 29,733; vol. 40, no. 30,486; ibid., series 2, vol. 12, no. 11,684; vol. 14, no. 12,284; vol. 27, no. 26,822; vol. 31, no. 30,759; vol. 36, nos. 36,571 and 37,569. For Bahçesaray, see ibid., series 1, vol. 27, no. 20,449, and vol. 39, no. 29,983.

38. Druzhinina, *Iuzhnaia,* p. 70; Haxthausen, vol. 2, p. 125.

39. Druzhinina, *Iuzhnaia,* p. 236.

40. *P.S.Z.,* series 2, vol. 8, nos. 5994 and 6373.

41. Pinson, pp. 40–41; *P.S.Z.,* series 2, vol. 31, no. 30,152 (removal of shore inhabitants).

42. *P.S.Z.,* series 2, vol. 36, no. 32,526a.; 36,571, 37,514, and 37,731.

43. Sumarokov, *Dosugi Krymskago Sud'i,* vol. 1, p. 158; S. D. Shiriaev, "Pomeshchich'ia kolonizatsiia i russkie usad'by v Krymu," *Krym* 2, no. 4, (1927), pp. 169–86; Raeff, pp. 1–52.

44. A. Skal'kovskii, *Khronologicheskoe obozrenie istorii novorossiiskogo kraia 1730–1823* (Odessa, 1836), vol. 1, p. 221.

45. Nadinskii, *Ocherki,* vol. 1, p. 105; Druzhinina, *Severnoe,* pp. 123–24, 129; Druzhinina, *Iuzhnaia,* pp. 240–41; *P.S.Z.,* series 1, vol. 27, no. 20,988; vol. 25, no. 19,229; vol. 28, no. 23,229.

46. Sumarokov, *Dosugi Krymskago Sud'i,* vol. 1., p. 158; an extreme position is presented in Vardges A. Mikaelian, *Na krymskoi zemle* (Erevan, 1974), p. 139, who states that the "removal of the Turkish and Tatar yoke" in the Crimea made it possible for "the peoples living there" to practice their own culture.

47. Johann H. Schnitzler, *Description de la Crimée,* (Paris, 1855) p. 67.

48. *P.S.Z.,* series 2, vol. 35, no. 36,297; vol. 37, nos. 37,859 and 38,307.

49. *P.S.Z.,* series 2, vol. 51, no. 56,221; ibid., series 3, vol. 13, no. 9877; vol. 14, no. 10,933.

10. The Crimean Tatar National Awakening

1. Haxthausen, vol. 2, p. 99; Druzhinina, *Severnoe,* p. 139.

2. Edward D. Clarke, *Travels to Russia, Tartary, and Turkey* (New York, 1970), pp. 359–60, 368, 465.

3. Ernest J. Simmons, *Pushkin* (Cambridge, Mass., 1937), p. 116.

4. Seymour, pp. 248–49, 251.

5. Nadinskii, *Ocherki,* vol. 1, pp. 97, 119, 123.

6. *P.S.Z.,* series 1, vol. 22, no. 15,708; I. F. Aleksandrov, "O musul'manskom dukhovenstve," pp. 211–12.

7. Aleksandrov, pp. 212–13.

8. *P.S.Z.,* series 2, vol. 6, no. 5033.

9. Ibid., vol. 7, no. 5770; vol. 8, no. 6591; vol. 9, no. 6774; vol. 14, no. 12,622; vol. 30, no. 29,903; ibid., series 3, vol. 11, no. 7754. Figure for 1910 in Edige Kirimal, *Der nationale Kampf der Krimtürken* (Emsdetten, 1952), p. 15.

10. Arsenii I. Markevich, "Nachal'naia stranitsa istorii Simferopol'skoi gimnazii," *ITUAK* 50 (1913), pp. 236–40.

11. *P.S.Z.,* series 2, vol. 5, no. 4167.

12. Demidoff, pp. 80, 185.

13. *P.S.Z.,* series 2, vol. 34, nos. 34,147 and 34,647; B. Veselovskii, *Istoriia zemstva za sorok let* (St. Petersburg, 1909), vol. 1, pp. 718, 723. In Simferopol' district the number of schools increased from 4 to 20; in Evpatoriia there were 10, in Perekop 11; in Ialta district 13, and Feodosiia 28. By contrast, in those districts whose population was not primarily Tatar, the number of schools was much higher: Berdiansk, 151; Dneprovsk, 66; and Melitopol', 112.

14. Veselovskii, *Istoriia zemstva,* vol. 1, pp. 634–39, 680, 695; see *Sbornik po shkol'noi statistike tavricheskoi gubernii,* no. 2 (Simferopol', 1903) for figures on Tatar "national" schools funded in large part from revenues collected by the local zemstvos.

15. Veselovskii, *Istoriia zemstva,* vol. 1, p. 695.

16. Serge Zenkovsky, *Pan-Turkism and Islam in Russia* (Cambridge, Mass., 1960), pp. 24–25; B. Spuler, *The Muslim World,* vol. 2, p. 92.

17. The most complete biographical account of Gaspirali is found in Cafer Seidahmet, *Gaspirali Ismail Bey: Dilde, Fikirde, İşte Birlik* (Istanbul, 1934). His early life is briefly discussed in Charles W. Hostler, *Turkism and the Soviets* (London, 1957), pp. 123–24. His ideas are most clearly presented in Edward Lazzerini, "Ismail Bey Gasprinskii and Muslim Modernism in Russia," (Ph.D. dissertation, University of Washington, 1973), and in his article "Ĝadidism at the Turn of the Twentieth Century: a View from Within," *Cahiers* (April–June 1975), pp. 245–77.

18. Hostler, p. 124; Lemercier-Quelquejay, "The Crimean Tatars," p. 20.

19. Isabelle Kreindler, "Educational Policies Toward the Eastern Nationalities in Tsarist Russia: a Study of Il'minskii's System," (Ph.D. dissertation, Columbia University, 1969), pp. 84–85.

20. Hugh Seton-Watson, *The Russian Empire 1801–1917* (Oxford, 1967), pp. 502–3; Zeki Veledi Toğan, *Bügünkü Türkili* (Istanbul, 1947), p. 551, quoted in Hostler, pp. 105–6.

21. Cited in Lazzerini, "Ismail Bey Gasprinskii," p. 17.

22. A. Bennigsen and Chantal Lemercier-Quelquejay, *La presse et le mouvement national chez les musulmans de Russie avant 1920* (Paris, 1964), pp. 35, 40.

23. Gerhard von Mende, *Der nationale Kampf der Russlandtürken* (Berlin, 1936), p. 216.

24. Zenkovsky, p. 35.

25. Bennigsen and Lemercier-Quelquejay, *Presse,* pp. 40–41; Edige Kirimal, "The Crimean Tatars," *Studies on the Soviet Union* (new series, 1970), vol. 10, no. 1, p. 77.

26. Zenkovsky, pp. 33–34; Bennigsen, *Islam,* p. 41.

27. Hostler, pp. 133–34; Seton-Watson, p. 612; Zenkovsky, pp. 41–42; Kirimal, *Der nationale,* pp. 17–18.

28. M. Szeftel, "The Reform of the Electoral Law to the State Duma on June 3, 1907," *Liber Memoralis Georges de Lagarde* (London, 1968), p. 331.

29. Bennigsen and Lemercier-Quelquejay, *Presse,* pp. 138–39.

30. Kirimal, *Der nationale,* pp. 19–20.

31. Bennigsen and Lemercier-Quelquejay, *Presse,* p. 141.

32. Ibid.; Arslan Krichinskii, *Ocherki russkoi politiki na okrainakh,* pt. 1, "K istorii religioznykh pritesnenii krymskikh tatar," (Baku, 1919), pp. 234–35.

33. Krichinskii, *Ocherki,* pp. 234–35.

34. Bennigsen and Lemercier-Quelquejay, *Presse,* p. 142.

35. Kirimal, "The Crimean Tatars," p. 78.

36. G. E. von Grunebaum, "Problems of Muslim Nationalism," in Richard Frye, *Islam and the West* (Gravenhage, 1957), p. 25.

11. *The Russian Revolution and the Tatars*

1. Kirimal, *Der nationale,* p. 25.

2. Ibid., pp. 28–29; Krichinskii, *Ocherki,* pp. 21–22, 36.

3. Zenkovsky, pp. 124–25.

4. V. Elagin, "Natsionalisticheskie illiuzii krymskikh tatar v revoliutsionnye gody," *Novyi vostok* 5 (1925), p. 192.

5. Zenkovsky, p. 127; Kirimal, *Der nationale,* pp. 30–31.

6. "Les étapes de la politique islamique russe," *Revue du monde musulman* vols. 55–56 (1923), pp. 146–47; Kirimal, *Der nationale,* p. 31; H. Revelstein, *Die Not der Fremdvölker ünter dem russischen Joche* (Berlin, 1916), pp. 96–100.

7. The most complete and authoritative discussion of these months is to be found in Kirimal, *Der nationale,* pp. 33–164.

8. Ibid., p. 35.

9. Ibid., pp. 36–37; Bennigsen and Lemercier-Quelquejay, *Islam,* p. 70.

10. Kirimal, "The Crimean Tatars," p. 79.

11. Nadinskii, *Ocherki,* vol. 2, pp. 8–14.

12. Richard Pipes, *The Formation of the Soviet Union,* (Cambridge, Mass., 1957) p. 77; Zenkovsky, pp. 140–42, 150; N. N. Agarwal, *Soviet Nationalities Policy* (Agra, 1969), p. 63.

13. Nadinskii, *Ocherki,* vol. 2, p. 27.

14. Bennigsen and Lemercier-Quelquejay, *Islam,* pp. 70–71.

15. Kirimal, *Der nationale,* pp. 56–57.

16. Kirimal, "Kirim Türklerinin 1917–1920 ihtilal yillarinda milli-kurtuluş hareketi," *Dergi* 48 (1967), p. 56; Nadinskii, *Ocherki,* vol. 2, pp. 27–28 (he mistakenly gives the date as June 23); for population figures see Partiinyi arkhiv krymskogo obkoma KP Ukrainy, *Bor'ba za sovetskuiu vlast' v Krymu* (Simferopol', 1957), vol. 1, p. 5; Kirimal, *Der nationale,* pp. 116–18, writes that the 1897 census gave Tatar percentages of the various districts as follows: Perekop: Tatars 24.1%, Russian-Ukrainian 44.6%; Evpatoriia: Tatars 42%, Russian-Ukrainian 38%; Simferopol': Tatars 41.8%, Russian-Ukrainian 37.7%; Feodosiia: Tatars 37.2%, Russian-Ukrainian 42.2%; Ialta: Tatars 60.2%, Russian-Ukrainian 29.9%; Sevastopol': Tatars 1.5%, Russian-Ukrainian 95.9%; city of Balaklava: Tatars 0.7%, Russians 17.4%, Greeks 76.2%; Kerch: Tatars 5%, Russian-Ukrainian 72.1%.

17. Seidahmet, *La Crimée,* p. 72; Nadinskii, *Ocherki,* vol. 2, p. 37.

18. Pipes, p. 81.

19. Seidahmet, *La Crim*ée, pp. 114–17; Joseph Castagne, "Le Bolchevisme et l'Islam," *Revue du monde musulman* 51 (1922), pp. 143–44; Kirimal, *Der nationale,* pp. 107–14, for texts of the Tatar constitution.

20. Kirimal, *Der nationale,* pp. 119–31.

21. Zenkovsky, p. 160.

22. Text is in Castagne, pp. 5–6.

23. Ibid., pp. 7–9.

24. Pipes, p. 109.

25. Both quoted in Agarwal, pp. 187–89.

26. Nadinskii, *Ocherki,* vol. 2, pp. 38–40.

27. Ibid., pp. 46–47; Kirimal, *Der nationale,* pp. 131–64.

28. Nadinskii, *Ocherki,* vol. 2, p. 60.

29. Kirimal, *Der nationale,* pp. 135–62; Pipes, p. 185.

30. Bennigsen and Lemercier-Quelquejay, *Islam,* p. 86; Seidahmet, *La Crimée,* p. 78; Lemercier-Quelquejay, "The Crimean Tatars," p. 22; Pipes, p. 185.

31. Bennigsen and Lemercier-Quelquejay, *Islam,* p. 86; Pipes, p. 185; V. Elagin, who was the Secretary of the Bolshevik organization in Evpatoriia in these days, wrote later that Cihan "during the period of anarchy in February, 1918, was removed by sailors from the prison and shot without the knowledge of the Sevastopol' Ispolkom"; V. Elagin, "Natsionalisticheskie illiuzii," *Novyi vostok* 6, p. 210.

32. Kirimal, *Der nationale,* pp. 164–67; Lemercier-Quelquejay, "The Crimean Tatars," p. 22; Bennigsen and Lemercier-Quelquejay, *Islam,* p. 93.

33. Pipes, pp. 186–87; Kirimal, *Der nationale,* pp. 166–67; Nadinskii, *Ocherki,* vol. 2, pp. 73–81.

34. Pipes, pp. 186–87; Agarwal, p. 229; Partiinyi arkhiv krymskago obkom K.P. Ukrainy, *Khronika revoliutsionnykh sobytii v krymu 1917–1920 gg.* (Simferopol', 1969), p. 88.

35. Nadinskii,˙ *Ocherki,* vol. 2, pp. 82, 87; Kirimal, *Der nationale,* pp. 170–73; F. S. Zagorodskikh, "Bor'ba trudiashchikhsia protiv nemetsko-kaizerovskikh okkupantov v Krymu," *Bor'ba bolshevikov za uprochenie sovetskoi vlasti* (Simferopol', 1958), p. 10.

36. Kirimal, *Der nationale,* pp. 179–92.

37. Nadinskii, *Ocherki,* vol. 2, pp. 102–7. To make his point with what he considers irrefutable evidence, Nadinskii points out that "Seidahmet, a Turk, a German spy, appeared in 1951 in the service of the United States State Department as 'President of the Senate of the Crimean

Republic.'" (p. 107). Thus the inevitable conclusion: Seidahmet was, in 1918, in support of the "khanate principle."

38. Kirimal, *Der nationale,* pp. 194–95; A. Gukovskii, ed., "Krymskoe kraevoe pravitel'stvo v 1918/19," *Krasnyi arkhiv* 22 (1927), pp. 97–98.

39. Nalbandov's journal was published in Gukovskii, pp. 97–131.

40. Arslan Krichinskii, "General Maciej Sulkiewicz (1865–1920)," *Rocznik Tatarski* 1 (1932), p. 250. The text of the declaration is in Gukovskii, pp. 117–22.

41. Kirimal, *Der nationale,* pp. 199–200; Gukovskii, pp. 99, 111, 122–28.

42. Zagorodskikh, pp. 15–16. Why this caused greater hardship on the Tatars than the Soviet forced shipment of food to central Russian regions during the N.E.P. is anyone's guess.

43. Pipes, p. 187.

44. Kirimal, *Der nationale,* p. 201.

45. Ibid., pp. 210–17, 220–39.

46. Ibid., pp. 204–5.

47. Ibid., pp. 270–73; The text of their declaration is in Gukovskii, pp. 122 ff.

48. Seidahmet, *La Crimée,* pp. 80–83; Kirimal, *Der nationale,* pp. 278–79.

49. Kirimal, *Der nationale,* pp. 279–80; Bennigsen and Lemercier-Quelquejay, *Presse,* p. 252.

50. Pipes, pp. 187–88; Kirimal *Der nationale,* pp. 281–82.

51. Kirimal, *Der nationale,* p. 282; Pipes, p. 188; Bennigsen and Lemercier-Quelquejay, *Presse,* p. 252.

52. *Bor'ba bolshevikov za uprochenie sovetskoi vlasti,* pp. 78–123; Lemercier-Quelquejay, "The Crimean Tatars," p. 22, who says, "It was the political mistakes of the Whites who forced the Muslims into the arms of Communism."

53. Bennigsen and Lemercier-Quelquejay, *Presse,* p. 252; Seidahmet, *La Crimée,* pp. 90–94.

12. The Crimean ASSR (1921–1941)

1. Castagne, pp. 5–9.

2. Ibid., pp. 9–10.

3. Ibid., p. 12.

4. Ibid., pp. 11–15.

5. Pipes, p. 189; Chirva, ed., *Ocherki po istorii kryma* (Simferopol' 1964), vol. 3, p. 11, indicates that there were no Tatars in the upper echelons of the party at this time. The Central Committee of the Krym Revkom included R. S. Zemliachki, Bela Kun, B. Ul'ianov, and Zemlichka.

6. Essad Bey, *Histoire du Géupéou, la police secrète de l'URSS, 1917–1933* (Paris, 1934), p. 96; Anatolii Marchenko, "Nikolai Bystrykh," in G. Anan'ev and M. Smirnov, eds. *Sbornik pogranichniki* (Moscow, 1973), p. 5–29.

7. The figure 60,000–70,000 is provided by Kirimal, "The Crimean Turks," in Institute for the Study of the USSR, *Genocide in the USSR, Studies in Group Destruction* (New York, 1958), p. 20. The Soviet account: P. V. Nadinskii, "Bor'ba krymskoi partorganizatsii za vosstanovlenie narodnogo khoziaistva," in *Bor'ba bolshevikov za uprochenie sovetskoi vlasti,* pp. 125–26.

8. Kirimal, *Der nationale,* pp. 286–87.

9. Pipes, p. 190.

10. Lemercier-Quelquejay, "The Tatars," pp. 22–23; Kirimal, *Der nationale,* p. 287; The chairman of this republic was to be Iurii Gaven, "a Bolshevik whose views on the nature of autonomy left no doubt that he would follow closely directives of Moscow," Pipes, pp. 189–90.

11. Castagne, pp. 148–49.

12. Ibid., pp. 149–50.

13. Ibid., p. 150.

14. Ibid., pp. 150–51.

15. Peter J. Potichnyj, "The Struggle of the Crimean Tatars," *Canadian Slavonic Papers* 17, nos. 2–3 (1975), p. 304.

16. M. Alaç, "Bolşeviklerin Ikinci Işgalinden Sonra Kirim'da Neler Oldu?," *Emel* 29 (1965), pp. 6–7.

17. Borys Lewytzkyj, *The Uses of Terror: The Soviet Secret Police, 1917–1970* (New York, 1972), p. 43; Pipes, p. 190.

18. Alaç, pp. 6–7; Kirimal, in *Genocide*, pp. 20–21.

19. Kirimal, in *Genocide*, p. 21; Kirimal, *Der nationale*, p. 288.

20. Castagne, pp. 151–52, quoting from a Russian newspaper in Paris, on January 31, 1922.

21. Ibid., p. 152.

22. Ibid., p. 152.

23. Lemercier-Quelquejay, "The Tatars," p. 23; Bennigsen and Lemercier-Quelquejay, *Islam*, p. 70.

24. S. A. Gamalov, "Natsional'nye men'shinstva kryma," *Krym* 2, no. 4 (1927), p. 187.

25. "KrASSR," in *B.S.E.* 1st ed (1937), vol. 35, p. 318, G. I. Khazanov, "Partiinaia organizatsiia kryma v bor'be za pobedu kholkoznogo stroia," *Bor'ba bolshevikov za uprochenie,* p. 202.

26. Bennigsen and Lemercier-Quelquejay, *Islam*, p. 107.

27. Lemercier-Quelquejay, "The Tatars," p. 23; Kirimal, *Der nationale*, pp. 289–90.

28. Bennigsen and Lemercier-Quelquejay, *Islam*, p. 112, quoting from A. K. Bochagov, *Milli Firka* (Simferopol', 1930), pp. 83–84; Alaç, p. 8.

29. Kirimal, "Mass Deportations and Massacres in the Crimea," *Cultura Turcica* 1, no. 2 (1964), p. 256; Kirimal, in *Genocide*, p. 21; Temirçili, "Kirim'da Eğitim Meseleleri Hakkinda Bazi Notlar," *Emel* 20 (1964), pp. 11–12.

30. Alaç, p. 9; Kirimal, *Der nationale*, p. 291, argues that nothing anti-Semitic should be inferred in Ibrahimov's protests since "Jews had been participating all along in Tatar life, including being represented in the Kurultay." According to Chirva, *Ocherki*, vol. 3, p. 67, Ibrahimov was charged with "participation in the murders of the first Soviet government in the Crimea in 1918, support of kulak bandit sheikhs, and embezzlement."

31. Alaç, p. 9; Kirimal, *Der nationale*, pp. 291–92; Lemercier-Quelquejay, "The Crimean Tatars," p. 23.

32. Chirva, *Ocherki*, vol. 3, p. 205.

33. Quoted in Robert Conquest, *The Nation Killers* (New York, 1970) p. 58.

34. Alaç, p. 10; Lemercier-Quelquejay, "The Crimean Tatars," p. 23.

35. "Çobanzade Bekir Sitki," *Emel* 46 (1968), p. 17; Gare Le Compte, *Muslims of the USSR,* pp. 8–9. The second stage of course "increased both the flow of Russian terminology into the Turkic languages and the facility of Muslims to learn Russian," as Le Compte says on p. 9.

36. Alaç, p. 9; Potichnyj, p. 305; Kirimal, "Mass Deportations," p. 256; Chirva, *Ocherki*, vol. 3, p. 192. See A. Mochanov, "K voprosu o proiskhozhdenii islama," in *Anti-religioznyi sbornik* 1 (Simferopol', 1929), pp. 57–69, for information about the religious aspect of the alphabet reform.

37. Quoted in Rudolf Schlesinger, ed., *The Nationalities Problem and Soviet Administration* (London, 1956), pp. 98, 107–8; Chirva, *Ocherki*, vol. 3, p. 72, says that "in the land commission of Jankoy region were a former count, a daughter of a priest, the wife of a former police official, a former pomeshchik, a former gendarme, etc."

38. Grigorii Aleksandrov, "Istreblenie krymskikh tatar," *Sotsialisticheskii vestnik* 3 (1950), p. 51.

39. Kirimal, "The Crimean Turks," p. 22.

40. Chirva, *Ocherki*, vol. 3, pp. 205, 216–18.

41. Kirimal, in *Genocide*, p. 22.

42. Quoted in Kirimal, "Mass Deportations," p. 257; Alaç, p. 10.

43. A. Semin, "Krymskaia partiinaia organizatsiia v gody zaversheniia rekonstruktsii narod-nogo khoziaistva i pobedy sotsializma v SSSR," in *Bor'ba bolshevikov za uprochenie*, p. 254.

44. Quoted in Schlesinger, p. 245.

45. Kirimal, *Der nationale*, p. 296.

46. Temirçili, pp. 13–14; Necip Abdulhamitoğlu, *Türksüz Kirim: Yüzbinlerin Sürgünü* (Istanbul, 1974), pp. 34–37; *B.S.E.*, quoted in Conquest, p. 58.

47. Kirimal, *Der nationale*, p. 257.

48. N. N. Agarwal, *Soviet Nationalities Policy* (Agra, 1969), p. 293.

49. Alaç, p. 10.

50. Kirimal, "Mass Deportations," p. 258.

51. Potichnyj, p. 305; Bennigsen and Lemercier-Quelquejay, *Presse*, p. 284; Kirimal, *Der nationale*, pp. 297–99; Kirimal, in *Genocide*, p. 22.

52. All accounts are quoted in Kirimal, "Mass Deportations," pp. 258–59; Kirimal, *Der nationale*, pp. 300–301.

53. Quoted in Schlesinger, p. 174.

54. S. P. Pisarev, "Iz istorii krymskikh tatar," *Politicheskii dnevnik 1964–1970* (Amsterdam, 1972), p. 701.

55. Komitet po planirovke iuzhnogo berega kryma, *Sotsialisticheskaia rekonstruktsiia iuzh-nogo berega kryma* (Simferopol', 1935), p. 175.

56. Komitet po planirovke, pp. 447–48, 543; On p. 449, one finds the following population figures for the southern shore:

Nationality	Urban	Rural	Total
Tatars	15.69%	84.20%	35.84%
Russians	52.45	11.15	40.38
Ukrainians	8.14	1.95	6.44
Jews	6.19	0.18	4.35
Germans	0.45	0.22	0.39
Greeks	10.47	1.41	7.70
Armenians	2.53	0.17	1.81
Bulgarians	0.22	0.11	0.19
Others	3.86	0.61	2.90
Total	100.00%	100.00%	100.00%

57. *B.S.E.* 1st ed. (1937), vol. 35, pp. 305–18.

58. Lemercier-Quelquejay, "The Crimean Tatars," p. 23.

13. The Crimean Tatars in World War II

1. Quoted in Alexander Werth, *Russia at War, 1941–1945* (New York, 1964), p. 581.

2. Decree published in full in Abdulhamitoğlu, pp. 143–46; and in part in Conquest, pp. 186–87.

3. Alexander Dallin, *German Rule in Russia 1941–1945* (London, 1957), pp. 51–52, 253–54.

4. Patrik von zur Mühlen, *Zwischen Hakenkreuz und Sowjetstern* (Dusseldorf, 1971), p. 46; Germany, Heer. 11 Armee, *Wir erobern die Krim* (Neustadt, 1943), pp. 277–78.

5. Werth, p. 599; Dallin, p. 254.

6. Dallin, p. 255.

7. Ibid., p. 258.

8. Werth, p. 173; Michel Luther, "Die Krim unter deutscher Besatzung im zweiten Weltkrieg," *Forschungen zur osteuropäischen Geschichte* 3 (Berlin, 1956), pp. 29–30.

9. Dallin, p. 259; Werth, pp. 208, 252; Lemercier-Quelquejay, "The Crimean Tatars,", p. 24; *Wir erobern die Krim.*

10. Abdulhamitoğlu, pp. 42–43; Potichnyj, pp. 305–6.

11. Luther, p. 35; Dallin, p. 258; The autobiography of Ulküsal is currently being published in *Emel* 87 (1975) and following; Mühlen, pp. 119–23.

12. Kirimal, in *Genocide,* p. 24; Abdulhamitoğlu, pp. 43–44.

13. Abdulhamitoğlu, pp. 43–44; Kirimal, in *Genocide,* p. 24; Borys Lewytzkyj, *Uses of Terror* (New York, 1972), p. 157.

14. Mühlen, p. 60; Lemercier-Quelquejay, "The Crimean Tatars," p. 24; Joachim Hoffmann, *Deutsche und Kalmyken 1942 bis 1945* (Freiburg, 1974), discusses the Kalmyk participation. See Norbert Müller, *Wehrmacht und Okkupation 1941–1944* (Berlin, 1971), for an unsympathetic account of military occupation policy. Luther points out that the Germans were generally pleased with the success of these Tatar volunteers, p. 62.

15. Dallin, p. 260.

16. Ibid., p. 264; Mühlen, p. 123, supports Dallin's view.

17. Luther, pp. 42–43.

18. Abdulhamitoğlu, pp. 52–56; Orhan Ozkirim, "Ikinci Dünya Savaşinda Kirim Türkleri ile Almanlar arasindaki Münasebetler," *Emel* 25 (1964), pp. 15–20. Luther, pp. 46–47, also credits General Manstein.

19. Luther, pp. 45–46, 52–53; Dallin, p. 260 (who claims that the Karaims were spared).

20. Mühlen, p. 123; Dallin, p. 261.

21. Mühlen, p. 124; Abdulhamitoğlu, pp. 45–46.

22. Ozkirim, p. 17; Abdulhamitoğlu, pp. 49–50.

23. Abdulhamitoğlu, p. 50; Mühlen, p. 185; Ivan G. Genov, *Chetyre vremeni goda i dnevnik partizana* (Moscow, 1969), pp. 76–84.

24. Mühlen, p. 184, repeats the view of Tatar favoritism; Abdulhamitoğlu, pp. 51–52.

25. Abdulhamitoğlu, pp. 52–54; Ozkirim, pp. 17–18; Dallin, p. 261; Temirçili, "2-inci Cihan Savaşi Sirasinda Alman Işgalinde Kirim Türklerinin Kültür ve Eğitim Işleri," *Emel* 23 (1964), pp. 20–21.

26. Abdulhamitoğlu, pp. 59–61; Otto Brautigam, *So bat es sich zugetragen . . . Ein Leben als Soldat und Diplomat* (Wurzburg, 1968), discusses the Tatars in the Vlasov army.

27. Pisarev, pp. 701–2; Potichnyj, p. 307; Ekaterina Shamko, *Partizanskoe dvizhenie v krymu* (Simferopol', 1959), p. 155, for biographical information on Mokrousov. L. D. Solodovnik, et al., *Istoriia mist i sil ukrains'koi SSR: Krims'ka Oblast'* (Kiev, 1974), mentions that he left the Crimea, but gives no reason.

28. Shamko, *Partizanskoe,* pp. 17, 81; Ivan Kozlov, *V krymskom podpol'e: vospominaniia* (Moscow, 1947), pp. 77, 90, 324, as cited by John Armstrong, *The Politics of Totalitarianism* (New York, 1961), pp. 151, 160.

29. Armstrong, p. 151.

30. Ekaterina Shamko, "Plamia nad krymom," *Geroi podpol'ia* 2 (Moscow, 1972), p. 49.

31. C. Aubrey Dixon and Otto Heilbrunn, *Communist Guerilla Warfare* (New York, 1955), p. 121.

32. Genov, p. 47.

33. Kirimal, "Mass Deportations," p. 260, who states that 128 Tatar villages in the mountains were destroyed by the partisans. Interestingly the memoir of a Soviet partisan leader corroborates a number of these charges: Genov, p. 90 (attacks on Beshui); on p. 168, Genov writes that "the Germans tried to discredit the partisans in the eyes of the populace and set up fake 'partisan detachments' which destroyed the villages of Prolom, Alaç, Karae El, etc." Surely the Tatars knew the difference between Russians and Germans, however.

34. Kirimal, "Kirim Türkleri," *Emel* 59, p. 14, citing *Lenin Bayragi* (July 8, 1969), p. 4.

35. Kirimal, "Kirim Türkleri," *Emel* 59, pp. 12–14; Luther, p. 57, cites a few other Tatars executed by the Germans, one of whom had been a "commander of a partisan sabotage battalion."

36. I. Osmanov, "Zaiavlenie v sviazi s arestom," (1968) *Arkhiv Samizdat*, no. 85. The death of his father is reported in *Krym v period velikoi otechestvennoi voiny 1941–1945* (Simferopol', 1973), p. 446, note 8: "A. O. Osmanov, from November, 1941, was political instructor of the partisan group, later commissar of the brigade. He was killed in battle, January 24, 1944."

37. *Krym v period velikoi . . .* , pp. 63, 92, 109, 210; D. Karov, *Partizanskoe dvizhenie v SSSR v 1941–1945 gg.* (Munich, 1954), p. 97, writes that "in the Crimea, the Central Staff of Partisan activities succeeded in creating a number of anti-German Tatar units, in 1943, under command of local Communist leaders."

38. *Krym v period velikoi . . .* , pp. 227–30.

39. Ibid., p. 300.

40. Ibid., pp. 321, 327. Other documents about Tatar participation are found on pp. 333, 347–48.

41. Shamko, *Partizanskoe*, p. 6.

42. Pisarev, p. 701; *A Chronicle of Current Events* nos. 28–31 (London, 1975), pp. 147–148. Ironically, Solodovnik, pp. 66–67, presents information on and a photo of Ahmet Khan Sultan, without identifying him as a Tatar. Indeed, the general categorization used in this and other Soviet volumes is: Tatar, when collaborators are meant (whatever their real nationality); and Soviet patriot (even if a Tatar) when partisans are discussed.

An interesting instance of Soviet censorship on the Crimea occurs in General A. I. Eremenko's memoir, *Gody vozmezdiia, 1943–1944* (Moscow, 1969), pp. 129 and 135, where the clumsy method of multiple footnotes is used (i.e., note 3–9, 13–14) to cover up deletions made after galley proofs were set. These portions of the book read as though information is missing. The topic is the behavior of the Crimean population under German administration.

43. Osman Turkay, "The Tragedy of the Crimean Tatars," *Index on Censorship* 3, no. 1 (1974), p. 70. Dagci's other novels include *Onlar da Insandi* [They Too Were Human Beings], *Badem Dalina Asili Bebekler* [Dolls Hanged on the Almond Tree], and *Üsüyen Sokak* [Cold Street].

44. Mühlen, pp. 124, 186–87; Dallin, pp. 267–68.

45. Dallin, p. 266; Abdulhamitoğlu, pp. 69–71.

46. Werth, p. 573.

47. Ibid., p. 838.

48. A. Krasnov Levitin, " 'Svet v okontse' k arestu Gen. Grigorenko, (24 mai 1969)," *Arkhiv Samizdat*, no. 269, p. 7.

14. The Deportation of the Crimean Tatars and Their Struggle for Rehabilitation

1. Conquest, p. 105; Lewytzkyj, *Uses of Terror*, p. 231.

2. Institute for the Study of the USSR, *Key Officials of the Government of the USSR and Union Republics* (Munich, 1962), p. 569; Lewytzkyj, *Uses of Terror*, p. 231.

3. Abdulhamitoğlu, pp. 71–74; Sheehy, pp. 10–11; Kirimal, "Mass Deportations," pp. 261–62. The "letter" was published as "Otkrytoe pis'mo v zashchitu krymskikh tatar," *Arkhiv Samizdat*, no. 101.

4. Kirimal, "Mass Deportations," pp. 261–62. General Eremenko, in charge of the reconquest of the Crimea in 1944, makes no mention at all of the Tatars or their deportation in *Gody* . . . ; neither does Chirvy, *Ocherky*, vol. 4. pp. 100–101, in discussing events of April–June, 1944. Of recent Soviet works on the Crimea, only Solodovnik, in *Istoriia mist* . . . , says, in an obscure footnote on p. 68, that the "Tatars were wrongly charged for crimes during the war, and are now residing in the Uzbek SSR. . . . "

5. Their partisan activities are mentioned in *Krym v period velikoi* . . . , doc. no. 222, p. 333.

6. *Krym v period velikoi* . . . , doc. no. 232, pp. 347–48, for a list of those given this award.

7. Kirimal, in *Genocide*, pp. 26–27.

8. Osman Turkay, pp. 77–78.

9. Kirimal, in *Genocide*, p. 25.

10. Conquest, p. 47.

11. Simon Wolin and Robert Slusser, eds. *The Soviet Secret Police* (New York, 1957), p. 192.

12. Werth, p. 581.

13. S. Enders Wimbush and Ronald Wixman, "The Mesketian Turks: A New Voice in Soviet Central Asia," *Canadian Slavonic Papers* 17, nos. 2–3 (1975), pp. 320–40.

14. Kirimal, "Kirim Türkleri," *Emel* 59, p. 16; *Geografischeskaia atlas SSSR* (Moscow, 1950), p. 104.

15. Feridun Cemal Erkin, *Les Relations Turco-Soviétiques et la Question des Détroits* (Ankara, 1968), pp. 286–87.

16. Jonathan Knight, "American Statecraft and the 1946 Black Sea Straits Controversy," *Political Science Quarterly* 90, no. 3 (1975), p. 452; Erkin, pp. 300–301.

17. Erkin, pp. 310–12.

18. Pisarev, p. 704, also mentions "Stalin's intentions against Turkey strongly influenced him on the question of the Crimean Tatars."

19. Abdulhamitoğlu, pp. 76–80; Sheehy, p. 11; Conquest, pp. 105, 161; Kirimal, "Mass Deportations," p. 262; the *Chronicle of Current Events* 31 (London, 1975), pp. 147–48, adds the following data: "238,000 people were deported in all, of which 113,000 were children (under 18) and 93,000 women. From the nine villages (census of 1971) 9494 people were deported, including 5078 children, 3280 women, 532 resistance and underground workers, and 347 sick people and invalids."

20. Wolin and Slusser, p. 151; Abdulhamitoğlu, pp. 75–76.

21. Cited in Sheehy, p. 11; and in Abdulhamitoğlu, p. 76.

22. Abdulhamitoğlu, pp. 77–78; *Arkhiv Samizdat*, no. 101.

23. Abdulhamitoğlu, pp. 56–57.

24. Ibid., pp. 67–68; Lemercier-Quelquejay, "The Crimean Tatars," p. 24.

25. A. Krasnov Levitin, p. 7.

26. The Petition of 115 is published in Abdulhamitoğlu, pp. 97–98.

27. Sheehy, p. 12; Abdulhamitoğlu, p. 97; Conquest, p. 107.

28. Solodovnik, pp. 233, 238, 248, 274, 393, 446.

29. V. Al'tman, "Sessiia po istorii Kryma," *Voprosy istorii* 2 (1948), pp. 179–184; discussed in Abdulhamitoğlu, pp. 102–3.

30. *B.S.E.* 2nd ed (1953), vol. 23, pp. 551–53; Sheehy, p. 12; in the recent Ukrainian history of the Crimea, Solodovnik, p. 17, the only illustration concerning the Tatars is the 1955 painting by Iu. Fastenka of "slave market in Kefe." Solodovnik, throughout, constantly refers to Ukrainian and Russian nationalists in the section on prerevolutionary and revolutionary history; only the Tatar nationalists are given the epithet *bourgeois*.

31. *Pravda,* June 4, 1952.

32. Potichnyj, p. 308.

33. Ibid., p. 307; See also Borys Lewytzkyj, *Die Sowjetukraine 1944–1963* (Cologne, 1964), p. 91, who points out this same problem.

34. *Tretya sessiia Ukrainskoi Natsionalnoi Radi: Materialy i dokumenty* (Munich, 1954); cited in Kirimal, "Mass Deportations," p. 265.

35. In 1959, the population of the Crimea (except for Sevastopol') had a total of 856,000 Russians and 267,000 Ukrainians, Abdulhamitoğlu, p. 116.

36. Chirva, *Ocherky,* vol. 4, pp. 106–8.

37. Il'ia Liuksemburg, "Novyi Vavilon na beregakh Syrdar'i," *Posev* (Sept, 1973), p. 37.

38. Sheehy, p. 12; Conquest, p. 185.

39. Werth, p. 581.

40. Sheehy, p. 13.

41. Ibid., p. 30, citing a five volume survey of Soviet languages published by the Institute of Linguistics in 1966. On *Lenin Bayragi*'s founding, see Abdulhamitoğlu, p. 133.

42. Abdulhamitoğlu, pp. 135–36.

43. Ibid., p. 136; Sheehy, p. 13.

44. Lewytzkyj, *Politische Opposition,* pp. 310, 314.

45. Mustafa Cemilev, "Pis'mo P.G. Grigorenko o perezhitom krymskimi tatarami v 1962," *Arkhiv Samizdat,* no. 281 (Nov. 1968); sentences reported in Lewytzkyj, *Politische Opposition,* pp. 314–15, and in Abdulhamitoğlu, pp. 136–38.

46. Potichnyj, p. 311; Abdulhamitoğlu, pp. 137–39; Sheehy, pp. 13–14.

47. Sheehy, p. 14.

48. Lewytzkyj, *Politische Opposition,* pp. 310–12, 315.

49. Ibid., names in the tables, pp. 284–316; Abdulhamitoğlu, pp. 140–41; Sheehy, p. 14.

50. Sheehy, pp. 14–15.

51. Ibid., p. 15; names of arrested are in Lewytzkyj, *Politische Opposition,* tables on pp. 284–316.

52. Sheehy, p. 16; Abdulhamitoğlu, pp. 141–43.

53. List of those sentenced are in Lewytzkyj, *Politische Opposition,* pp. 284–316.

54. Conquest, pp. 186–87; Published also in *Emel* 47 (1968), pp. 3–6; Abdulhamitoğlu, pp. 143–46; Sheehy, p. 16.

15. "The Right to Return"

1. Sheehy, p. 17.

2. Abdulhamitoğlu, pp. 151–52.

3. The published *Arkhiv Samizdat* includes many such reports, such as "Akt, sostavlennyi otdukhaiushchimi v sele 'Rybach'e' v Krymu," no. 319; Umer Çobanov, "Otryvok iz pis'ma bezdaty," no. 311; "Otryvok iz 'Informatsii' krymskikh tatar z avril-iun 1968," no. 313; "Kratkaia zapis' besedy gruppy krymskikh tatar s predsedatelem Leninskogo raiispolkoma krymskoi oblasti Kuznetsovym," no. 312; Sheehy, pp. 17–18, describes some other cases.

4. "Vyderzhki iz pis'ma krymskikh tatar v Politbiuro TsK KPSS," *Arkhiv Samizdat,* no. 309.

5. *Arkhiv Samizdat,* no. 314; Abdulhamitoğlu, pp. 155–56, who gives a detailed description of these events; Sheehy, p. 18.

6. Sheehy, p. 18.

7. Potichnyj, p. 312.

8. *Arkhiv Samizdat,* no. 309(b).

9. *Arkhiv Samizdat,* no. 309(g). Eight other letters published by Abdulhamitoğlu (pp. 158–67), express similar experiences.

10. *Chronicle of Current Events* 28–31, p. 132.

11. Potichnyj, p. 313.

12. *Chronicle of Current Events* 28–31, p. 136.

13. *Christian Science Monitor,* Nov. 12, 1975 (Mark Brayn).

14. *Chronicle of Current Events* 25–26 (London, October 1972), pp. 200–202. See also a letter of support for Muzafarov from Vladimir Maksimov in *Khronika Zashchity Prav v SSSR,* 5–6, Nov. 1973 (New York, 1974), pp. 33–34.

15. Peter Reddaway, *Uncensored Russia* (New York, 1972), p. 256.

16. Sheehy, p. 19; Potichnyj, p. 315; *Emel* 51 (1969), pp. 8–9; Abraham Rothberg, *The Heirs of Stalin* (Ithaca, 1972), p. 237; Abdulhamitoğlu, pp. 170–73.

17. Reddaway, p. 461 (note 3), pp. 254–55.

18. *Arkhiv Samizdat,* no. 77. Another delegation sent to the Uzbek authorities was led by the Tatar scientist Rollan Kadiev in early summer, *Arkhiv Samizdat,* no. 40.

19. Published in Reddaway, pp. 249–51; also in Abraham Brumberg, ed., *In Quest of Justice* (New York, 1970), pp. 204 ff.; and *Arkhiv Samizdat,* no. 45.

20. "Informatsiia," *Arkhiv Samizdat,* no. 291; "Vsenarodnyi protest," *Arkhiv Samizdat,* no. 379; "Kirima dönmekte olan Kirim Türklerinin durumu," *Emel* 64 (1971), pp. 18–19.

21. The *Chronicle*'s account is published in Reddaway, pp. 254–55; Sheehy, p. 20.

22. *Arkhiv Samizdat,* no. 255; "Sürgündeki Kirimlilar," *Emel* 64 (1971), pp. 35–37.

23. This Information Bulletin is summarized in *Chronicle of Current Events* 18 (London, 1971), pp. 126–27.

24. This petition is published in *Chronicle of Current Events* 19–20 (London, 1971), pp. 182–84.

25. *Chronicle of Current Events* 27 (London, 1973), p. 302.

26. *Arkhiv Samizdat,* no. 281, p. 15; Lewytzkyj, *Politische Opposition,* pp. 300–315.

27. Lewytzkyj, *Politische Opposition,* pp. 283–99.

28. *Arkhiv Samizdat,* no. 281, p. 16; Abdulhamitoğlu, pp. 179–82, for a complete coverage of the trial; Reddaway, pp. 266–68.

29. Sheehy, p. 20.

30. Abdulhamitoğlu, pp. 184–85.

31. Sheehy, p. 21.

32. Sheehy, pp. 20–23; Abdulhamitoğlu, pp. 184–92, for a complete report.

33. Abdulhamitoğlu, pp. 191–92; Sheehy, p. 21.

34. Lewytzkyj, *Politische Opposition,* p. 312; *Arkhiv Samizdat,* no. 255; on Gabay, see Abdulhamitoğlu, pp. 193–94, and on Cemilev, pp. 194–96.

35. Abdulhamitoğlu, pp. 196–97; *Emel* 64 (1971), p. 37.

36. *Chronicle of Current Events* 18 (1971), p. 127.

37. Lewytzkyj, *Politische Opposition,* pp. 286, 312–13.

38. *Chronicle of Current Events* 19–20 (1971), pp. 244–45; and 22–23 (1972), p. 84.

39. *Krym v period velik . . . ,* p. 445 (note 16).

40. *Chronicle of Current Events* 28–31, pp. 127–28.

41. *Chronicle of Current Events* 27 (1972), p. 303; *Posev* (December, 1974), p. 12; *Chronicle of Current Events* 28–31, pp. 127–31.

42. *Christian Science Monitor,* April 15–16, 20, 1976 (Elizabeth Pond). The *Monitor* was the only U.S. newspaper that saw the event as something beyond Sakharov himself.

43. Sheehy, p. 5.

44. George Saunders (ed), *Samizdat: Voices of the Soviet Opposition* (New York, 1974), p. 278.

45. Grigorenko's speech is published in Brumberg, pp. 208–13; also *Arkhiv Samizdat*, no. 76.

46. Abdulhamitoğlu, pp. 208–10, for Tatar reactions to Kosterin, and pp. 210–20 on Grigorenko.

47. Saunders, p. 296.

48. Ibid., pp. 304, 308.

49. Ibid., pp. 325–27; Reddaway, pp. 258–59.

50. Reddaway, p. 249.

51. *Arkhiv Samizdat*, no. 580.

52. Abdulhamitoğlu, pp. 220–22; Potichnyj, p. 317.

53. *Arkhiv Samizdat*, no. 269; Barbara Jancar, "Religious Dissent in the Soviet Union," in Rudolf L. Tokes, *Dissent in the USSR* (Baltimore, 1975), pp. 214–15.

54. Abdulhamitoğlu, pp. 222–25; Rothberg, p. 293.

55. Cited in Peter Dornan, "Andrei Sakharov: the Conscience of a Liberal Scientist," in Tokes, p. 369; complete text in Andrei D. Sakharov, *Sakharov Speaks* (New York, 1974), p. 95.

56. *Sakharov Speaks*, p. 229.

57. Kirimal, in *Genocide*, p. 91.

58. Ibid., pp. 87–88.

59. Ibid., p. 88.

60. *Lenin Bayragi*, December 21, 1968, and April 5, 1969.

61. Kirimal, in *Genocide*, p. 91.

62. Ibid., pp. 92–93; *Emel* 59, pp. 16–19; *Dergi* 52 (1968), p. 74; Abdulhamitoğlu, pp. 227–37; Sheehy, pp. 22–23.

63. "Krym," *B.S.E.* 3rd ed (1973), vol. 13, pp. 509–11.

64. Abdulhamitoğlu, p. 242.

65. Reddaway, p. 253.

Bibliography

Abdul Gaffar. *Umdetüt-Tevarih.* Istanbul, 1924. Türk Tarih Encumeni Mecmuasi, Ilave XI, pp. 1–207.

Abdülhamitoğlu, Necip. *Türksüz Kirim: Yüzbinlerin Sürgünü.* Istanbul, 1974.

Abrahamowicz, Zygmunt. "Turkic Geographic Names Qači and Qači Sarayi in the Crimea." *Folia Orientalia* 6 (1964): 244–47.

Adler, B. "Die Krim-Karäer in geschichtlicher, demographischer und volkskundlicher Beziehung." *Baessler Archiv* 17 (1934): 103–33.

Agarwal, N. N. *Soviet Nationalities Policy.* Agra, 1969.

Akçokrakly, O. "Krymsko-tatarskie i turetskie istoricheskie dokumenty XVI–XIX vv., vnov' postupivshie v krymskii tsentral'nyi arkhiv." *Biulletin Tsentr. Arkh. Upravleniia KrASSR* 2 (1932): 12–16.

―――. *Novoe v istorii Chufut Kale.* Simferopol', 1928.

―――. *Staro-krymskii nadpisi XIII–XV vv.* Simferopol', 1927.

―――. "Tatarskie dokumenty XV–XIX vv., khraniiashchiesia v Tsentr. arkhive KrASSR." *Biulletin Tsentr. Arkh. Upravleniia KrASSR* 2 (1931): 13–19.

―――. *Tatarskie tamgi v Krymu.* Simferopol', 1927.

Akin, I. *Bolşevizm felaketi ve kirim halk mücadelesi.* Immenstadt, 1947.

Alaç, M. "Bolşeviklerin Ikinci Işgalinden Sonra Kirim'da Neler Oldu?" *Emel* 29 (1965): 5–20.

―――. "Kirim'da Salomon Krym Hükumeti." *Emel* 27 (1965): 10–15.

Alekberli, M. A. *Bor'ba ukrainskogo naroda protiv turetsko-tatarskoi agressii.* Saratov, 1961.

Aleksandrov, Grigorii. "Istreblenie krymskikh tatar." *Sotsialisticheskii vestnik.* Paris, 1950.

Aleksandrov, I. F. "O musul'manskom dukhovenstve i upravlenii dukhovnymi delami musulman v krymu posle ego prisoedinenie k rossii." *ITUAK* 51 (1914):207–20.

Allen, Samuel, Jr. "The Zemstvo as a Force for Social and Civic Regeneration in Russia." Ph.D. dissertation, Clark University, 1969.

Altdorffer, H. "Kongress der musulmanischen Geistlichen." *Die neue Orient* 1, no. 10 (1917).

―――. "Die Kongresse der Mohammedaner Russlands in Kasan." *Die neue Orient* 2, no. 1 (1917).

Al'tman, V. "Sessiia po istorii Kryma." *Voprosy istorii* 2 (1948):179–84.

Amanton, Victor. *Notices sur les diverses populations du Gouvernement de la Tauride, et specialement de la Crimée.* Besançon, 1854.

AN SSSR. *Pushkin, polnoe sobranie sochinenie.* Vol. 4. Moscow, 1937.

AN UkSSR. *Istoriia goroda-geroia Sevastopolia, 1917–1957.* Kiev, 1958.

Anderle, Alfred. "Antibolschewismus und 'Ostforschung' bei der Vorbereitung des zweiten Weltkrieges." *Wissenschaftliche Zeitschrift der Martin-Luther Universität* 9 (Halle/Wittenberg, 1959).

Anderson, M. S. "The Great Powers and the Russian Annexation of the Crimea, 1783–1784." *Slavonic and East European Review* 37 (1958):17–41.

Andrievskii, A. *Kommissiia 1749 g. dlia razbora vzaimnykh pretenzii tatar' i zaporozhtsev.* Kiev, 1894.

d'Aragon, Marquis. "Le voyage de l'imperatrice Catherine II en Crimée d'après une relation inédite." *Revue des deux mondes* 15 (July 1893):394–418.

Arbatli, Omer. "Kirim'da Rüştiye Mekteplerinin Açilmasi ve Tesirleri." *Emel* 26 (1965):19–30.

Arikan, Sabri. *Zagadnienie pánstwa krymskiego.* Posen, 1939.

Arkas, Z. "Nachalo i deistviia russkago flota na Chernom mor'e s 1778 po 1798 god." *ZOOID* 4 (1860):261–310.

Arkhiv Samizdat. 1968–. Collection of documents published irregularly. Munich.

"Arkhiv voenno-pokhodnoi kantseliarii grafa P. A. Rumiantseva-Zadunaiskago." *Chteniia* 56 (1866), 96 (1876).

Armstrong, John A. *The Politics of Totalitarianism.* New York, 1961.

d'Askoli, Emiddio Dortelli. "Opisanie chernago moria i tatarii, 1634." *ZOOID* 24 (1902):89–180.

Aslanapa, O. "Kirim'da Türk Eserleri ve Mimar Sinan'in Yaptiği Cami." *Türk Kültürü* 28 (1965):229–40.

Atlas, M. *Bor'ba za soveti, ocherki po istorii sovetov v krymu, 1917–1918.* Simferopol', 1933.

Azaria Iliia, Karaim Rabbi. "Sobytiia sluchivshiiasia v krymu v tsarstvovanie Shagin Gereia Khana." *Vremennik imperatorskago moskovskago obshchestva istorii i drevnostei rossiiskikh* 24 (1854):101–34.

Babenko, N. A. *Obzor deiatel'nosti perekopskago zemstva za 1866–1896 gg.* Simferopol', 1897.

Babichev, G. *Pokolenie otvazhnykh komsomol'tsy kryma—aktivnye pomoshchniki partii v velikoi otechestvennoi voine.* Simferopol', 1958.

Bachmakoff, A. *Cinquante siècles d'évolution ethnique autour de la Mer Noire.* Paris, 1937.

Bagalei, D. I. "Ocherki iz istorii kolonizatsii stepnoi okrainy Moskovskago gosudarstva." *Chteniia* 138, no. 3 (1886):1–264.

Bagiev, I. *Zemel'naia reforma i batrachestvo.* Simferopol', 1929.

Bakhchisarai: Putevoditel'. Simferopol', 1967.

Bakhrushin, S. V. "Osnovnye momenty istorii krymskogo khanstva." *Istoriia v shkole* 3 (1936):29–61.

Bantysh-Kamenskii, Dmitrii. *Istoriia maloi rossii.* Moscow, 1822.

Bantysh-Kamenskii, N. N. *Reestr delam krymskogo dvora s 1474 po 1779 g.* Simferopol', 1893.

Baranchenko, V. *Gaven.* Moscow, 1967.

Baranowski, Bohdan. *Chlop polski w walce z tatarami.* Warsaw, 1952.

————. "Turcja i Krym Wobec Walk Polsko-Kozackich w r. 1625." *Ziemia Czerwienska* 3 (1937).

Barsamov, N., and A. Polkanov. *Feodosiia: Proshloe goroda i arkheologicheskie pamiatniki.* Feodosiia, 1927.

Barthold, W. "Ak Masdjid." *E.I.* Vol. 1, p. 312.

Bashkirov, A. S. "Istoriko-arkheologicheskii ocherk kryma." In *Krym: Putevoditel'.* Simferopol', 1914. Pp. 172–226.

Baskakov, N. A. *Vvedenie v izuchenie tiurkskikh iazykov.* Moscow, 1962.

Battal-Taymas, A. "La littérature des tatars de Crimée." *Philologiae Turcicae Fundamenta* 2 (Wiesbaden, 1964):785–92.

Beauplan. *Description d'Ukrainie qui sont plusieurs Provinces du Royaume de Pologne* (Rouen, 1660). Also, in Russian translation, *Opisanie Ukrainy* (St. Petersburg, 1832).

Béla, Juhasz. *Magyar hadifoglyok a Krimi tatár rabságban 1657-töl.* Szeged, 1926.

Belokurov, S. *O posol'skom prikaze.* Moscow, 1906.

Benenson, M. E. *Ekonomicheskie ocherki kryma.* Simferopol', 1919.

Bennigsen, A., and Chantal Lemercier-Quelquejay. *Islam in the Soviet Union.* New York, 1967.

————. "Le Khanat de Crimée du XVIe siècle de la tradition mongole à la suzeraineté ottomane d'après un document inédit des Archives ottomanes." *Cahiers* 13 (1972):321–37.

————. "La Moscovie, l'Empire ottoman et la crise successorale de 1577–1588 dans le Khanat de Crimée." *Cahiers* 14 (1973):453–87.

————. *La presse et le mouvement national chez les musulmans de Russie avant 1920.* Paris, 1964.

————. "La Russie du XVIIIe siècle dans les archives de l'Empire ottoman." *La Russie de l'Europe.* Paris, Moscow (1970):307–23.

Benzing, Johannes. "Berliner politische Veröffentlichungen der Türken aus der Sowjetunion." *Welt des Islam* 18 (1936).

Berezhkov, M. N. "Drevneishaia kniga krymskikh posol'skikh del (1474–1505)." *ITUAK* 21:27–55.

————. "Krymskiye dela v starom tsarskom arkhive XVI v. na osnovanii sovremennoi arkhivnoi opisi." *ITUAK* 19:93–100.

————. "Nur'saltan, tsaritsa Krymskaia." *ITUAK* 27 (1897):1–17.

————. "Plan zavoevaniia Kryma, sostavlennyi Iuriem Krizhanichem." *ZhMNP* 127 (October 1891):483–517; 128 (November 1891):65–119.

————. "Russkie plenniki i nevol'niki v krymu." *Arkheologicheskii S'ezd: Trudy* 6, no. 2 (Odessa):342–72.

Berezin, I. "Tarkhannye iarlyki krymskikh khanov." *ZOOID* 8 (1872):1–23.

Berinder, Mihnea, and Gilles Veinstein. "Règlements de Süleyman Ier concernant le liva de Kefe." *Cahiers* 16 (1975):57–104.

Bert'e-Delagard, A. L. "K istorii Khristianstva v krymu." *ZOOID* 28 (1910):1–108.

————. "Tsennost' monetnykh nominalov v krymskom khanstve." *ITUAK* 51 (1914):153–85.

Bliumenfeld, G. F. *Krymsko-tatarskoe zemlevladenie: istoriko-iuridicheskii ocherk.* Odessa, 1888.

Bochagov, A. *Milli Firka: natsionalnaia kontrrevoliutsiia v krymu.* Simferopol', 1930.

Bodaninskii, I. *Arkheologicheskoe i etnograficheskoe izuchenie tatar v krymu.* Simferopol', 1930.

———. "Tatarskie 'Durbe' mazolei v krymu: iz istorii iskusstva krymskikh tatar." *ITOIAE* 1, no. 58 (1927):195–201.

Bogdanova, N. A., and I. I. Loboda. *Bakhchisaraiskii istoriko-arkheologicheskii muzei.* Simferopol', 1964.

Bogorodnitskii, V. "O krymsko-tatarskom narechii." In his *Etiudy po tatarskomu iazykoznaniiu.* Kazan, 1933.

Boi za krym. Simferopol', 1945.

Boiadzhiev, T. *Krymsko-tatarskaia molodezh' v revoliutsii.* Simferopol', 1930.

Bolgari, P. *Chernomorskii flot.* Moscow, 1967.

Bor'ba bolshevikov za uprochenie sovetskoi vlasti, vosstanovlenie i razvitie narodnogo khoziaistva kryma. Simferopol', 1958.

Bor'ba bol'shevikov za vlast' sovetov v krymu. Simferopol', 1957.

Bor'ba za sovetskuiu vlast' v krymu: Dokumenty i materialy. Vol. 1, Simferopol', 1957. Vol. 2, Simferopol', 1961.

Borozdin, I. "Sovremennaia krymskaia respublika." *Novyi vostok* 19 (1927):99–120.

———. "Novye danniye po zoloto ordinskoi kulture v krymu." *Novyi vostok* 16–17 (1927):256–74.

Borzenko, A., and A. Negri. "Bakhchisaraiskaia, arabskaia i turetskaia nadpisi khanskago dvortsa, mecheti, kladbishcha." *ZOOID* 2 (1848):489–529.

Botero, Giovanno. *Relationi Universali.* Brescia, 1599.

Bozgöz, Aziz. "Zincirli Medrese Meselesi ve Çelebicihan-Kirimtayef düellosu." *Emel* 38 (1967):7–15.

Brautigam, Otto. *So bat es sich zugetragen . . . Ein Leben als Soldat und Diplomat.* Wurzburg, 1968.

Bronevskii, M. "Collections out of Martin Broniovius . . . contayning a Description of Tataria. . . . " *Purchas His Pilgrimes* XIII (Glasgow, 1906):pp. 461–91. Also in Russian translation, "Opisanie Kryma (Tartariae Descriptio)." *ZOOID* 6 (1867):333–67.

Brükner, A. G. "Puteshestvie Ekateriny II v Krym." *Istoricheskii vestnik* 21 (1885):5–23, 242–64, 444–509.

Brumberg, Abraham, ed. *In Quest of Justice.* New York, 1970.

Brun, V. "Materialy kasaiushchiesia kryma i moldavii: turetskie fermany (1578–1761)." *ZOOID* 11 (1879):467–72.

Brusali Mehmed Tahir. *Idare-i osmaniye zamaninda Kirim müellifleri.* Istanbul, 1916–1917.

"Bumagi Imperatritsy Ekateriny II." *SIRIO* 10, 13, 27.

Bunegin, Maksim. *Revoliutsiia i grazhdanskaia voina v krymu (1917–1920 gg.).* Simferopol', 1927.

Bütün Kirim. Simferopol', 1925.

Cahiers du monde russe et soviétique. Vol. 1. Paris, 1960–.

Castagne, Joseph. "Le Bolchevisme et l'Islam: les organisations soviétiques de la Russie musulmane." *Revue du monde musulman* 51 (1922).

Cemilev, Mustafa. "Pis'mo P. G. Grigorenko o perezhitom krymskimi tatarami v 1962." *Arkhiv Samizdat,* no. 281 (Nov. 1968).

Cevdet, Ahmet. *Cevdet Tarihi.* 2nd ed. Istanbul, 1854–1891.

Chatskaya, C. "Chansons tatars de Crimée." *Journal asiatique* 208 (1926):341–69.

Chirva, I. *Krym revoliutsionnyi: istoriko-partiinyi ocherk.* Kiev, 1963.

———. ed. *Ocherki po istorii kryma.* Vols. 3 and 4. Simferopol, 1964–1967.

Chojeckie, Edmund. *Wspomnienia z podrózy po krymie.* Warsaw, 1845.

Chowaniec, Czeslaw. "Soboieski wobec Tatarszczyzny 1683–1685." *Kwartalnik Hist.* 42 (1928):52–66.

Chronicle of Current Events 18–31 (London, 1971–1975).

Chteniia v imperatorskom obshchestve istorii i drevnostei rossiiskikh pri moskovskom universitete. Moscow, 1846–1918.

Clarke, Edward D. *Travels to Russia, Tartary, and Turkey.* New York, 1907.

Çobanzade, B. *Nauchnaia grammatika krymsko-tatarskogo iazyka.* Simferopol', 1925.

———. "Son Devir Kirim Edebiyati." *Emel* 48 (1968):24–31.

"Çobanzade Bekir Sitki." *Emel* 46 (1968):17.

Conquest, Robert. *The Nation Killers: The Soviet Deportation of Nationalities.* New York, 1970.

———. *Soviet Nationalities Policy in Practice.* London, 1967.

Craven, Elizabeth Lady. *A Journey through the Crimea to Constantinople in 1783.* London, 1789.

Czaplinski, Wladyslaw. "Sprawa najazdow tatarskich na Polske w pierwszej polovie XVII w." *Kwartalnik Historyczny* 70, no. 3 (1963):713–20.

Czolowski, A. "Tatarzy w karpatach w 1594 r. (Epizod z najazdow tatarskich na Polski)." *Zloty Szlak* (1939).

D., V. "Otryvok iz puteshestviia po kryma. Pis'mo XVIII v." *Syn' otechestva.* Pt. 36 (1817).

Dağci, Cengiz. *Badem Dalina Asili Bebekler.* Istanbul, 1970.

———. *Onlar Da Insandi.* Istanbul, 1958.

———. *O Topraklar Bizimdi.* Istanbul, 1972.

———. *Üşüyen Sokak.* Istanbul, 1972.

Dallin, Alexander. *German Rule in Russia 1941–1945.* London, 1957.

Degtiarev, P., and R. Vul'. *U literaturnoi karty kryma.* Simferopol', 1965.

Dehérain, Henri. "La mission du Baron de Tott et de Pierre Ruffin auprès du Khan de Crimée de 1767–1769." *Revue de l'histoire des colonies françaises* 15, no. 1 (1923):1–32.

Demidoff, Anatole de. *Travels in the Krimea and Southern Russia in 1837.* London, 1853.

Derzhavin, N. "Bolgarskiia kolonii novorossiiskago kraia." *ITUAK* 41 (1908):1–237.

Desaive, Dilek. "Le Khanat de Crimée dans les Archives Ottomanes." *Cahiers* 13, no. 4 (1972):560–83.

"Diariusz expeditiey Jego Mości Pana Stanislawa Zolkiewskiego przeciu Tatarom w 1618 g." *Kwartalnik Historyczny* (1899).

"Diplomaticheskaia perepiska Imperatritsy Ekateriny II." *SIRIO* 135.

Dixon, C. Aubrey, and Otto Heilbrunn. *Communist Guerilla Warfare.* New York, 1955.

Dmitriev, N. "Krymskaia iazykovaia ekspeditsii." *Revoliutsiia i pis'mennost'* 2 (Moscow, 1936.).

Doerfer, Gerhard. "Das Krimosmanische." *Philologiae Turcicae Fundamenta* 2 (1964):272–80.

———. "Das Krimtatarische." *Philologiae Turcicae Fundamenta* 2 (1964):369–90.

Dogel. "Diplomaticheskii kodeks materialov o rossii i polshe." Pt. 3 "Otnosheniia polshi k kazakam, krimu i turtsiiu." *ZhMNP* 11 (1842), 6 (1843).

Dombrovskii, F. *Dvorets krymskikh khanov v bakhchisarae.* Simferopol', 1863.

———. "Istoriko-statisticheskii ocherk g. bakhchisaraia." *Novorossiiskii kalendar na 1849 g.* Pp. 380–96.

Dornan, Peter. "Andrei Sakharov: the Conscience of a Liberal Scientist." In Rudolf L. Tokes, ed., *Dissent in the USSR.* Baltimore, 1975. Pp. 354–417.

Dovnar-Zapol'skii, M. V. "Zametka o krymskikh delakh v Metrike Litovskoi." *ITUAK* 26 (1897):11–23.

Dragomanov. *Pro ukrainskikh kozakiv, tatar ta turkiv.* Kiev, 1876.

Druzhinina, E. I. *Iuzhnaia ukraina v 1800–1825 gg.* Moscow, 1970.

———. *Kiuchuk-kainardzhiiskii mir 1774 goda: ego podgotovka i zakliuchenie.* Moscow, 1955.

———. "Nachalo nauchnogo izucheniia kryma." *Voprosy sotsial'no-ekonomicheskoi istorii i istochnikovedeniia perioda feodalizma v rossii.* Moscow, 1961.

———. *Severnoe prichernomor'e v 1775–1800 gg.* Moscow, 1959.

Dubrovin, N. F. *Prisoedinenie kryma k rossii: reskripty, pis'ma, reliatsii, doneseniia.* 4 vols. St. Peterburg, 1885–1889.

———. "Bumagi Kniazia Grigoriia Aleksandrovicha Potemkina-Tavricheskago, 1774–1788 gg." *Sbornik voenno-istoricheskikh materialov* 6 (1893).

Dubrovskiy, V. "Türk Kirima dair Tarihi Kaynak ve Araştirmalar." *Dergi* 4 (1956):53–76.

———. *Ukraina i Krim v Istoricheskikh Vzaeminakh.* Geneva, 1946.

Efetov, S. B., and V. I. Filonenko. "Pesni krymskikh tatar." *ITOIAE* 1:69–84.

Ekonomicheskoe sostoianie gorodskikh poselenii Evropeiskoi Rossii v 1861–1862 gg. Pt. 1, "Tavricheskaia guberniia." St. Petersburg, 1863.

Elagin, V. "Natsionalisticheskie illiuzii krymskikh tatar v revoliutsionnie gody." *Novyi vostok,* 5 (1925):190–216; 6 (1925):205–25.

———. *Revoliutsiia i grazhdanskaia voina v krymu.* Simferopol', 1927.

Emel (Istanbul, 1960–).

Encyclopaedia of Islam (new edition). Leiden, 1960–.

Eremenko, A. I. *Gody vozmezdiia, 1943–1944.* Moscow, 1969.

Ergüven, A. Riza. "Halim Giray." *Türk Dili* 2, no. 18 (new series, 1953):349–53.

Erkin, Feridun Cemal. *Les Relations Turco-Soviétiques et la Question des Détroits.* Ankara, 1968.

Ernst, N. L. "Bakhchisaraiskii Khanskii dvorets i arkhitektor vel. kn. Ivana III friazin Aleviz Novyi." *ITOIAE* 2 (Simferopol', 1928):39–54.

Ertaylan, Ismail Hikmet. *Gazi Geray Han, Hayati ve Eserleri.* Istanbul, 1958.

Essad Bey. *Histoire du Guépéou, la police secrète de l'URSS 1917–1933.* Paris, 1934.

Eszer, A. "Emido Dortelli d'Ascoli O.P. und die II. Krim-Mission der Dominikaner (1624–1635)." *Archivum Fratrum Praedicatorum* 38 (1968):165–258.

Evarnitskii, D. *Istoriia zaporozhskikh kazakov i tavricheskaia guberniia.* St. Petersburg, 1865.

Falev, P. A. "Poslovitsy, pogovorki i primety krymskikh tatar." *ITUAK* 52 (1915): 1–67.

Feridun Bey. *Münşeat-i Selatin.* 2 vols. Istanbul, 1849.

Ferrand, Monsieur de. "Relation de sieur Ferrand, médecin du Kan des Tatares." In Jean Bernard, ed. *Recueil de voyages au nord.* 2nd ed. Amsterdam, 1732. Vol. 4, pp. 516–34.

Fevret, A. "Les tatars de Crimée." *Revue du monde musulman* 3 (1907):75–105.

Filonenko, V. I. *Zagadki krymskikh tatar.* Simferopol', 1926.

Firkovich, Z. A. *Sbornik starinnykh gramot i uzakonenii rossiiskoi imperii kasatel'no prav i sostoianiia russko-poddannykh karaimov.* St. Petersburg, 1890.

Fisher, A. "The Administration of Subordinate Nationalities in Multinational Empires." In J. Pelenski, ed. *State and Society in Europe in the 16th and 17th Centuries.* Warsaw, forthcoming.

———. "Azov in the Sixteenth and Seventeenth Centuries." *Jahrbücher für Geschichte Osteuropas* 21, no. 2 (1973).

———. "Crimean Separatism in the Ottoman Empire." In W. Haddad and W. Ochsenwald, eds. *Nationalism in a Non-National State: The Dissolution of the Ottoman Empire.* Columbus, forthcoming.

———. "Enlightened Despotism and Islam under Catherine II." *Slavic Review* (Dec. 1968):542–53.

———. "Muscovite-Ottoman Relations in the 16th and 17th Centuries." *Humaniora Islamica* 1 (1973):207–17.

———. "Muscovy and the Black Sea Slave Trade." *Canadian-American Slavic Studies* 6, no. 4 (1972):575–94.

———. "Les rapports entre l'Empire ottoman et la Crimée: l'aspect financier." *Cahiers* 13 (1972):368–81.

———. *The Russian Annexation of the Crimea 1772–1783.* Cambridge, 1970.

Fursenko, V. I. *Doklad simferopol'skoi gorodskoi upravy.* Simferopol', 1892.

Gabaev, G. S. "Zakonodatel'nye akty i drugie dokumenty o voennoi sluzhbe krymskikh tatar v riadakh voiskovykh chastei." *ITUAK* 51 (1914):135–52.

Gablits, K. I. *Fizicheskoe opisanie tavricheskoi oblasti po ee mesto polozheniiu i po vsem trem tsarstvam prirody.* St. Petersburg, 1785.

Gamalov, S. A. "Natsional'nye men'shinstva kryma." *Krym* 2, no. 4 (Moscow, 1927):pp. 184–93.

Gavriil arkhiepiskop khersonskii i tavricheskii. "Pereselenie grekov iz kryma v azovskaia guberniia." *ZOOID* 1 (1844):197–204.

Genov, Ivan G. *Chetyre vremeni goda: dnevnik partizana.* Moscow, 1969.

Geograficheskaia atlas SSSR. Moscow, 1950.

Gerasimov, D. *Oblast', v kotoroi my zhivem: ocherk o kryme.* Simferopol', 1959.

Germany, Heer. 11 Armee. *Wir erobern die Krim.* Neustadt, 1943.

Geroi boev za krym. Simferopol', 1972.

Gidalevich, A. I. *Mediko-topograficheskoe opisanie goroda Simferopolia.* Simferopol', 1891.

Ginzburg, M. "Omer, pri dvornyi zhivopisets i dekorator krymskikh khanov Selamet i Krym Gireyev." *Sredi kollektsionerov* 1–2 (1924):22–27.

———. "Tatarskoe iskusstvo v Krymu." *Sredi kollektsionerov* 11–12 (1921):1, 3 (1922).

Giray, Hamdi. *Kirim Tarihi.* Kostenze, 1935.

Glavani, X. *Relation de la Crimée par le S. Xaverio Glavani Consul de France à Bakche Seray Capitale de cette peninsule et premier médecin du Kan, 1723.* Paris, Archive National–Marine 2 JJ 80.

Glazik, J. P. *Die Islammission der Russich-Orthodoxen Kirche.* Munster, 1959.

Gökbilgin, Ozalp. *1532–1577 yillarda arasinda Kirim Hanliğinin Siyasi Durumu.* Ankara, 1973.

———. *Tarih-i Sahib Giray Han.* Ankara, 1973.

Gökbilgin, Ozalp, and Dilek Desaive. "Le khanat de crimée et les campagnes militaires de l'Empire ottoman fin du XVIIe–début du XVIIIe siècle." *Cahiers* 11, no. 1 (1970):110–17.

Gokolov, D. *Progulka po krymu s tsel'iu oznakomit's nim.* Odessa, 1869.

Goldstein, M. "Sovyet Hareketine uğrayan Kirim Türk Halki ve Onun Milli Kültürü." *Emel* 59 (1970):24–32.

Golobutskii, V. A. *Zaporozhskoe kazachestvo.* Kiev, 1957.

Gore, Montague. *Description of Some of the Principal Harbours and Towns of the Krimea.* 2nd ed. London, 1854.

Gorka, Olgierd. *Liczebność Tatarów Krymskich i ich Wojsk.* Warsaw, 1936.

Gözaydin. *Kirim.* Istanbul, 1948.

Grant, Anthony. *An Historical Sketch of the Crimea.* London, 1855.

Grechaniuk, N., and P. Popov. *Moriaki chernomorskogo flota v bor'be za vlast' sovetov.* Simferopol', 1957.

Grigorovich, N. *Kantsler Kniaz A. A. Bezborodko v sviazi s sobytiiami ego vremeni.* *SIRIO* 26.

Grunebaum, G. E. von. "Problems of Muslim Nationalism." In Richard Frye. *Islam and the West.* Gravenhage, 1957.

Grylev, A. N. *Dnepr, karpaty, krym: Osvobozhdenie pravoberezhnoi ukrainy i kryma v 1944 godu.* Moscow, 1970.

Gubenko, G. N. *Revoliutsionnoe dvizhenie v tavricheskoi gubernii v 1905–1907 gg.* Simferopol', 1955.

Gukovskii, A. ed. "Krymskoe kraevoe pravitel'stvo v 1918/19 g." *Krasnyi arkhiv* 22 (1927):92–152.

Guthrie, Maria. *A Tour Performed in the Years 1795–96 Through the Taurida, or Crimea.* London, 1802.

Hadzy Mehmed Senai z Krymu. *Historia Chana Islam Gereja III.* Edited by Olgierd Gorka and Zbigniew Wojcik. Warsaw, 1971.

Halim Giray Sultan. *Gülbün-i Hanan.* Istanbul, 1871.

Hammer-Purgstall, Joseph von. *Geschichte der Chane der Krim.* Wien, 1856.

Hanoğlu, R. Hikmet. "Kirim Edebiyati Halk Edebiyati, Tercuman ve Zamanimiz edebiyati Devirleri." *Emel* 13 (1962):19–21.

Hasan, Abdullah Og. "Birinci Mengili Giray Han Yarliği." *Türkiyat Mecmuasi* 4 (1934):99–109.

Haxthausen, Baron von. *The Russian Empire: Its People, Institutions, and Resources.* 2 vols. London, 1856.

Hingley, Ronald. *The Russian Secret Police.* London, 1970.

Hoffmann, Joachim. *Deutsche und Kalmyken 1942 bis 1945.* Freiburg, 1974.

Holderness, Mary. *New Russia: Journey from Riga to the Crimea.* London, 1823.

Hopstein, E. *Bibliografiia bibliograficheskikh ukazatelei literatury o kryme.* Simferopol', 1930.

Horn, Maurycy. "Chronologia i zasieg najazdow tatarskich na ziemie rzeczypospolitej polskiej w latach 1600–1647." *Studia i materialy do historii wojskowosci* 8, no. 1 (1963).

———. *Skutki ekoniczne najazdow tatarskich z lat 1605–1633 na rus czerwona.* Warsaw, 1964.

Hostler, Charles W. *Turkism and the Soviets.* London, 1957.

Howorth, Henry H. *History of the Mongols from the 9th to the 19th Century.* Part 2. London, 1880.

Hrushevsky, M. *A History of the Ukraine.* New Haven, 1941.

Iakobson, A. L. "Armianskaia srednevekovaia arkhitektura v krymu." *Vizantiiskii vremennik* 8 (1956):166–91.

———. *Krym v srednie veka.* Moscow, 1973.

———. *Rannesrednevekovye sel'skie poseleniia iugo-zapadnoi tavridi.* Leningrad, 1970.

Ianson, Iu. *Krym: ego khlebopashestvo i khlebuaia torgovlia.* St. Petersburg, 1870.

"Iarlyki krymskikh khanov." *ZOOID* 2 (1848):675–79.

"Iarlyki tokhtamysha i seadet'-geraia." *ZOOID* 1 (1844):337–48.

Iashchurzhinskii, Kh. P. "Iuzhno-russkie plenniki v krymu." *ITUAK* 47 (1912).

Igel'strom. "Arkhiv Grafa Igel'stroma." *Russkii arkhiv* 4 (1886):345–71.

Inalcik, Halil. "C. S. Kirimer." *Emel* 28 (1965):15–19.

———. "Çerkes: Ottoman Period." *E.I.* Vol. 2, pp. 24–25.

———. "Dawlat Giray." *E.I.* Vol. 2, pp. 178–79.

———. "Eyalet." *E.I.* Vol. 2, pp. 721–24.

———. "Ghazi Giray I." *E.I.* Vol. 2, p. 1046.

———. "Ghazi Giray II." *E.I.* Vol. 2, pp. 1046–47.

———. "Giray." *Islam Ansiklopedisi.* Istanbul, 1948. Vol. 4, pp. 783–89.

———. "Hadjdji Giray." *E.I.* Vol. 3, pp. 43–45.

————. "Kirim Hanliği." *Islam Ansiklopedisi.* 1955. Vol. 6, pp. 746–56.

————. "Kirim Türk Yurdunun Yok Edilişi." *Emel* 24 (1964):37–42.

————. "Yeni Vesikalara Göre Kirim Hanliğinin Osmanli Tabiliğine Girmesi ve Ahidname Meselesi." *Belleten* 8, no. 31 (1944):185–229.

Institut Istorii, AN SSSR. *Sevastopol'skoe vooruchennoe vosstanie v noiabre 1905 goda: dokumenty i materialy.* Moscow, 1957.

Institute for the Study of the USSR. *Key Officials of the Government of the USSR and Union Republics.* Munich, 1962.

"Istoricheskaia spravka ob obrazovanii v tavricheskoi gubernii tatarskikh dvorian-kikh rodov." *ZOOID* 23 (1901):41–45.

Istoricheskie mesta i pamiatniki kryma. Simferopol', 1960.

"Istoricheskoe i diplomaticheskoe sobranie del proiskhodivskikh mezhdu rossiiskimi velikimi kniaziami i byvshimi v kryme tatarskimi tsariami s 1462 po 1553 god." *ZOOID* 4 (1863).

Iurchenko, I. "Opisanie Perekopskikh." *ZOOID* 11 (1879):479–86.

Ivanics, Mary. "Formal and Linguistic Peculiarities of 17th Century Crimean Tatar Letters Addressed to Princes of Transylvania." *Acta Orientalia Hungaricae* 29 no. 2:213–24.

Ivanov, I. "Snosheniia malorossiiskoi kollegii v 1752 godu s krymskim khanom." *ZOOID* 5:842–46.

Ivanov, P. A. "Ocherk deiatel'nosti na iuge rossii admirala grafa N. S. Mordvinova." *ITUAK* 23:24–70.

Izvestiia tavricheskago uchennago arkhivnago kommissii. Odessa, 1866–1916.

Izvestiia tavricheskogo obschchestva istorii, arkheologii i etnografii. Odessa, 1874–1917.

Jablonowski, S. "Diariusz napadu tatarskiego w r. 1692." *Kwartalnik Historyczny* (1890):287–91.

Jancar, Barbara Wolfe. "Religious Dissent in the Soviet Union." In Tokes, *Dissent in the USSR.* Baltimore, 1975. Pp. 191–230.

Kalendar' i pamiatnaia knizhka tavricheskoi gubernii na 1896 god. Simferopol', 1896.

Karabiber, Osman. *Kirimli Bir Türkün Rusyadaki Maceralari.* Ankara, 1954.

Kargalov, V. V. *Na stepnoi granitse: oborona 'krymskoi ukrainy' russkogo gosudarstva v pervoi polovine XVI stoletiia.* Moscow, 1974.

Karov, D. *Partizanskoe dvizhenie v SSSR v 1941–1945 gg.* Munich, 1954.

Karpov, Gennadii. "Otnosheniia moskovskago gosudarstva k krymu i turtsii v 1508–1517 godakh." *Izvestiia moskovskago univ.,* no. 4 (1865):213–44.

Karskii, M. V. "Krym v tsarstvovanie Imperatora Nikolaia I." *Odesskii listok,* no. 166 (1896).

————. "O snosheniiakh prussii s krymskim khanstvom." *Odesskii listok,* no. 158 (1896).

Kaszczenko, A. *Bisurmanska newolia w ukrajunskij naridnij poezji.* Katerynoslaw, 1917.

Kazimirski, M. M., and A. Jaubert. "Prècis de l'histoire des Khans de Crimée." *Journal asiatique* 12 (1833):349–480.

Kellner-Heinkele, Barbara. *Aus den Aufzeichnungen des Said Giray Sultan.* Freiburg, 1975.

Kharizomenov, S. A. "Formov zemlevladeniia u krymskikh tatar." *Iuridicheskii vestnik,* no. 5 (1887).

Khartakhai, F. "Istoricheskaia sud'ba krymskikh tatar." *Vestnik evropy* 2 (1866):182–236.

Kirichenko, N. K. *Vtoroi orden na znameni kryma.* Simferopol', 1972.

Kirim Şiirleri. Kostanza, 1935.

"Kirima dönmekte olan Kirim Türklerinin durumu." *Emel* 64 (1971):18–34.

Kirimal, Edige. "1917 ihtilalinden sonra Kirim-Türk ailesiyle kadinin durumu." *Dergi* 3 (1955):13–30.

———. "Çarlik Rusyasi Hakimiyeti altinda Kirim." *Dergi* 46 (1966):51–61.

———. "The Crimean Tatars." *Studies on the Soviet Union* (new series, 1970). Vol. 10, no. 1, pp. 70–97.

———. "The Crimean Turks." In Institute for the Study of the USSR. *Genocide in the USSR, Studies in Group Destruction.* New York, 1958. Pp. 20–29.

———. "Kirim Türkleri." *Emel* 59 (1970):4–23.

———. "Kirim Türklerinin 1917–1920 ihtilal yillarinda milli-kurtuluş hareketi." *Dergi* 48 (1967):55–69.

———. "Kirim Türklerinin Yigit Halim Halk Destani Hakkinda Bazi Kayitlar." *Dergi* 20 (1958):32–38.

———. "Kirimda Sovyetlerin Din Siyaseti." *Dergi* 1 (1955):55–67.

———. "Kirimda Topyekün Tehcir ve Katliam." *Emel* 15 (1963):35–40. 16 (1963):32–40. 18 (1963):21–25.

———. "Mass Deportations and Massacres in the Crimea." *Cultura Turcica* 1, no. 2 (1964):253–65.

———. *Der nationale Kampf der Krimtürken.* Emsdetten, 1952.

———. "Sovyet Rusya Hakimiyeti altinda Kirim." *Dergi* 49 (1967):59–66.

———. "Sürgündeki Kirimlilara Dair." *Emel* 62 (1971):40–47.

Kirimli Yiğit. *W odpowiedzi ukrainskim imperjalistom.* Wilna, 1939.

Kirimsar. "Cafer Seydahmet Kirimer." *Emel* 63 (1971):17–32.

———. "Cafer Seydahmet Kirimer." *Emel* 65 (1971):21–45.

Kirpenko, G. K. "Ordera Kniazia Platona A. Zubova praviteliu tavricheskoi oblasti za 1796 g." *ITUAK* 26 (1897):1–10.

Kleemanns, Nikolaus. *Reisen in der Krim.* Wien, 1771.

Knight, Jonathan. "American Statecraft and the 1946 Black Sea Straits Controversy." *Political Science Quarterly* 90, no. 3 (1975).

Koch, Karl. *Die Krim und Odessa.* Leipzig, 1865.

Kocowski, S. *Wyprawa Tatarow na Wegry przez Polske w 1594 r.* Lublin, 1948.

Koehler, Paule. "Le Khanat de Crimée en Mai 1607 vu par un voyageur français." *Cahiers* 12, no. 3 (1971):316–26.

Köhlin, H. "Some Remarks on Maps of the Crimea and the Sea of Azov." *Imago Mundi* 15 (1960):84–88.

Kolankowski, L. "Problem Krymu w dziejach jagiellonskich."*Kwartalnik Historycz-nyi* 49 (1935):279–300.

Koll', L. P. "Khadzhi-Girei Khan i ego politika (po genuezskim istochnikam). Vzgliad po politicheskiia snosheniia Kafy s tatarami v XV veke." *ITUAK* 50 (1913):99–139.

———. "O sud'be nekotorykh istoricheskikh zdanii v Starom Krymu i Feodosii." *ITUAK* 35 (1903):10–17.

Komiakhov, V. G. *Opyt razvitiia sadovodstva i vinogradarstva v krymskoi oblasti Ukrainskoi SSR.* Moscow, 1958.

Komitet po planirovke iuzhnogo berega kryma. *Sotsialisticheskaia rekonstruktsiia iuzhnogo berega kryma.* Simferopol', 1935.

Köppen, P. I. *Krymskii sbornik.* St. Petersburg, 1837.

Korotkov, I. S., and G. A. Koltunov. *Osvobozhdenie kryma.* Moscow, 1959.

Korsh, F. E. "Universaly Petra Velikago k budzhatskam i krymskim tataram." *Drevnosti vostochnyia* 1, no. 3 (1893).

Kortepeter, C. M. "Gazi Giray II, Khan of the Crimea, and Ottoman Policy in Eastern Europe and the Caucasus, 1588–1594." *Slavonic and East European Review* 54, no. 102 (1966):139–66.

———. *Ottoman Imperialism during the Reformation: Europe and the Caucasus.* New York, 1973.

———. "Ottoman Imperial Policy and the Economy of the Black Sea Region in the Sixteenth Century." *Journal of the American Oriental Society* 86 (1966):86–113.

Kowalski, Tadeusz, and Jozef Dutkiewicz. "Jarlyk tatarski z r. 1177 H. (1763 D.)." *Rocznik Orientalistyczny* 2 (1919–1924):213–19.

Kozhevnikov, M. V. *Zakon o zeml'noi reforme v krymu.* Simferopol', 1929.

Kozlov, I. ed. *Desiat' let sovetskogo kryma: sbornik posviashchennyi desiati letiiu sovetizatsii krymu 1920–1930.* Simferopol', 1930.

Kraelitz-Greifenhorst, Friedrich. "Aufforderungs- und Kontributions- schreiben des Tataren-Hans Murad Giraj vom Jahre 1683 an Wr. Neustadt." *Mitteilungen zur osmanischen Geschichte* 1 (1921–1922):223–31.

Kreindler, Isabelle, "Educational Policies Toward the Eastern Nationalities in Tsarist Russia: a Study of Il'minskii's System." Ph.D. dissertation, Columbia University, 1969.

Krichinskii, Arslan. *Bor'ba s prosveshcheniem i kulturoi krymskikh tatar.* Baku, 1920.

———. "General Maciej Sulkiewicz (1865–1920)." *Rocznik Tatarski* 1 (1932).

———. *Ocherki russkoi politiki na okrainakh.* Pt. 1, "K istorii religioznikh pritesnenii krymskikh tatar." Baku, 1919.

Krizhanich, Iurii. *Politika.* Moscow, 1965.

"Krym."*B.S.E.* 3rd ed. 1973. Vol. 13, pp. 509–11.

Krym revoliutsionnyi. Simferopol', 1968.

Krym v boiakh i trude. Simferopol', 1967.

Krym v period velikoi otechestvennoi voiny 1941–1945 (Sbornik dokumentov i materialov. Simferopol', 1973.

Krym v velikoi otechestvennoi voine sovetskogo soiuza 1941–1945 gg. Simferopol', 1963.

Krym za 50 let sovetskoi vlasti. Simferopol', 1970.

"Krymskaia avtonomnaia sovetskaia sotsialisticheskaia respublika." *B.S.E.* 1st ed. 1937.

Krymskaia oblast'. Gosudarstvennyi arkhiv. *Krymskii oblastnoi gosudarstvennyi arkhiv. Putevoditel'.* Simferopol', 1961.

"Krymskaia oblast'." *B.S.E.* 3rd ed. 1973. Vol. 13, p. 514.

"Krymskaia oblast'." *B.S.E.* 2nd ed. 1953. Vol. 23, pp. 551–53.

Krymskie legendy. Simferopol', 1957.

"Krymskie tatary."*Khronika zashchity prav v SSSR* 5–6, Nov. 1973 (New York, 1974). Pp. 33–38.

Krymskii, A. "Literatura krymskikh tatar.": *Studii z krymu.* Kiev, 1930. pp. 165–91.

Krymskii oblastnoi komitet kommunisticheskoi partii Ukrainy. *Bor'ba bol'shevikov za uprochenie sovetskoi vlasti, vosstanovlenie i razvitie narodnogo khoziaistva kryma.* Simferopol', 1958.

"Krymskoe murzachestvo." *Perevodchik,* nos. 32–33 (1888).

Kuftin, B. A. *Yilishche krymskikh tatar v sviazi s istoriei zaseleniia poluostrova.* Moscow, 1925.

Kulakovskii, Iulian. *Proshloe tavridy.* Kiev, 1914.

Kurat, Akdes N. *IV–XVIII Yüzyillarda Karadeniz Küzeyindeki Türk Kavimleri ve Devletleri.* Ankara, 1972.

———. *Türkiye ve Idil Boyu.* Ankara, 1966.

Kurganov, I. A. *Natsii SSSR i russkii vopros.* Frankfurt, 1961.

Kurtoğlu, Fevzi, "Ilk Kirim Hanlarinin Mektuplari." *Belleten* 3 (1941):641–55.

Langlès, L. "Notice chronologique des Khans de Crimée composée principalement d'après les Auteurs Turcs et Persans." In Georges Forster. *Voyage du Bengale à Petersburg.* Paris, 1802. Vol. 3, pp. 327–492.

Lashkov, F. F. "Arkhivnyia dannyia o beilikakh v krymskom khanstve." *Arkheologicheskii S'ezd: Trudy* 6, no. 4 (1889):96–110.

———. Istoricheskii ocherk krymsko-tatarskago zemlevladeniia." *ITUAK* 23 (1895):71–117.

———. "K voprosu o kolichestve naseleniia tavricheskoi gubernii v nachale XIX stoletiia." *ITUAK* 53 (1916):158–76.

———. "Krymskaia dela 1775–1776 gg." *ZOOID* 18 (1895):87–118.

———. "Krymsko-turetskiia dela 80-x godov XVIII stoletiia." *ZOOID* 17 (1894):155–62.

———. *Pamiatniki diplomaticheskikh snoshenii krymskago khanstva s moskovskim gosudarstvom v XVI i XVII vv.* Simferopol', 1891.

———. "Reestr delam krymskogo dvora s 1474 po 1779 g. uchenennyi destvitelnym statskim sovetnikom N. Bantysh-Kamenskim v 1808 g." *ITUAK* 14–18.

———. "Sbornik dokumentov po istorii krymsko-tatarskago zemlevladeniia." *ITUAK* 26 (1897):24–154.

———. *Sel'skaia obshchina v krymskom khanstve.* Simferopol', 1887.

———. "Shagin-Girei, poslednii krymskii khan." *Kievskaia starina* (Sept. 1886): 36–80.

————. "Statisticheskiia svedeniia o Kryme, soobshchennyia kaimakamami v 1783 godu." *ZOOID* 14 (1886):91–156.

Laskovskii, V. P. "Praviteli tavridy." *ITUAK* 35 (1903):24–26.

Lazzerini, Edward. "Ismail Bey Gasprinskii and Muslim Modernism in Russia." Ph.D. dissertation, University of Washington, 1973.

————. "Ǧadidism at the Turn of the Twentieth Century: A View from Within." *Cahiers* (April–June 1975):245–77.

Le Compte, Gare. *Muslims of the USSR*. Munich: Institute for the Study of the USSR, n.d.

Lemercier-Quelquejay, Chantal. "Les expeditions de Devlet Giray contre Moscou en 1571 et 1572." *Cahiers* 13, no. 4 (1972):555–59.

————. "Les khanats de Kazan et de Crimée face à la Moscovie en 1521 d'après un document inédit des archives du musée du palais de Topkapi." *Cahiers* 12, no. 4 (1971):480–90.

————. "Les missions orthodoxes en Pays Musulmans de moyenne–et basse– Volga, 1552–1865," *Cahiers* 8, no. 3 (1967):369–403.

————. "The Crimean Tatars: A Retrospective Summary."*Central Asian Review* 16, no. 1 (1968):15–25.

"Les étapes de la politique islamique russe." *Revue du monde musulman* 55–56 (1923):93–166.

"Les nouveaux problèmes islamo-bolchevistes." *Revue du monde musulman* 55–56 (1923):167–245.

"Lettre à M. le marquis de Torcy, ministre et sec. d'état, sur le nouvel établissement de la mission des pères Jesuites dans la Crimée." *Lettres édifiantes et curieuses, écrites des missions étrangères, mémoires du Levant*. 2nd ed. Lyon, 1819. Vol 2, pp. 174–213.

Levitin, A. Krasnov. "'Svet v okontse' k arestu Gen. Grigorenko (May 24, 1969)." *Arkhiv Samizdat*, no. 269.

Levitskii, G. I. "Pereselenie tatar iz kryma v turtsiiu." *Vestnik evropy*, no. 5 (1882):596–639.

Lewytzkyj, Borys. *Die sowjetische Nationalitätenpolitik nach Stalins Tod (1953– 1970)*. Munich, 1970.

————. *Die Sowjetukraine 1944–1963*. Köln, 1964.

————. *Politische Opposition in der Sowjetunion 1960–1972*. Munich, 1972.

————. *The Uses of Terror: The Soviet Secret Police, 1917–1970*. New York, 1972.

Ley, Francis. *Le Maréchal de Münnich et la Russie au XVIIIe Siècle*. Paris, 1959.

Litvin, M. "Izvlechenie iz sochineniia Mikhaila Litvina, 1550 g." *Memuary otno-siashchiesia k istorii iuzhnoi rusi*, no. 1. Kiev, 1890.

————. "O nravakh tatar, litovtsev i moskvitian." *Arkhiv istoriko-iuridicheskikh svedenii, otnosiaschikhsia do rossii* 2, no. 2. Moscow, 1854.

de Liuk. "Opisanie perekopskikh i nogaiskikh tatar . . . zhana de Liuka, monakha dominikanskago ordena, 1625." *ZOOID* 11 (1879):473–93.

Liuksemburg, Il'ia. "Novyi Vavilon na beregakh Syrdar'i." *Posev* (Sept. 1973):37.

Loenertz, R. "Le origini della missione secentesca dei Domenicani in Crimea." *Archivum Fratrum Praedicatorum* 5 (1935):261–88.

Loewenthal, Rudolf. "The Extinction of the Krimchaks in World War II." *American Slavic and East European Review* 10, no. 2 (1951):130–36.

Lokhvitskii, A. "O vykupe plennykh u tatar." *Moskovskii vedemosti,* nos. 124–26. 1855.

Lopukhin, I. V. *Zapiski.* Moscow, 1860.

Luther, Michel. "Die Krim unter deutscher Besatzung im zweiten Weltkrieg." *Forschungen zur osteuropäischen Geschichte* 3 (1956):28–98.

M., and E. L. *Putevoditel' po krymu.* Odessa, 1872.

Machanov, A. E. *Bor'ba tsarskoi rossii i turtsii za obladanie krymskim khanstvom.* Simferopol', 1929.

Maistrenko, Ivan. "Natsional'no-vizvol'nii rukh krimskikh tatar ta ikh vzaemini z ukrainoiu." *Ukrains'kii somostiinik* 12, nos. 7–8 (1971):2–14.

Majewski, Wieslaw. "Najazd tatarow w lutym 1695 r." *Studia i materialy do historii wojskowosci* 9, no. 1 (1964):125–78.

Makedonskii, M. *Plamia nad krymom.* Simferopol', 1969.

Maksimenko, M. *Krest'ianskoe dvizhenie v tavricheskoi gubernii nakanune i posle otmeny krepostnogo prava.* Simferopol', 1957.

———. *Mestnye sovety kryma v poslevoennyi period 1945–1958.* Kiev, 1972.

Malinowsky, J. A. *Die deutschen katholischen Kolonien am Schwarzen Meere.* Stuttgart, 1923.

Malov, E. A. *O novokreshchenskoi kontore.* Kazan, 1873.

Malowist, Marian. *Kaffa-Kolonia Genuenska na Krymie i problem wschodni w latach 1453–1475.* Warsaw, 1947.

Manstein. "Opisanie bakhchisaraiskogo dvortsa." *Otechestvennie zapiski* 19, no. 31 (1824):75–84.

Manstein, Erich von. *Lost Victories.* Chicago, 1958.

Marchenko, Anatolii. "Nikolai Bystrykh." *Sbornik pogranichniki.* Moscow, 1973. pp. 5–29.

Markevich, Arsenii I. "A. S. Pushkin i krym." *ITUAK* 30 (1899):25–58.

———. "Getmanstvo Barabasha." *Russkii vestnik* 1 (1841):468–92.

———. "Imperatritsa Ekaterina II i Krym." *ITUAK* 27 (1897):18–37.

———. "K istorii khanskago bakhchisaraiskago dvortsa." *ITUAK* 23:130–76.

———. "Kratkii ocherk deiatel'nosti generalisimusa A. V. Suvorova v kryma." *ITUAK* 31 (1901):1–26.

———. *Krym v russkoi poezii.* Simferopol', 1897.

———. "Nachal'naia stranitsa istorii Simferopol'skoi gimnazii." *ITUAK* 50 (1913):236–40.

———. "Opyt ukazatelia knig i statei, kasaiushchikhsia kryma i tavricheskoi gubernii voobshche." *ITUAK* 28 (1898):92–185; 32–33 (1902):47–128.

———. "Pereseleniia krymskikh tatar v turtsiiu v sviazi s dvizheniem naseleniia v krymu." *Izvestiia AN SSSR,* series 7, no. 4 (1928):375–405.

———. "Prebyvanie v krymu moskovskogo gontsa pod'iachego Vasiliia Aitemirova v 1692–1695." *ITUAK* 9 (1890):48–61.

———. *Simferopol': Ego istoricheskie sud'by.* Simferopol', 1924.

———. *Taurica: Opyt ukazatelia sochinenii kasaiushchikhsia kryma i tavricheskoi gubernii voobshche.* Simferopol', 1894.

———. "Tavricheskaia guberniia vo vremia krymskoi voiny." *ITUAK* 37 (1905): 1–260.

Mart'ianov, G. P. "Posledniaia emigratsiia tatar iz kryma v 1874 g." *Istoricheskii vestnik* 6 (1886).

Materialy k otchety Simferopol'skogo soveta X sozyva. Simferopol', 1934.

Matuz, J. "Eine Beschreibung des Khanats der Krim aus dem Jahre 1669." *Acta Orientalia* 28 (1964):29–151.

———. "Qalga." *Turcica: revue d'études turques* 2:101–29.

McNeill, William H. *Europe's Steppe Frontier.* Chicago, 1964.

Meksin, D. *Sel'skoe khoziaistvo kryma.* Simferopol', 1939.

Mel'nik, K. "Svedeniia o pokhode v krym Mikhail Doroshenka (1628 g.)." *Kievskaia starina* November, 1896.

Mende, Gerhard von. *Der nationale Kampf der Russlandtürken.* Berlin, 1936.

Mertvago, D. B. "Zapiski Dmitriia Borisovicha Mertvago 1760–1824." Appendix to *Russkii arkhiv* (1867).

Mikaelian, Vardges A. *Istoriia armianskoi kolonii v krymu.* Erevan, 1964.

———. *Na krymskoi zemle.* Erevan, 1974.

Milner, Thomas. *The Crimea, Its Ancient and Modern History: The Khans, the Sultans, and the Czars.* London, 1855.

Mironov, M. "K istorii pogranichnykh nashikh snoshenii s krymskim khanstvom." *Kievskaia starina* (Feb. 1885):339–56.

Mochanov, A. "K voprosu o proiskhozhdenii islama." In Narodnyi komissariat prosveshcheniia Krym. ASSR. *Anti-religioznyi sbornik* 1 (Simferopol', 1929):57–69.

Mokrousov, A. V. *V gorakh kryma.* Simferopol', 1940.

Mordvinov. "Mnenie Mordvinova otnositel'no kryma." *Arkhiv grafov mordvinovykh* 3 1902. Pp. 193–213.

Mubarek, Mehmed. *Meskukat-i Kirimiye.* Istanbul, 1900.

Muftizade, Izmail. "Ocherk voennoi sluzhby krymskikh tatar s 1783 po 1889 god." *ITUAK* 30 (1899):1–24.

Mühlen, Patrik von zur. *Zwischen Hakenkreuz und Sowjetstern (Der Nationalismus der sowjetischen Orientvölker im zweiten Weltkrieg).* Dusseldorf, 1971.

Müller, Norbert. *Wehrmacht und Okkupation 1941–1944.* Berlin, 1971.

Mundt, Theodor. *Krim Girai, ein Bundesgenosse Friedrichs des Grossen.* Berlin, 1855.

Münecimbaşi, Ahmed Dede. *Münecimbaşi Tarihi.* Istanbul, 1973.

Murzakevich, N. "'Otvod' zemli grekam, v 1780 g. pereseliavshimsia iz kryma k azovskomu moriu." *ZOOID* 4 (1860):359–63.

Müstecip, Naci. "Kurultay nasil Toplandi." *Emel* 11 (1937):12–37.

Muzei vostochnykh kul'tur (Moscow). *Vystavka nauchno-issledovatel'skikh rabot ekspeditsii po izucheniiu tatarskoi kultury v krymu 1925–26.* Moscow, 1927.

Nadinskii, P. N. *Ocherki po istorii kryma.* Vols. 1 and 2. Simferopol', 1951–1957.

———. *Suvorov v krymu.* Simferopol', 1947.

Nadler, V. K. *Odessa v pervye epokhi ee sushchestvovaniia.* Odessa, 1893.

Narodnoe khoziaistvo krymskoi oblasti: statisticheskii sbornik. Simferopol', 1957.

Necati Efendi. "Zapiski Mukhammeda Nedjati Efendi." *Russkaia starina* (March, 1894).

Negri, A. "Istoriia krymskikh khanov: Perevod turetskoi rukopisi." *ZOOID* 2 (1848):680–87.

Neruchev, M. V. *Ocherk pozemel'nykh otnoshenii v tavricheskoi gubernii.* Simferopol', 1907.

"Neue tatarische Zeitungen." *Der neue Orient.* Vol. 1.

Nikiforov, A. "Donesenie residenta Aleksandr Nikiforova 1764 g. o nizlozhenii Krym-Girei." *ZOOID* 1 (1844):375–79.

Nolde, Boris. *La formation de l'empire russe.* 2 vols. Paris, 1952–1953.

Novikova, M. *Krymskie otkrytiia.* Simferopol', 1970.

Novosel'skii, A. A. *Bor'ba moskovskago gosudarstva s tatarami v XVII veke.* Moscow, 1948.

Ö[zkirim], O[rhan]. 'Ikinci Dunya Savaşinda Kirim Türkleri ile Almanlar Arasindaki münasebetler." *Emel* 25 (1964):15–20.

"Obrashchenie tatarskikh detei." *Khronika zashchity prav v SSSR,* no. 12, Nov.–Dec. 1974 (New York, 1975).

Odabash, A., and I. S. Kaia. *Rukovodstvo dlia obucheniia krymsko-tatarskomu iazyku.* 1st ed. Simferopol', 1924.

Oktay, Selim. *Kirim Istiklal Davasi.* Kostanza, 1939.

Olesnitskii, A. *Pesni krymskikh turok.* Moscow, 1910.

Oliphant, Laurence. *The Russian Shores of the Black Sea.* New York, 1854.

"Opisanie dvortsa khana krymskago i stolichnago ego goroda bakhchisaraia, uchinennoe, po prikazu grafa Munikha." *Otechestvennyi zapiski* 19, no. 51 (1824):75–100.

Ortekin, Hasan. *Çorabatir Destani.* Istanbul, 1939.

———. *Kirim Hanlarinin Şeceresi.* Istanbul, 1938.

Osmanov, I. "Aaiavlenie v sviazi s arestom." (1968) *Arkhiv Samizdat,* no. 85.

Osvobozhdenie kryma ot anglo-frantsuzskikh interventov. Simferopol, 1940.

Otar, Ibrahim. "Cafer Seydahmet Kirimer." *Emel* 1 (1960): 18–26.

———. "Çelebi Cihan." *Emel* 44 (1968):4–13.

Otchet Simferopol'skogo gorodskogo soveta XI sozyva o rabote za period s 1935 po 1938 god: Materialy dlia dokladchikov. Simferopol', 1939.

Ozenbaşli, Ahmed. *Çarlik Hakimiyetinde Kirim Faciasi Yahut Tatar Hicretleri.* Simferopol', 1925.

———. "Kirim Tatar Tarihine Ait Bazi Kayitlar." *Ana Yurt,* no. 1 (Simferopol', 1943).

Ozerov, M. *Po sledam geroev revoliutsii.* Simferopol', 1967.

Paget, R. T. *Manstein: His Campaigns and His Trial.* London, 1951.

Pallas, P. S. *Travels Through the Southern Provinces of the Russian Empire, in the Years 1793 and 1794.* 2 vols. London, 1812.

"Pamiatniki diplomaticheskikh snoshenii moskovskogo gosudarstva s krymskoiu i nogaiskoiu ordami i s turtsiei." *SIRIO* 53.

Pamiati pavshikh za sovetskii krym, 1918–1920: Sbornik statei i vospominanii. Simferopol', 1940.

Parkinson, John. *A Tour of Russia, Siberia, and the Crimea, 1792–1794.* Edited by William Collier. London, 1971.

Partiinyi arkhiv krymskogo obkoma K.P. Ukrainy. *Bor'ba za sovetskuiu vlast' v Krymu: dokumenty i materialy.* Vol. 1, 1917–1918. Simferopol', 1957.

————. *Khronika revoliutsionnykh sobytii v krymu 1917–1920 gg.* Simferopol', 1969.

————. *V bor'be za sovetskii krym.* Simferopol', 1958.

Pasmanik, Daniil S. *Revoliutsionnye gody v krymu.* Paris, 1926.

Pelenski, Jaroslaw. *Russia and Kazan: Conquest and Imperial Ideology.* The Hague, 1974.

Petrun', F. "Khans'ki Iarliki na Ukrainsk'ki zemli." *Skhidnii Svit* 2 (1928):170–87.

Peysonnel, M. de. *Traité sur le commerce de la Mer Noire.* 2 vols. Paris, 1787.

Pinson, Mark. "Russian Policy and the Emigration of the Crimean Tatars to the Ottoman Empire, 1854–1862." *Güney-Doğu Avrupa Araştirmalari Dergisi* 1 (1972):37–56.

Pipes, Richard. *The Formation of the Soviet Union.* Cambridge, Mass., 1957.

Pisarev, S. P. "Iz istorii krymskikh tatar." *Politicheskii dnevnik 1964–1970.* Amsterdam, 1972.

Pisateli Krymy: literaturnyi al'manakh. Moscow, 1928.

"Pis'ma grafa N. I. Panina k Imperatritse Ekaterine Velikoi." *Arkhiv kniazia vorontsova.* 1882. Vol. 26, p. 153.

"Pis'ma pravitelia tavricheskoi oblasti V.V. Khokhovskago praviteliu kantseliarii V.S. Popovu." *ZOOID* 10 (1877):235–361.

Piwarski, Kazimierz. "Sprawa posrednictwa tatarskiego w wojnie polsko-tureckiej 1692–1693." *Studia Historica* (1958):1351–72.

Poliakovskaia, S. V. *Kul'turnoe stroitel'stvo v krymu.* Simferopol', 1939.

"Politicheskaia perepiska Imperatritsy Ekateriny II." *SIRIO* 87, 97, 118.

Politicheskii dnevnik 1964–1970. Amsterdam, 1972.

Polnoe sobranie zakonov rossiiskoi imperii. 3 series. St. Petersburg, 1830–1917.

Potichnyj, Peter J. "The Struggle of the Crimean Tatars." *Canadian Slavonic Papers* 17, nos. 2–3 (1975):302–19.

"Prebyvanie iezuitov v krymu." *ZOOID* 4 (1860):466–67.

Priroda i naselenie rossii. Pt. 4, *Narody Evropeiskoi rossii,* no. 3, Krym i kavkaz [on Crimea and Caucasus]. St. Petersburg, 1906.

Pulaski, Kazimierz. "Trzy poselstwa Lawryna Piaseczynskiego do Kazi Gireja, hana Tatarow perekopskich 1601–1603." *Przew. Nauk i Liter.* 39 (1911):135–45, 244–56, 358–66, 467–80, 553–66, 645–60, 756–68, 845–64, 945–60.

Puteshestvie po tavride v 1820. St. Petersburg, 1823.

Raeff, Marc. "The Style of Russia's Imperial Policy and Prince G. A. Potemkin." In G. N. Grob, ed. *Statesmen and Statecraft of the Modern West.* Barre, Mass., 1967. Pp. 1–52.

Raevskii, V. G. "Otkrytie v simferopole okruzhnago suda." *ITUAK* 52 (1915): 216–24.

Rambaud, A. "Les Tatars de Crimée." *Revue politique et littéraire* 2 (1875).

"Rasporiazheniia svetleishago kniazia G.A. Potemkina-Tavricheskago kasatel'no ustroeniia tavricheskoi oblasti." *ZOOID* 12 (1881):249–329.

Reddaway, Peter, ed. *Uncensored Russia: Protest and Dissent in the Soviet Union.* New York, 1972.

Rempel', L. I. *Komsomol v krymu.* Simferopol', 1927.

———. *Povstantsy v krymu.* Simferopol', 1927.

Retovskii, O. "Genuezsko-tatarskiia monety goroda Kaffa." *ITUAK* 27 (1897):49–104; 29 (1899):1–52; 32–33 (1902):1–17.

Reuilly, J. *Voyage en Crimée et sur les bords de la Mer Noire.* Paris, 1806.

Revelstein, H. *Die Not der Fremdvölker ünter dem russischen Joche.* Berlin, 1916.

Revkomy kryma: sbornik dokumentov i materialov. Simferopol', 1968.

Revoliutsionnoe dvizhenie v tavricheskoi gubernii v 1905–1907 gg: sbornik dokumentov i materialov. Simferopol', 1955.

Riza Seiid Mukhammed. *Asseb o Sseiiar' ili Sem' Planet'.* Kazan, 1832.

Rothberg, Abraham. *The Heirs of Stalin: Dissidence and the Soviet Regime, 1953–1970.* Ithaca, 1972.

Rudnev, S. P. "Lichnyi sostav pervykh sudov v tavricheskoi gubernii." *ITUAK* 52 (1915):225–33.

Rugard, M. *Krim—und Kaukasus—Fahrt Bilder aus Russland.* Breslau, 1891.

Rypka, J. "Briefwechsel der Hohen Pforte mit den Krimchanen im II Bande von Feriduns Munšeat." *Festschrift Georg Jakob.* 1937. Pp. 241–69.

Safonov, S. "Ostatki grecheskikh legionov v rossii, ili nyneshnee naselenie balaklavy." *ZOOID* 1 (1844):205–56.

Sakharov, Andrei D. *Sakharov Speaks.* New York, 1974.

Samojlovič, A. "Beiträge zur Bienenzucht in der Krim im 14.–17. Jahrhundert." *Festschrift Georg Jacob.* 1937. Pp. 270–75.

———. "K istorii krymsko-tatarskogo literaturnogo iazyka." *Vestnik nauchnogo obshchestva tatarovedeniia.* Kazan, 1927.

———. "Krymsko-tatarskie skorogovorki." *Sbornik muzeia arkheologii i etnografii* 5, no. 1 (1918).

———. *Opyt kratkoi krymsko-tatarskoi grammatiki.* St. Petersburg, 1916.

———. "Poslovitsy, pogovorki i primety krymskikh tatar." *ITUAK* 52 (1915).

Şapşal, S. "Kirim karai türkleri." *Türk Yili.* Istanbul, 1928.

Sarkisyanz, Emanuel. *Geschichte der orientalischen Völker Russlands bis 1917: Eine Ergänzung zur ostslawischen Geschichte Russlands.* Munich, 1961.

Saunders, George, ed. *Samizdat: Voices of the Soviet Opposition.* New York, 1974.

Savelov, L. M. "Iz istorii snoshenii moskvy s krymom pri tsaŗe Mikhaile Feodoroviche. Posel'stvo S.I. Tarbeeva v krym 1626–1628." *ITUAK* 39 (1906):1–105.

———. "Perepiska patriarkha Ioakima s voevodami, byvshimi v krymskikh pokhodakh 1687 i 1689 godov." *ITUAK* 40 (1907):1028.

———. "Posylki v krym v XVII veke." *ZOOID* 24 (1902):73–82.

Sbornik imperatorskogo russkogo istoricheskogo obshchestva. St. Petersburg, 1867–1916.

Sbornik po shkol'noi statistike tavricheskoi gubernii, no. 2. Simferopol', 1903.

Scheel, Helmuth. "Ein Schreiben des Kirim Giray Khan an den Prinzen Heinrich, den Bruder Friedrichs des Grossen." *Jean Deny Armağani.* Ankara, 1958. Pp. 213–20.

Schlesinger, Rudolf, ed. *The Nationalities Problem and Soviet Administration.* London, 1956.

Schnitzler, Johann H. *Description de la Crimée, surtout au point de vue de ses lignes de communication.* Paris, 1855.

Schütz, E. "Eine Armenische Chronik von Kaffa aus der ersten Hälfte des 17. Jahrhunderts." *Acta Orientalia* 29, no. 2 (1975):133–86.

Seidahmet, Cafer. *La Crimée: passé-présent, revendications des tatars.* Lausanne, 1921.

———. *Gaspirali Ismail Bey: Dilde, Fikirde, Işte Birlik.* Istanbul, 1934.

———. "Mübarek Çoban." *Emel* 10 (1962):15–20.

———. *Rus Tarihinin Inkilaba, Bolşevizme ve Cihan Inkilabina Sürüklenmesi.* Istanbul, 1948.

Sekirinskii, S. Z. "Iz istorii razvitiia promyshlennosti v krymu v pervoi polovine XIX veka." *Izvestiia krymskogo otdela geograficheskogo obshchestva SSSR* 6 (Simferopol', 1961):169–84.

———. "K voprosu o zaselenii kryma v kontse XVIII veka." *Izvestiia krymskogo pedagogicheskogo instituta* 23, no. 6 (1957):73–87.

———. "Nekotorye cherty razvitiia sel'skogo khoziaistva kryma i prilegaiushchikh k nemu zemel' iuzhnoi ukrainy v kontse XVIII–pervoi polovine XX v." *Ezhegodnik po agrarnoi istorii vostochnoi evropy, 1960 g.* Kiev, 1962.

Seniutkin, M. "Voennyia deistviia dontsov protiv krymskago khana Devlet-Gireia i samozvantsva Pugacheva v 1773 i 1774 godakh." *Sovremennik* 46 (1856):43–131.

Sergeev, A. "Doklad Imperatritse Ekaterine II-oi po vstuplenii Eia na Prestol, izobrazhaiushchii sistemu Krymskikh Tatar, ikh opasnost' dlia Rossii i pretenziiu na nikh." *ITUAK* 53 (1916):190–93.

———. "Nogaitsy na molochnykh vodakh." *ITUAK* 48 (1912):1–144.

———. "Ukhod tavricheskikh nogaitsev v turtsiiu." *ITUAK* 48 (1912).

Serk, Ivan. "Pis'mo k khanu krymskomu voiska zaporozhskago nizovago koshevago atamana Ivana Serka." *Russkaia starina* 8, no. 7 (1873):88–92.

Seton-Watson, Hugh. *The Russian Empire 1801–1917.* Oxford, 1967.

Seymour, H. D. *Russia on the Black Sea and the Sea of Azof.* London, 1855.

Shamko, Ekaterina. *Partizanskimi tropami.* Simferopol', 1969.

———. *Partizanskoe dvizhenie v krymu.* Simferopol', 1959.

———. "Plamia nad krymom." *Geroi podpol'ia.* Moscow, 1972. Vol. 2, pp. 47–82.

———. "Stoiali nasmert'." In V.E. Bystrov, ed. *Sovetskie partizany.* 2nd ed. Moscow, 1963. Pp. 412–49.

Shchebal'skii, P. K. "Potemkin i zaselenie novorossiiskago kraia." In V. A. Dashkov, ed. *Sbornik antropologicheskikh i etnograficheskikh statei o rossii.* Moscow, 1868. Pp. 130–43.

Sheehy, Ann. *The Crimean Tatars and Volga Germans: Soviet Treatment of Two National Minorities.* London, 1971.

Sheva, O. *Krim v ukrains'kii literaturi.* Simferopol', 1963.

Shiriaev, S. D. "Pomeshchich'ia kolonizatsiia i russkie usad'by v krymu v kontse XVIII i per. pol. XIX veka." *Krym* 2, no. 4 (1927):169–86.

Shmal'ts, G. "Vzgliad na poluostrov krym v zemledel'cheskom i promyshlennom otnoshenii." *Trudy vol'nogo ekonomicheskogo obshchestva* 1 (1842):79–81.

Shmidt, S. O. "Russkie polonianiki v krymu i sistema ikh vypkupa v seredine XVI v." In AN SSSR. Inst. Ist. *Voprosy sotsial'no-ekonomicheskoi istorii i istochnikovedeniia perioda feodalizma rossii.* Moscow, 1961. Pp. 30–34.

Shumilov. V. N., ed. *Tsentral'nyi gosudarstvennyi arkhiv drevnikh aktov: putevoditel'.* Pt. 1. Snosheniia rossii s krymom [Relations of Russia with Crimea.] Moscow, 1946. Pp. 85–87.

Shustov, B. *Krymskaia ASSR.* Moscow, 1927.

Simmons, Ernest J. *Pushkin.* Cambridge, Mass., 1937.

Simon, Gerhard. "Die nationale Bewegung der Krimtataren." 2 pts. *Berichte des Bundesinstituts für ostwissenschaftliche und internationale Studien* 30–31 (1975).

Skal'kovskii, A. *Khronologicheskoe obozrenie istorii novorossiiskago kraia 1730–1823.* Vol. 1 (Odessa, 1836).

―――. "O Nogaiskikh tatarakh zhivushchikh v tavricheskoi gubernii." *ZhMNP* 40, no. 12:147–90.

―――. *Opyt statisticheskogo opisaniia novorossiiskogo kraia.* 2 vols. Odessa, 1850.

―――. "Zaniatie kryma v 1783 g., materialy dlia istorii novorossiiskogo kraia." *ZhMNP* 30, no. 2 (1841):1–44.

Smirnov, N. A. *Rossiia i turtsiia v XVI–XVII vv.* 2 vols. Moscow, 1946.

Smirnov, V. D. "Krymsko-tatarskiia gramoty." *ITUAK* 50 (1913):140–78.

―――. *Krymskoe khanstvo pod verkhovenstvom otomanskoi porty do nachala XVIII veka.* St. Petersburg, 1887.

―――. *Krymskoe khanstvo pod verkhovenstvom otomanskoi porty v XVIII stoletie.* Odessa, 1889.

―――. *Sbornik nekotorykh vazhnykh izvestii i ofitsial'nykh dokumentov kasatel'no turtsii, rossii, i kryma.* St. Petersburg, 1881.

―――. "Tatarsko-khanskie iarlyki iz kollektsii tavricheskoi uchenoi arkhivnoe komissii." *ITUAK* 54 (1917).

―――. "Tavricheskaia moneta: ocherk istorii Feodosiiskogo dvora." *Gornyi zhurnal* (1892):1–60.

Sokhan', M. *Perekop: istoriko-kraevedcheskii ocherk.* Simferopol', 1962.

Sokolnicki, Michel. "La Sultane Ruthene." *Belleten* 23 (1959):229–40.

Solodovnik, L. D., et al. *Istoriia mist i sil ukrains'koi SSR: Krims'ka oblast'.* Kiev, 1974.

Solov'ev, S. M. *Istoriia rossii s drevneishikh vremen.* Moscow, 1959–1965. 29 vols, in 15.

Sovetov, V. *Rasstrel sovetskogo pravitelstvo krymskoi respubliki tavridi.* Simferopol', 1933.

―――. *Sotsial-demokratie v krymu.* Simferopol', 1933.

Sovetskomu krymu dvadtsat' let, 1920–1940. Simferopol', 1940.

"Sovyet Dökümanlarindan: Kirim Tatarlari Adalet Huzurunda." *Emel* 51 (1969): 12–15.

"Sovyetler Birliğindeki Kirim Türklerinin Isteklerine Dair Belge." *Emel* 62 (1971):31–39.

Soysal, Abdullah. *Hanlik Devrinde Kirim Türk Kulturu.* Istanbul, 1941.

———. *Jarlyki krymskie z czasov Jana Kazimierza.* Warsaw, 1939.

———. "Kirim Hanliğinda Asilzadeler." *Emel* 83 (1974):14–23.

———. *Z Dziejow Krymu: Politika-kultura-emigracja.* Warsaw, 1938.

Spuler, B. "Baghče Saray." *E.I.* Vol. 1, pp. 893–94.

———. "Die Grenze des Grossfürstentums Litauen im Südosten gegen Türken und Tataren." *Jahrbücher für Geschichte Osteuropas* 6, nos. 2–4 (1941):152–70.

———. *Die Krim.* Berlin, 1944.

———. "Die Krim unter russischer Herrschaft." *Blick in der Wissenschaft* 8 (1948).

———. *The Muslim World.* vol. 2, *The Mongol Period.* Leiden, 1960.

Statistika rossiiskoi imperii. Vol. 22, *Glavneishiia dannyia pozemel'noi statistiki po obsledovaniiu 1889 g.* No. 41, "Tavricheskaia guberniia." St. Petersburg, 1895.

Stepanov, E. *Partizanskimi tropami.* Simferopol', 1951.

Steven, Kh. "Kratkoe opisani imp. Nikitskogo sada v tavricheskoi gubernii." *Ukrainskii zhurnal* 15 (1824).

Struve, *Travels in the Crimea.* London, 1802.

Sumarokov, P. I. *Dosugi krymskago sud'i ili vtoroe puteshestvie v Tavridu.* 2 vols. St. Petersburg, 1803–1805.

———. *Reise durch die Krim und Bessarabien im Jahre 1799.* Leipzig, 1802.

Sumner, B. H. *Peter the Great and the Ottoman Empire.* London, 1949.

"Sürgündeki Kirimlilar." *Emel* 64 (1971):35–37.

Svin'in, P. "Nablindeniia puteshestvennika v 1827 godu o vygodakh vinogradnogo sadovodstva v krymu." *Otechestvennye zapiski,* no. 96, 1828.

Szapszal, H. "Znaczenie opisu podrozy Ewlija Czelebiego dla dziejow Chanatu Krymskiego." *Rocznik Orientalistyczny* 8 (1931–1932).

Tardy, L., and I. Vasaray. "A. Taranowskis Bericht über seine Gesandtschaftsreise in der Tartarei (1569)." *Acta Orientalia Hungaricae* 28, no. 2 (1974).

Tatarchevskii, A. "Puteshestvie i deiatel'nost barona Totta, v kachestve konsula v krymu v 1767 g." *Izvestiia Kiev. Univ.,* no. 10 (1873):1–24.

Tatarinov, P. *Ocherk tavricheskoi gubernii v istoriko-geograficheskom otnoshenii.* Simferopol', 1894.

Temirçili. "2-inci Cihan Savaşi Sirasinda Alman Işgalinde Kirim Türklerinin Kültür ve Eğitim Işleri." *Emel* 23 (1964):19–23.

———. "Kirim'da Eğitim Meseleleri Hakkinda Bazi Notlar." *Emel* 20 (1964):11–14.

Ter-Abramov, M. *Istoriia kryma s geograficheskimi i uchenymi issledovaniiami.* Feodosiia, 1865.

Thounmann, M. *Description de la Crimée.* Strasbourg, 1786.

Tiapkin, V. "Perevod s shertnyia gramoty, kakovu dal Murat Girei Khan poslannikam, stol'niku Vasil'iu Tiapkinu, da d'iaku Nikite Zotovu." *Drevniaia Rossiskaia Vivliofika.* Vol. 15, pp. 1–5.

————. "Spisok s stateinago spiska . . . Tiapkina . . . ," *ZOOID* 2 (1850):568–658.

Toğan, Zeki Veledi. *Bügünkü Türkili.* Istanbul, 1947.

Tokes, Rudolf L. *Dissent in the USSR.* Baltimore, 1975.

Toktar, Kerim. "Kirim Türklerinin Kamplardaki Kültür Çalişmalarina Dair." *Emel* 41 (1967):17–19.

Tolunay, M. *Kirimin Osmanli Imparatorluğuna Eklenmesi Meselesi.* Istanbul, 1934.

Torcy. "Lettre d'Monseigneur le Marquis de Torcy sur le nouvel établissement de la Mission des Pères Jésuites en Krimée." *Nouveaux mémoires des missions de la Compagnie de Jésus dans le Levant.* Paris, 1715. Vol. 1, pp. 1–135.

de Tott. *Mémoires de Baron de Tott, sur les Turcs et les Tatares.* 4 vols. Hamburg, 1785.

Troinitskii, N. A. *Obshchii svod' po imperii resul'tatov razrabotki dannykh pervoi vseobshchei perepisi naseleniia 28 ian. 1897.* Vols. 1 and 2. St. Petersburg, 1905.

Tsarskii, I. "Zhurnal puteshestviia Ekateriny II v Krym, 1787 g." *ZOOID* 3 (1852):273–89.

Turkay, Osman. "The Tragedy of the Crimean Tatars." *Index on Censorship* 3, no. 1 (1974):67–78.

U., A. "O zaselenii kryma novymi poselentsami." *Russkii vestnik* 63, no. 5 (1866):256–68.

Ulianitskii, V. *Russkiia konsul'stva za granitseiu v XVIII veke.* 2 vols. Moscow, 1899.

Ülküsal, M. *Dobruca'daki Kirim Türklerinde Atasözleri ve Deyimler.* Ankara, 1970.

————. *Dobruca ve Türkler.* Ankara, 1966.

————. " 'Emel' ve Kirim Davasi." *Emel* 76 (1973):1–14.

————. *Ikinci Dünya Savaşinda, 1941–1942, Berlin Hatiralari ve Kirim'in Kurtuluş Davasi.* Istanbul, 1976.

Unat, F. R. "Kirimin Osmanli Idaresinden Çiktiği Günlere Ait Bir Vesika: Necati Efendi Sefaretname Veya Sesgüzeştnamesi." *Türk Tarih Kurumu Yayinlari,* series 9, vol. 3 (1943):367–74.

Uralgiray, Yusuf. "Hocam Mehmet Niyazi." *Emel* 67 (1971):9–32.

————. *Karithat al-Qirim al-Islamiya fi'l-ittihad as-sovyeti.* Cairo, 1950.

Utz, Viktor. *Die Besitzverhältnisse der Tataren bauern im kreise Simferopol.* Tubingen, 1911.

Uzunçarşili, I. H. *Osmanli Tarihi.* Vol. 4, pt. 1. Ankara, 1956.

V plameni i slave: ocherki o geroiakh grazhdanskoi voiny. Simferopol', 1972.

Vakhidov, Seiid. "Iarlyk khana Sakhib-Gireia." *Nauchnoe obshchestvo tatarovedeniia, Kazan: Vestnik* 1–2 (1926):29–37.

————. "Issledovanie iarlyka Sahib-Girei Khana." *Kazan Univ.: Obshchestvo arkheologii, istorii i etnografii: Izvestiia* 30, no. 1 (1925):61–92.

Vanzetti, Titus. *Excursion en Crimée, faite dans l'automne de 1835.* Odessa, 1836.

Vardys, V. Stanley. "The Case of the Crimean Tatars." *Russian Review* 30, no. 2 (1971).

Vasinkova, S. I. *Krym i gornye tatary.* St. Petersburg, 1904.

Veinstein, Gilles. "La révolte des mirza tatars contre le Khan, 1724–1725." *Cahiers* 12 (1971):327–38.

———. "Aspects économiques d'Azaq dans la première moitié du XVIe siècle." *Turcica* 8 (1976).

———. "Les Tatars de Crimée et la seconde élection de Stanislas Leszczynski." *Cahiers* 11 (1970):24–92.

———. "Missionaires jésuites et agents français en Crimée au début du XVIIIe siècle." *Cahiers* 10 (1969):416–42.

Vel'iaminov-Zernov, V. V. *Materialy dlia istorii krymskago khanstva.* St. Petersburg, 1864.

Verlinden, Charles. *L'Esclavage dans l'Europe médiévale.* Vol. 1. Brugge, 1955.

———. "La colonie vénitienne de Tana, centre de la traite des esclaves au XIV et au début du XV siècle." *Studi in onore di Gino Luzzatto.* Milan, 1950. Vol. 2, Pp. 1–25.

Vernadsky, G. *The Tsardom of Moscow 1547–1682.* New Haven, 1969.

Veselovskii, B. *Istoriia zemstva za sorok let.* 2 vols. St. Petersburg, 1909.

Veselovskii, N. I. *Tatarskoe vliianie na russkii posol'skii tseremonial' v moskovskii period russkoi istorii.* St. Petersburg, 1911.

Vitte, Iu. "O sel'skom khoziaistve v khersonskoi, tavricheskoi i ekaterinoslavskoi guberniiakh." *Zhurnal ministerstva gosudarstvennykh imushchestv,* no. 10 (1844).

Voina v tylu vraga Vol. 1. Moscow, 1974.

Vol'fson, B. *Izgnanie germanskikh okkupantov iz kryma.* Simferopol', 1939.

———. "Prisoedinenie kryma k rossii v 1783 godu."*Istoricheskii zhurnal* 3 (1941): 56–67.

Voloshinov, L. *Oktiabr' v krymu i severnoi tavrii.* Simferopol', 1960.

Vorontsov, M. L. "Opisanie sostoianiia del vo vremia Gosudaryni Imperatritsy Elizavetu Petrovny." *Arkhiv Kniazia Vorontsova* Moscow, 1882. Vol. 25, pp. 308–10.

Vsevolozhskii, N. S. "Krym i Odessa." *Syn otechestva* 3, pt. 3 (1838):1–52.

"Vyezd posledniago krymskago khana Shagin-Gireia iz rossii v turtsiiu, v 1787 godu." *ZOOID* 13 (1883):132–56.

"Vymiranie tatar' v Bakhchisarae." *Perevodchik,* no. 15 1889.

"Vysochaishe reskripty Imperatritsy Ekateriny II i ministerskaia perepiska po delam krymskim." *Chteniia* 79 (1871):1–168.

Werth, Alexander. *Russia at War 1941–1945.* New York, 1964.

Wertheimer, Fritz. *Durch Ukraine und Krim.* Stuttgart, 1918.

Widajawicz, J. "Napady Kozakow, Tatarow i Turkow na Buszcze." *Kwartalnik Historyczny* 43.

Willis, Richard. *A Short Account of the Ancient and Modern State of Crim-Tartary.* London, 1787.

Wimbush, S. Enders, and Ronald Wixman. "The Mesketian Turks: A New Voice in Soviet Central Asia." *Canadian Slavonic Papers* 17, nos. 2–3 (1975):320–40.

Wojcik, Zbigniew. "Mediacja tatarska miedzy Polska a Turcja w roku 1672." *Przeglad Historyczny* 53, no. 1 (1962):32–50.

———. "Rywalizacja polsko-tatarska o Ukraine na przelomie lat 1660–1661." *Przeglad Historyczny* 45 (1954):609–34.

———. "Some Problems of Polish-Tatar Relations in the Seventeenth Century: the

Financial Aspects of the Polish-Tatar Alliance in the Years 1654–1666." *Acta Poloniae Historica* 13 (1966):87–102.

Wolin, Simon, and Robert Slusser, eds. *The Soviet Secret Police.* New York, 1957.

Wolinski, Janusz. "Posrednictwo tatarskie w wojnie polsko-tureckiej 1674–1675." *Polityka Narodow.* 1934. Vol. 4, pp. 480–507.

Wrangell, Baronne L. de. *Visages de Crimée.* Paris, 1939.

Yapp, M. E. "The Golden Horde and Its Successors." *The Cambridge History of Islam.* Vol. 1. Cambridge, 1970.

Zaatov, O. *Polnyi russko-tatarskii slovar'.* Simferopol', 1906.

Zagorodskikh, F. S. *Bor'ba s denikinshchinoi i interventsiei v krymu.* Simferopol', 1940.

———. "Bor'ba trudiashchikhsia protiv nemetsko-kaizerovskikh okkupantov v Krymu." *Bor'ba bolshevikov za uprochenie sovetskoi vlasti.* Simferopol', 1958.

Zagorovskii, E. A. *Voennaia kolonizatsiia novorossii pri Potemkine.* Odessa, 1913.

Zajaczkowski, Ananiasz, ed. *La chronique des steppes kiptchak: Tevarih-i Dešt-i Qipčak.* Warsaw, 1966.

———. "'Letopis' Kipchaksoi stepi, kak istochnik po istorii kryma." In A. S. Tveritinova. *Vostochnye istochniki po istorii narodov iugo-vostochnoi i tsentral'noi evropy.* Moscow, 1969. Vol. 2, pp. 10–28.

Zapiski imperatorskago odesskago obshchestva istorii i drevnostei. Odessa, 1844–1916.

Zdan, M. "Kilka slow o sladach Tatarszczyzny na terytorium wojewodztwa lwowskiego." *Rocznik Tatarski* 2.

Zemskii, V. G. "Iz sel'sko-khoziaistv. deiatel'nosti tavricheskago zemstva." *Khoziain,* no. 24 (1904).

"Zemstva tavridy i narodnoe obrazovanie." *Krymskii vestnik,* no. 120 (1898).

Zenkovsky, Serge. *Pan-Turkism and Islam in Russia.* Cambridge, Mass., 1960.

Zertsalov, A. N. *Ob oskorblenii tsarskikh poslov v krymu v XVII veke.* Moscow, 1893.

Zettersteen, K. V. *Türkische, tatarische und persische Urkunden im Schwedischen Reichsarchiv.* Uppsala, 1945.

Zhurnal ministerstva narodnago prosveshcheniia. St. Petersburg, 1846–1917.

Zimnicki, Wladyslaw. "Jarlyk Maksud ben Selamet Girej Chana z r. 1767." *Rocznik Orientalistyczny* 8 (1931–1932):161–66.

Index

LITHUANIAN S.S.R.

ESTONIAN S.S.R.

LATVIAN S.S.R.

BELORUSSIAN S.S.R.

MOLDAVIAN S.S.R.

UKRAINIAN
S.S.R.

Crimea

GEORGIAN S.S.R.

ARMENIAN
S.S.R.

RUSS